T0331865

Applications of Advanced Machine Intelligence in Computer Vision and Object Recognition:

Emerging Research and Opportunities

Shouvik Chakraborty
University of Kalyani, India

Kalyani Mali
University of Kalyani, India

A volume in the Advances in
Computational Intelligence and
Robotics (ACIR) Book Series

Published in the United States of America by
   IGI Global
   Engineering Science Reference (an imprint of IGI Global)
   701 E. Chocolate Avenue
   Hershey PA, USA 17033
   Tel: 717-533-8845
   Fax: 717-533-8661
   E-mail: cust@igi-global.com
   Web site: http://www.igi-global.com

Library of Congress Cataloging-in-Publication Data

Names: Chakraborty, Shouvik, 1992- editor. | Mali, Kalyani, 1962- editor.
Title: Applications of advanced machine intelligence in computer vision and
   object recognition : emerging research and opportunities / Shouvik
   Chakraborty and Kalyani Mali, editors.
Description: Hershey, PA : Engineering Science Reference, 2020. | Includes
   bibliographical references and index. | Summary: "This book explores
   recent developments and advancements in object recognition using
   artificial intelligence"-- Provided by publisher.
Identifiers: LCCN 2019043979 (print) | LCCN 2019043980 (ebook) | ISBN
   9781799827368 (hardcover) | ISBN 9781799827375 (paperback) | ISBN
   9781799827382 (ebook)
Subjects: LCSH: Computer vision. | Machine learning.
Classification: LCC TA1634 .A64 2020 (print) | LCC TA1634 (ebook) | DDC
   006.3/843--dc23
LC record available at https://lccn.loc.gov/2019043979
LC ebook record available at https://lccn.loc.gov/2019043980

British Cataloguing in Publication Data
A Cataloguing in Publication record for this book is available from the British Library.

All work contributed to this book is new, previously-unpublished material.
The views expressed in this book are those of the authors, but not necessarily of the publisher.

For electronic access to this publication, please contact: eresources@igi-global.com.

Advances in Computational Intelligence and Robotics (ACIR) Book Series

ISSN:2327-0411
EISSN:2327-042X

Editor-in-Chief: Ivan Giannoccaro, University of Salento, Italy

MISSION

While intelligence is traditionally a term applied to humans and human cognition, technology has progressed in such a way to allow for the development of intelligent systems able to simulate many human traits. With this new era of simulated and artificial intelligence, much research is needed in order to continue to advance the field and also to evaluate the ethical and societal concerns of the existence of artificial life and machine learning.

The **Advances in Computational Intelligence and Robotics (ACIR) Book Series** encourages scholarly discourse on all topics pertaining to evolutionary computing, artificial life, computational intelligence, machine learning, and robotics. ACIR presents the latest research being conducted on diverse topics in intelligence technologies with the goal of advancing knowledge and applications in this rapidly evolving field.

COVERAGE

- Cyborgs
- Fuzzy Systems
- Agent technologies
- Evolutionary Computing
- Computer Vision
- Brain Simulation
- Algorithmic Learning
- Robotics
- Natural Language Processing
- Automated Reasoning

IGI Global is currently accepting manuscripts for publication within this series. To submit a proposal for a volume in this series, please contact our Acquisition Editors at Acquisitions@igi-global.com or visit: http://www.igi-global.com/publish/.

Titles in this Series

For a list of additional titles in this series, please visit:
http://www.igi-global.com/book-series/advances-computational-intelligence-robotics/73674

Smart Systems Design, Applications, and Challenges
João M.F. Rodrigues (Universidade do Algarve, Portugal & LARSyS, Institute for Systems and Robotics, Lisbon, Portugal) Pedro J.S. Cardoso (Universidade do Algarve, Portugal & LARSyS, Institute for Systems and Robotics, Lisbon, Portugal) Jânio Monteiro (Universidade do Algarve, Portugal & INESC-ID, Lisbon, Portugal) and Célia M.Q. Ramos (Universidade do Algarve, Portugal & CIEO, ortugal)
Engineering Science Reference • © 2020 • 459pp • H/C (ISBN: 9781799821120) • US $245.00

Deep Learning Applications and Intelligent Decision Making in Engineering
Karthikrajan Senthilnathan (VIT University, India) Balamurugan Shanmugam (Quants IS & CS, India) Dinesh Goyal (Poornima Institute of Engineering and Technology, India) Iyswarya Annapoorani (VIT University, India) and Ravi Samikannu (Botswana International University of Science and Technology, Botswana)
Engineering Science Reference • © 2020 • 335pp • H/C (ISBN: 9781799821083) • US $245.00

Implementing Computational Intelligence Techniques for Security Systems Design
Yousif Abdullatif Albastaki (Ahlia University, Bahrain) and Wasan Awad (Ahlia University, Bahrain)
Information Science Reference • © 2020 • 332pp • H/C (ISBN: 9781799824183) • US $195.00

Managerial Challenges and Social Impacts of Virtual and Augmented Reality
Sandra Maria Correia Loureiro (Business Research Unit (BRU-IUL), Instituto Universitário de Lisboa (ISCTE-IUL), Lisboa, Portugal)
Engineering Science Reference • © 2020 • 318pp • H/C (ISBN: 9781799828747) • US $195.00

701 East Chocolate Avenue, Hershey, PA 17033, USA
Tel: 717-533-8845 x100 • Fax: 717-533-8661
E-Mail: cust@igi-global.com • www.igi-global.com

Table of Contents

Detailed Table of Contents

Mousomi Roy, University of Kalyani, India
Shouvik Chakraborty, University of Kalyani, India
Kalyani Mali, University of Kalyani, India

Encryption is one of the most frequently used tools in data communications to prevent unwanted access to the data. In the field of image encryption, chaos-based encryption methods have become very popular in the recent years. Chaos-based methods provide a good security mechanism in image communication. In this chapter, chaotic skew-tent map is adapted to encode an image. Seventy-two bit external key is considered (besides the initial parameters of the chaotic system) initially, and after some processing operations, 64 bit internal key is obtained. Using this key, every pixel is processed. The internal key is transformed using some basic operations to enhance the security. The decryption method is very simple so that authentic users can retrieve the information very fast. Every pixel is encrypted using some basic mathematical operations. The values of various test parameters show the power and efficiency of the proposed algorithm, which can be used as a safeguard for sensitive image data and a secure method of image transmission.

Rohini A. Bhusnurmath, Karnataka State Akkamahadevi Women's
University, India
Prakash S. Hiremath, KLE Technological University, India

This chapter proposes the framework for computer vision algorithm for industrial application. The proposed framework uses wavelet transform to obtain the multiresolution images. Anisotropic diffusion is employed to obtain the texture component. Various feature sets and their combinations are considered obtained from texture component. Linear discriminant analysis is employed to get the distinguished features. The k-NN classifier is used for classification. The proposed method is experimented on benchmark datasets for texture classification. Further, the method is extended to exploration of different color spaces for finding reference standard. The thrust area of industrial applications for machine intelligence in computer vision is considered. The industrial datasets, namely, MondialMarmi dataset for granite tiles and Parquet dataset for wood textures are experimented. It was observed that the combination of features performs better in YCbCr and HSV color spaces for MondialMarmi and Parquet datasets as compared to the other methods in literature.

Mousomi Roy, University of Kalyani, India

Biological data analysis is one of the most important and challenging tasks in today's world. Automated analysis of these data is necessary for quick and accurate diagnosis. Intelligent computing-based solutions are highly required to reduce the human intervention as well as time. Artificial intelligence-based methods are frequently used to analyze and mine information from biological data. There are several machine learning-based tools available, using which powerful and intelligent automated systems can be developed. In general, the amount and volume of this kind of data is quite huge and demands sophisticated tools that can efficiently handle this data and produce results within reasonable time by extracting useful information from big data. In this chapter, the authors have made a comprehensive study about different computer-aided automated methods and tools to analyze the different types of biological data. Moreover, this chapter gives an insight about various types of biological data and their real-life applications.

Chapter 4

Image segmentation has been an active topic of research for many years. Edges characterize boundaries, and therefore, detection of edges is a problem of fundamental importance in image processing. Edge detection in images significantly reduces the amount of data and filters out useless information while preserving the important structural properties in an image. Edges carry significant information about the image structure and shape, which is useful in various applications related with computer vision. In many applications, the edge detection is used as a pre-processing step. Edge detection is highly beneficial in automated cell counting, structural analysis of the image, automated object detection, shape analysis, optical character recognition, etc. Different filters are developed to find the gradients and detect edges. In this chapter, a new filter (kernel) is proposed, and the compass operator is applied on it to detect edges more efficiently. The results are compared with some of the previously proposed filters both qualitatively and quantitatively.

Chapter 5

Plant disease is the major threat to the productivity of the plants. Identification of the plant diseases is the key to prevent the losses in the productivity and quality of the yield. It is a very challenging task to identify diseases detection on the plant for sustainable agriculture, where it requires a tremendous amount of work, expertise in the plant disease, and also requires excessive processing time. Hence, image processing is used here for detection of diseases in multi-horticulture plants such as alternaria alternata, anthracnose, bacterial blight, and cercospora leaf spot and also addition with the healthy leaves. In the first stage, the leaf is classified as healthy or unhealthy using the KNN approach. In the second stage, they classify the unhealthy leaf using PNN, SVM, and the KNN approach. The features are like GLCM, Gabor, and color are used for classification purposes. Experimentation is conducted on the authors own dataset of 820 healthy and unhealthy leaves. The experimentation reveals that the fusion approach with PNN and SVM classifier outperforms KNN methods.

Chapter 6

Mousomi Roy, University of Kalyani, India

Computer-aided biomedical data and image analysis is one of the inevitable parts for today's world. A huge dependency can be observed on the computer-aided diagnostic systems to detect and diagnose a disease accurately and within the stipulated amount of time. Big data analysis strategies involve several advanced methods to process big data, such as biomedical images, efficiently and fast. In this work biomedical image analysis techniques from the perception of the big data analytics are studied. Big data and machine learning-based biomedical image analysis is helpful to achieve high accuracy results by maintaining the time constraints. It is also helpful in telemedicine and remote diagnostics where the physical distance of the patient and the domain experts is not a problem. This work can also be helpful in future developments in this domain and also helpful in improving present techniques for biomedical data analysis.

Chapter 7

Rajalingam B., Priyadarshini College of Engineering and Technology, India
Priya R., Annamalai University, India
Bhavani R., Annamalai University, India
Santhoshkumar R., Annamalai University, India

Image fusion is the process of combining two or more images to form a single fused image, which can provide more reliable and accurate information. Over the last few decades, medical imaging plays an important role in a large number of healthcare applications including diagnosis, treatment, etc. The different modalities of medical images contain complementary information of human organs and tissues, which help the physicians to diagnose the diseases. The multimodality medical images can provide limited information. These multimodality medical images cannot provide comprehensive and accurate information. This chapter proposed and examines some of the hybrid multimodality medical image fusion methods and discusses the most essential advantages and disadvantages of these methods. The hybrid multimodal medical image fusion algorithms are used to improve the quality of fused multimodality medical image. An experimental result of proposed hybrid fusion techniques provides the fused multimodal medical images of highest quality, shortest processing time, and best visualization.

Chapter 8

An Overview of Biomedical Image Analysis From the Deep Learning
Perspective 197

Shouvik Chakraborty, University of Kalyani, India
Kalyani Mali, University of Kalyani, India

Biomedical image analysis methods are gradually shifting towards computer-aided
solutions from manual investigations to save time and improve the quality of the
diagnosis. Deep learning-assisted biomedical image analysis is one of the major
and active research areas. Several researchers are working in this domain because
deep learning-assisted computer-aided diagnostic solutions are well known for their
efficiency. In this chapter, a comprehensive overview of the deep learning-assisted
biomedical image analysis methods is presented. This chapter can be helpful for
the researchers to understand the recent developments and drawbacks of the present
systems. The discussion is made from the perspective of the computer vision, pattern
recognition, and artificial intelligence. This chapter can help to get future research
directions to exploit the blessings of deep learning techniques for biomedical image
analysis.

Chapter 9

Segmentation-Free Word Spotting in Handwritten Documents Using Scale
Space Co-HoG Feature Descriptors..219

Prabhakar C. J., Kuvempu University, India

In this chapter, the author present a segmentation-free-based word spotting method
for handwritten documents using Scale Space co-occurrence histograms of oriented
gradients (Co-HOG) feature descriptor. The chapter begin with introduction to word
spotting, its challenges, and applications. It is followed by review of the existing
techniques for word spotting in handwritten documents. The literature survey reveals
that segmentation-based word spotting methods usually need a layout analysis step
for word segmentation, and any segmentation errors can affect the subsequent word
representations and matching steps. Hence, in order to overcome the drawbacks of
segmentation-based methods, the author proposed segmentation-free word spotting
using Scale Space Co-HOG feature descriptor. The proposed method is evaluated
using mean Average Precision (mAP) through experimentation conducted on popular
datasets such as GW and IAM. The performance of the proposed method is compared
with existing state-of-the-segmentation and segmentation-free methods, and there
is a considerable increase in accuracy.

Preface

Since long time, humans are trying to make a machine intelligent. Intelligent systems are useful in various real-life applications. In some occasions, intelligent computing systems are efficient enough to replace the humans. Automated intelligent systems are very useful in various applications like automated production lines in various manufacturing factories, biomedical image analysis for automated disease detection, traverse some risk prone zones, etc. Computer vision is a domain of modern scientific research where a researchers try to impose some intelligence on a machine so that it can mimic the human visual system or sometimes it can be used to perform certain tasks which are cannot be performed by the human visual systems. Computer vision-based systems help us to understand an image by analyzing an acquired image and can take certain actions against it. The computer vision-based methods are very useful in constructing intelligent robotic systems. The methods and algorithms which are involves in the discussion of computer vision is the basis of the automated understanding of a scene. From the computer science perspective, computer vision is generally used to extract useful patterns and information from a single image or a collection of images. The image or images under consideration can be of various forms. For example, computer vision-based systems may need to extract useful information from the captured images of a single object, taken by more than one camera. A video sequence may also be necessary to process. The data can also be captured by a biomedical image acquisition device and the data can be high dimensional. The domain of computer vision is focused to apply several theories and models for different types of images to explore hidden patterns and extract complex information from these images. Object detection is somewhat related and based on the computer vision and machine intelligence systems. Object detection is frequently used to recognize different objects from an image or a collection of images. It has various applications in different disciplines. Object detection is generally performed by extracting and analyzing features of different objects. In general humans can differentiate among several objects of an image by observing some specific features of an object. Computer vision-based methods can differentiate several objects and recognize class of different objects. To do that, knowledge about the features of a particular object should be already known to the intelligent system. Here, machine learning plays a vital role. Object can be detected and recognized by using machine learning or deep learning approaches. It has different real time applications including face detection, automated surveillance systems, biomedical image analysis, continuous object monitoring like tracking a ball etc. The recent developments in the field of computer vision and object detection are very promising and various real-life applications can be observed in different domains. The advancements in this domain is quite satisfactory but still, the level of intelligence achieved can improved in various ways. Moreover, the existing methods are not very straightforward to apply directly to the real-world problems. Further research is necessary to achieve better performance. Although in some occasions, computer vision-based methods outperform the human vision but in most of the cases computer vision based methods is not compatible with the efficiency of the human vision systems. It is necessary to understand the developments of the computer vision-based systems and the drawbacks in the existing systems so that it can be overcome. Considering the impacts of the computer vision systems in daily life, it is our responsibility to improve the computer vision-based system so that our lifestyle and the quality of Living can be uplifted. The blessings of computer vision converted many dreams into reality. This book will help in understanding the present scenario and also helps in for the development in this field. This book is comprehensive enough to be understood by various people of different profession. The book is suitable for the research persons, industry experts, undergraduate and postgraduate students etc. Is bid book will provide significant knowledge about the computer vision and object recognition which can be used in several real-life applications as well as it is helpful for the further research. A brief description of the constituent chapters of this book is given below.

CHAPTER 1: A ROBUST IMAGE ENCRYPTION METHOD USING CHAOTIC SKEW-TENT MAP

This chapter is dealing with the image security. Authors proposes a novel image encryption method using chaos theory. The chaotic skew-tent map is used to secure the images. This method is a symmetric method of image encryption. The proposed method is compared with other standard methods and the efficiency of the proposed method is proved using both visual and numerical analysis.

CHAPTER 2: ANISOTROPIC DIFFUSION-BASED COLOR TEXTURE ANALYSIS FOR INDUSTRIAL APPLICATION

This work is based on the computer vision and aimed to solve the image classification problem by analyzing the texture features. Authors show an industrial application of the proposed system to process multiplication images. The texture features are obtained by applying the anisotropic diffusion method. The proposed method is tested on the two industrial data sets. The classification is performed by using the k-NN classifier. Different combination of the features are tested and compared with the other standard methods available in the literature.

CHAPTER 3: A BRIEF OVERVIEW ON INTELLIGENT COMPUTING-BASED BIOLOGICAL DATA AND IMAGE ANALYSIS

Automated analysis of biological data and images is always a challenging task. Advanced computing methods are helpful in fast and accurate analysis of the biological data. In general, biomedical data analysis is an inevitable step of various tasks like automated disease analysis, DNA analysis, diagnostic etc. Automated analysis of biological data can reduce the inherent errors which are associated with the manual investigations. Moreover, limited time is an another constraint for these types of applications. This chapter presents an overview about the advancements in this domain and highlight the scope of further development.

CHAPTER 4: AN ADVANCED APPROACH TO DETECT EDGES OF DIGITAL IMAGES FOR IMAGE SEGMENTATION

Edge detection is one of the fundamental problems in computer vision. Edges are helpful to interpret different regions of an image separately. Various methods are available in literature which are proposed to solve the problem of edge detection. This chapter proposes a novel method to solve the problem of edge detection. The detected edges using the proposed method looks very promising. A comparative study shows that the proposed method outperforms various standard edge detection methods. Both visual and numerical analysis of the proposed method establish the efficiency and effectiveness of the proposed method in edge detection.

CHAPTER 5: FUSION APPROACH-BASED HORTICULTURE PLANT DISEASES IDENTIFICATION USING IMAGE PROCESSING

Plant disease is a major threat for the productivity of the crop. To overcome this problem, it is necessary to detect the disease so that appropriate preventive measures can be taken. Manual investigations of the plant diseases requires huge amount of time and effort. Moreover, domain knowledge is essential to study and detect various diseases. This chapter proposes a new method to detect different plant diseases using machine learning and computer vision. In the first stage, the leaves are classified in two classes i.e. healthy and unhealthy. If a particular leaf is found to be unhealthy then, further classification is performed to determine the disease. Author build a database of total 820 leaves which includes both healthy and unhealthy classes. Different classifiers are used to classify the images and a comparative study is presented.

CHAPTER 6: A GENERALIZED OVERVIEW OF THE BIOMEDICAL IMAGE PROCESSING FROM THE BIG DATA PERSPECTIVE

This chapter presents the biomedical image analysis problem from the big data perspective. Generally, modern biomedical image acquisition tools produce a large volume of high dimensional data. Without having any efficient and sophisticated methods, it is very difficult to process such a huge amount of data. This chapter presents the state-of-the-art solutions to handle large volume of biomedical data using various methods of big data analytics.

CHAPTER 7: IMAGE FUSION TECHNIQUES FOR DIFFERENT MULTIMODALITY MEDICAL IMAGES BASED ON VARIOUS CONVENTIONAL AND HYBRID ALGORITHMS FOR DISEASE ANALYSIS

This objective of this article is discuss the image fusion methods to analyse and extract useful information from the biomedical images of various modalities. An image of a certain modality is not enough in various occasions to explain an issue. To properly analyse a disease, it is necessary to study various modalities and combine the the obtained information. This process can be automated by applying some intelligent computer vision based methods. This article talks about some of the recent methods that can fuse the biomedical images of different modalities and can extract useful information from the combined source. Moreover, a new method is proposed to solve the same problem and it is compared with some of the existing methods to prove the effectiveness of it.

CHAPTER 8: AN OVERVIEW OF BIOMEDICAL IMAGE ANALYSIS FROM THE DEEP LEARNING PERSPECTIVE

In this chapter, authors discussed the recent developments in deep learning based biomedical image analysis. Deep learning is an active topic of research and has several applications in biomedical image analysis. Deep learning based object and region of interest detection, segmentation, classification, feature extraction etc. are discussed in the context of biomedical image analysis. Researchers can get an overview of the fundamental concepts of the deep learning methods and the recent developments in the deep learning technologies.

CHAPTER 9: SEGMENTATION-FREE WORD SPOTTING IN HANDWRITTEN DOCUMENTS USING SCALE SPACE CO-HOG FEATURE DESCRIPTORS

In this work, author proposes a method to detect words from a handwritten document. The main advantage of the proposed method is that it doesn't depend on the segmentation. That is why, this method is called segmentation free word spotting method. Author discusses the challenges of the existing methods as well as gives the literature review in the present context. The proposed work is compared with the existing segmentation based as well as segmentation free method and the proposed method is proved to be efficient compared with many existing methods.

This book contains ten chapters which are covering different aspects of the intelligent computing systems for the advancement of the computer vision and object recognition systems. This book proposes a comprehensive approach towards intelligent computing-based computer vision and object recognition covering both intelligent systems and computer vision related challenges. Recent and advanced methods discussed in a lucid language. Therefore, this book will be highly beneficial in understanding the state-of-the-art developments and also opens the scope of further research.

Shouvik Chakraborty
University of Kalyani, India

Kalyani Mali
University of Kalyani, India

Acknowledgment

"Thinking is the hardest work there is, which is probably the reason so few engage in it." – Henry Ford

We are really thankful to our parents, spouse, children, other family members, colleagues and friends for their priceless support and love through all our life. We dedicate this book to all of them. We are grateful to the all peoples who support, read, wrote, and provides valuable insights through the book development journey. Moreover, we are really grateful to all the esteemed authors who shares their knowledge through this book.

Special thanks to the IGI-Global development and publisher team, who stand beside us always as well as our readers, who gave us their heartiest blessings and hope, this small contribution will inspire and help them.

Shouvik Chakraborty
University of Kalyani, India

Kalyani Mali
University of Kalyani, India

Intorduction

To the readers of this book:

Stephen Hawking, the famous theoretical physicist, cosmologist, and author once said that "Success in creating AI could be the biggest event in human history. Unfortunately, it might also be the last, unless we learn how to avoid the risks". This book, *Applications of Advanced Machine Intelligence in Computer Vision and Object Recognition: Emerging Research and Opportunities* is completely dedicated towards the application and study of the advanced computing tools along with the artificial intelligence-based computing resources for modern computer vision and object recognition purposes. Before applying anything new, one must have an idea about the advantages and risks associated with it. To achieve success in the field of research, researches must be aware about the recent developments in the concerned fields as well as the available technologies which will serve as a base of further research. Otherwise it will be very difficult to proceed after a certain height. Efforts given in developing something new should be worthy otherwise researchers can get stuck under a certain level.

This book can help the researchers, students, industry experts and other interested persons to understand the developments in the field of computer vision and object recognition. Computer Vision helps a machine to get an eye and digital image processing helps to understand the scene. With the help of artificial intelligence and Machine Learning, machine becomes more powerful and intelligent. It is an active research area and there are several sections of this domain that can be improved. This field demands continuous enhancements and improvement in terms of methods and applications to support the quality and accuracy of services in different sectors like health care, security etc. From the study of the literature it is understood that this has got promising scope for further research in the areas of object detection and identification, automated disease analysis, quality control etc. With the development of sophisticated hardware for imaging, advanced image analysis is increasingly essential in real life. Readers of this book can easily get an essence of the state-of-the-art research in this domain and can exploit various information and references in further research.

Shouvik Chakraborty
University of Kalyani, India

Kalyani Mali
University of Kalyani, India

Chapter 1
A Robust Image Encryption Method Using Chaotic Skew–Tent Map

Mousomi Roy
University of Kalyani, India

Shouvik Chakraborty
iD https://orcid.org/0000-0002-3427-7492
University of Kalyani, India

Kalyani Mali
University of Kalyani, India

ABSTRACT

Encryption is one of the most frequently used tools in data communications to prevent unwanted access to the data. In the field of image encryption, chaos-based encryption methods have become very popular in the recent years. Chaos-based methods provide a good security mechanism in image communication. In this chapter, chaotic skew-tent map is adapted to encode an image. Seventy-two bit external key is considered (besides the initial parameters of the chaotic system) initially, and after some processing operations, 64 bit internal key is obtained. Using this key, every pixel is processed. The internal key is transformed using some basic operations to enhance the security. The decryption method is very simple so that authentic users can retrieve the information very fast. Every pixel is encrypted using some basic mathematical operations. The values of various test parameters show the power and efficiency of the proposed algorithm, which can be used as a safeguard for sensitive image data and a secure method of image transmission.

DOI: 10.4018/978-1-7998-2736-8.ch001

INTRODUCTION

At present, digital images are used as a frequent medium to transfer messages. Therefore it is very important to secure the digital images. Many real life applications demand reliable, fast and secured encryption of images. Some examples of the real life scenarios where the security of the images are vital are: army image databases, video conferencing, various medical images and their automated analysis results (Chakraborty, Chatterjee, Dey, Ashour, & Shi, 2018; Chakraborty, Mali, Chatterjee, Banerjee, Roy, Deb, et al., 2018;. Chakraborty, Mali, Chatterjee, Banerjee, Roy, Dutta, et al., 2018; Shouvik Chakraborty, Chatterjee, Dey, et al., 2017; Chakraborty et al., 2019; S. Hore et al., 2016; Hore et al., 2015; M. Roy et al., 2017; Roy et al., 2017), online personal photographs, images in social networking sites etc. This requirement is the main inspiration of image encryption systems. In the last decade, a good number of encryption algorithms (Ahmad, Alam, Umayya, Khan, & Ahmad, 2018; Bourbakis & Alexopoulos, 1992; Chakraborty, Seal, Roy, & Mali, 2016; Chang, Hwang, & Chen, 2001; H. K. C. Chang & Liu, 1997; Chen, Mao, & Chui, 2004; Cheng, 2000; Fridrich, 1998; Jui-Cheng & Jiun-In Guo, n.d.; Li & Zheng, 2002; Li, Zheng, Mou, & Cai, n.d.; Liu & Xia, 2017; Mali, Chakraborty, Seal, & Roy, 2015; Refregier & Javidi, 1995; Scharinger, 1998; Seal, Chakraborty, & Mali, 2017; Yen, J.-C. Guo, 2000; Yen & Guo, 1999; Zhang & Chen, 2008) are proposed by many scientists based on various principles. Among these algorithms, chaos based encryption methods are well known for their security, complexity, speed etc. The digital images are not similar in nature like a text data. They possess some certain properties like: redundant data, high correlation value, less sensitive i.e. a small modification in the value of any pixel of the digital image does not heavily reduce the details and quality of the image. Some of the features of the image may not be always directly visible (Chakraborty, Chatterjee, Ashour, Mali, & Dey, 2017; Chakraborty, Chatterjee, Das, & Mali, 2020; Chakraborty & Mali, 2018; Chakraborty, Mali, Chatterjee, Banerjee, Sah, et al., 2017; Chakraborty, Roy, & Hore, 2016; Hore, Chatterjee, Chakraborty, & Shaw, 2016). The popular text encryption methods like DES, AES, IDEA are not suitable for digital images because of their high computational time and computational power (Seal, Chakraborty, & Mali, 2017). Digital image encryption systems should not take very high time for real life applications (Seal et al., 2017). If an encryption process with high degree of security takes too much time then, that method cannot be used in practical situations.

Many chaos based image encryption algorithms are proposed in recent years. Some of them are discussed here in brief. Bourbakis and Alexopoulos (1992) (Bourbakis & Alexopoulos, 1992) developed an image encryption technique which uses the SCAN language for encryption and compression simultaneously. Fridrich (Fridrich, 1998) illustrated a symmetric block encryption scheme that uses two-dimensional standard baker map. Scharinger (Scharinger, 1998) developed a chaotic image encryption technique based on Kolmogorov-flow, where the total image is considered as a single block and permutation is done using a key-controlled chaotic process. Yen and Guo (Yen & Guo, 1999) developed an image encryption method called BRIE. It is based on the logistic map. Cheng and Guo (Jui-Cheng & Guo, n.d.) also proposed a technique called CKBA (Chaotic Key Based Algorithm). CKBA uses a binary sequence as a key and it is generated using a chaotic system. Li and Zheng (2002) (Li & Zheng, 2002) pointed out some loop holes in the encryption method described in the references (Jui-Cheng & J Guo, n.d.; Yen & Guo, 1999) and also proposed some possible improvements. Li et al. (S. Li et al., n.d.) presented a video encryption scheme. It uses multiple digital chaotic systems and it is known as CVES (i.e. Chaotic Video Encryption Scheme). Recently, Chen et al. (Chen et al., 2004) developed a symmetric image encryption method in which a 2D chaotic map is generalized to 3D. This scheme employs the 3D cat map. N.K. Pareek et al. (Pareek, Patidar, & Sud, 2006) proposed an image encryption technique using chaotic logistic map. Chakraborty et. al. proposed a new image encryption method based on logistic map and DNA substitution method (Chakraborty, Seal, et al., 2016). Metaheuristic algorithms have several applications (Chakraborty, Mali, Banerjee, et al., 2018; Chakraborty, Mali, Chatterjee, Anand, et al., 2018; Chakraborty et al., 2018; Chakraborty, Seal, & Roy, 2015; Chakraborty, Mali, Chatterjee, Banerjee, Mazumdar, et al., 2017; Chakraborty, Mali, Chatterjee, Banerjee, Sah, et al., 2017; Sarddar, Chakraborty, & Roy, 2015) in different domains including image encryption. Ahamad et. al. developed a chaotic map based methods optimized with particle swarm optimization (Ahmad et al., 2018). In (Wang, Liu, & Zhang, 2015), authors proposed a new image encryption method which is based on simulated annealing (Chakraborty & Bhowmik, 2015; Shouvik Chakraborty & Bhowmik, 2013, 2015) and chaos theory. Some security related issues of chaotic cryptography is discussed in (Muhammad & Ozkaynak, 2019).An extended chaotic map based encryption method is proposed in (Meshram, Lee, Meshram, & Li, 2019). This work is based on the 1 dimensional model for cryptographic transformation. A cryptanalysis study is performed on the chaos based image encryption systems in (Wong, Yap, Goi, & Wong, 2019). A cellular automata and chaos based image encryption method is proposed in (Li, Belazi, Kharbech, Talha, & Xiang, 2019). Hilbert curves and H-Fractals based a chaotic image encryption scheme is proposed in (Xuncai Zhang, Wang, Zhou, & Niu, 2019). In this work, SHA 3 algorithm is used to compute the hash value of the image.

The properties of the chaotic maps have drawn the attention of scientists to develop encryption algorithms based on it. The chaotic maps have some basic characteristics e.g. ergodicity, sensitivity to initial condition (system parameter) etc (Roy, Chakraborty, et al., 2019; Mousomi Roy, Mali, et al., 2019). In this context, a new image encryption method is proposed depending on chaotic skew-tent maps to satisfy the requirements of the fast and secure image transfer. In the proposed encryption method an external key of 72-bit and skew-tent map is employed. The initial parameter for the skew-tent map can be used as an another set of key. In the proposed encryption process, some basic operators are applied to encrypt the pixels of an digital image. To make the algorithm more robust against any kinds of attack, after each encryption of a four bit block, the internal key is modified by substitution method and after the completion of a row, the internal key is modified using the chaotic sequence.

INTRODUCTION TO CHAOS THEORY

Chaos theory is one of the major areas of study in mathematics and physics. It is dependent on the nature of the dynamic systems. These systems are highly sensitive to their initial conditions. Very little differences in initial conditions (e.g errors due to rounding in numerical computation) generates widely diverging results for such systems. Therefore long term prediction is very difficult in reality. It is very interesting phenomena because these systems are deterministic, i.e. their future nature is totally determined by their initial parameters and no random elements involved in it. The systems are not predictable if the initial conditions are not known earlier. Edward Lorenz summarized the chaos theory. Chaotic behavior can be observed in different natural systems, like weather and climate. Since long time, Chaos theory is being used in the cryptography. The concept of confusion and diffusion can be modeled well by the chaos theory (Wang & Zhao, 2010). DNA computing and chaos theory together provides an efficient way to encrypt an image (Babaei, 2013; Chakraborty, Seal, et al., 2016).

A chaotic map is a map that possesses some sort of chaotic behavior. Maps can be parameterized using a continuous-time or a discrete-time parameter. Discrete maps normally uses the form of an iterated function. Chaotic maps can 1, 2 or 3 dimensional. Examples of some chaotic maps are: Logistic map, tent map, Arnold's cat map, Baker's map e.t.c. In this paper, skew-tent map is adapted for the image encryption purpose and it is discussed below.

Skew-Tent Map

The skew-tent map is ergodic and has uniform non-variant density function in its interval. It is one of the simplest kind of 1D chaotic maps and it is defined in equation 1 (Pareek, Patidar, & Sud, 2010).

$$x_{i+1} = F\left(\alpha, x_i\right) = \begin{cases} \dfrac{x_i}{\alpha}, x_i = [0, \alpha) \\ \dfrac{1 - x_i}{1 - \alpha}, x_i = (\alpha, 1] \end{cases} \tag{1}$$

Where α is the parameter of the system and x_i is the initial condition of the map. The system parameter α, determines the position of the top of the tent in the interval [0,1]. A sequence computed by iterating $F(\alpha,x)$, is expansionary everywhere in the interval [0,1]. Figure 1 shows the orbits of the skew-tent map for the system parameter 0.4. Figure 2 shows the bifurcation diagram and figure 3 shows the sensitivity of chaotic skew tent map on initial condition and system parameter (α).

Figure 1. The orbits of the skew tent map for system parameter value 0.4

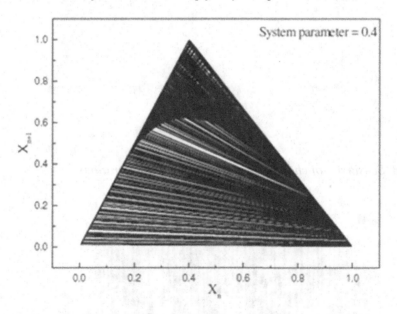

Random Bit Generation Using Chaotic Map (Pseudo Noise(PN) Sequences)

A pseudo random bit generator (PRBG) algorithm is deterministic in nature, that uses a random binary sequence of length k called seed and generates a binary sequence of length l>>k, and it is called pseudo random sequence. The output of a PRBG is not exactly random. The key idea is to take a very small and truly random sequence of length k and then expand it to a much larger sequence of length l in such a way

Figure 2. Bifurcation diagram for tent map

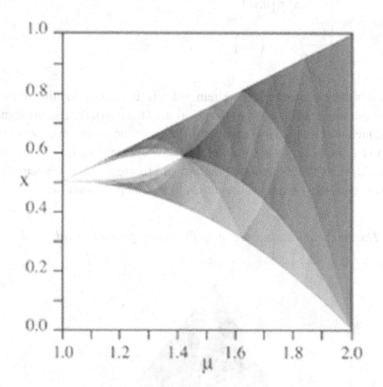

Figure 3. Sensitivity of chaotic skew tent map for 250 iterations

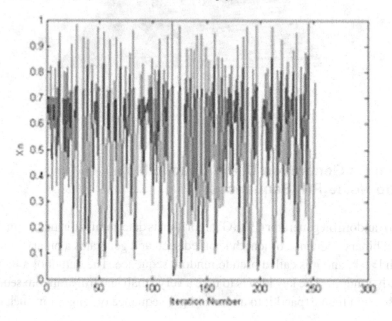

that it cannot efficiently be distinguished between output sequence of PRBG and really random sequence.

In this work, a Chaotic tent map based Bit Generator is used where two skew-tent maps are chosen. They are piecewise linear chaotic maps. The system parameter for both the chaotic maps is kept same.

Let $f_1(x_0,\alpha)$ and $f_2(y_0,\alpha)$ be two piecewise linear chaotic maps given in equation 2.

$$x_{i+1} = f_1(\alpha, x_i)$$
$$y_{i+1} = f_2(\alpha, y_i) \tag{2}$$

Where α is the system parameter and is same for both chaotic tent maps, x_i and y_i are the initial conditions and x_{i+1} and y_{i+1} are their new corresponding states.

The chaotic tent map produces the binary sequences by comparing the generated outputs of the piecewise linear chaotic maps using equation 3.

$$g(x_{n+1}, y_{n+1}) = \begin{cases} 0, & x_{n+1} < y_{n+1} \\ 1, & otherwise \end{cases} \tag{3}$$

PROPOSED APPROACH

Encryption Method

The proposed encryption procedure is based on the chaotic system. The first step is to process the 72 bits randomly predetermined external key. A chaotic sequence of length 36 bits is generated using two skew-tent maps. The initial condition of the skew-tent map can serve as an another set of keys which makes the encryption process stronger. Now, this 36 bit sequence is reversed and concatenated with the original sequence to generate a 72 bits chaotic sequence. This procedure is shown in figure 4. Now, a XOR operation is to be performed between the external key and the concatenated chaotic sequence and then the result of the XOR operation is inverted (by applying NOT operator). So, 72 bit processed key is obtained in this method. Now, every 9th bit of the key is discarded to get a 64 bit internal key. The key discarding process is illustrated in figure 5. This is the first step of the encryption algorithm. Now, a 64 bit chaotic sequence is obtained using the skew-tent map.

Now every pixel of the image is processed as discussed next. At first, a pixel is converted into 8 bit binary form and reversed. 8 bits are taken from the processed internal key and XOR operation is performed with the reversed sequence and the

Figure 4. Generation of 72 bit chaotic sequence

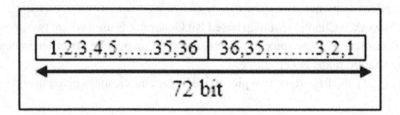

Figure 5. The key discarding process

1	2	3	4	5	6	7	8	9
10	11	12	13	14	15	16	17	18
19	20	21	22	23	24	25	26	27
28	29	30	31	32	33	34	35	36
37	38	39	40	41	42	43	44	45
46	47	48	49	50	51	52	53	54
55	56	57	58	59	60	61	62	63
64	65	66	67	68	69	70	71	72

result of the XOR operation is inverted and the inverted sequence is converted into the decimal form and stored as an encoded pixel. When 64 bit key gets exhausted (i.e. 8 pixels are processed) then the last 8 encoded pixels are taken and only the pixels of the even positions are considered. These pixels are converted into binary and reversed. The new key is generated by replacing the bytes in the even positions of the old key with the corresponding reversed bit sequence generated in the previous step. This process changes the key after 8 pixels and increases the security. This process is shown in figure 6.

When a row gets completed, generate a completely new key by doing XOR operation between the last operated key and the chaotic sequence generated at beginning. So for every row, we get a completely new key for each row. The key is frequently changed which makes this algorithm more secure against cryptographic attacks. At last transpose the image to get the ultimate encrypted image. The encryption algorithm is given below.

Figure 6. The key modification process

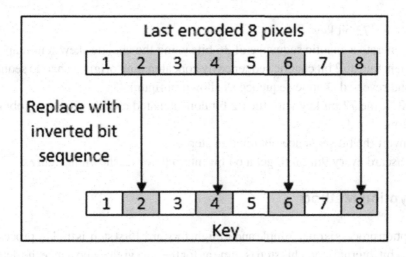

Algorithm 1: Chaotic Skew-Tent Map based Encryption

1. Key processing - generate 64 bit internal key from 72 bits external key
2. Generate a chaotic sequence of 64 bit length using skew-tent map
3. For each pixel repeat steps 3 to 9
4. Convert a pixel value to a 8 bit binary sequence
5. Reverse the sequence obtained in step 4.
6. Take 8 bits from the internal key and perform XOR operation with the reversed sequence
7. Reverse the result obtained in step 6 and convert it into decimal form and store it as an encrypted pixel
8. When 64 bit key gets exhausted (i.e. 8 pixels are covered) then perform the following (as in figure 6):
   a. Take the last 8 pixels those are covered by the key and consider only the pixels of the even positions
   b. Convert the pixel values (already encrypted) in binary and reverse it
   c. Generate the new key by replacing the bytes in the even positions of the old key with the corresponding reversed bit sequence generated in step 8.b.
9. When a row gets completed, generate a completely new key by doing key XOR chaotic sequence generated in step 2 and for next rows generate new chaotic sequence using skew-tent map
10. Transpose the generated encoded image to get the final image

Algorithm 2: Key Processing

1. Take a 72 bit key
2. Generate a chaotic sequence of 36 bits using the chaotic skew-tent map
3. Generate a 72 bit chaotic sequence by concatenating original chaotic sequence and reversed chaotic sequence as shown in figure 4.
4. XOR the 72 bit key with the 72 bit concatenated chaotic sequence (obtained from step 3)
5. Invert the bit sequence obtained in step 4
6. Discard every 9th bit to get a 64 bit internal key as shown in figure 5

Decryption Method

Decryption process is quite simple and straight forward. First step, is the key processing to get 64 bit internal key. This step is same as for the encryption and hence the detailed discussion is omitted. After generating the internal key using the key processing algorithm, the encrypted image is transposed. Then a chaotic sequence of length 64 bits is generated using two chaotic skew-tent maps. Now for each pixel, an encrypted pixel value is converted to 8 bit binary form and reversed it. Now 8 bits are taken from the internal key and XOR operation is performed with the reversed sequence. The result of the XOR operation is reversed and converted into decimal form and stored as a decrypted pixel. When the 64 bit key gets exhausted (i.e. 8 pixels are covered) then the last 8 pixels those are covered by the key are taken and only the pixels of the even positions are considered. The pixel values are converted (before decryption) into binary and reversed. The new key is generated by replacing the bytes in even positions of the old key with the corresponding reversed bit sequence generated in the previous step. A completely new key is generated at the completion of every row, by performing XOR operation between key and the chaotic sequence generated at beginning using skew-tent map. The decryption process is completely lossless in nature. The algorithm for the decryption process is given below.

Algorithm 3: Chaotic Skew-Tent Map based Decryption

1. Key processing - generate 64 bit internal key from 72 bits external key
2. Transpose the encoded image
3. Generate a chaotic sequence of 64 bit length using two skew-tent maps
4. For each pixel repeat steps 3 to 10
5. Convert an encrypted pixel value to 8 bit binary form
6. Reverse the sequence obtained in step 5
7. Take 8 bit from the internal key and perform XOR with the reversed sequence

8. Reverse the result and convert it into decimal form and store it as a decrypted pixel

9. When 64 bit key gets exhausted (i.e. 8 pixels are covered) then perform the following (as in figure 5):

   a. Take the last 8 pixels those are covered by the key and consider the pixels that belongs to the even positions

   b. Convert the pixel values (encrypted i.e. before decryption) in binary and reverse it

   c. Generate the new key by replacing the bytes of the even positions of the old key with the corresponding reversed bit sequence generated in step 9. b.

10. When a row gets completed, generate a completely new key by performing XOR operation between the last operated key and the chaotic sequence generated in step 3.

EXPERIMENTAL RESULTS AND ANALYSIS

The target of the image cryptographic algorithms is to protect the original image and generate an image that is difficult to understand by vision as well as by statistical analysis. It must be resilient against any cryptographic attacks. The proposed algorithm degrades the image quality during the encryption technique but at the end of the decryption, the original image is restored. Visual inspection may not be always sufficient to test the quality of the encryption algorithm. Automated image quality evaluation methods that are based on statistical, mathematical and computational algorithms are necessary because of the variability and inconsistency between different human observers (Mali, Chakraborty, & Roy, 2015). In this work, the quality of the encrypted image is assessed by some standard parameters. In the following sections, details of the different evaluation parameters along with the results are given.

Statistical Analysis

Correlation Coefficients

Correlation coefficients is computed in three different direction i.e. horizontal, vertical and diagonal. Correlation coefficients are calculated for the selected pairs using equation 4 (Shouvik Chakraborty, Seal, et al., 2016).

$$R_{xy} = COV(xy) / \sqrt{D(x)} \sqrt{D(y)} \qquad (4)$$

where,

$$COV(xy) = \frac{1}{T} \sum_{i=1}^{T} \left((x_i - E(x))(y_i - E(y)) \right) \qquad (5)$$

$$E(x) = \frac{1}{T} \sum_{i=1}^{T} x_i, \; E(y) = \frac{1}{T} \sum_{j=1}^{T} y_j \qquad (6)$$

$$D(x) = \frac{1}{T} \sum_{i=1}^{T} (x_i - E(x_i))^2, \; D(y) = \frac{1}{T} \sum_{i=1}^{T} (y_i - E(y_i))^2 \qquad (7)$$

where x, and y in the above equations are the gray-scale values of the two adjacent pixels in the image, and T is the total pair of pixels, randomly selected from the image. Table 1 provides the comparison among the proposed approach and some other benchmark approaches. Table 2 shows the results obtained by applying the proposed approach on some standard images.

Table 1. Comparison of correlation coefficients in original and encrypted images

Encryption Method	Test Image	Horizontal		Vertical		Diagonal	
		Original	Encrypted	Original	Encrypted	Original	Encrypted
Proposed	Lena	0.8956	-0.028	0.9521	-0.0022	0.8563	0.0009
	Lake	0.9252	-0.0486	0.9266	0.0274	0.8794	-0.0134
Tedmori and Najdawi (Tedmori & Al-Najdawi, 2014)	Lena	0.919	0.0023	0.927	0.0042	0.962	0.0053
	Lake	0.987	0.0025	0.936	0.0015	0.927	0.0105
Ye (Ye, 2011)	Lena	0.904	0.0020	0.903	0.0042	0.953	0.0088
	Lake	0.976	-0.0730	0.904	-0.0038	0.912	0.0191
Sethi and Sharma (Sethi & Sharma, n.d.)	Lena	0.913	0.0031	0.920	0.0049	0.925	0.0062
	Lake	0.942	-0.0016	0.922	0.0036	0.887	0.0144
Huang and Nien (Huang & Nien, 2009)	Lena	0.916	0.0058	0.929	0.0092	0.946	0.0058
	Lake	0.982	0.0074	0.898	0.0084	0.924	0.0146
Liu et. Al. (Liu & Xia, 2017)	Lena	0.9792	−0.0028	0.9888	0.0081	0.9653	0.0091
	Lake	0.9657	0.0071	0.9630	−0.0080	0.9401	0.0060
Chakraborty et. al. (Shouvik Chakraborty, Seal, et al., 2016)	Lena	0.946	-0.0055	0.973	-0.0075	0.921	0.0026
	Lake	0.958	-0.0025	0.958	0.00977	0.929	0.0127

Table 2. Correlation coefficients in original and encrypted images based on the proposed encryption algorithm results

Test Image	Horizontal			Vertical			Diagonal		
	Org	Enc	Dec	Org	Enc	Dec	Org	Enc	Dec
Lena	0.8956	-0.028	0.8956	0.9521	-0.0022	0.9521	0.8563	0.0009	0.8563
Lake	0.92528	-0.04867	0.92528	0.92668	0.02740	0.92668	0.87946	-0.01349	0.87946
Living-Room	0.90160	-0.03038	0.90160	0.90361	-0.00386	0.90361	0.83162	- 0.0001	0.83162
Pirate	0.90890	-0.0066	0.90890	0.92973	0.00271	0.92973	0.85770	0.00824	0.85770
Peeper	0.92380	-0.01252	0.92380	0.94345	-0.00212	0.94345	0.87391	-0.00516	0.87391
Jetplane	0.8935	-0.0177	0.8935	0.87816	-0.00471	0.87816	0.8054	-0.00029	0.8054
House	0.95695	-0.03927	0.95695	0.95191	0.00239	0.95191	0.92093	-0.00235	0.92093
Cameraman	0.92066	-0.0109	0.92066	0.95381	0.00601	0.95381	0.88938	-0.00505	0.88938
Mandril	0.87287	-0.00801	0.87287	0.87699	-0.01512	0.87699	0.81707	0.00332	0.81707
Hestain	0.87359	-0.00966	0.87359	0.86943	0.00376	0.86943	0.78323	-0.00042	0.78323
Walkbridge	0.92548	-0.03009	0.92548	0.88750	0.01004	0.88750	0.84897	0.01141	0.84897
Woman Darkhair	0.97802	-0.01415	0.97802	0.98019	0.00166	0.98019	0.96302	0.00302	0.96302

PSNR

PSNR is an abbreviation for Peak Signal to Noise Ratio. PSNR is a well-known parameter that can be computed using equation 8 (Chakraborty, Seal, et al., 2016). The PSNR results in an undefined value under one condition only; i.e., when the original image is compared to itself. In that case, the MSE value in the denominator part of the equation 8 would result in a zero value, and hence, a division by zero situation occurs.

$$PSNR = 10 \log_{10} \left(\frac{L^2}{MSE} \right) \tag{8}$$

where the parameter MSE represent Mean Squared Error and given in equation 9.

$$MSE = \frac{1}{N} \sum_{i=0, j=0}^{N,N} \left(x_{ij} - y_{ij} \right)^2 \tag{9}$$

Here, N is the number of pixels in the frame and x_{ij}, y_{ij} are the ith and j^{th} pixels in the original and processed frames, respectively. L is the dynamic range of pixel values (L can ranges from 0 to 255 for gray-scale images). Table 3 provides the comparison of the proposed approach and some other benchmark approaches. Table 4 shows the results obtained after applying the proposed approach on some standard images.

Table 3. Comparison of PSNR values

Test Image	Proposed		Tedmori and Najdawi (Tedmori & Al-Najdawi, 2014)		Samsom and Sastry (Samson & U., 2012)		Sethi and Sharma (Sethi & Sharma, n.d.)		Huang and Nien (Huang & Nien, 2009)		Chakraborty et. al. (Shouvik Chakraborty, Seal, et al., 2016)	
	O-D	O-E	O-D	O-E	O-D	O-E	O-D	O-E	O-D	O-E	O-D	O-E
Lena	Undefined	0.0092	Undefined	0.0017	40.22	0.113	69.70	0.036	45.78	0.154	Undefined	0.0049
Lake	Undefined	0.0083	Undefined	0.0043	33.49	0.098	43.65	0.072	51.83	0.127	Undefined	0.0043

Table 4. PSNR values of some standard images obtained using proposed approach

Test Image	PSNR	
	O-D	O-E
Lena	Undefined	0.0092
Lake	Undefined	0.0083
Living-Room	Undefined	0.0096
Pirate	Undefined	0.0091
Peeper	Undefined	0.0089
Jetplane	Undefined	0.0081
House	Undefined	0.0088
Cameraman	Undefined	0.0085
Mandril	Undefined	0.0097
Hestain	Undefined	0.0094
Walkbridge	Undefined	0.0089
Woman Darkhair	Undefined	0.0083

Differential Attacks: NPCR and UACI

If one small modification in the actual image generates a significant change in the encrypted image, this shows that the encryption technique can resist differential attacks efficiently. To test the influence of only one pixel change in the plain image over the whole encrypted image (the attacker can make a slight change (e.g. modify one pixel) of the original image to find some meaningful relationships), two frequently used measures are Number of Pixels Change Rate (NPCR) and Unified Average

Changing Intensity(UACI). NPCR and UACI can be defined using equation 10 and equation 11 respectively (Chakraborty, Seal, et al., 2016).

$$NPCR = \frac{\sum_{i=j=1}^{m,n} D(i,j)}{w \times h} \times 100\%$$

(10)

$$UACI = \frac{1}{w \times h} \left[\sum_{i,j}^{m,n} \frac{\left| C_1(i,j) - C_2(i,j) \right|}{255} \right] \times 100\%$$

(11)

Where C1 and C2 are two encrypted images corresponding to two original images with subtle change e.g., one pixel difference. The parameters 'w' and 'h' represents the width and the height of the image, D(i, j) is a bipolar array with the same size as image C1 and it can be determined using equation 12 (Chakraborty, Seal, et al., 2016).

$$D(i,j) = \begin{cases} 1 \, if \, C_1(i,j) = C_2(i,j) \\ 0 \, Otherwise \end{cases}$$

(12)

Table 5 provides the comparison among proposed approach and some other benchmark approaches. Table 6 shows the results obtained by applying the proposed approach on some standard images.

Table 5. Comparison of NPCR and UACI values

Test Image	Proposed		Tedmori and Najdawi (Tedmori & Al-Najdawi, 2014)		Ye (Ye, 2011)		Sethi and Sharma (Sethi & Sharma, n.d.)		Huang and Nien (Huang & Nien, 2009)		Chakraborty et. al. (Shouvik Chakraborty, Seal, et al., 2016)	
	NPCR%	UACI%	NPCR%	UACI%	NPCR%	UACI%	NPCR%	UACI%	NPCR%	UACI%		
Lena	99.683	28.604	99.941	38.981	99.105	36.241	95.124	20.113	99.214	27.481	99.932	39.520
Lake	99.609	31.669	99.953	40.874	98.642	37.121	34.124	98.642	98.349	27.628	99.85	40.303

Entropy

If an encryption method produces an encrypted image as output whose entropy is less than 8 bits, then there would be a chance of predictability. It can create some problems for in terms of the security. The entropy of an image is calculated using equation 13.

Table 6. NPCR and UACI values of some standard images obtained using proposed approach

Test Image	Proposed Approach	
	NPCR	UACI
Lena	99.683%	28.604%
Lake	99.609%	31.669%
Living-Room	99.548%	27.326%
Pirate	99.530%	28.745%
Peeper	99.603%	29.636%
Jetplane	99.622%	32.327%
House	99.615%	29.858%
Cameraman	99.597%	30.606%
Mandril	99.658%	27.358%
Hestain	99.683%	28.269%
Walkbridge	99.518%	29.455%
Woman Darkhair	99.536%	31.694%

$$H(s) = -\sum_{i=0}^{N-1} p(s_i) \log_2 p(s_i) \tag{13}$$

Here $p(s_i)$ is the probability of presence of the symbol s_i [27] [22]. The entropy of an image shows the distribution of the gray scale values. Higher entropy information is obtained in more uniform distributions. Table 7 provides the comparison of entropy values between proposed approach and some other benchmark approaches. Table 8 shows the results obtained by applying the proposed approach on various standard images.

Table 7. Comparison of the entropy values

Method	Images	
	Lena	Lake
Proposed	7.991	7.998
Tedmori and Najdawi (Tedmori & Al-Najdawi, 2014)	7.998	7.996
Ye (Ye, 2011)	7.989	6.574
Sethi and Sharma (Sethi & Sharma, n.d.)	7.247	7.160
Huang and Nien (Huang & Nien, 2009)	6.732	7.826

Table 8. Entropy values of some standard images obtained by applying the proposed approach

Test Image	Proposed Approach		
	Original	Encrypted	Decrypted
Lena	7.40406	7.982175	7.40406
Lake	7.475101	7.980997	7.475101
Living-Room	7.340895	7.980417	7.340895
Pirate	7.290901	7.982927	7.290901
Peeper	7.547372	7.982726	7.547372
Jetplane	6.735717	7.980006	6.735717
House	5.728775	7.955951	5.728775
Cameraman	7.044226	7.980038	7.044226
Mandril	7.149238	7.979089	7.149238
Hestain	7.217699	7.981043	7.979723
Walkbridge	7.605784	7.978831	7.605784
Woman Darkhair	7.269206	7.98054	7.269206

Analysis of the Key Space

In the proposed algorithm, a 72 bit symmetric encryption key is used. In the domain of cryptography, algorithms that use the same key for encryption and decryption process are called symmetric key methods. The 72bit key is not dependent on image and it is preprocessed and then applied on the image. The internal key undergoes a substitution step after each block of 64 bits and a completely new key is generated after the complete processing of every row using a skew-tent map. Symmetric key encryption methods are much faster than public key encryption. It makes the key unpredictable and resilient against cryptographic attacks.

For the sake of the security, the key space must be large enough to make the brute force attacks infeasible. The proposed scheme has 2^{64} different combinations of the internal key and 2^{72} different combinations of the external key. An image encryption method with such a long key space is sufficient for reliable and secure uses in the practical applications. Moreover, the initial parameters of the chaotic skew-tent map is also very difficult to predict and hence, it provides two layers of security. Here, we have 3 initial keys (α, x_0, y_0) for the two chaotic skew-tent maps. Now, if the precision of the α is (2×10^{-15}), and precision of x_0 and y_0 is (1.5×10^{-16}) then the secret key space = $[(2 \times 10^{-15}) \times (1.5 \times 10^{-16}) \times (1.5 \times 10^{-16})]^{-1}$ = $[4.5 \times 10^{-47}]^{-1} \approx 2.2 \times 10^{46}$.

Histogram Analysis

The histogram of an image describes how pixels in an image are distributed by plotting the number of pixels for each intensity levels. The histogram of the encrypted images is significantly different from the histogram of the original and hence it does not provide any useful information to perform any statistical analysis attack on the encrypted image.

Figure 7. In the first row, Histogram representation of the Cameraman standard image (from left to right Original, Encrypted and Decrypted),From second row, top to bottom Correlation coefficients of Original, Encrypted and Decrypted, left to right Correlation coefficients in Horizontal, Vertical and Diagonal directions are plotted

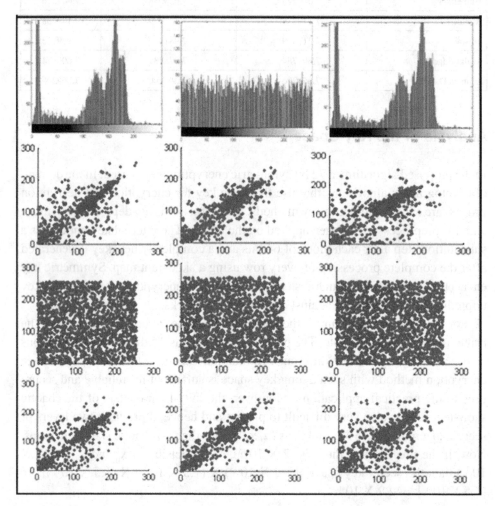

Figure 8. From top to bottom, Standard images "Cameraman", "Hestain", "House" and "Jetplane", from right to left, the figure present the original, encrypted and decrypted algorithms results.

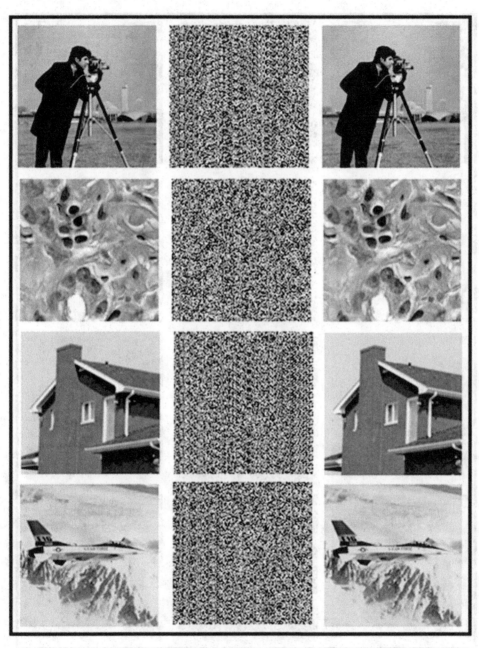

Figure 9. From top to bottom, Standard images "Lake", "Lena", "Livingroom" and "Mandril", from right to left, the figure present the original, encrypted and decrypted algorithms results.

Figure 10. From top to bottom, Standard images "Peppers", "Pirate", "Walkbridge" and "Woman Drakhair", from right to left, the figure present the original, encrypted and decrypted algorithms results.

Figure 7. shows an example (for the cameraman image) of plotting the histogram of the original, encrypted, and decrypted along with the correlation coefficients. Figure 8 to Figure 10 gives some of the results obtained using the proposed encoding/decoding algorithms. These results are obtained by applying the proposed method on some standard test images.

CONCLUSION

This proposed work is based on image manipulation using chaotic map. Encryption procedure is simple, secure and robust that makes the method suitable for the real life communications and the decryption process follows exactly the opposite way of the encryption method. The proposed approach changes the key, after processing every 8 pixels and also creates a new key for every row. The proposed approach also provides a two level security by using a key set for the chaotic maps and an another external key. This makes our approach resilient, robust and cogent enough in comparison to the other approaches available. Not only visual inspection but, different parameters are used to test and prove the viability of the approach and it has been found to be satisfactory. Various security and statistical analysis tests are carried out in order to evaluate the robustness of the proposed work. Results are compared against benchmark algorithms which describes the effectiveness of the proposed work. This work can be highly beneficial in secured digital communication that can save many precious data from unauthorized access.

REFERENCES

Ahmad, M., Alam, M. Z., Umayya, Z., Khan, S., & Ahmad, F. (2018). An image encryption approach using particle swarm optimization and chaotic map. International Journal of Information Technology, 1–9. doi:10.100741870-018-0099-y

Babaei, M. (2013). A novel text and image encryption method based on chaos theory and DNA computing. *Natural Computing*, *12*(1), 101–107. doi:10.1007/s11047-012-9334-9

Bourbakis, N., & Alexopoulos, C. (1992). Picture data encryption using scan patterns. *Pattern Recognition*, *25*(6), 567–581. doi:10.1016/0031-3203(92)90074-S

Chakraborty, S., & Bhowmik, S. (2013). Job Shop Scheduling using Simulated Annealing. First International Conference on Computation and Communication Advancement, 1(1), 69–73. Retrieved from https://scholar.google.co.in/citations?user=8lhQFaYAAAAJ&hl=en

Chakraborty, S., & Bhowmik, S. (2015). An Efficient Approach to Job Shop Scheduling Problem using Simulated Annealing. *International Journal of Hybrid Information Technology*, *8*(11), 273–284. doi:10.14257/ijhit.2015.8.11.23

Chakraborty, S., & Bhowmik, S. (2015). Blending roulette wheel selection with simulated annealing for job shop scheduling problem. Michael Faraday IET International Summit 2015, 100(7). doi:10.1049/cp.2015.1696

Chakraborty, S., Chatterjee, S., Ashour, A. S., Mali, K., & Dey, N. (2017). Intelligent Computing in Medical Imaging: A Study. In N. Dey (Ed.), *Advancements in Applied Metaheuristic Computing* (pp. 143–163)., doi:10.4018/978-1-5225-4151-6.ch006

Chakraborty, S., Chatterjee, S., Chatterjee, A., Mali, K., Goswami, S., & Sen, S. (2018). Automated Breast Cancer Identification by analyzing Histology Slides using Metaheuristic Supported Supervised Classification coupled with Bag-of-Features. 2018 Fourth International Conference on Research in Computational Intelligence and Communication Networks (ICRCICN), 81–86. doi:10.1109/ICRCICN.2018.8718736

Chakraborty, S., Chatterjee, S., Das, A., & Mali, K. (2020). Penalized Fuzzy C-Means Enabled Hybrid Region Growing in Segmenting Medical Images. doi:10.1007/978-981-13-8930-6_3

Chakraborty, S., Chatterjee, S., Dey, N., Ashour, A. S., Ashour, A. S., Shi, F., & Mali, K. (2017). Modified cuckoo search algorithm in microscopic image segmentation of hippocampus. *Microscopy Research and Technique*, *80*(10), 1051–1072. doi:10.1002/jemt.22900 PubMed

Chakraborty, S., Chatterjee, S., Dey, N., Ashour, A. S., & Shi, F. (2018). Gradient approximation in retinal blood vessel segmentation. 2017 4th IEEE Uttar Pradesh Section International Conference on Electrical, Computer and Electronics, UPCON 2017, 2018–Janua. 10.1109/UPCON.2017.8251120

Chakraborty, S., & Mali, K. (2018). Application of Multiobjective Optimization Techniques in Biomedical Image Segmentation—A Study. In Multi-Objective Optimization (pp. 181–194). doi:10.1007/978-981-13-1471-1_8

Chakraborty, S., Mali, K., Banerjee, S., Roy, K., Saha, D., & Chatterjee, S. ... Majumder, S. (2018). Bag-of-features based classification of dermoscopic images. 2017 4th International Conference on Opto-Electronics and Applied Optics, Optronix 2017, 2018–Janua. 10.1109/OPTRONIX.2017.8349977

Chakraborty, S., Mali, K., Chatterjee, S., Anand, S., Basu, A., & Banerjee, S. ... Bhattacharya, A. (2018). Image based skin disease detection using hybrid neural network coupled bag-of-features. 2017 IEEE 8th Annual Ubiquitous Computing, Electronics and Mobile Communication Conference, UEMCON 2017, 2018–Janua. 10.1109/UEMCON.2017.8249038

Chakraborty, S., Mali, K., Chatterjee, S., Banerjee, S., Mazumdar, K. G., & Debnath, M. ... Roy, K. (2017). Detection of skin disease using metaheuristic supported artificial neural networks. 2017 8th Annual Industrial Automation and Electromechanical Engineering Conference (IEMECON), 224–229. 10.1109/IEMECON.2017.8079594

Chakraborty, S., Mali, K., Chatterjee, S., Banerjee, S., Roy, K., & Deb, K. ... Prasad, N. (2018). An integrated method for automated biomedical image segmentation. 2017 4th International Conference on Opto-Electronics and Applied Optics, Optronix 2017, 2018–Janua. 10.1109/OPTRONIX.2017.8349978

Chakraborty, S., Mali, K., Chatterjee, S., Banerjee, S., Roy, K., & Dutta, N. ... Mazumdar, S. (2018). Dermatological effect of UV rays owing to ozone layer depletion. 2017 4th International Conference on Opto-Electronics and Applied Optics, Optronix 2017, 2018–Janua. 10.1109/OPTRONIX.2017.8349975

Chakraborty, S., Mali, K., Chatterjee, S., Banerjee, S., Sah, A., & Pathak, S., ... Roy, D. (2017). Bio-medical image enhancement using hybrid metaheuristic coupled soft computing tools. 2017 IEEE 8th Annual Ubiquitous Computing, *Electronics and Mobile Communication Conference (UEMCON)*, 231–236. 10.1109/ UEMCON.2017.8249036

Chakraborty, S., Raman, A., Sen, S., Mali, K., Chatterjee, S., & Hachimi, H. (2019). Contrast Optimization using Elitist Metaheuristic Optimization and Gradient Approximation for Biomedical Image Enhancement. 2019 Amity International Conference on Artificial Intelligence (AICAI), 712–717. doi:10.1109/ AICAI.2019.8701367

Chakraborty, S., Roy, M., & Hore, S. (2016). A Study on Different Edge Detection Techniques in Digital Image Processing. In Feature Detectors and Motion Detection in Video Processing (pp. 100–122). doi:10.4018/978-1-5225-1025-3.ch005

Chakraborty, S., Seal, A., & Roy, M. (2015). An Elitist Model for Obtaining Alignment of Multiple Sequences using Genetic Algorithm. *2nd National Conference NCETAS 2015*, 4(9), 61–67.

Chakraborty, S., Seal, A., Roy, M., & Mali, K. (2016). A novel lossless image encryption method using DNA substitution and chaotic logistic map. *International Journal of Security and Its Applications*, *10*(2), 205–216. doi:10.14257/ijsia.2016.10.2.19

Chang, C., Hwang, M., & Chen, T. (2001). A new encryption algorithm for image cryptosystems. *Journal of Systems and Software*, *58*(2), 83–91. doi:10.1016/S0164-1212(01)00029-2

Chang, H. K. C., & Liu, J. L. (1997). A linear quadtree compression scheme for image encryption. *Signal Processing Image Communication*, *10*(4), 279–290. doi:10.1016/S0923-5965(96)00025-2

Chen, G., Mao, Y., & Chui, C. K. (2004). A symmetric image encryption scheme based on 3D chaotic cat maps. *Chaos, Solitons, and Fractals*, *21*(3), 749–761. doi:10.1016/j.chaos.2003.12.022

Cheng, H., & Li, X. (2000). Partial encryption of compressed images and videos. *IEEE Transactions on Signal Processing*, *48*(8), 2439–2451. doi:10.1109/78.852023

Fridrich, J. (1998). Symmetric ciphers based on two-dimensional chaotic maps. *International Journal of Bifurcation and Chaos in Applied Sciences and Engineering*, *8*(6), 1259–1284. doi:10.1142/S021812749800098X

Hore, S., Chakraborty, S., Chatterjee, S., Dey, N., Ashour, A. S., Van Chung, L., & Le, D.-N. (2016). An integrated interactive technique for image segmentation using stack based seeded region growing and thresholding. *Iranian Journal of Electrical and Computer Engineering*, *6*(6). doi:10.11591/ijece.v6i6.11801

Hore, S., Chakroborty, S., Ashour, A. S., Dey, N., Ashour, A. S., Sifaki-Pistolla, D., ... Chaudhuri, S. R. B. (2015). Finding Contours of Hippocampus Brain Cell Using Microscopic Image Analysis. *Journal of Advanced Microscopy Research*, *10*(2), 93–103. doi:10.1166/jamr.2015.1245

Hore, S., Chatterjee, S., Chakraborty, S., & Kumar Shaw, R. (2016). Analysis of Different Feature Description Algorithm in object Recognition. In Feature Detectors and Motion Detection in Video Processing (pp. 66–99). doi:10.4018/978-1-5225-1025-3.ch004

Huang, C. K., & Nien, H. H. (2009). Multi chaotic systems based pixel shuffle for image encryption. *Optics Communications*, *282*(11), 2123–2127. doi:10.1016/j.optcom.2009.02.044

Jui-Cheng & Guo. (n.d.). A new chaotic key-based design for image encryption and decryption. 2000 IEEE International Symposium on Circuits and Systems. Emerging Technologies for the 21st Century. Proceedings (IEEE Cat No.00CH36353), 4, 49–52. 10.1109/ISCAS.2000.858685

Li, A., Belazi, A., Kharbech, S., Talha, M., & Xiang, W. (2019). Fourth Order MCA and Chaos-Based Image Encryption Scheme. *IEEE Access : Practical Innovations, Open Solutions*, *7*, 66395–66409. doi:10.1109/ACCESS.2019.2911559

Li, S., & Zheng, X. (2002). Cryptanalysis of a chaotic image encryption method. Proceedings - IEEE International Symposium on Circuits and Systems, 2, 708–711. 10.1109/ISCAS.2002.1011451

Li, S., Zheng, X., Mou, X., & Cai, Y. (n.d.). Chaotic Encryption Scheme for Real-Time Digital Video. Retrieved from http://epubs.surrey.ac.uk/532414/1/SPIE_EI2002.pdf

Liu, Z., & Xia, T. (2017). *Novel two dimensional fractional-order discrete chaotic map and its application to image encryption*. Applied Computing and Informatics; doi:10.1016/J.ACI.2017.07.002

Mali, K., Chakraborty, S., & Roy, M. (2015). A Study on Statistical Analysis and Security Evaluation Parameters in Image Encryption. International Journal for Scientific Research & Development, 3. Retrieved from www.ijsrd.com

Mali, K., Chakraborty, S., Seal, A., & Roy, M. (2015). An Efficient Image Cryptographic Algorithm based on Frequency Domain using Haar Wavelet Transform. *International Journal of Security and Its Applications*, *9*(12), 279–288. doi:10.14257/ijsia.2015.9.12.26

Meshram, C., Lee, C. C., Meshram, S. G., & Li, C. T. (2019). An efficient ID-based cryptographic transformation model for extended chaotic-map-based cryptosystem. *Soft Computing*, *23*(16), 6937–6946. doi:10.1007/s00500-018-3332-5

Muhammad, Z. M. Z., & Ozkaynak, F. (2019). Security Problems of Chaotic Image Encryption Algorithms Based on Cryptanalysis Driven Design Technique. *IEEE Access : Practical Innovations, Open Solutions*, *7*, 99945–99953. doi:10.1109/ACCESS.2019.2930606

Pareek, N. K., Patidar, V., & Sud, K. K. (2006). Image encryption using chaotic logistic map. *Image and Vision Computing*, *24*(9), 926–934. doi:10.1016/j.imavis.2006.02.021

Pareek, N. K., Patidar, V., & Sud, K. K. (2010). A random bit generator using chaotic maps. *International Journal of Network Security*, *10*(1), 32–38.

Refregier, P., & Javidi, B. (1995). Optical image encryption based on input plane and Fourier plane random encoding. *Optics Letters*, *20*(7), 767. doi:10.1364/OL.20.000767 PubMed

Roy, M., Chakraborty, S., Mali, K., Chatterjee, S., Banerjee, S., & Chakraborty, A. … Roy, K. (2017). Biomedical image enhancement based on modified Cuckoo Search and morphology. 2017 8th Industrial Automation and Electromechanical Engineering Conference, IEMECON 2017. 10.1109/IEMECON.2017.8079595

Roy, M., Chakraborty, S., Mali, K., Chatterjee, S., Banerjee, S., & Mitra, S., … Bhattacharjee, A. (2017). Cellular image processing using morphological analysis. 2017 IEEE 8th Annual Ubiquitous Computing, Electronics and Mobile Communication Conference (UEMCON), 237–241. 10.1109/UEMCON.2017.8249037

Roy, M., Chakraborty, S., Mali, K., Mitra, S., Mondal, I., & Dawn, R. … Chatterjee, S. (2019). A dual layer image encryption using polymerase chain reaction amplification and dna encryption. 2019 International Conference on Opto-Electronics and Applied Optics, Optronix 2019. doi:10.1109/OPTRONIX.2019.8862350

Roy, M., Mali, K., Chatterjee, S., Chakraborty, S., Debnath, R., & Sen, S. (2019). A Study on the Applications of the Biomedical Image Encryption Methods for Secured Computer Aided Diagnostics. 2019 Amity International Conference on Artificial Intelligence (AICAI), 881–886. doi:10.1109/AICAI.2019.8701382

Samson, C., & U, V. (2012). A Novel Image Encryption Supported by Compression Using Multilevel Wavelet Transform. International Journal of Advanced Computer Science and Applications, 3(9), 178–183. doi:10.14569/IJACSA.2012.030926

Sarddar, D., Chakraborty, S., & Roy, M. (2015). An Efficient Approach to Calculate Dynamic Time Quantum in Round Robin Algorithm for Efficient Load Balancing. *International Journal of Computers and Applications*, *123*(14), 48–52. doi:10.5120/ijca2015905701

Scharinger, J. (1998). Secure and fast encryption using chaotic Kolmogorov flows. 1998 Information Theory Workshop. ITW, 124–125. doi:10.1109/ITW.1998.706468

Seal, A., Chakraborty, S., & Mali, K. (2017). A new and resilient image encryption technique based on pixel manipulation, value transformation and visual transformation utilizing single–Level haar wavelet transform. In Advances in Intelligent Systems and Computing (Vol. 458). doi:10.1007/978-981-10-2035-3_61

Seal, A., Chakraborty, S., & Mali, K. (2017). A New and Resilient Image Encryption Technique Based on Pixel Manipulation (pp. 603–611). Value Transformation and Visual Transformation Utilizing Single–Level Haar Wavelet Transform. In Proceedings of the First International Conference on Intelligent Computing and Communication; doi:10.1007/978-981-10-2035-3_61.

Sethi, N., & Sharma, D. (n.d.). A novel method of image encryption using logistic mapping. Retrieved from http://citeseerx.ist.psu.edu/viewdoc/download?doi=10.1 .1.436.7858&rep=rep1&type=pdf

Tedmori, S., & Al-Najdawi, N. (2014). Image cryptographic algorithm based on the Haar wavelet transform. *Information Sciences*, *269*, 21–34. doi:10.1016/j. ins.2014.02.004

Wang, X., Liu, L., & Zhang, Y. (2015). A novel chaotic block image encryption algorithm based on dynamic random growth technique. *Optics and Lasers in Engineering*, *66*, 10–18. doi:10.1016/j.optlaseng.2014.08.005

Wang, X., & Zhao, J. (2010). An improved key agreement protocol based on chaos. *Communications in Nonlinear Science and Numerical Simulation*, *15*(12), 4052–4057. doi:10.1016/j.cnsns.2010.02.014

Wong, K. W., Yap, W. S., Goi, B. M., & Wong, D. C. K. (2019). Differential Cryptanalysis on Chaotic Based Image Encryption Scheme. *IOP Conference Series. Materials Science and Engineering*, *495*(1), 012041. doi:10.1088/1757-899X/495/1/012041

Ye, R. (2011). A novel chaos-based image encryption scheme with an efficient permutation-diffusion mechanism. *Optics Communications*, *284*(22), 5290–5298. doi:10.1016/j.optcom.2011.07.070

Yen, J., & Guo, J. (1999). A new image encryption algorithm and its VLSI architecture. 1999 IEEE Workshop on Signal Processing Systems. SiPS 99. Design and Implementation (Cat. No.99TH8461), 430–437. 10.1109/SIPS.1999.822348

Yen, J.-C., & Guo, J.-I. (2000). Efficient hierarchical chaotic image encryption algorithm and its VLSI realisation. *IEE Proceedings. Vision Image and Signal Processing*, *147*(2), 167. doi:10.1049/ip-vis:20000208

Zhang, X., & Chen, W. (2008). A new chaotic algorithm for image encryption. ICALIP 2008 - 2008 International Conference on Audio, Language and Image Processing, Proceedings, 889–892. 10.1109/ICALIP.2008.4590187

Zhang, X., Wang, L., Zhou, Z., & Niu, Y. (2019). A Chaos-Based Image Encryption Technique Utilizing Hilbert Curves and H-Fractals. *IEEE Access : Practical Innovations, Open Solutions*, 7, 74734–74746. doi:10.1109/ACCESS.2019.2921309

KEY TERMS AND DEFINITIONS

Chaos-Based Cryptography: A domain of cryptography where the application of the chaos theory plays a vital role.

Digital Data Protection: Protection of digital data against different types of attacks.

Image Security: Protect digital images from unauthorized access.

Lossless Decryption: 100% data can be recovered at the time of decryption.

Pixel-Level Encryption: An encryption method where the algorithm operates in the pixel level.

Robust Method: The results are reliable, and the method can be applied in different situations.

Secure Data Communication: A way of data communication to prevent intruders.

Skew-Tent Map: It is one kind of chaotic map.

Chapter 2
Anisotropic Diffusion–Based Color Texture Analysis for Industrial Application

Rohini A. Bhusnurmath

(iD) https://orcid.org/0000-0002-9908-5651
Karnataka State Akkamahadevi Women's University, India

Prakash S. Hiremath
KLE Technological University, India

ABSTRACT

This chapter proposes the framework for computer vision algorithm for industrial application. The proposed framework uses wavelet transform to obtain the multiresolution images. Anisotropic diffusion is employed to obtain the texture component. Various feature sets and their combinations are considered obtained from texture component. Linear discriminant analysis is employed to get the distinguished features. The k-NN classifier is used for classification. The proposed method is experimented on benchmark datasets for texture classification. Further, the method is extended to exploration of different color spaces for finding reference standard. The thrust area of industrial applications for machine intelligence in computer vision is considered. The industrial datasets, namely, MondialMarmi dataset for granite tiles and Parquet dataset for wood textures are experimented. It was observed that the combination of features performs better in YCbCr and HSV color spaces for MondialMarmi and Parquet datasets as compared to the other methods in literature.

DOI: 10.4018/978-1-7998-2736-8.ch002

INTRODUCTION

Computer vision task in artificial intelligence aims in recognizing the patterns in images. The focus is to identify patterns in images based on textural information. Applications of texture analysis in object recognition in various image processing modalities have made the task of efficient texture feature extraction more imperative and challenging. There is a definite need to develop novel algorithms which are faster and more accurate in texture representation and classification. In this direction, some authors have investigated the diffusion model based texture analysis in an attempt to address the challenges in texture classification. There is a constant need to increase recognition accuracy. Further, the traditional techniques of machine learning often require human expertise and knowledge to develop features tailor made for a particular application. Thus, the success of artificial intelligence lies in developing strong features rather than just machine learning algorithms that implement them. Therefore, the intelligent machine learning techniques do need robust textural features for accurate pattern analysis.

Texture analysis has been a prominent aspect in computer vision and image processing. A survey of texture analysis is given in (Tuceryan & Jain, 1998; Pietikainen, 2000; Petrou & Sevilla, 2006; Xie, 2008; Hermanson & Wiedenhoeft, 2011; Ahmadvand & Daliri, 2016a, Heurtier, 2019). The chrominance information is also incorporated into texture features in (Paschos, 2000; Mirmehdi & Petrou, 2000; Bombardier & Schmitt, 2010; Bianconi, et al., 2013; Hiremath & Bhusnurmath, 2014c; Hoang, 2018; Porebski, et al., 2018). A number of feature learning methods for texture classification based on statistical features have been proposed in recent years (Lu, et al., 2015a-2015d; Doost & Arimani, 2013; Zhu & Wang, 2012). It is observed that there is no universal set of textural features that serve the purpose of a recognition method for different tasks. In image analysis, texture recognition techniques deal with various textures present in the images. These texture measures must be robust and invariant to texture structures. The low computational complexity is necessary for any real time application of the methods.

Texture classification can generally be used as an idea to solve many real world problems. Many computer vision algorithms today use the idea of texture classification to accomplish the task. These pattern recognition algorithms often view the subject of interest as different textures, and classify those accordingly using texture analysis techniques.

Grading is the problem of automatic recognition of products which has wide applications in industrial products. The examples of such products include, textile (Sheriff et al., 2018), ceramic tiles (Fernandez et al. 2011; Ferreira & Giraldi 2017), leather (Murinto et al., 2018; Liong et al.,2019). In the industries such as parquet (Bianconi, et al., 2013; Bello-Cerezo, et al., 2019), wood (Jahanbanifard et al., 2019;

31

Hiremath, & Bhusnurmath, 2016c, 2016d, 2017b; Bhusnurmath & Hiremath, 2019; Shustrov, et al., 2019), natural stone (Bianconi, et al., 2015), etc.

Texture classification techniques are popularly used in industrial applications in grading products based on visual appearance (CIE 2006; Eugene, 2008). These systems employ image processing techniques with the help of two main visual features: texture and colour (CIE, 2006). The examples of a computer vision application in the areas of industrial automation that involve texture classification are wood classification and granite tiles classification which is done manually and is subjective. Hence, there is an emergent need to perform this task automatically.

Wood Texture Identification

The appearance of the wood surface plays a key role in determining the price and quality. Selection of flooring wood under goes rigorous selection criteria. The color tone and fiber type decides the grading of wood. To fulfill this requisite, radical improvement in wood quality standards are attempted to be met by producers. Thus, wood classification is of prime importance. The process of manual wood identification is subjective. It is time consuming to become skilled. Thus, this is the thrust area for developing image processing techniques for the task of automatic wood recognition.

Wood species recognition is a task that is currently conducted mainly by wood experts. However, these experts have to be trained for a period of time before they are qualified to accomplish the task. There are more species of trees compared to temperate countries, so it is more challenging to identify all the species easily. The experts will have to study the characteristics observed on the surface and to make a decision on which species it is. Close resemblance of certain species with the others will cause further difficulty in accomplishing the task. The time required to identify the species of a piece of wood can therefore vary from a couple of minutes to hours or days depending on their difficulty. On the other hand, the identification time is also related to the expertise and experience of the wood experts themselves.

Wood species recognition is not only required in the studies of wood in wood firms and research labs. In reality, wood species recognition is required in a wide range of areas, including the industry, forensics and conservation. In the industry, recognition of the species will ensure that the wood materials delivered are the correct species. This is important due to the different characteristics of different wood species. If the wood materials that are not strong enough are used in building roof truss or furniture, they may collapse after a period of time which might threaten human lives. Identifying the species at immigration customs will also avoid endangered species to be illegally exported which will assist in conserving these species (Hermanson & Wiedenhoeft, 2011). While in forensics, the species of wood collected from the crime scene could be a clue to solve the crime (Lew, 2005).

Identification of wood type from the wood product is done using computer vision algorithm in (Labati, et al., 2009). Rubber wood board classification using color descriptors and histogram of hue is described in Kurdthongmee (2008). Hrcka (2008) investigated that the CIE Lab color space descriminates the European spruce and common beech. Classification of woods, namely, oak, beech tree and cherry tree on HSV and CIE Lab space is employed in Faria et al. (2008). Color features and fuzzy reasoning classifier is used in Bombardier and Schmitt (2010) using HSV and CIE Lab color spaces in wood recognition. More recently color based wood identification is experimented in Bianconi et al. (2013). In (Hiremath & Bhusnurmath 2017a), authors have explored method for texture analysis based on anisotropic diffusion and multiresolution local directional binary patterns (LDBP).

Granite Tiles Identification

Granite industry is another thrust area of automated identification of granite plates which are similar in visual appearance. Granite tiles are popularly used in pavement covering and façade cladding because of its strength and beautiful appearance. The rate of granite depends on visual appearance just like an ornamental material. Different colors (green, black, etc.) and textures (homogeneous, speckled, etc.) are available in commercial granite. The visual appearance, flatness of slab and dimensions of blocks decides its standard (Shadmon, 2005). Granites are usually identified by a generic name and the colour, for example "Baltic Brown", "Emerald Pearl" or "Imperial Pink". However, this nomenclature is different in every country. The standardization of nomenclature is given in (Standard EN 12440:2000). This nomenclature helps commercially rather than in automatic grading process. Only visual appearance may not be sufficient to decide the quality. It leads to the controversy between customers and suppliers resulting in rejection of orders. There is no uniform visual appearance in the plates of the lot. This results in late delays and heavy charges to suppliers. As a solution granite industry has adopted quality control by visual inspection using skilled operators. This type of inspection is subjective and non repetitive. Many methods have been developed for granite classification in past few years. Initially, the methods for granite classification were based on color features such as chromaticity moments (Paschos, 2000). Later, approaches like used were co-occurrence matrices (Paclík, et al., 2005), Gabor filter banks (Bianconi & Fernández, 2006; Lepisto, et al., 2005) and coordinated clusters representation (Guillen, et al., 2007; Kurmyshev, et al., 2007). Researchers have considered the crystalline structure of granite which is more prominent in characteristics as compared to the color information. Larer, in Bianconi et al. (2009), authors have considered the texture features and color jointly. The variation in classification accuracy obtained by these authors is mainly due to the acquisition procedure of images. Other factors affecting are noise, image size, degree of similarity in granite textures.

In Bianconi et al. (2012) authors reviewed that majority of methods are based on texture features. Dogan and Akay (2010) employed AdaBoost and sum, difference histograms for classification of marble slabs. The gray scale histogram based method for recognition of tiles is presented in Topalova and Tzokev (2010). Bianconi and Fernandez (2006) employed different Gabor filter banks for granite classification. Fernandez et al. (2011) have employed variants of LBP and coordinated clusters for classification of granite. Bianconi et al. (2012) have presented an approach for classification of granite tiles, in which colour and textural features are extracted and support vector machine is used as classifier. Gonzalez et al. (2013) have used texture and color descriptors for identification of granite tiles. Fernandez et al. (2013) have described a general framework for texture analysis based on histograms of equivalent patterns. Texture analysis based on local binary patterns is used in Kylberg and Sintorn (2013). Paci et al. (2013) have proposed various feature extraction approaches and their combinations, which are compared for granite texture classification. In a recent work, Bianconi et al. (2015) tested the robustness of the methods based on variants of LBP on different datasets including granite tiles dataset.

Image processing methods take the input as RGB images obtained with industrial cameras (Bianconi, et al. 2013). These images are used 'as is' or are transformed to other color spaces for experimentation. Such methods aim to obtain global statistical descriptors which represents the content of color images. To design recognition system for granite tiles and wood grading based on computer vision techniques, key factors are the choice of the appropriate descriptors and the right colour space.

The objectives of study in the proposed chapter are: Firstly, to explore AD based color texture descriptors using wavelet transform in industrial applications for granite tiles identification and wood identification. Secondly, to evaluate the robustness of the proposed method for different industrial benchmark datasets. Thirdly, to study the effect of combination of feature sets on texture classification. Fourth, to find the reference standard. Finally, to obtain the better classification accuracy.

PROPOSED METHOD

The proposed method encompasses the extraction of texture features from luminance component and statistical moment features from the two pure chrominance components of color texture image.

1.   The directional information of luminance component of input image of sample is extracted by applying Haar wavelet transform.

2.   The texture component is yielded from directional information using anisotropic diffusion.
3.   The first and second order statistical features are obtained from texture component.
4.   Feature vector is formed by combining texture features obtained from luminance component and statistical moment features of chrominance components.

The classification is performed using k-NN classifier. The brief discussion of these steps is given below.

Wavelet Transform

The one level of Haar wavelet transform (WT) is used for experimentation. This yields diagonal (D), vertical (V) and horizontal (H) subbands. The one level decomposition is more effective in representing directional information. The multilevel decomposition compresses the information. The detailed theory of the WT is given in (Mallat, 1989a). The WT is briefly described in the Appendix 1.

Anisotropic Diffusion

The anisotropic diffusion (AD) is applied on directional subbands D, V and H of WT applied image to obtain texture components. The basic idea of the partial differential equation (PDE) based AD filter (Perona & Malik, 1990) is described in the Appendix 2.

Feature Sets

The feature extraction is done using texture components obtained after the Step 2. The texture descriptors used for the experimentation are of first order (F1), second order (F2 to F9) and their combinations are also considered (F10 to F30). The feature sees are described in the Appendix 3.

TEXTURE CLASSIFICATION

The proposed methodology for the texture classification includes two procedures: (1) Training procedure and (2) Testing procedure. The colour images in the datasets are used to extract the features.

Training Procedure

Input the image of colour material sample I (in RGB). The colour sample is then converted to HSV (or Lab or YCbCr) space, where V (or Y or L) is the luminance component I_{lmn}. The luminance (I_{lmn}) and chrominance components of the color image I are extracted. I_{lmn} is subjected to Haar WT, to obtain diagonal (D), vertical (V) and horizontal (H) components. The AD is applied on D, V and H components of I further texture approximations I_{Htxr}, I_{Vtxr}, I_{Dtxr} are obtained. Different statistical features defined in the Tables 22 and 23 are calculated for image texture approximations I_{Htxr}, I_{Vtxr}, I_{Dtxr}. For chrominance components, mean and standard deviation are computed. The combined features of luminance and chrominance components form feature vector F. It is stored with class label. This procedure is repeated to form training feature set (TF) using all the training images. The discriminant feature set TFLDA is obtained by applying LDA on TF. TFLDA is used for texture classification.

Testing Procedure

Input the test image colour material sample I_{test}. The sample I_{test} is converted to HSV (or Lab or YCbCr) space, where V (or L or Y) is the luminance component $I_{testlmn}$. The luminance ($I_{testlmn}$) and chrominance components of the color image I_{test} are extracted. $I_{testlmn}$ is subjected to Haar WT to obtain diagonal (D), vertical (V) and horizontal (H) components. The AD is applied on D, V and H components of I_{test} to obtain texture approximations $I_{testDtxr}$, $I_{testVtxr}$, $I_{testHtxr}$. Different statistical features as in Tables 22 and 23 are computed for image texture approximations $I_{testHtxr}$, $I_{testVtxr}$, $I_{testDtxr}$. For chrominance components, mean and standard deviation are calculated. The combined features of luminance and chrominance components form feature vector F_{test}. The $F_{testLDA}$ vector is obtained by projecting F_{test} on TFLDA components. The k-NN classifier is used for classification (Duda, et al., 2001) of material sample. The two-fold experimentation is repeated five times.

The Fig. 1 shows the overview of the proposed method based on wavelet transform and PDE approach for colour texture analysis.

The Figs. 2 and 3 show the pictorial representation of feature extraction in RGB and other colour spaces (HSV, YCbCr and Lab).

EXPERIMENTAL RESULTS AND DISCUSSION

The experiments are implemented using MATLAB 7.9 software on Intel(R) Core(TM) i3-2330M @ 2.20GHz with 4 GB RAM. The proposed methodology is experimented on four gray scale benchmark datasets, namely, Brodatz (1966), VisTex (online), Oulu (2005), Kylberg (2012), a color dataset Oulu (2005) and two industrial datasets

Figure 1. The overview of proposed method for colour texture analysis

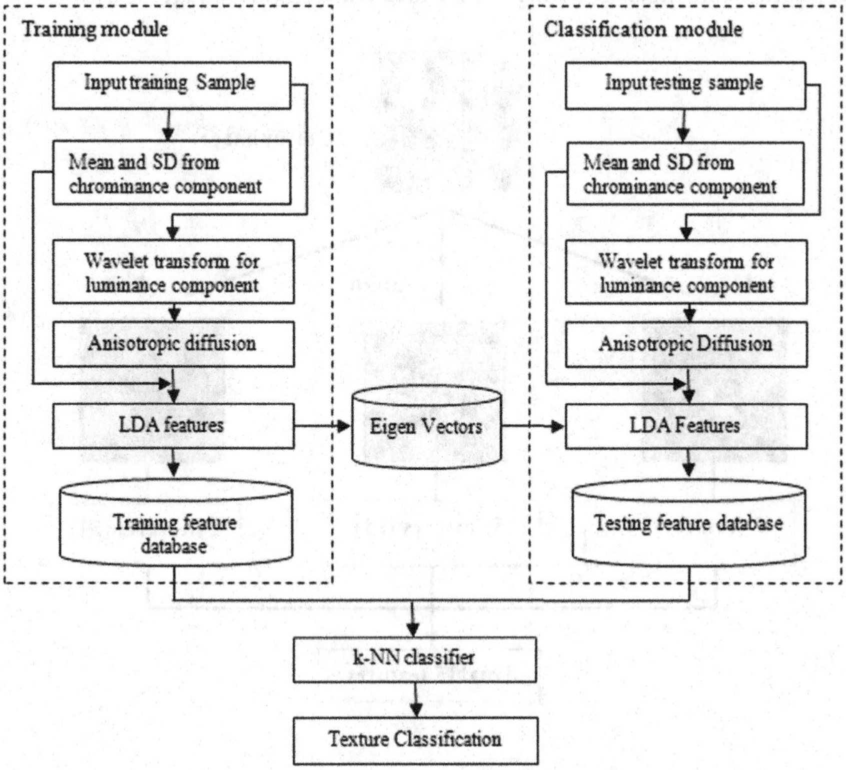

of color texture images representing real life materials, namely, Parquet dataset (2012) for wood and MondialMarmi dataset (2011) for granite tiles. The FigS. 4 to 7 shows the samples images from benchmark datasets. The properties of benchmark datasets and industrial datasets are given in the Tables 1 and 2.

The five sample texture images of each of the benchmark datasets are displayed in the Fig. 4 to Fig. 7, respectively.

The Tables 3 and 4 show sample images of materials namely, hard wood and granite tiles from each of the two industrial datasets.

Benchmark Datasets

The experimental results obtained with four benchmark datasets in gray scale for the proposed method, method in Hiremath & Bhusnurmath (2013a, 2014a) based on nonsubsampled contourlet transform (NSCT) and local directional binary patterns (LDBP) and the method in Hiremath & Bhusnurmath (2014b, 2015) based on partial differential equation (PDE) and LDBP is given in the Table 5.

Figure 2. Pictorial representation of feature extraction using Multi-spectral approach in RGB space considering feature set F1 and Oulu texture image 'tile'

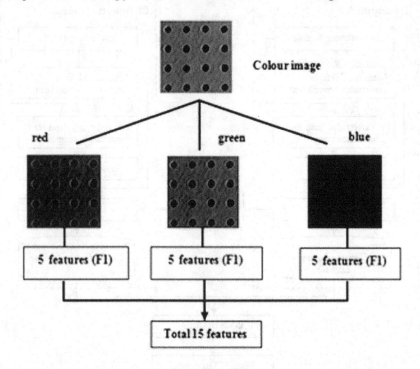

Figure 3. Pictorial representation of feature extraction using Multi-spectral approach in HSV/YCbCr/Lab space considering feature set F1 and Oulu texture image 'tile'

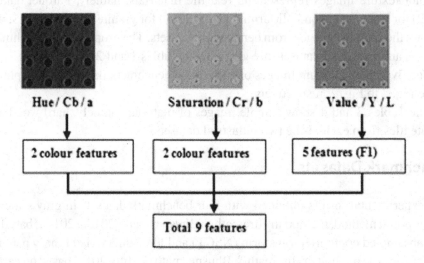

Table 1. Properties of benchmark datasets

Dataset name	Number of classes	Number of sub images per class	Total number of sub mages	Size of image in pixels	Size of sub image pixels	Image format
Brodatz (1966)	16	16	256	256x256	64 x 64	gif
VisTex (online)	19	16	304	512x512	128x128	ppm
Kylberg (2012)	28	2560	71680	576x576	144x144	png
Oulu (2005)	16	16	256	512x512	128x128	ppm

Table 2. Properties of the industrial datasets used for experimentation.

Dataset name	Number of classes	Number of sub images per class	Total number of sub mages	Size of image in pixels	Size of sub image pixels	Image format
Parquet (2012)	14	192	2688	1200x300	150 x 150	bmp
MondialMarmi (2011)	12	64	768	544x544	136 x 136	bmp

Figure 4. Sample texture images from Brodatz dataset (from left to right): D3, D4, D6, D11, D16

Figure 5. Sample texture images from VisTex dataset (from left to right): Bark0, Bark6, Bark8, Bark9, Brick1

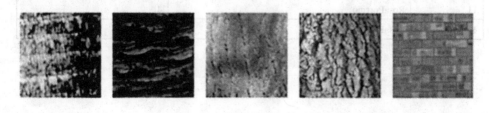

Figure 6. Sample texture images from Kylberg dataset (from left to right): blanket1-a-p1, rug1-a-p1, rice2-a-p1, sand1-a-p1, blanket2-a-p2

Figure 7. Sample texture images from Oulu dataset (from left to right): Clouds, Fabric7, Leaves, Metal, Food1

Table 3. Granite tiles samples used in the experimentation

SI No.	Image Name	Samples/Class
1	AcquaMarina	4
2	AzulCapixaba	4
3	AzulPlatino	4
4	BiancoCristal	4
5	BiancoSardo	4
6	GialloNapoletano	4
7	GialloOrnamentale	4
8	GialloSantaCecilia	4
9	GialloVeneziano	4
10	RosaBeta	4
11	RosaPorriño_A	4
12	RosaPorriño_B	4

Table 4. Hardwood parquet samples used in the experimentation

Wood Class Code	Tones	Samples/Tone
IRK_01	3	4
OAK_01	4	3
OAK_02	2	6
OAK_03	2	6
OAK_04	3	4
OAK_05	2	6
OAK_06	3	4
OAK_07	3	4
OAK_08	3	4
OAK_09	3	4
OAK_10	2	6
OAK_11	2	6
TEK_01	3	4
TEK_02	3	4

It is observed from the Table 5 that the classification accuracy of the proposed method is computationally less expensive (in terms of training and testing times) as compared to the methods in (Hiremath & Bhusnurmath 2013a, 2014a) and (Hiremath & Bhusnurmath 2014b, 2015).

The summarized result of the experimentation carried out on color dataset, Oulu (2005), is given in the Table 6 (Hiremath & Bhusnurmath 2016b). It is observed from the Table 6 that the HSV color space gives better classification accuracy as compared to the other color spaces explored and that of the gray scale.

The Table 7 shows the performance comparison of the proposed method with the state-of-the-art methods using Oulu dataset.

It is observed from the Table 7 that the proposed method, based on WT and PDE, features extracted in HSV colour space, is effective in achieving better classification accuracy as compared to the state-of-the-art methods in the literature. The experimental results demonstrate the efficacy of the proposed feature extraction method for the colour texture classification. The results are found to be encouraging.

The texture classification method based on wavelet transform and anisotropic diffusion (WT+PDE), which has been proposed in (Hiremath & Bhusnurmath 2016a, 2017c, Bhusnurmath & Hiremath 2017d) and experimented on color spaces in (Hiremath & Bhusnurmath 2016b), yields higher classification rate in the HSV space, as compared to the other methods proposed in the (Hiremath & Bhusnurmath

Table 5. Comparison of classification accuracy, training time and testing time of the proposed method and the methods of the (Hiremath & Bhusnurmath 2013a, 2014a) and (Hiremath & Bhusnurmath 2014b and 2015) using the four gray scale datasets: Brodatz, VisTex, Kylberg and Oulu.

Dataset	Method	Approach	Classification accuracy (%)	Training time (sec.)	Testing time (sec.)	Diffusion step
Brodatz	Proposed Method	WT+PDE	98.75	8.18	0.51	10
	Hiremath & Bhusnurmath (2014b, 2015)	PDE+LDBP	98.98	14.92	0.93	15
	Hiremath & Bhusnurmath (2013a, 2014a)	NSCT +LDBP	98.44	278.50	12.42	-
VisTex	Proposed Method	WT+PDE	97.43	16.45	0.87	8
	Hiremath & Bhusnurmath (2014b, 2015)	PDE+LDBP	98.55	69.05	3.63	65
	Hiremath & Bhusnurmath (2013a, 2014a)	NSCT +LDBP	96.38	343.05	11.33	-
Kylberg	Proposed Method	WT+PDE	100	1434.71	1.65	1
	Hiremath & Bhusnurmath (2014b, 2015)	PDE+LDBP	100	7575.67	2.77	15
	Hiremath & Bhusnurmath (2013a, 2014a)	NSCT +LDBP	83.42	48771.46	1930.46	-
Oulu	Proposed Method	WT+PDE	98.36	18.36	1.15	10
	Hiremath & Bhusnurmath (2014b, 2015)	PDE+LDBP	99.84	135.97	8.50	200
	Hiremath & Bhusnurmath (2013a, 2014a)	NSCT +LDBP	99.68	291.48	10.06	-

Table 6. Comparison of classification accuracy (%) of the proposed method obtained by using different colour spaces, and the corresponding computation cost (training and testing time), optimal feature set and diffusion step using Oulu color dataset.

Parameters / Colour space	RGB	HSV	YCbCr	Lab	Gray
Classification accuracy (%)	97.11	**99.45**	98.36	98.44	98.36
Training time (sec.)	25.73	**24.28**	8.60	21.86	18.36
Testing time (sec.)	1.61	**1.52**	0.54	1.37	1.15
Optimal feature set	F5	**F17**	F22	F26	F17
Optimal no. of diffusion step	2	**8**	6	8	10

Table 7. The performance comparison of the proposed method with states-of-the-art methods, in terms of classification accuracy using Oulu color dataset for HSV color space (Hiremath & Bhusnurmath 2016b)

Method	Classification accuracy (%)
Selvan & Ramakrishnan (2007)	92.81
Sengur (2008)	97.63
Chang et al. (2010)	97.87
Abdulmunim (2012)	98.81
Proposed method	**99.45**

2014b, 2015). Hence, in the present Chapter, the colour texture classification method developed in the (Hiremath & Bhusnurmath 2016b) is adopted for industrial automation problems, namely, granite tiles and wood texture identification. The proposed recognition system is useful in automatic computer vision tool for grading of the granite tiles and wood.

The experimental results obtained with the proposed method for two industrial datasets are discussed below.

Wood Texture Analysis

The Table 8 to Table 12 show the classification accuracy, corresponding training time and testing time using optimal diffusion steps for different feature sets (F1 to F30) using Parquet dataset (wood textures), for RGB, YCbCr, HSV and Lab colour spaces. The method is also experimented in gray scale for comparative analysis of results.

Table 8. The classification accuracy (CA), corresponding training time (TrTm) and testing time (TsTm) using optimal diffusion steps (DS) for different feature sets using Parquet dataset, for RGB colour space.

Sl. No.	Feature set	CA(%)	TrTm (sec.)	TsTm (sec.)	DS	Sl. No.	Feature set	CA(%)	TrTm (sec.)	TsTm (sec.)	DS
1	F1	84.57	210.33	0.02	5	16	F16	74.86	729.51	0.13	10
2	F2	49.50	1568.65	0.08	7	17	F17	92.10	547.90	0.06	8
3	F3	92.10	263.51	0.01	7	18	F18	91.51	635.47	0.06	8
4	F4	91.96	391.11	0.01	9	19	F19	89.96	440.00	0.05	1
5	F5	94.21	428.50	0.02	7	20	F20	44.24	281.82	0.05	1
6	F6	93.79	138.45	0.02	1	**21**	**F21**	**95.15**	**433.75**	**0.04**	**6**
7	F7	89.34	300.25	0.01	8	22	F22	93.67	243.50	0.05	4
8	F8	63.75	113.07	0.01	1	23	F23	94.28	663.49	0.05	9
9	F9	44.24	105.34	0.02	1	24	F24	94.83	780.59	0.05	8
10	F10	94.96	283.12	0.03	7	25	F25	93.04	414.38	0.04	7
11	F11	92.87	415.28	0.05	8	26	F26	94.71	745.22	0.03	9
12	F12	92.20	595.58	0.07	8	27	F27	95.02	446.09	0.04	9
13	F13	44.53	604.26	0.09	6	28	F28	94.54	492.21	0.03	7
14	F14	62.47	561.73	0.12	3	29	F29	44.24	123.85	0.03	1
15	F15	73.03	642.27	0.09	6	30	F30	58.44	1735.11	0.11	9

The Table 13 shows the comparison of optimal classification accuracy (CA) attained among thirty feature sets, experimented using Parquet database for different colour spaces. The corresponding testing time, feature set, training time and optimal number of diffusion steps are shown in the Table 13.

It is evident from the Table 13 that the HSV colour space gives better classification accuracy 96.57% as compared to the experimented colour spaces. The better classification accuracy is obtained for the feature set F12 with testing time of 0.02 sec and training time of 237.56 sec.

The Table 14 shows the comparison of classification accuracy obtained by the proposed method and other methods in the literature using Parquet dataset. No of features and classifier used in experimentation is also reported.

The experimental results show improved classification accuracy as compared to the other method in the literature. In addition, the reduction in computational cost is achieved owing to diffusion based approach (Hiremath & Bhusnurmath 2016b).

Table 9. The classification accuracy (CA), corresponding training time (TrTm) and testing time (TsTm) using optimal diffusion steps (DS) for different feature sets using Parquet dataset, for HSV colour space.

Sl. No.	Feature set	CA(%)	TrTm (sec.)	TsTm (sec.)	DS	Sl. No.	Feature set	CA(%)	TrTm (sec.)	TsTm (sec.)	DS
1	F1	82.60	151.85	0.01	10	16	F16	40.07	227.35	0.05	4
2	F2	93.09	554.79	0.03	6	17	F17	96.12	200.67	0.02	6
3	F3	91.63	161	0.01	10	18	F18	95.85	232.41	0.02	4
4	F4	92.18	123.36	0.01	3	19	F19	95.89	172.69	0.03	2
5	F5	93.87	143.55	0.01	1	20	F20	38.79	119.48	0.02	10
6	F6	93.51	127.44	0.01	5	21	F21	96.44	247.62	0.02	10
7	F7	88.88	92.50	0.01	2	22	F22	96.20	204.80	0.02	8
8	F8	40.98	80.72	0.01	1	23	F23	96.42	207.03	0.02	2
9	F9	34.06	75.27	0.01	1	24	F24	96.16	251.60	0.02	8
10	F10	94.96	91.44	0.01	2	25	F25	92.91	118.99	0.01	2
11	F11	96.07	116.82	0.02	2	26	F26	95.90	273.76	0.02	10
12	**F12**	**96.57**	**237.56**	**0.02**	**8**	27	F27	94.18	114.77	0.01	2
13	F13	96.43	205.37	0.03	2	28	F28	94.63	198.23	0.01	5
14	F14	96.16	279.22	0.03	10	29	F29	38.21	110.52	0.02	4
15	F15	95.39	254.31	0.04	6	30	F30	93.87	615.51	0.04	10

Granite Tiles Texture Analysis

The Table 15 to Table 19 show the classification accuracy, corresponding training time and testing time using optimal diffusion steps for different feature sets (F1 to F30) using MondialMarmi dataset, for different colour spaces. The optimal number of diffusion steps is the diffusion step at which the best classification results are obtained for a given feature set.

The Table 20 presents the comparison of optimal classification accuracy (CA) attained among the thirty feature sets, experimented using MondialMarmi dataset for different colour spaces. The corresponding testing time, feature set, training time and optimal number of diffusion steps are shown in the Table 20. It is evident from the Table 20 that the better classification accuracy of 99.58% is obtained for YCbCr colour space as compared to the other colour spaces. The accuracy is obtained for the feature set F21 with testing time of 0.0040 sec. and training time of 36.03 sec.

Table 10. The classification accuracy (CA), corresponding training time (TrTm) and testing time (TsTm) using optimal diffusion steps (DS) for different feature sets using Parquet dataset, for YCbCr colour space.

Sl.No.	Feature set	CA(%)	TrTm (sec.)	TsTm (sec.)	DS	Sl. No.	Feature set	CA(%)	TrTm (sec.)	TsTm (sec.)	DS
1	F1	82.40	193.37	0.01	10	16	F16	37.07	252.31	0.05	4
2	F2	94.09	551.03	0.03	8	17	F17	96.14	229.29	0.03	7
3	F3	92.13	170.80	0.01	9	**18**	**F18**	**96.55**	**262.84**	**0.03**	**8**
4	F4	89.03	179.51	0.01	9	19	F19	95.96	204.51	0.03	2
5	F5	92.39	149.07	0.01	2	20	F20	36.38	140.02	0.03	4
6	F6	91.73	158.53	0.01	9	21	F21	95.10	284.02	0.01	10
7	F7	90.31	94.46	0.01	2	22	F22	96.10	178.74	0.02	9
8	F8	44.11	89.31	0.01	2	23	F23	95.13	252.49	0.02	10
9	F9	34.06	100.97	0.01	4	24	F24	95.40	238.94	0.02	8
10	F10	94.91	131.83	0.01	7	25	F25	93.40	128.70	0.01	4
11	F11	95.90	183.16	0.02	10	26	F26	94.44	254.35	0.02	10
12	F12	96.07	243.15	0.02	10	27	F27	94.87	180.57	0.02	9
13	F13	96.30	231.01	0.02	6	28	F28	94.87	197.57	0.01	6
14	F14	95.84	257.85	0.03	8	29	F29	34.63	111.62	0.01	4
15	F15	95.79	285.79	0.04	9	30	F30	94.51	578.01	0.05	9

The Table 21 shows the comparison of classification accuracy obtained by the proposed method and other methods in the literature using MondialMarmi dataset. The feature set size and classifier used is also reported in the table. The increased classification accuracy of the proposed method as observed in the Table 21, is due to the AD and wavelet transform.

The analysis of experimental results indicates the efficacy of the proposed method (WT+PDE) in grading of the industrial materials for hardwood and granite tiles.

CONCLUSION

The classification accuracy using the proposed method, which is achieved with reduced computational time cost, compares well with the methods described in the (Hiremath & Bhusnurmath 2013a, 2014a) and (Hiremath & Bhusnurmath 2014b, 2015). The experimental results show the effectiveness of the proposed

Table 11. The classification accuracy (CA), corresponding training time (TrTm) and testing time (TsTm) using optimal diffusion steps (DS) for different feature sets using Parquet dataset, for Lab colour space.

Sl. No.	Feature set	CA(%)	TrTm (sec.)	TsTm (sec.)	DS	Sl. No.	Feature set	CA(%)	TrTm (sec.)	TsTm (sec.)	DS
1	F1	84.60	132.06	0.01	9	16	F16	33.53	226.27	0.04	2
2	F2	94.50	561.48	0.03	10	17	**F17**	**96.48**	**234.28**	**0.02**	**9**
3	F3	91.31	157.44	0.01	10	18	F18	95.59	251.56	0.02	8
4	F4	90.83	178.96	0.01	10	19	F19	95.65	187.44	0.02	1
5	F5	93.10	209.08	0.01	10	20	F20	32.32	128.83	0.02	3
6	F6	95.94	117.98	0.01	5	21	F21	95.43	184.30	0.01	5
7	F7	85.72	143.53	0.01	9	22	F22	95.59	171.12	0.02	9
8	F8	48.57	76.39	0.01	1	23	F23	94.48	246.12	0.02	9
9	F9	32.32	86.58	0.01	3	24	F24	95.07	249.77	0.02	7
10	F10	93.85	107.66	0.01	5	25	F25	93.79	179.59	0.02	9
11	F11	93.71	181.37	0.02	6	26	F26	94.59	243.57	0.01	7
12	F12	95.38	253.45	0.02	9	27	F27	92.44	163.48	0.02	6
13	F13	95.73	231.42	0.02	5	28	F28	95.40	244.67	0.02	9
14	F14	95.29	263.56	0.03	7	29	F29	32.32	110.50	0.02	3
15	F15	94.92	266.30	0.04	7	30	F30	93.79	612.17	0.05	8

feature extraction method in colour texture classification. The results are found to be encouraging. In this chapter, the colour texture feature set developed in the (Hiremath & Bhusnurmath 2016b) is evaluated for the purpose of grading of industrial products. The effectiveness of automatic recognition of wood and granite tiles through computer vision at reduced computational cost is achieved. The proposed method meets the criteria of real time processing of being computationally low-cost. Hence, it is suitable for developing expert system for automatic recognition of textures of the material products based on visual characteristics. The examples include products like leather, parquet, granite and fabric. Also, it is observed that the selection of color space is application dependent. The combination of feature descriptors amplifies the classification result. The experimental results demonstrate effectiveness of the proposed method in terms of increased recognition accuracy with reduced computational cost. The experimental results exhibit the potential of such an approach for computer vision application such as automatic recognition of wood and granite tiles textures.

Table 12. The classification accuracy (CA), corresponding training time (TrTm) and testing time (TsTm) using optimal diffusion steps (DS) for different feature sets using Parquet dataset, for gray scale.

Sl. No.	Feature set	CA(%)	TrTm (sec.)	TsTm (sec.)	DS	Sl. No.	Feature set	CA (%)	TrTm (sec.)	TsTm (sec.)	DS
1	F1	72.25	84.84	0.0109	8	16	F16	41.83	247.27	0.0522	2
2	F2	94.07	525.91	0.0260	6	17	F17	95.34	229.35	0.0288	6
3	F3	86.46	129.16	0.0102	10	18	F18	95.15	314.62	0.0257	8
4	F4	85.61	77.48	0.0106	2	19	F19	94.74	343.57	0.0310	10
5	F5	54.38	107.48	0.0216	1	20	F20	35.63	184.53	0.0264	8
6	F6	89.04	70.32	0.0107	3	21	F21	94.08	294.74	0.0229	10
7	F7	84.11	93.41	0.0093	6	22	F22	94.49	100.05	0.0247	2
8	F8	40.09	80.73	0.0085	5	23	F23	93.67	217.27	0.0224	2
9	F9	35.58	105.02	0.0112	8	24	F24	94.63	275.30	0.0199	6
10	F10	92.10	129.83	0.0128	10	25	F25	91.89	159.66	0.0230	6
11	F11	93.82	164.94	0.0231	10	26	F26	93.57	204.98	0.0118	2
12	F12	94.57	209.25	0.0203	8	27	F27	93.13	222.48	0.0146	10
13	**F13**	**95.34**	**191.75**	**0.0364**	**4**	28	F28	93.04	236.18	0.0213	6
14	F14	94.14	337.35	0.0417	10	29	F29	35.58	153.61	0.0223	8
15	F15	93.90	309.16	0.0411	7	30	F30	92.46	761.24	0.0473	8

Table 13. Comparison of optimal classification accuracy (CA) of the proposed method experimented on different colour spaces and the corresponding training time, testing time, optimal feature set and diffusion steps using Parquet dataset.

Parameters	Colour space				
	Gray	RGB	HSV	YCbCr	Lab
CA (%)	95.34	95.15	**96.57**	96.55	96.48
Training time (sec.)	191.75	433.75	**237.56**	262.84	234.28
Testing time (sec.)	0.03	0.04	**0.02**	0.03	0.02
Optimal feature set	F13	F21	**F12**	F18	F17
Optimal no. of diffusion step	4	6	**8**	8	9

Table 14. Comparison of classification accuracy (CA) for the proposed method and other methods in the literature using Parquet dataset.

Method	CA(%)	Number of features	Classifier
Proposed method	**96.57**	**13**	**k-NN, k=3**
Bianconi et al. (2013)	89.8	12	k-NN, k=1

Table 15. The classification accuracy (CA), corresponding training time (TrTm) and testing time (TsTm) using optimal diffusion steps (DS) for different feature sets using MondialMarmi dataset, for RGB colour space.

Sl. No.	Feature set	CA(%)	TrTm (sec.)	TsTm (sec.)	DS	Sl. No.	Feature set	CA (%)	TrTm (sec.)	TsTm (sec.)	DS
1	F1	86.08	23.49	0.0044	2	16	F16	80.27	182.62	0.0111	9
2	F2	43.42	450.94	0.0100	9	17	F17	81.13	130.89	0.0068	7
3	F3	95.42	18.88	0.0043	1	18	F18	73.08	117.95	0.0076	2
4	F4	94.94	107.40	0.0043	10	19	F19	78.88	149.51	0.0070	7
5	**F5**	**98.69**	**120.45**	**0.0039**	**8**	20	F20	61.94	57.12	0.0064	2
6	F6	93.52	72.56	0.0048	7	21	F21	80.73	120.83	0.0055	8
7	F7	96.10	91.93	0.0043	10	22	F22	78.67	62.90	0.0061	5
8	F8	54.23	30.29	0.0043	2	23	F23	72.58	150.33	0.0057	7
9	F9	38.33	19.12	0.0045	1	24	F24	81.48	171.73	0.0055	10
10	F10	57.33	69.40	0.0052	7	25	F25	47.17	61.12	0.0049	4
11	F11	78.31	119.96	0.0065	10	26	F26	95.15	162.63	0.0047	9
12	F12	90.10	167.97	0.0071	10	27	F27	56.21	98.11	0.0054	7
13	F13	77.60	179.07	0.0087	10	28	F28	82.94	129.46	0.0101	7
14	F14	76.23	177.70	0.0101	9	29	F29	38.33	25.72	0.0052	1
15	F15	76.67	168.00	0.0099	7	30	F30	61.29	511.62	0.0115	8

Table 16. The classification accuracy (CA), corresponding training time (TrTm) and testing time (TsTm) using optimal diffusion steps (DS) for different feature sets using MondialMarmi dataset, for HSV colour space.

Sl. No.	Feature set	CA(%)	TrTm (sec.)	TsTm (sec.)	DS	Sl. No.	Feature set	CA (%)	TrTm (sec.)	TsTm (sec.)	DS
1	F1	92.58	30.87	0.0035	1	16	F16	73.15	87.15	0.0058	3
2	F2	60.10	194.99	0.0060	9	17	F17	98.00	80.52	0.0051	6
3	F3	97.58	57.92	0.0035	7	18	F18	98.65	75.08	0.0044	1
4	F4	98.88	50.76	0.0035	1	19	F19	98.10	84.67	0.0047	5
5	F5	98.98	82.80	0.0034	10	20	F20	38.71	51.11	0.0052	1
6	F6	97.92	45.88	0.0040	1	21	F21	98.92	59.62	0.0049	5
7	F7	97.94	45.61	0.0035	1	22	F22	98.63	44.27	0.0048	3
8	F8	34.58	44.04	0.0043	1	23	F23	99.33	57.64	0.0041	1
9	F9	38.71	43.48	0.0042	1	24	F24	98.88	62.15	0.0040	4
10	F10	99.33	44.46	0.0042	1	25	F25	97.48	40.92	0.0121	2
11	F11	99.00	76.19	0.0041	10	**26**	**F26**	**99.54**	**67.64**	**0.0037**	**8**
12	F12	98.67	94.42	0.0043	10	27	F27	99.06	54.65	0.0041	8
13	F13	91.92	79.52	0.0047	2	28	F28	98.79	52.22	0.0064	1
14	F14	73.29	97.72	0.0053	8	29	F29	38.71	36.87	0.0042	1
15	F15	60.15	81.08	0.0051	1	30	F30	61.42	151.03	0.0057	3

Table 17. The classification accuracy (CA), corresponding training time (TrTm) and testing time (TsTm) using optimal diffusion steps (DS) for different feature sets using MondialMarmi dataset, for YCbCr colour space.

Sl. No.	Feature set	CA(%)	TrTm (sec.)	TsTm (sec.)	DS	Sl. No.	Feature set	CA(%)	TrTm (sec.)	TsTm (sec.)	DS
1	F1	90.65	14.87	0.0037	4	16	F16	64.83	61.66	0.0059	10
2	F2	54.54	120.11	0.0050	2	17	F17	98.06	38.41	0.0044	5
3	F3	98.19	12.73	0.0040	2	18	F18	98.02	38.67	0.0043	2
4	F4	97.63	35.93	0.0038	10	19	F19	97.58	53.92	0.0045	9
5	F5	99.33	29.81	0.0036	4	20	F20	39.25	16.29	0.0047	1
6	F6	96.69	28.86	0.0042	9	**21**	**F21**	**99.58**	**36.03**	**0.0040**	**6**
7	F7	97.25	29.67	0.0047	10	22	F22	97.92	15.19	0.0046	2
8	F8	39.79	22.79	0.0038	7	23	F23	99.19	46.70	0.0039	8
9	F9	39.25	9.42	0.0041	1	24	F24	99.40	53.25	0.0039	10
10	F10	98.81	11.94	0.0042	2	25	F25	97.75	33.24	0.0042	10
11	F11	98.48	26.24	0.0043	4	26	F26	99.35	41.44	0.0036	5
12	F12	98.79	48.36	0.0046	8	27	F27	98.98	36.83	0.0040	10
13	F13	93.29	52.76	0.0052	8	28	F28	98.83	30.48	0.0045	3
14	F14	66.69	50.55	0.0050	6	29	F29	39.25	10.27	0.0043	1
15	F15	38.10	56.51	0.0054	8	30	F30	59.06	141.77	0.0055	9

Table 18. The classification accuracy (CA), corresponding training time (TrTm) and testing time (TsTm) using optimal diffusion steps (DS) for different feature sets using MondialMarmi dataset, for Lab colour space.

Sl. No.	Feature set	CA(%)	TrTm (sec.)	TsTm (sec.)	DS	Sl. No.	Feature set	CA(%)	TrTm (sec.)	TsTm (sec.)	DS
1	F1	89.85	27.02	0.0036	4	16	F16	65.08	83.85	0.0062	8
2	F2	47.77	147.36	0.0047	2	17	F17	96.88	74.72	0.0053	10
3	F3	97.38	33.78	0.0036	4	18	F18	97.75	65.45	0.0052	4
4	F4	96.48	52.73	0.0039	8	19	F19	97.02	82.79	0.0044	10
5	F5	98.88	57.53	0.0035	6	20	F20	39.27	53.67	0.0100	8
6	F6	94.48	44.32	0.0037	9	21	F21	98.73	67.68	0.0055	9
7	F7	94.88	48.64	0.0036	10	22	F22	97.13	41.41	0.0054	5
8	F8	41.88	38.74	0.0037	6	23	F23	98.96	66.54	0.0052	6
9	F9	39.27	42.51	0.0041	8	**24**	**F24**	**99.19**	**55.52**	**0.0045**	**2**
10	F10	98.29	40.68	0.0040	6	25	F25	95.50	44.64	0.0053	6
11	F11	98.10	60.79	0.0043	10	26	F26	99.10	65.13	0.0037	6
12	F12	98.52	65.85	0.0047	4	27	F27	98.69	42.00	0.0111	4
13	F13	92.00	77.66	0.0046	8	28	F28	98.15	66.69	0.0042	8
14	F14	68.17	78.74	0.0054	7	29	F29	39.27	46.33	0.0044	8
15	F15	37.83	93.86	0.0057	8	30	F30	60.25	177.70	0.0062	4

Table 19. The classification accuracy (CA), corresponding training time (TrTm) and testing time (TsTm) using optimal diffusion steps (DS) for different feature sets using MondialMarmi dataset, for gray scale.

Sl. No.	Feature set	CA(%)	TrTm (sec.)	TsTm (sec.)	DS	Sl. No.	Feature set	CA(%)	TrTm (sec.)	TsTm (sec.)	DS
1	F1	73.56	26.41	0.0052	9	16	F16	46.17	60.69	0.0115	8
2	F2	62.33	126.57	0.0091	2	17	F17	96.38	47.35	0.0062	10
3	F3	91.19	20.45	0.0077	8	18	F18	96.98	51.36	0.0062	8
4	F4	89.54	25.52	0.0110	6	19	F19	96.27	44.84	0.0119	5
5	F5	65.21	26.12	0.0285	1	20	F20	39.67	13.80	0.0145	1
6	F6	91.83	32.50	0.0090	10	21	**F21**	**98.63**	**36.12**	**0.0103**	**7**
7	F7	88.29	32.32	0.0099	10	22	F22	96.35	24.02	0.0059	7
8	F8	40.83	31.08	0.0036	9	23	F23	98.13	43.09	0.0071	6
9	F9	39.67	6.63	0.0055	1	24	F24	98.50	42.88	0.0086	6
10	F10	97.23	17.50	0.0058	4	25	F25	93.73	25.83	0.0118	8
11	F11	97.19	44.72	0.0070	10	26	F26	98.46	51.01	0.0046	10
12	F12	97.35	57.67	0.0119	7	27	F27	96.90	18.33	0.0095	2
13	F13	93.83	55.65	0.0074	8	28	F28	97.46	33.13	0.0054	5
14	F14	61.90	64.55	0.0098	9	29	F29	39.67	6.72	0.0058	1
15	F15	56.65	58.51	0.0114	7	30	F30	60.06	146.40	0.0105	2

Table 20. Comparison of optimal classification accuracy (CA) of the proposed method experimented on different colour spaces and the corresponding training time, testing time, optimal feature set and diffusion steps for MondialMarmi dataset.

Parameters	Colour space				
	Gray	RGB	HSV	YCbCr	Lab
CA (%)	98.63	98.69	99.54	**99.58**	99.19
Training time (sec.)	36.12	120.45	67.64	**36.03**	55.52
Testing time (sec.)	0.0103	0.0039	0.0037	**0.0040**	0.0045
Optimal feature set	F21	F5	F26	**F21**	F24
Optimal no. of diffusion step	7	8	8	**6**	2

Table 21. Comparison of classification accuracy (CA) for the proposed method and other methods in the literature using MondialMarmi dataset.

Method	CA(%)	Number of features	Classifier
Proposed method	**99.58**	**11**	**k-NN, k=3**
Bianconi et al. (2015)	93.90	512	SVM+GPC
Paci et al. (2013)	96.56	60	k-NN, k=1
Kylberg & Sintorn (2013)	95.80	4116	k-NN, k=1
Fernandez et al. (2013)	93.35	725	k-NN, k=1
Gonzalez et al. (2013)	97.50	216	k-NN, k=1
Bianconi et al. (2012)	98.50	30	SVM
Fernandez et al. (2011)	97.40	325	k-NN, k=1

ACKNOWLEDGMENT

Authors are indebted to the reviewers for critical comments which substantially increased the quality of the chapter.

REFERENCES

Abdulmunim, M. E. (2012). Color Texture Classification using Adaptive Discrete Multiwavelets Transform. *Eng. & Tech. Journal, 30*(4), 615–627.

Ahmadvand, A., & Daliri, M. R. (2016a). A review on texture analysis methods in biomedical image processing. *OMICS Journal of Radiology, 5*(02), 2. doi:10.4172/2167-7964.1000e136

Ahmadvand, A., & Daliri, M. R. (2016b). Rotation invariant texture classification using extended wavelet channel combining and LL channel filter bank. *Knowledge-Based Systems, 97*, 75–88. doi:10.1016/j.knosys.2016.01.015

Amadasun, M., & King, R. (1989). Textural features corresponding to texural properties. *IEEE Transactions on Systems, Man, and Cybernetics, 19*(5), 1264–1274. doi:10.1109/21.44046

Bello-Cerezo, R., Bianconi, F., Di Maria, F., Napoletano, P., & Smeraldi, F. (2019, February). Comparative evaluation of hand-crafted image descriptors vs. off-the-shelf CNN-based features for colour texture classification under ideal and realistic conditions. *Applied Sciences (Basel, Switzerland), 9*(4), 738. doi:10.3390/app9040738

Bhusnurmath, R. A., & Hiremath, P. S. (2017d). LDA based Discriminant Features for Texture Classification Using WT and PDE Approach. In *Third International Conference on Cognitive Computing and Information Processing (CCIP 2017), Bengaluru, Karnataka, India, Communications in Computer and Information Science (CCIS)*. Springer. DOI: 10.1007/978-981-10-9059-2_18

Bhusnurmath, R.A., & Hiremath, P.S., (2019). *WT and PDE approach for forest species recognition in macroscopic images.* doi:10.1007/978-981-13-9184-2_23

Bhusnurmath, R. A., & Hiremath, P. S. (2019). WT and PDE approach for forest species recognition in macroscopic images. CCIS, 1036, 258–269. Doi:10.1007/978-981-13-9184-2_23

Bianconi, F., & Fernandez, A. (2006). Granite texture classification with Gabor filters. *Proc. of the 18th International Congress on Graphical Engineering.* doi: 10.1.1.107.1400

Bianconi, F., Fernández, A., González, E., Caride, J., & Calviño, A. (2009). Rotation-invariant colour texture classification through multilayer CCR. *Pattern Recognition Letters, 30*(8), 765–773. doi:10.1016/j.patrec.2009.02.006

Bianconi, F., Fernandez, A., González, E., & Saetta, S. A. (2013). Performance analysis of colour descriptors for parquet sorting. *Expert Systems with Applications, 40*(5), 1636–1644. doi:10.1016/j.eswa.2012.09.007

Bianconi, F., Gonzalez, E., & Fernandez, A. (2015). Dominant local binary patterns for texture classification: Labelled or unlabelled? *Pattern Recognition Letters, 65,* 8–14. doi:10.1016/j.patrec.2015.06.025

Bianconi, F., Gonzalez, E., Fernandez, A., & Saetta, S. A. (2012). Automatic classification of granite tiles through colour and texture features. *Expert Systems with Applications, 39*(12), 11212–11218. doi:10.1016/j.eswa.2012.03.052

Bombardier, V., & Schmitt, E. (2010). Fuzzy rule classifier: Capability for generalization in wood color recognition. *Engineering Applications of Artificial Intelligence, 23*(6), 978–988. doi:10.1016/j.engappai.2010.05.001

Brodatz, P. (1966). *Textures: A Photographic Album of Artists and Designers.* Dover Publication.

Chang, J.-D., Yu, S.-S., Chen, H.-H., & Tsai, C.-S. (2010). HSV-based Color Texture Image Classification using Wavelet Transform and Motif Patterns. *Journal of Computers, 20*(4), 63–69.

CIE. (2006). *A framework for the measurement of visual appearance, Tech. Rep. CIE 175*. International Commission on Illumination.

Daubechies, I. (1992). *Ten Lectures on Wavelets*. Montpellier, VT: Capital City Press. doi:10.1137/1.9781611970104

Dogan, H., & Akay, O. (2010). Using adaboost classifiers in a hierarchical framework for classifying surface images of marble slabs. *Expert Systems with Applications*, *37*(12), 8814–8821. doi:10.1016/j.eswa.2010.06.019

Doost, H. R. E., & Amirani, M. C. (2013). Texture classification with local binary pattern based on continues wavelet transformation. *International Journal of Advanced Research in Electrical. Electronics and Instrumentation Engineering*, *2*(10), 4651–4656.

Duda, R. O., Hart, P. E., & Stork, D. (2001). *Pattern Classification* (2nd ed.). New York: Wiley Publications.

Eugene, C. (2008). Measurement of "total visual appearance": a CIE challenge of soft metrology. *Proceedings of the 12th IMEKO TC1-TC7 Joint Symposium on Man, Science & Measurement*, 61–65.

Faria, J., Martins, T., Ferreira, M., & Santos, C. (2008). A computer vision system for color grading wood boards using fuzzy logic. *Proceedings of the IEEE international symposium on industrial electronics (ISIE 2008)*, 345–350. 10.1109/ISIE.2008.4677036

Fernandez, A., Alvarez, M. X., & Bianconi, F. (2013). Texture Description Through Histograms of Equivalent Patterns. *Journal of Mathematical Imaging and Vision*, *45*(1), 76–102. doi:10.100710851-012-0349-8

Fernandez, A., Ghita, O., Gonzalez, E., Bianconi, F., & Whelan, P. F. (2011). Evaluation of robustness against rotation of LBP, CCR and ILBP features in granite texture classification. *Machine Vision and Applications*, *22*(6), 913–926. doi:10.100700138-010-0253-4

Ferreira, A., & Giraldi, G. (2017). Convolutional neural network approaches to granite tiles classification. *Expert Systems with Applications*, *84*, 1–11. doi:10.1016/j.eswa.2017.04.053

Gonzalez, E., Bianconi, F. Alvarez, M.X. & Saetta, S.A. (2013). *Automatic Characterization of the Visual Appearance of Industrial Materials through Colour and Texture Analysis: An Overview of Methods and Applications*. Hindawi Publishing Corporation. doi:10.1155/2013/503541

Guillen-Bonilla, J. T., Kurmyshev, E. V., & Fernández, A. (2007). Quantifying a similarity of classes of texture images. *Applied Optics, 46*(23), 5562–5570. doi:10.1364/AO.46.005562 PMID:17694100

Haralick, R. M., Shanmugam, K., & Dinstein, I. (1973). Textural features for image classification. *IEEE Transactions on Systems, Man, and Cybernetics, SMC-3*(6), 610–621. doi:10.1109/TSMC.1973.4309314

Hermanson, J. C., & Wiedenhoeft, A. C. (2011). A brief review of machine vision in the context of automated wood identification systems. *The International Association of Wood Anatomists Journal, 32*(2), 233–250. doi:10.1163/22941932-90000054

Heurtier, A. H. (2019). Texture Feature Extraction Methods: A Survey. *IEEE Access: Practical Innovations, Open Solutions, 7*, 8975–9000. doi:10.1109/ACCESS.2018.2890743

Hiremath, P.S. & Bhusnurmath, R.A. (2013a). Texture image classification using nonsubsampled contourlet transform and local directional binary pattern. *International Journal of Advanced Research in Computer Science and Software Engineering, 3*(7), 819-827.

Hiremath, P.S. & Bhusnurmath R.A., (2014a). A novel approach to texture classification using NSCT and LDBP. *IJCA*, 36-42.

Hiremath, P. S., & Bhusnurmath, R. A. (2014b). Texture Classification Using Anisotropic Diffusion and Local Directional Binary Pattern Co-Occurrence Matrix. ERCICA 2014, 2, 763-769.

Hiremath, P. S., & Bhusnurmath, R. A. (2014c). RGB – Based Color Texture Image Classification Using Anisotropic Diffusion and LDBP. LNAI, 8875, 101–111, DOI doi:10.1007/978-3-319-13365-2_10

Hiremath, P.S. & Bhusnurmath, R.A., (2015). Diffusion Approach for Texture Analysis Based on LDBP. *International Journal of Computer Engineering and Applications, 9*(7), 108-121.

Hiremath, P.S. & Bhusnurmath, R.A. (2016a). PDE based features for texture analysis using wavelet transform. *International Journal on Cybernetics & Informatics, 5*(1), 143-155. Doi:10.5121/ijci.2016.5114

Hiremath, P. S., & Bhusnurmath, R. A. (2016b). Colour Texture Classification Using Anisotropic Diffusion and Wavelet Transform. *Seventh International Conference on Advances in Communication, Network, and Computing- CNC 2016*, 44-61. DOI: 10.1515/9783110469608-006

Hiremath, P. S., & Bhusnurmath, R. A. (2016c). Applications Of Texture Analysis Based On Anisotropic Diffusion. *UGC Sponsored National Conference on Recent Trends in Image Processing and Pattern Recognition (RTIP2R)*, 116 -128.

Hiremath, P.S. & Bhusnurmath, R.A. (2016d). Industrial Applications of Colour Texture Classification Based on Anisotropic Diffusion. *CCIS, 653,* 293–304. Doi:10.1007/978-981-10-4859-3_27

Hiremath, P.S. & Bhusnurmath, R.A. (2017a). Multiresolution LDBP Descriptors for Texture Classification Using Anisotropic Diffusion With an Application To Wood Texture Analysis. *Pattern Recognition Letters, 89*, 8-17. DOI: 10.1016j. patrec.2017.01.015

Hiremath, P.S. & Bhusnurmath, R.A. (2017b). Performance analysis of anisotropic diffusion descriptors in applications of colour texture Classification. *International Journal of Computer Vision and Image Processing, 7*(2), 50-63. Doi:10.4018/ IJCVIP.2017040104

Hiremath, P. S., & Bhusnurmath, R. A. (2017c). Texture Classification Using PDE Approach and Wavelet Transform. *Pattern Recognition and Image Analysis*, 27(3), 473–479. doi:10.1134/S1054661817030154

Hoang, V. T. (2018). *Multi color space LBP-based feature selection for texture classification*. Thesis.

Hrcka, R. (2008). Colour modelling as a tool for wood grading. *Proceedings of COST E53 – Quality control for wood and wood products*, 165–170.

Internet: University of Oulu texture database. (2005). http://www.outex.oulu.fi/ outex.php

Jahanbanifard, M., Gravendeel, B., Lens, F., & Verbeek, F. (2019). Ebony wood identification to battle illegal trade. *Biodiversity information science and standards*. doi:10.3897/biss.3.37084

Kurdthongmee, W. (2008). Colour classification of rubberwood boards for fingerjoint manufacturing using a SOM neural network and image processing. *Computers and Electronics in Agriculture, 64*(2), 85–92. doi:10.1016/j.compag.2008.04.002

Kurmyshev, E., Poterasu, M., & Guillén-Bonilla, J. T. (2007). Image scale determination for optimal texture classification using coordinated cluster representation. *Applied Optics, 46*(9), 1467–1476. doi:10.1364/AO.46.001467 PMID:17334437

Kylberg, G. (2012). *Kylberg Texture Dataset v. 1.0*. http://www.cb.uu.se/~gustaf/texture/

Kylberg, G., & Sintorn, I. M. (2013). Evaluation of noise robustness for local binary pattern descriptors in texture classification. *EURASIP Journal on Image and Video Processing*, *2013*(1), 17. doi:10.1186/1687-5281-2013-17

Labati, R., Gamassi, M., Piuri, V., & Scotti, F. (2009). A low-cost neural-based approach for wood types classification. *Proc. of the international conference on computational intelligence for measurement systems and applications*, 199-203. 10.1109/CIMSA.2009.5069947

Laws, K. I. (1980). Rapid texture identification. *SPIE*, *238*, 376–380.

Lepisto, L., Kunttu, I., & Visa, A. (2005). Rock image classification using color features in Gabor space. *Journal of Electron. Imaging, 14*(4), 1–3.

Lew, Y. L. (2005). *Design of an intelligent wood recognition system for the classification of tropical wood species* (Master Thesis). Universiti Teknologi Malaysia, Malaysia.

Liong, S. T., Gan, Y. S., Liu, K. H., Binh, T. Q., Le, C. T., Wu, C. A., . . . Yen-Chang, H. (2019). *Efficient Neural Network Approaches for Leather Defect Classification*. arXiv:1906.06446 (cs.CV)

Lu, J., Liong, V. E., Wang, G., & Moulin, P. (2015a). Joint feature learning for face recognition. *IEEE Transactions on Information Forensics and Security, 10*(7), 1371–1383. doi:10.1109/TIFS.2015.2408431

Lu, J., Liong, V. E., & Zhou, J. (2015b). Simultaneous local binary feature learning and encoding for face recognition. *IEEE International Conference on Computer Vision (ICCV'15)*. 10.1109/ICCV.2015.424

Lu, J., Liong, V. E., & Zhou, J. (2015d). Cost-sensitive local binary feature learning for facial age estimation. *IEEE Transactions on Image Processing, 24*(12), 5356–5368. doi:10.1109/TIP.2015.2481327 PMID:26415174

Lu, J., Liong, V. E., Zhou, X., & Zhou, J. (2015c). Learning compact binary face descriptor for face recognition. *IEEE Transactions on Pattern Analysis and Machine Intelligence, 37*(10), 2041–2256. doi:10.1109/TPAMI.2015.2408359 PMID:26340256

Mallat, S. G. (1989a). A theory of multiresolution signal decomposition: The wavelet representation. *IEEE Transactions on Pattern Analysis and Machine Intelligence, 11*(7), 674–693. doi:10.1109/34.192463

Mandelbrot, B. B. (1982). *The Fractal Geometry of Nature*. San Francisco, CA: Freeman.

Mirmehdi, M., & Petrou, M. (2000). Segmentation of colour textures. *IEEE Transactions on Pattern Analysis and Machine Intelligence*, 22(2), 142–159. doi:10.1109/34.825753

MondialMarmi. (2011). *A granite image database for colour and texture analysis, v1.1*. http://dismac.dii.unipg.it/mm

Murinto, M., Prahara, A., Winiari, S., Pramudi, I., & Dewi. (2018). Pre-Trained convolutional neural network for classification of tanning leather image. *International Journal of Advanced Computer Science and Applications, 9*. doi:10.14569/IJACSA.2018.090129

Paci, M., Nanni, L., & Severi, S. (2013). An ensemble of classifiers based on different texture descriptors for texture classification. *Journal of King Saud University-Science, 25*, 235-244.

Paclik, P., Verzakov, S., & Duin, R. P. W. (2005). Improving the maximum likelihood co-occurrence classifier: A study on classification of inhomogeneous rock images. *Lecture Notes in Computer Science, 3540*, 998–1008. doi:10.1007/11499145_101

Parquet: Parquet image database. (2012). http://dismac.dii.unipg.it/parquet/data.html

Paschos, G. (2000). Fast color texture recognition using chromaticity moments. *Pattern Recognition Letters, 21*(9), 837–841. doi:10.1016/S0167-8655(00)00043-X

Perona, P., & Malik, J. (1990). Scale-Space and Edge Detection Using Anisotropic Diffusion. *IEEE Transactions on Pattern Analysis and Machine Intelligence, 12*(7), 629–639. doi:10.1109/34.56205

Petrou, M., & Sevilla, P. G. (2006). Image processing dealing with texture. West Sussex, UK: John Wiley & Sons.

Pietikainen. (2000). *Texture analysis in machine vision*. Singapore: World Scientific Publishing.

Porebski, A., Hoang, V. T., Vandenbroucke, N., & Hamad, D. (2018). Multi-color space local binary pattern-based feature selection for texture classification, 15 pages J. *Electron. Imag., 27*(1). doi:10.1117/1.JEI.27.1.011010

Rosenfeld, A., & Weszka, J. (1980). Picture Recognition. In K. Fu (Ed.), *Digital Pattern Recognition* (pp. 135–166). Springer-Verlag. doi:10.1007/978-3-642-67740-3_5

Selvan, S., & Ramakrishnan, S. (2007). SVD-based Modeling for Image Texture Classification using Wavelet Transformation. *IEEE Transactions on Image Processing*, *16*(11), 2688–2696. doi:10.1109/TIP.2007.908082 PMID:17990746

Sengur, A. (2008). Wavelet transform and adaptive neuro-fuzzy inference system for color texture classification. *Expert Systems with Applications*, *34*(3), 2120–2128. doi:10.1016/j.eswa.2007.02.032

Shadmon, A. (2005). Stone Absolute (by any other name). *Litos, 78*.

Sheriff, M., AntoBennet, M., Pavithra, B., & Suvetha, P. (2018). Manufacturing defect detection in textile industry using neural network. *International Journal of Pure and Applied Mathematics*, *119*, 197–205.

Shustrov, D., Eerola, T., Lensu, L., Kälviäinen, H., & Haario, H. (2019). *Fine-grained wood species identification using convolutional neural networks*. doi:10.1007/978-3-030-20205-7_6

Standard EN 12440:2000: Natural stone—denomination criteria.

Topalova, I. & Tzokev, A. (2010). Automated texture classification of marble shades with real-time PLC neural network implementation. *The 2010 international joint conference on Neural networks*, 1–8.

Tuceryan, M., & Jain, A. (1998). Texture analysis. In *Handbook of Pattern Recognition and Vision*. World Scientific.

VisTex. (n.d.). https://vismod.media.mit.edu/vismod/imagery/VisionTexture

Weszka, J. S., Dyer, C. R., & Rosenfeld, A. (1976). A comparative study of texture measures for terrain classification. *IEEE Transactions on Systems, Man, and Cybernetics*, *6*(4), 269–286. doi:10.1109/TSMC.1976.5408777

Wu, C.-M., & Chen, Y.-C. (1992). Statistical feature matrix for texture analysis. *CVGIP. Graphical Models and Image Processing*, *54*(5), 407–419. doi:10.1016/1049-9652(92)90025-S

Xie, X. (2008). A review of recent advances in surface defect detection using texture analysis techniques. *ELCVIA. Electronic Letters on Computer Vision and Image Analysis*, *7*(3), 1–22. doi:10.5565/rev/elcvia.268

Zhu, C., & Wang, R. (2012). Local multiple patterns based multi-resolution gray-scale and rotation invariant texture classification. *Information Sciences*, *187*, 93–108. doi:10.1016/j.ins.2011.10.014

APPENDIX 1

Wavelet Transform

The implementation and theoretical aspects of wavelet based algorithms are discussed in (Daubechies, 1992; Mallat, 1989a). Wavelet functions have been defined in order to be suitable for a specific application. The continuous wavelet transform of a 1-D signal g(x) is defined by the Eqs. (1) and (2):

$$\left(W_\psi g\right)(a,b) = \int g(x)\psi^*_{(a,b)}(x)dx \tag{1}$$

and

$$\psi_{a,b} = a^{-1/2}\psi\left((x-a)/b\right) \tag{2}$$

where a represents the scaling factor, b represents the translation parameter related to the location of the window, and $\psi^*(x)$ is the transforming function. The 2-D wavelet transform is performed by a product of 1-D filters. The transform is calculated by applying a filter bank to the textured image. The rows and columns of an image are processed separately and down sampled by a factor of 2 in each direction. In the present chapter, the Haar wavelet is employed for the wavelet transform of an image, and is defined as:

$$\dot{E}(t) = \begin{cases} 1 & , 0 <= t <= \frac{1}{2} \\ -1 & , \frac{1}{2} <= t <= 1 \\ 0 & , \text{ otherwise} \end{cases} \tag{3}$$

APPENDIX 2

Anisotropic Diffusion

Anisotropic diffusion (Perona and Malik, 1990) is normally implemented by means of an approximation of the generalized diffusion equation as given in the Eq. (4).

$$I_s^{t+\Delta t} = I_s^t + \frac{\lambda}{|\eta_s|}\sum_{p\in\eta_s} c\left(\nabla I_{s,p}^t\right)\nabla I_{s,p}^t \tag{4}$$

where i'_s is the discretely sampled image, s denotes the pixel position in a discrete two-dimensional (2-D) grid, and $0 \le \lambda \le 1/4$ is a scalar that controls the numerical stability, $\bar{\eta}_s$ is the number of pixels in the window (usually four, except at the image boundaries), and $\nabla i'_{s,p} = i'_p - i'_s, \forall p \in \bar{\eta}_s$. The advantages of anisotropic diffusion include intra-region smoothing and edge preservation. Using the Eq. (B4) each new image in the family is computed by applying this equation to the previous image. Consequently, anisotropic diffusion is an iterative process where a relatively simple set of computation are used to compute each successive image in the family and this process is continued until a sufficient degree of smoothing is obtained (so as to obtain better texture component). Two diffusion coefficients are given in the Eqs. (B5) and (B6) (Perona and Malik, 1990).

$$c(x) = \frac{1}{1 + (x/k)^2} \tag{5}$$

and

$$c(x) = \exp\left[-(x/k)^2\right] \tag{6}$$

where k is an edge magnitude parameter. In the anisotropic diffusion method, the gradient magnitude is used to detect an image edge or boundary as a step discontinuity in intensity.

APPENDIX 3

Feature Sets

Various first order and second order descriptors obtained are tabulated in the Table 22. The first order descriptor considers individual pixel value. The second order descriptors take into account the relationship between neighboring pixel values. The various feature sets based on first order descriptor (F1) and second order descriptors (F2-F9) considered in the present study are tabulated in the Table 22 (Hiremath & Bhusnurmath, 2016a). Further, the various combinations of these feature sets (F10-F30) listed in the Table 22 are also explored to investigate the effect on classification accuracy.

Table 22. The different feature sets based on first order descriptor (F1) and second order descriptors (F2-F9) (Hiremath & Bhusnurmath, 2016a)

Feature set	Description	Features extracted	Feature set	Description	Features extracted
F1	First order statistics	Skewness, mean, standard deviation, kurtosis and median.	F6	Law's texture energy measures (Laws, 1980)	Six texture energy measures
F2	Haralick features (Haralick et al., 1973)	entropy, homogeneity, contrast, energy, maximum probability, cluster shade and cluster prominence	F7	Fractal dimension texture analysis (Mandelbrot, 1982)	roughness of a surface
F3	Gray level difference statistics (Weszka et al., 1976)	contrast, homogeneity, energy, entropy and mean	F8	Fourier power spectrum (Rosenfeld & Weszka, 1980)	radial sum and angular sum
F4	Neighborhood gray tone difference matrix (Amadasun & King, 1989)	busyness, complexity, coarseness, contrast and texture strength	F9	Shape	size(x,y), area, perimeter and perimeter^2 /area
F5	Statistical feature matrix (Wu & Chen, 1992)	coarseness, contrast, period and roughness			

Table 23. The combinations (F10-F30) of feature sets given in the Table 22 (Hiremath & Bhusnurmath, 2016a).

Feature set name	Feature set combination	Feature set name	Feature set combination
F10	F1+F3	F21	F1+F3+F5
F11	F1+F3+F4	F22	F1+F3+F6
F12	F1+F3+F4+F5	F23	F1+F4+F5
F13	F1+F3+F4+F5+F6	F24	F3+F4+F5
F14	F1+F3+F4+F5+F6+F7	F25	F6+F7
F15	F1+F3+F4+F5+F6+F7+F8	F26	F4+F5
F16	F1+F3+F4+F5+F6+F7+F8+F9	F27	F3+F4
F17	F1+F3+F5+F6	F28	F5+F6
F18	F3+F4+F5+F6	F29	F8+F9
F19	F1+F4+F5+F6	F30	F2+F4

Chapter 3
A Brief Overview on Intelligent Computing–Based Biological Data and Image Analysis

Mousomi Roy
University of Kalyani, India

ABSTRACT

Biological data analysis is one of the most important and challenging tasks in today's world. Automated analysis of these data is necessary for quick and accurate diagnosis. Intelligent computing-based solutions are highly required to reduce the human intervention as well as time. Artificial intelligence-based methods are frequently used to analyze and mine information from biological data. There are several machine learning-based tools available, using which powerful and intelligent automated systems can be developed. In general, the amount and volume of this kind of data is quite huge and demands sophisticated tools that can efficiently handle this data and produce results within reasonable time by extracting useful information from big data. In this chapter, the authors have made a comprehensive study about different computer-aided automated methods and tools to analyze the different types of biological data. Moreover, this chapter gives an insight about various types of biological data and their real-life applications.

DOI: 10.4018/978-1-7998-2736-8.ch003

INTRODUCTION

In the field of diagnosis and medical research, analysis of biological data is inevitable. We can explore and extract some precious information from various types of biological data. To mine some knowledge from these data requires the involvement of the domain experts. Although humans are highly intelligent, there are some inherent problems associated with the human observers. For example, experiments done by the humans are subject to errors. It may also happen that, same data when diagnosed two times by the same observer may produce the different results. It is purely subjective and depends on the present state of the observer (Chakraborty, Chatterjee, et al., 2017a; Hore et al., 2015).

In general, biological sources generates a huge amount of data which is often considered as the big data (Prabha, Rai, & Singh, n.d.). Detailed study of these data is required for generating any useful information from the raw form. Now, humans are hardly capable of handling such a huge amount of data in a stipulated amount of time. This is an another problem associated with the human observers. Moreover, the analysis of these data is significant in the diagnostic field to provide proper treatment. The inaccuracies in the diagnostic process can be very costly in terms of the life of the patients.

Automated systems are highly beneficial in analyzing and mining useful information from the biological datasets. The term 'data mining' is a well-known technology which is used to find hidden information from large databases and big data. The exploration process is often known as 'knowledge discovery'. Now a days, it is very hard to think the world without computers. The technical explosion in the automated systems makes the life easier. Automated systems are highly efficient and can mimic the diagnostic process as made by a human expert. Modern applications can effectively search the ocean of the data and discover useful information with high accuracy and in moderate time (Chakraborty, Chatterjee, Ashour, Mali, & Dey, 2017).

Most of the computer aided diagnostic systems are based on the artificial intelligence (AI) based tools. Artificial intelligence mimics the human intelligence and helps a machine to behave intelligently ("Artificial intelligence," n.d.). In general, it can induce the cognitive nature in a machine. AI based tools provides the power to a computer to perform certain tasks very efficiently like humans (even better in some situation) (Boden, 1998).

In recent years, a huge growth in Artificial intelligence based technologies can be observed that can change the standard of the life. Artificial intelligence provides a way to make a machine learn. This technology is known as machine learning which is the blessing of artificial intelligence. Machine learning algorithms are used to make a machine learn and to avoid programming for each and every problem instance

(Mitchell, 1997). These algorithms follows a set of rules for learning as well as for producing results. The performance of these algorithms are measured in terms of the accuracy and some other parameters. The machine learning based approaches can be broadly categorized as given follows:

i. **Unsupervised Learning**: In this type of learning, there is no predefined knowledge about the class of the object. Algorithm tries to find out some pattern so that it can identify the class of the unknown object. The classification operation is based on some hypothesis. To draw a conclusion, all of the hypothesis must be evaluated (Karaboga & Basturk, 2007). There is no so called 'supervision' or guidance for the algorithms, It predicts the natural grouping of the objects.

ii. **Supervised Learning**: Here, some data are used whose classes are known to train the classifier. After the training phase, testing is performed on the known datasets. The deviation of the result from the actual one and predicted one is considered as the error. The main objective of these kind of algorithms is to train the classifier in such a way so that the error will be minimized (Chakraborty et al., 2017). There are several models proposed in the literature that follows the supervised learning methods. For example, Artificial Neural Networks, Support Vector Machine etc. Several hybrid models are found in literature which are based on the metaheurictic algorithms such as GA (Chakraborty, Seal, & Roy, 2015), SA (Chakraborty & Bhowmik, 2015; SChakraborty & Bhowmik, 2013, 2015), CS (S. Chakraborty, Chatterjee, et al., 2017a; Mousomi Roy et al., 2017) to adjust the input weights to enhance the accuracy.

iii. **Reinforcement Learning**: This type of learning uses two data sets, one is used to train the system and another one is used to test the system. So, the algorithm gather knowledge from one dataset and apply it on another dataset.

The difference among supervised, unsupervised and reinforcement learning can be visualized in figure 1 (Wang, Chaovalitwongse, & Babuska, 2012).

This work gives a comprehensive review on the intelligent computing methods and automated systems that has been applied on different types of biological data.

DIFFERENT TYPES OF BIOLOGICAL DATA

Biological data are those raw facts and figures that are generated from different biological sources. Nucleic Acids Research has published a list of 180 data repository in 2016 (Rigden, Fernández-Suárez, & Galperin, 2016). The biological data can be broadly categorized in three ways as follows: ("List of biological databases," n.d.)

Figure 1. Comparison of supervised, unsupervised and reinforcement learning

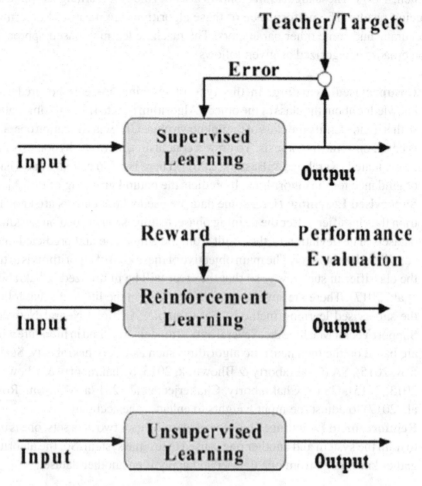

i. **Nucleic Acid**: This type of data are collected from sources based on nucleic acid. There are basically four sources from which this type of data are collected as discussed below:

a. **DNA**: This type of data is generally consist of DNA profiles. DNA data is highly beneficial and frequently used to study various genetic disorders and diseases, genetic fingerprinting etc. DNA based data are stored in various DNA data banks. Some of the DNA data banks are forensic, medical, national, corporate etc.

b. **Gene Expression**: The term 'Gene Expression' is associated with almost every living organisms. Gene expression is the method where the information of genes is utilized to generate a product (e.g. proteins, RNA etc.).

c. **Phenotype**: The term 'phenotype' indicates various observable characteristics of the living organisms. Sometimes this type of data is manually generated and recorded. Some example of the data repository that stores phenotype data are PHI base, RGD etc.

d. **RNA**: RNA data are collected from different types of RNAs like non-coding RNAs and some other elements of RNA.

ii. **Amino Acid/Protein**: This kind of data are collected by analyzing amino acids and proteins. This category is also having four classifications as discussed below:

a. **Protein Sequence**: Protein sequence denotes the sequence of the amino acids in a protein. It can be sequenced straight way or can be derived from the DNA sequences ("Protein primary structure," n.d.).

b. **Protein Structure**: This database is constructed based on different structures of protein that has been computed experimentally. It provides an easier way to access various data related to the structure of the protein.

c. **Protein Model**: This type of data is concerned about the protein structure model.

d. **Interaction**: Different data about molecular interaction along with protein-protein interaction fall under this category.

iii. **Miscellaneous**: Some other type of data belong to this category. Some of them are listed below:

a. **Signal Transduction Pathway**: The term 'Signal transduction' indicates the process by which a signal (chemical or physical) transmits from a cell. In general, there is a sequence of operations happen in the transmission process of a signal. Signal transduction pathway related data deals with it.

b. **Metabolic Pathway**: This type of data deals with the details of the series of chemical reactions associated with a cell.

c. **Exosomal**: It deals with the data about the exosomes. Exosomes are vesicles derived from the cells and it is present in the fluids (e.g. blood, urine etc.) of almost all possible eukaryotic cells ("Exosome (vesicle)," n.d.).

d. **Mathematical Model**: It is the mathematical representation of different biological processes.

e. **Taxonomic**: This type of data is used for species identification

Different categories of the biological data can be visualized from figure 2.

Figure 2. Different categories of biological data

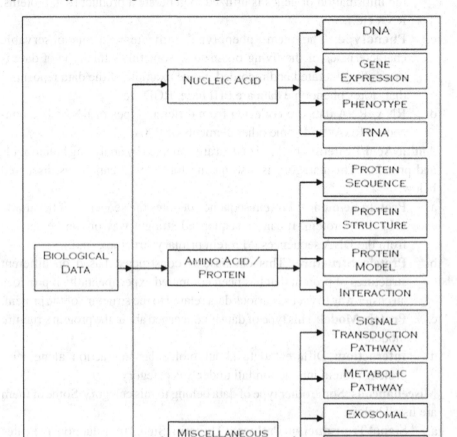

Nowadays, the biomedical images are considered as one of the major source of data which is helpful in automated disease analysis and diagnostic purposes (Chakraborty, Chatterjee, et al., 2017b; Hore et al., 2015). Biological images are processed using various advanced computing methods to extract meaningful information and interpret the biological significance of the extracted results (Chakraborty, Chatterjee, Dey, Ashour, & Shi, 2018; Chakraborty, Roy, & Hore, 2018; Chakraborty, Chatterjee, et al., 2017; Shouvik Chakraborty, Chatterjee, Das, & Mali, 2020; Shouvik Chakraborty & Mali, 2018; Hartley et al., 2014; Hore, Chatterjee, Chakraborty, & Shaw, 2016). Sometimes, the security of the biomedical images becomes one of the major concerns because these types of images often contain sensitive and private information of the patients and other species which is vulnerable for attack (Chakraborty, Seal, Roy, & Mali, 2016; Mali, Chakraborty, & Roy, 2015; Mali, Chakraborty, Seal, & Roy, 2015; Roy, Chakraborty, et al., 2019; Roy, Mali, et al., 2019; Seal, Chakraborty, & Mali, 2017). Therefore, biomedical image analysis and its security is necessary and in most of the cases, it is inevitable for the diagnostic process (Chakraborty et al., 2018, 2017, 2019).

Analysis of biological data and image has several applications like personalized medicine. It demands processing, storing and analyzing huge amount of biological data in a restricted time period. Tools for big data analysis tools along with artificial intelligence based techniques are used to perform computation and mine information from the biological big data and images (Datta et al., 2018; Hore et al., 2016). Sometimes, fully automated systems are not preferable because of its inherent limitations. In some situations some interactive systems are used which is semi-automatic kind in nature.

INTELLIGENT COMPUTING BASED BIOLOGICAL DATA AND IMAGE ANALYSIS

As discussed above, biological data can be considered as the big data and intelligent computing tools are required to process these data efficiently. In this section, some related work is discussed to process various types of biological data.

Among the different types of biological data, gene expression data is one of the most important and frequently used. In most of the cases gene expression data analysis involves DNA microarrays. Different operations can be performed on the microarray data to mine and extract different type of information. Different types of work has been proposed on gene expression data including pattern recognition, clustering, identification of consensus modules etc. Table 1 gives an overview of different methods intelligent computing tools that has been used to mine information from microarray gene expression data.

In table 2, some of the recent methods for biomedical image analysis is illustrated. There are several methods which are based on the advanced computational methods like deep learning, metaheuristic optimization (Chakraborty & Bhowmik, 2015; Chakraborty, Mali, Chatterjee, et al., 2018b; Chakraborty & Bhowmik, 2013, 2015, Chakraborty et al., 2017, 2015; Roy et al., 2017; Sarddar, Chakraborty, & Roy, 2015), IoT etc (Chakraborty, Roy, & Hore, 2016) which are highly beneficial to get accurate results from anywhere in the globe (Chakraborty, Mali, Banerjee, et al., 2018; Chakraborty, Mali, Chatterjee, et al., 2018a; Chakraborty et al., 2017; Roy et al., 2018).

Table 1. Overview of different methods for microarray gene expression data analysis

Method	Prime objective	Brief Description	Dataset
Zhang et. al. (H. Zhang, Yu, & Singer, 2003)	Tumor Classification	It is a decision tree based approach where forest of classification trees has been used to classify tumors	Leukemia and lymphoma ("Lymphoma/Leukemia Molecular Profiling Project," n.d.)
Busygin et. al. (Busygin, Jacobsen, Kramer, Krämer, & Ag, 2002)	Microarray Biclustering	A node-driven clustering technique has been proposed	Leukemia
Tan et. al. (Tan, Dowe, & Dix, 2007)	Building a classification model	A tree based classification model has been proposed to analyze microarray data. In this paper, Partial Least-Squares regression method has been used to select the features.	Leukaemia, Breast cancer, Central nervous system (CNS), Colon tumour, Lung cancer, Prostate cancer and Prostate cancer outcome ("GEDatasets," n.d.)
Tang et. al. (Tang, Zhang, Zhang, & Ramanathan, 2001)	Unsupervised clustering of microarray data	This work presents an interrelated bi-clustering method based on iterative row column clustering method.	Multiple sclerosis
Getz et. al. (Getz, Gal, Kela, Notterman, & Domany, 2003)	Analyze microarray data related to breast and colon cancer	A new bi-clustering method has been proposed to extract information from gene expression data. It helps to identify important sub matrices from gene expression data.	Breast and colon cancer (Notterman, Alon, Sierk, & Levine, 2001)
Shipp et. al. (Shipp et al., 2002)	Prediction of the outcome of diffuse large b-cell lymphoma	Tumor classification work based on machine learning	Lymphoma (Shipp et al., 2002)
Peterson et. al. (Peterson & Coleman, 2008)	Classification of microarray data	A machine learning based approach to classify microarray gene expression data using ROC curves.	Cancer Data (Peterson & Coleman, 2008)
Cheng et. al. (Cheng & Church, 2000)	Knowledge mining from gene expression data using biclustering	Determine some sub matrices with low score of 'mean squared residue'. It is useful in finding co-regulation pattern.	Yeast and Human (Cheng & Church, 2000)
Yang et. al. (Yang, Wang, Wang, & Yu, 2003)	Accelerate and improve the biclustering process for gene expression data	A new method has been proposed to enhance the biclustering process. The proposed algorithm has been termed as 'FLOC'	Yeast ("Harvard Molecular Technologies," n.d.)
Golub et. al. (Golub et al., 1999)	Cancer classification	Class predition and discovery method has been proposed for cancer based gene expression data.	Leukemia (Golub et al., 1999)
Pique-Regi (Pique-Regi, Ortega, & Asgharzadeh, 2005)	'Sequential Diagonal Linear Discriminant Analysis' method for gene expression data	In this work, a novel algorithm has been developed to perform 'Sequential Diagonal Linear Discriminant Analysis'. In this approach, both gene selection and classification has been integrated.	(Neuroblastoma, Prostate, Leukemia, Colon (Pique-Regi et al., 2005)
Guo et. al. (Guo, Hastie, & Tibshirani, 2007)	Linear discriminant analysis for gene expression data	A new method has been proposed called 'shrunken centroids regularized discriminant analysis' which is modification of linear discriminant analysis for microarray gene expression data	Tamayo (Ramaswamy et al., 2001), Golub (Golub et al., 1999), Brown data
Cho el. al. (Cho & Dhillon, 2008)	Clustering of microarray data	A modification of 'Minimum Sum-Squared Residue Coclustering (MSSRCC)' method has been proposed for gene expression data.	Colon cancer, Leukemia, Lung cancer, and Mixed-Lineage Leukemia, synthesis ("Co-clustering Software," n.d.)
Liu et. al. (X. Liu & Wang, 2007)	Biclustering of gene expression data	In this work, a new similarity score has been developed that can be used to solve the biclustering problem in gene expression data.	Colon cancer (Murali & Kasif, 2003)
Brown et. al.(Brown et al., 2000)	Knowledge mining from gene expression data	In this work, support vector machine based knowledge mining is used to extract information from microarray gene expression data.	Yeast
Guyon et. al. (Guyon, Weston, Barnhill, & Vapnik, 2002)	Cancer classification using gene expression data	Gene selection and classification to classify cancer data using Recursive Feature Elimination (RFE) method and support vector machine.	Leukemia
Kluger et. al. (Kluger, Basri, Chang, & Gerstein, 2003)	Biclustering of gene expression data	A new method has been developed for biclustering microarray data.	lymphoma, leukemia, breast cancer, central nervous system (Pomeroy et al., 2002), embryonal tumors

continued on following page

Table 1. Continued

Method	Prime objective	Brief Description	Dataset
Van Uitert et. al. (van Uitert, Meuleman, & Wessels, 2008)	Biclustering of gene expression data	A new algorithm has been developed to mine biclusters. Different biclusters with varying no of rows and coloumns can be detected.	TRANSFAC (Wingender, 2000)
Zhang et. al. (X. Zhang et al., 2006)	Classification of microarray data	A new method has been developed to choose biomarkers for efficient classification. Recursive support vector machine has been used for this purpose.	Simulated, SELDI proteomics (Shi et al., 2006; Xu et al., 2004)
Zhang et. al. (H. H. Zhang, Ahn, Lin, & Park, 2006)	Gene selection	A new technique based on support vector machine has been developed to select better genes from a dataset. It will further help in the classification process.	Simulated, UNC breast cancer dataset (Perou et al., 2000; Sotiriou et al., 2003; van 't Veer et al., 2002)
Ayadi et. al. (Ayadi, Elloumi, & Hao, 2009)	Biclustering of DNA microarray data	A biclustering algorithm was proposed based on bicluster enumeration tree.	Synthetic dataset
Shamir et. al. (Shamir et al., 2005)	Microarray data analysis	EXPANDER is the acronym for EXPression ANalyzer and DisplayER. It is a set of programs to analyse microarray data.	Various datasets
Chen et. al. (Chen & Chang, 2009)	Biclustering of microarray data	A new method has been proposed based on Condition-Enumeration tree to perform clustering on microarray data.	Synthetic, yeast (Tavazoie, Hughes, Campbell, Cho, & Church, 1999), Small, Round Blue Cell Tumors (Khan et al., 2001), ALL-AML (Brunet, Tamayo, Golub, & Mesirov, 2004)
Sill et. al. (Sill, Kaiser, Benner, & Kopp-schneider, 2011)	Biclustering of gene expression data	A new method has been proposed for biclustering with stability selection.	Lung cancer (Bhattacharjee et al., 2001)
Tanay et. al. (Tanay, Sharan, & Shamir, 2002)	Biclustering of gene expression data	In this method, a graph theoretic approach has been taken to find the most significant biclusters from gene expression data.	Yeast, human clinical, lymphoma
O'Neill et. al. (O'Neill & Song, 2003)	Analysis of microarray data using neural network	A neural network based model has been proposed for near perfect prognosis using microarray data.	Lymphoma
Friedman et. al. (Friedman, Linial, Nachman, & Pe'er, 2000)	Bayesian network based analysis of gene expression data	In this work, Bayesian network has been adopted to show the interaction among genes.	Cell cycle (Spellman et al., 1998)
de Ferrari et. al. (De Ferrari & Aitken, 2006)	Identification of housekeeping genes	Naïve Bayes classifier has been used to identify and extract housekeeping genes from gene expression data	human, mouse and fruit fly
Helman et. al. (Helman, Veroff, Atlas, & Willman, 2004)	Classification of gene expression data	A Bayesian network based classifier has been developed to classify the gene expression data. The results have been cross validated to prove the efficiency of the proposed method.	MIT leukemia data (Golub et al., 1999), Princeton colon cancer data (Alon et al., 1999)
Demichelis et. al. (Demichelis, Magni, Piergiorgi, Rubin, & Bellazzi, 2006)	Managing heterogeneity in classification problems	In this work, a Naïve Bayes approach has been adopted to manage the problems that are generated during the classification process due to heterogeneity of the microarray data.	Simulated, TMA prostate cancer (Bismar et al., 2006)
Gusenleitner et. al. (Gusenleitner, Howe, Bentink, Quackenbush, & Culhane, 2012)	Biclustering of gene expression data	An iterative approach has been adopted for the biclustering of gene datasets. This method uses distribution parameter identification approach. The method is termed as 'iBBiG'.	Simulated, primary breast tumors (Kao, Chang, Hsu, & Huang, 2011), GeneChip Ontology Database (F. Liu, White, Antonescu, Gusenleitner, & Quackenbush, 2011)
Lazzeroni et. al. (Lazzeroni & Owen, 2002)	Biclustering of gene expression data	This work introduces a plaid model for two sided analysis of gene expression data. Two way ANOVA has been incorporated along with this method.	Yeast
Mankad et. al. (Mankad & Michailidis, 2014)	Biclustering of 3D gene expression data	This work focuses on the biclustering of 3D models of gene expression data using plaid model.	T-Cell data (Rangel et al., 2004)
Dettling (Dettling, 2004)	Tumor classification	This work combines the bagging and boosting scheme for tumor classification using microarray gene expression data.	Simulated, Leukemia (Golub et al., 1999), Colon (Alon et al., 1999), Prostate (Singh et al., 2002), Lymphoma (Alizadeh et al., 2000), SRBCT (Khan et al., 2001), Brain (Pomeroy et al., 2002)

continued on following page

Table 1. Continued

Method	Prime objective	Brief Description	Dataset
Long et.al. (Long & Vega, 2003)	Improve AdaBoost (Freund & Schapire, 1996) method	A modification to AdaBoost (Freund & Schapire, 1996)method has been developed for microarray data analysis	ALL-AML (Golub et al., 1999), colon cancer (Alon et al., 1999), breast cancer (West et al., 2001), Brain tumor (Pomeroy et al., 2002)
Li et.al. (Li, Ma, Tang, Paterson, & Xu, 2009)	Biclustering of gene expression data	A new qualitative biclustering algorithm has been proposed for gene expression data. This method is known as QUBIC which is the acronym for QUalitative BIClustering	Simulated, Some standard dataset (Prelić et al., 2006)
Ihmels et.al. (Ihmels, Bergmann, & Barkai, 2004)	Defining transcriptional modules	A new method has been developed to define transcriptional modules from gene expression data	Yeast S.cerevisiae

Table 2. Overview of different methods for biomedical image analysis

Method	Prime objective	Brief Description	Dataset
Song et.al. (Song et al., 2009)	Tumor segmentation from MRI data	Authors proposed a new method for automated tumor segmentation from the MRI data. It is a semi-supervised method where, a Bayesian Gaussian random field is used.	Not specified
Batmanghelich et. al. (Batmanghelich, Ye, Pohl, Taskar, & Davatzikos, 2011)	Classification of Normal Control and Alzheimer Disease and Mild Cognitive Impairment	A semi supervised method is proposed to reduce the dimension and to improve the quality of the disease detection and classification.	ADNI dataset ("ADNI I Alzheimer's Disease Neuroimaging Initiative," n.d.)
Pang et. al. (Pang, Du, Orgun, & Yu, 2019)	Increase the classification accuracy with more powerful deep learning architecture	A novel method is developed which integrates the features collected from shallow layers and deep layers. In this way, a fused CNN is developed.	ImageCLEFmed dataset ("ImageCLEFmedical I ImageCLEF / LifeCLEF - Multimedia Retrieval in CLEF," n.d.)
Long et. al. (L. D. Nguyen, Gao, Lin, & Lin, 2019)	Improve the performance of the classification	A feature concatenation based method is proposed with the ensemble method to improve the performance of the traditional CNN method.	2D Hela dataset (Boland & Murphy, 2001; "National Institute on Aging," n.d.), Pap-smear dataset (Jantzen, Norup, Dounias, & Bjerregaard, 2005), HEp-2 cell dataset (Foggia, Percannella, Soda, & Vento, 2013)
Cui et. al. (Cui et al., 2020)	Biomedical image segmentation and the current state-of-the-art.	A comprehensive study is presented about the biomedical image segmentation based on the graph theories and region based ANN.	Not specified
Kwon et. al. (Kwon, Won, Kim, & Paik, 2020)	Biomedical image segmentation	An ANN based uncertainty quantification method is proposed and applied on the biomedical images to improve the segmentation performance.	Ischemic Stroke Lesion Segmentation (Winzeck et al., 2018), DRIVE (Staal, Abràmoff, Niemeijer, Viergever, & Van Ginneken, 2004)
Sun et. al. (Sun, Tseng, Zhang, & Qian, 2016)	Breast cancer analysis	A three stage semi supervised method is proposed to analyze the breast cancer data.	Collected from an established in-house full-field data
Chakraborty et. al. (S. Chakraborty, Chatterjee, et al., 2017b)	Microscopic image segmentation	A modified cuckoo search based method is proposed for microscopic image segmentation.	Collected dataset of rat's hippocampus
Arefan et. al. (Arefan et al., 2019)	Risk prediction for the breast cancer	A deep learning based method which is used to predict the risk for the breast cancer	Collected/prepared dataset
Kesim et. al. (Kesim, Dokur, & Olmez, 2019)	Chest X-Ray image classification	A CNN based approach is proposed to classify the chest X-Ray images. A new architecture of the network is proposed. Moreover, the effects of the size of the input image is also determined.	ChestX-ray8 (X. Wang et al., 2017)

Some of the recent methods and developments in the field of biomedical image analysis is reported here. Various other intelligent computing based methods which are applied for biomedical image analysis can be explored from (Celebi, Codella, & Halpern, 2019; Shouvik Chakraborty, Chatterjee, et al., 2017; Cheplygina, de Bruijne, & Pluim, 2019; Moen et al., 2019; Nguyen, Son, Ashour, & Dey, 2019; Ørting et al., 2019).

CONCLUSION

In this article, a brief overview of the current-state-of-the-art research in the field of biological data and image analysis. Some of the recent articles and their major points are discussed briefly so that, an essence of the current trend in this domain can be easily understood. Several aspects and different domains of the biological data and image analysis are discussed. This work can be helpful for the basic understanding of the underlying subject and also helpful in the future developments in this domain. There are several articles which can be found in the literature that explains a specific approach which is proposed by the author(s) of a particular article but there must a way in which a good method can be easily identified and quickly accessed so that it can be used for the real life applications. It is necessary to understand the relation among several algorithms, their application domains and the corresponding output to create a generalized approach to improve the quality of the obtained results.

ACKNOWLEDGMENT

Author is highly grateful to the editors of the book Applications of Advanced Machine Intelligence in Computer Vision and Object Recognition: Emerging Research and Opportunities to create this chapter.

REFERENCES

Alizadeh, A. A., Eisen, M. B., Davis, R. E., Ma, C., Lossos, I. S., Rosenwald, A., ... Staudt, L. M. (2000). Distinct types of diffuse large B-cell lymphoma identified by gene expression profiling. *Nature*, *403*(6769), 503–511. doi:10.1038/35000501 PubMed

Alon, U., Barkai, N., Notterman, D. A., Gish, K., Ybarra, S., Mack, D., & Levine, A. J. (1999). Broad patterns of gene expression revealed by clustering analysis of tumor and normal colon tissues probed by oligonucleotide arrays. *Proceedings of the National Academy of Sciences of the United States of America, 96*(12), 6745–6750. doi:10.1073/pnas.96.12.6745 PubMed

Alzheimer's Disease Neuroimaging Initiative (ADNI). (n.d.). Retrieved November 20, 2019, from http://adni.loni.usc.edu/

Arefan, D., Mohamed, A. A., Berg, W. A., Zuley, M. L., Sumkin, J. H., & Wu, S. (2019). Deep learning modeling using normal mammograms for predicting breast cancer risk. Medical Physics, mp.13886. doi:10.1002/mp.13886

Artificial Intelligence. (n.d.). Retrieved January 22, 2018, from https://en.wikipedia.org/wiki/Artificial_intelligence

Ayadi, W., Elloumi, M., & Hao, J. K. (2009). A biclustering algorithm based on a Bicluster Enumeration Tree: Application to DNA microarray data. *BioData Mining, 2*(1), 9. doi:10.1186/1756-0381-2-9 PubMed

Batmanghelich, K. N., Ye, D. H., Pohl, K. M., Taskar, B., & Davatzikos, C. (2011). Disease classification and prediction via semi-supervised dimensionality reduction. Proceedings - International Symposium on Biomedical Imaging, 1086–1090. doi:10.1109/ISBI.2011.5872590

Bhattacharjee, A., Richards, W. G., Staunton, J., Li, C., Monti, S., Vasa, P., ... Meyerson, M. (2001). Classification of human lung carcinomas by mRNA expression profiling reveals distinct adenocarcinoma subclasses. *Proceedings of the National Academy of Sciences of the United States of America, 98*(24), 13790–13795. doi:10.1073/pnas.191502998

Bismar, T. A., Demichelis, F., Riva, A., Kim, R., Varambally, S., He, L., ... Rubin, M. A. (2006). Defining Aggressive Prostate Cancer Using a 12-Gene Model. *Neoplasia (New York, N.Y.), 8*(1), 59–68. doi:10.1593/neo.05664 PubMed

Boden, M. A. (1998). Creativity and artificial intelligence. *Artificial Intelligence, 103*(1–2), 347–356. doi:10.1016/S0004-3702(98)00055-1

Boland, M. V., & Murphy, R. F. (2001). A neural network classifier capable of recognizing the patterns of all major subcellular structures in fluorescence microscope images of HeLa cells. *Bioinformatics (Oxford, England), 17*(12), 1213–1223. doi:10.1093/bioinformatics/17.12.1213 PubMed

Brown, M. P., Grundy, W. N., Lin, D., Cristianini, N., Sugnet, C. W., & Furey, T. S. … Haussler, D. (2000). Knowledge-based analysis of microarray gene expression data by using support vector machines. Proceedings of the National Academy of Sciences of the United States of America, 97(1), 262–267. doi:10.1073/pnas.97.1.262

Brunet, J. P., Tamayo, P., Golub, T. R., & Mesirov, J. P. (2004). Metagenes and molecular pattern discovery using matrix factorization. *Proceedings of the National Academy of Sciences of the United States of America*, *101*(12), 4164–4169. doi:10.1073/pnas.0308531101 PubMed

Busygin, S., Jacobsen, G., Kramer, E., Krämer, E., & Ag, C. (2002). Double Conjugated Clustering Applied to Leukemia Microarray Data. Proceedings of the 2nd SIAM ICDM, Workshop on Clustering High Dimensional Data.

Celebi, M. E., Codella, N., & Halpern, A. (2019, March 1). Dermoscopy Image Analysis: Overview and Future Directions. *IEEE Journal of Biomedical and Health Informatics*, *23*(2), 474–478. doi:10.1109/JBHI.2019.2895803 PubMed

Chakraborty, S., & Bhowmik, S. (2013). Job Shop Scheduling using Simulated Annealing. First International Conference on Computation and Communication Advancement, 1(1), 69–73. Retrieved from https://scholar.google.co.in/citations?user=8lhQFaYAAAAJ&hl=en

Chakraborty, S., & Bhowmik, S. (2015). An Efficient Approach to Job Shop Scheduling Problem using Simulated Annealing. *International Journal of Hybrid Information Technology*, *8*(11), 273–284. doi:10.14257/ijhit.2015.8.11.23

Chakraborty, S., & Bhowmik, S. (2015). Blending roulette wheel selection with simulated annealing for job shop scheduling problem. Michael Faraday IET International Summit 2015, 100(7). doi:10.1049/cp.2015.1696

Chakraborty, S., Chatterjee, S., Ashour, A. S., Mali, K., & Dey, N. (2017). Intelligent Computing in Medical Imaging: A Study. In N. Dey (Ed.), *Advancements in Applied Metaheuristic Computing* (pp. 143–163)., doi:10.4018/978-1-5225-4151-6.ch006

Chakraborty, S., Chatterjee, S., Chatterjee, A., Mali, K., Goswami, S., & Sen, S. (2018). Automated Breast Cancer Identification by analyzing Histology Slides using Metaheuristic Supported Supervised Classification coupled with Bag-of-Features. 2018 Fourth International Conference on Research in Computational Intelligence and Communication Networks (ICRCICN), 81–86. doi:10.1109/ICRCICN.2018.8718736

Chakraborty, S., Chatterjee, S., Das, A., & Mali, K. (2020). Penalized Fuzzy C-Means Enabled Hybrid Region Growing in Segmenting Medical Images. doi:10.1007/978-981-13-8930-6_3

Chakraborty, S., Chatterjee, S., Dey, N., Ashour, A. S., Ashour, A. S., Shi, F., & Mali, K. (2017a). Modified cuckoo search algorithm in microscopic image segmentation of hippocampus. *Microscopy Research and Technique*, *80*(May), 1–22. doi:10.1002/jemt.22900 PubMed

Chakraborty, S., Chatterjee, S., Dey, N., Ashour, A. S., Ashour, A. S., Shi, F., & Mali, K. (2017b). Modified cuckoo search algorithm in microscopic image segmentation of hippocampus. *Microscopy Research and Technique*, *80*(10), 1051–1072. doi:10.1002/jemt.22900 PubMed

Chakraborty, S., Chatterjee, S., Dey, N., Ashour, A. S., & Shi, F. (2018). Gradient approximation in retinal blood vessel segmentation. 2017 4th IEEE Uttar Pradesh Section International Conference on Electrical, Computer and Electronics, UPCON 2017, 2018–Janua. 10.1109/UPCON.2017.8251120

Chakraborty, S., & Mali, K. (2018). Application of Multiobjective Optimization Techniques in Biomedical Image Segmentation—A Study. In Multi-Objective Optimization (pp. 181–194). doi:10.1007/978-981-13-1471-1_8

Chakraborty, S., Mali, K., Banerjee, S., Roy, K., Saha, D., & Chatterjee, S. ... Majumder, S. (2018). Bag-of-features based classification of dermoscopic images. 2017 4th International Conference on Opto-Electronics and Applied Optics, Optronix 2017, 2018–Janua. 10.1109/OPTRONIX.2017.8349977

Chakraborty, S., Mali, K., Chatterjee, S., Anand, S., Basu, A., & Banerjee, S., ... Bhattacharya, A. (2017). Image based skin disease detection using hybrid neural network coupled bag-of-features. 2017 IEEE 8th Annual Ubiquitous Computing, Electronics and Mobile Communication Conference (UEMCON), 242–246. 10.1109/UEMCON.2017.8249038

Chakraborty, S., Mali, K., Chatterjee, S., Banerjee, S., Mazumdar, K. G., & Debnath, M. ... Roy, K. (2017). Detection of skin disease using metaheuristic supported artificial neural networks. 2017 8th Annual Industrial Automation and Electromechanical Engineering Conference (IEMECON), 224–229. 10.1109/IEMECON.2017.8079594

Chakraborty, S., Mali, K., Chatterjee, S., Banerjee, S., Mazumdar, K. G., & Debnath, M. ... Roy, K. (2017). Detection of skin disease using metaheuristic supported artificial neural networks. 2017 8th Industrial Automation and Electromechanical Engineering Conference, IEMECON 2017, 224–229. 10.1109/IEMECON.2017.8079594

Chakraborty, S., Mali, K., Chatterjee, S., Banerjee, S., Roy, K., & Deb, K. ... Prasad, N. (2017). An integrated method for automated biomedical image segmentation. 2017 4th International Conference on Opto-Electronics and Applied Optics (Optronix), 1–5. 10.1109/OPTRONIX.2017.8349978

Chakraborty, S., Mali, K., Chatterjee, S., Banerjee, S., Roy, K., & Dutta, N. … Mazumdar, S. (2018a). Dermatological effect of UV rays owing to ozone layer depletion. 2017 4th International Conference on Opto-Electronics and Applied Optics, Optronix 2017, 2018–Janua. 10.1109/OPTRONIX.2017.8349975

Chakraborty, S., Mali, K., Chatterjee, S., Banerjee, S., Sah, A., & Pathak, S. … Roy, D. (2018b). Bio-medical image enhancement using hybrid metaheuristic coupled soft computing tools. 2017 IEEE 8th Annual Ubiquitous Computing, Electronics and Mobile Communication Conference, UEMCON 2017, 2018–Janua. 10.1109/UEMCON.2017.8249036

Chakraborty, S., Raman, A., Sen, S., Mali, K., Chatterjee, S., & Hachimi, H. (2019). Contrast Optimization using Elitist Metaheuristic Optimization and Gradient Approximation for Biomedical Image Enhancement. 2019 Amity International Conference on Artificial Intelligence (AICAI), 712–717. doi:10.1109/AICAI.2019.8701367

Chakraborty, S., Roy, M., & Hore, S. (2016). *A study on different edge detection techniques in digital image processing*. Feature Detectors and Motion Detection in Video Processing; doi:10.4018/978-1-5225-1025-3.ch005

Chakraborty, S., Roy, M., & Hore, S. (2018). A study on different edge detection techniques in digital image processing. In Computer Vision. Concepts, Methodologies, Tools, and Applications. doi:10.4018/978-1-5225-5204-8.ch070

Chakraborty, S., Seal, A., & Roy, M. (2015). An Elitist Model for Obtaining Alignment of Multiple Sequences using Genetic Algorithm. *2nd National Conference NCETAS 2015*, 4(9), 61–67.

Chakraborty, S., Seal, A., Roy, M., & Mali, K. (2016). A novel lossless image encryption method using DNA substitution and chaotic logistic map. *International Journal of Security and Its Applications*, 10(2), 205–216. doi:10.14257/ijsia.2016.10.2.19

Chen, J. R., & Chang, Y. I. (2009). A Condition-Enumeration Tree method for mining biclusters from DNA microarray data sets. *Bio Systems*, 97(1), 44–59. doi:10.1016/j.biosystems.2009.04.003 PubMed

Cheng, Y., & Church, G. M. (2000). Biclustering of expression data. Proceedings / … International Conference on Intelligent Systems for Molecular Biology; ISMB. International Conference on Intelligent Systems for Molecular Biology, 8, 93–103. 10.1007/11564126

Cheplygina, V., de Bruijne, M., & Pluim, J. P. W. (2019). Not-so-supervised: A survey of semi-supervised, multi-instance, and transfer learning in medical image analysis. *Medical Image Analysis*, *54*, 280–296. doi:10.1016/j.media.2019.03.009 PubMed

Cho, H., & Dhillon, I. S. (2008). Coclustering of human cancer microarrays using minimum sum-squared residue coclustering. *IEEE/ACM Transactions on Computational Biology and Bioinformatics*, *5*(3), 385–400. doi:10.1109/TCBB.2007.70268 PubMed

Co-clustering Software. (n.d.). Retrieved from http://www.cs.utexas.edu/users/dml/Software/cocluster.html

Cui, H., Wang, H., Yan, K., Wang, X., Zuo, W., & Feng, D. D. (2020). Biomedical image segmentation for precision radiation oncology. In Biomedical Information Technology (pp. 295–319). doi:10.1016/B978-0-12-816034-3.00010-9

Datta, S., Chakraborty, S., Mali, K., Baneijee, S., Roy, K., & Chatterjee, S. … Bhattacharjee, S. (2018). Optimal usage of pessimistic association rules in cost effective decision making. 2017 4th International Conference on Opto-Electronics and Applied Optics, Optronix 2017, 2018–Janua. 10.1109/OPTRONIX.2017.8349976

De Ferrari, L., & Aitken, S. (2006). Mining housekeeping genes with a Naive Bayes classifier. *BMC Genomics*, *7*(1), 277. doi:10.1186/1471-2164-7-277 PubMed

Demichelis, F., Magni, P., Piergiorgi, P., Rubin, M. A., & Bellazzi, R. (2006). A hierarchical Naïve Bayes model for handling sample heterogeneity in classification problems: An application to tissue microarrays. *BMC Bioinformatics*, *7*(1), 514. doi:10.1186/1471-2105-7-514 PubMed

Dettling, M. (2004). BagBoosting for tumor classification with gene expression data. *Bioinformatics (Oxford, England)*, *20*(18), 3583–3593. doi:10.1093/bioinformatics/bth447 PubMed

Exosome (vesicle). (n.d.). Retrieved from https://en.wikipedia.org/wiki/Exosome_(vesicle)

Foggia, P., Percannella, G., Soda, P., & Vento, M. (2013). Benchmarking HEp-2 cells classification methods. *IEEE Transactions on Medical Imaging*, *32*(10), 1878–1889. doi:10.1109/TMI.2013.2268163 PubMed

Freund, Y., & Schapire, R. R. E. (1996). Experiments with a New Boosting Algorithm. *International Conference on Machine Learning*, 148–156.

Friedman, N., Linial, M., Nachman, I., & Pe'er, D. (2000). Using Bayesian networks to analyze expression data. Journal of Computational Biology : A Journal of Computational Molecular Cell Biology, 7(3–4), 601–620. doi:10.1089/106652700750050961

GEDatasets. (n.d.). Retrieved from http://sdmc.lit.org.sg/GEDatasets

Getz, G., Gal, H., Kela, I., Notterman, D. A., & Domany, E. (2003). Coupled two-way clustering analysis of breast cancer and colon cancer gene expression data. *Bioinformatics (Oxford, England)*, *19*(9), 1079–1089. doi:10.1093/bioinformatics/btf876 PubMed

Golub, T. R., Slonim, D. K., Tamayo, P., Huard, C., Gaasenbeek, M., Mesirov, J. P., ... Lander, E. S. (1999). Molecular classification of cancer: Class discovery and class prediction by gene expression monitoring. *Science*, *286*(5439), 531–527. doi:10.1126/science.286.5439.531 PubMed

Guo, Y., Hastie, T., & Tibshirani, R. (2007). Regularized linear discriminant analysis and its application in microarrays. In Biostatistics (Oxford, England) (Vol. 8). doi:10.1093/biostatistics/kxj035

Gusenleitner, D., Howe, E. A., Bentink, S., Quackenbush, J., & Culhane, A. C. (2012). iBBiG: Iterative binary bi-clustering of gene sets. *Bioinformatics (Oxford, England)*, *28*(19), 2484–2492. doi:10.1093/bioinformatics/bts438 PubMed

Guyon, I., Weston, J., Barnhill, S., & Vapnik, V. (2002). Gene selection for cancer classification using support vector machines. *Machine Learning*, *46*(1–3), 389–422. doi:10.1023/A:1012487302797

Hartley, T. D. R., Catalyurek, U., Ruiz, A., Igual, F., Mayo, R., & Ujaldon, M. (2014). Biomedical image analysis on a cooperative cluster of GPUs and multicores. 25th Anniversary International Conference on Supercomputing Anniversary, 413–423. doi:10.1145/2591635.2667189

Harvard Molecular Technologies. (n.d.). Retrieved from http://arep.med.harvard.edu/

Helman, P., Veroff, R., Atlas, S. R., & Willman, C. (2004). A Bayesian network classification methodology for gene expression data. Journal of Computational Biology : A Journal of Computational Molecular Cell Biology, 11(4), 581–615. doi:10.1089/1066527041887294

Hore, S., Chakraborty, S., Chatterjee, S., Dey, N., Ashour, A. S., Van Chung, L., & Le, D.-N. (2016). An integrated interactive technique for image segmentation using stack based seeded region growing and thresholding. *Iranian Journal of Electrical and Computer Engineering*, *6*(6). doi:10.11591/ijece.v6i6.11801

Hore, S., Chakroborty, S., Ashour, A. S., Dey, N., Ashour, A. S., Sifaki-Pistolla, D., ... Chaudhuri, S. R. B. (2015). Finding Contours of Hippocampus Brain Cell Using Microscopic Image Analysis. *Journal of Advanced Microscopy Research*, *10*(2), 93–103. doi:10.1166/jamr.2015.1245

Hore, S., Chatterjee, S., Chakraborty, S., & Kumar Shaw, R. (2016). Analysis of Different Feature Description Algorithm in object Recognition. In Feature Detectors and Motion Detection in Video Processing (pp. 66–99). doi:10.4018/978-1-5225-1025-3.ch004

Ihmels, J., Bergmann, S., & Barkai, N. (2004). Defining transcription modules using large-scale gene expression data. *Bioinformatics (Oxford, England)*, *20*(13), 1993–2003. doi:10.1093/bioinformatics/bth166

ImageCLEFmedical. (n.d.). ImageCLEF / LifeCLEF - Multimedia Retrieval in CLEF. Retrieved November 20, 2019, from https://www.imageclef.org/2019/medical

Jantzen, J., Norup, J., Dounias, G., & Bjerregaard, B. (2005). Pap-smear Benchmark Data For Pattern Classification. NiSIS.

Kao, K.-J., Chang, K.-M., Hsu, H.-C., & Huang, A. T. (2011). Correlation of microarray-based breast cancer molecular subtypes and clinical outcomes: Implications for treatment optimization. *BMC Cancer*, *11*(1), 143. doi:10.1186/1471-2407-11-143 PubMed

Karaboga, D., & Basturk, B. (2007). A powerful and efficient algorithm for numerical function optimization: Artificial bee colony (ABC) algorithm. *Journal of Global Optimization*, *39*(3), 459–471. doi:10.1007/s10898-007-9149-x

Kesim, E., Dokur, Z., & Olmez, T. (2019). X-ray chest image classification by a small-sized convolutional neural network. *2019 Scientific Meeting on Electrical-Electronics and Biomedical Engineering and Computer Science*. doi:10.1109/EBBT.2019.8742050

Khan, J., Wei, J. S., Ringnér, M., Saal, L. H., Ladanyi, M., Westermann, F., ... Meltzer, P. S. (2001). Classification and diagnostic prediction of cancers using gene expression profiling and artificial neural networks. *Nature Medicine*, *7*(6), 673–679. doi:10.1038/89044 PubMed

Kluger, Y., Basri, R., Chang, J. T., & Gerstein, M. (2003). Spectral biclustering of microarray data: Coclustering genes and conditions. *Genome Research*, *13*(4), 703–716. doi:10.1101/gr.648603 PubMed

Kwon, Y., Won, J.-H., Kim, B. J., & Paik, M. C. (2020). Uncertainty quantification using Bayesian neural networks in classification: Application to biomedical image segmentation. *Computational Statistics & Data Analysis*, *142*, 106816. doi:10.1016/j.csda.2019.106816

Lazzeroni, L., & Owen, A. (2002). Plaid Models for Gene Expression Data. *Statistica Sinica*, *12*, 61–86. doi:10.1017/CBO9781107415324.004

Li, G., Ma, Q., Tang, H., Paterson, A. H., & Xu, Y. (2009). QUBIC: A qualitative biclustering algorithm for analyses of gene expression data. *Nucleic Acids Research*, *37*(15), e101. doi:10.1093/nar/gkp491 PubMed

List of biological databases. (n.d.). Retrieved from https://en.wikipedia.org/wiki/List_of_biological_databases

Liu, F., White, J. A., Antonescu, C., Gusenleitner, D., & Quackenbush, J. (2011). GCOD - GeneChip Oncology Database. *BMC Bioinformatics*, *12*(1), 46. doi:10.1186/1471-2105-12-46 PubMed

Liu, X., & Wang, L. (2007). Computing the maximum similarity bi-clusters of gene expression data. *Bioinformatics (Oxford, England)*, *23*(1), 50–56. doi:10.1093/bioinformatics/btl560 PubMed

Long, P. M., & Vega, V. B. (2003). Boosting and microarray data. *Machine Learning*, *52*(1–2), 31–44. doi:10.1023/A:1023937123600

Mali, K., Chakraborty, S., & Roy, M. (2015). A Study on Statistical Analysis and Security Evaluation Parameters in Image Encryption. *International Journal for Scientific Research & Development*, *3*, 2321–0613. Retrieved from www.ijsrd.com

Mali, K., Chakraborty, S., Seal, A., & Roy, M. (2015). An Efficient Image Cryptographic Algorithm based on Frequency Domain using Haar Wavelet Transform. *International Journal of Security and Its Applications*, *9*(12), 279–288. doi:10.14257/ijsia.2015.9.12.26

Mankad, S., & Michailidis, G. (2014). Biclustering Three-Dimensional Data Arrays With Plaid Models. *Journal of Computational and Graphical Statistics*, *23*(4), 943–965. doi:10.1080/10618600.2013.851608

Mitchell, T. M. (1997). Machine Learning. *Annual Review of Computer Science*. doi:10.1145/242224.242229

Moen, E., Bannon, D., Kudo, T., Graf, W., Covert, M., & Van Valen, D. (2019). Deep learning for cellular image analysis. *Nature Methods*, *16*(12), 1233–1246. doi:10.1038/s41592-019-0403-1 PubMed

Murali, T. M., & Kasif, S. (2003). Extracting conserved gene expression motifs from gene expression data. *Pacific Symposium on Biocomputing*, *88*, 77–88. doi: PubMed doi:10.1142/9789812776303_0008

National Institute on Aging. (n.d.). Retrieved November 20, 2019, from https://ome.grc.nia.nih.gov/iicbu2008/hela/index.html

Nguyen, G. N., Son, L. H., Ashour, A. S., & Dey, N. (2019). A survey of the state-of-the-arts on neutrosophic sets in biomedical diagnoses. *International Journal of Machine Learning and Cybernetics*, *10*(1), 1–13. doi:10.1007/s13042-017-0691-7

Nguyen, L. D., Gao, R., Lin, D., & Lin, Z. (2019). Biomedical image classification based on a feature concatenation and ensemble of deep CNNs. Journal of Ambient Intelligence and Humanized Computing. doi:10.100712652-019-01276-4

Notterman, D., Alon, U., Sierk, J., & Levine, J. (2001). Transcriptional gene expression profiles of colorectal adenoma, adenocarcinoma, and normal tissue examined by oligonucleotide arrays. *Cancer Research*, *61*, 3124–3130. Retrieved from https://www.ncbi.nlm.nih.gov/entrez/query.fcgi?cmd=Retrieve&db=PubMed&dopt=Citation&list_uids=11306497

O'Neill, M. C., & Song, L. (2003). Neural network analysis of lymphoma microarray data: Prognosis and diagnosis near-perfect. *BMC Bioinformatics*, *4*(1), 13. doi:10.1186/1471-2105-4-13 PubMed

Ørting, S., Doyle, A., van Hilten, A., Hirth, M., Inel, O., & Madan, C. R. … Cheplygina, V. (2019). A Survey of Crowdsourcing in Medical Image Analysis. Retrieved from https://arxiv.org/abs/1902.09159

Pang, S., Du, A., Orgun, M. A., & Yu, Z. (2019). A novel fused convolutional neural network for biomedical image classification. *Medical & Biological Engineering & Computing*, *57*(1), 107–121. doi:10.1007/s11517-018-1819-y PubMed

Perou, C. M., Sørile, T., Eisen, M. B., Van De Rijn, M., Jeffrey, S. S., Ress, C. A., ... Botstein, D. (2000). Molecular portraits of human breast tumours. *Nature*, *406*(6797), 747–752. doi:10.1038/35021093 PubMed

Peterson, L. E., & Coleman, M. A. (2008). Machine learning-based receiver operating characteristic (ROC) curves for crisp and fuzzy classification of DNA microarrays in cancer research. *International Journal of Approximate Reasoning, 47*(1), 17–36. doi:10.1016/j.ijar.2007.03.006 PubMed

Pique-Regi, R., Ortega, A., & Asgharzadeh, S. (2005). Sequential Diagonal Linear Discriminant Analysis (SeqDLDA) for microarray classification and gene identification. 2005 IEEE Computational Systems Bioinformatics Conference. Workshops and Poster Abstracts, 112–113. doi:10.1109/CSBW.2005.124

Pomeroy, S. L., Tamayo, P., Gaasenbeek, M., Sturla, L. M., Angelo, M., McLaughlin, M. E., ... Golub, T. R. (2002). Prediction of central nervous system embryonal tumour outcome based on gene expression. *Nature, 415*(6870), 436–442. doi:10.1038/415436a PubMed

Prabha, R., Rai, A., & Singh, D. P. (n.d.). Bioinformatics-Driven Big Data Analytics in Microbial Research. Big Data Analytics in Bioinformatics and Healthcare. doi:10.4018/978-1-4666-6611-5.ch012

Prelić, A., Bleuler, S., Zimmermann, P., Wille, A., Bühlmann, P., Gruissem, W., ... Zitzler, E. (2006). A systematic comparison and evaluation of biclustering methods for gene expression data. *Bioinformatics (Oxford, England), 22*(9), 1122–1129. doi:10.1093/bioinformatics/btl060 PubMed

Protein primary structure. (n.d.). Retrieved from https://en.wikipedia.org/wiki/Protein_primary_structure

Ramaswamy, S., Tamayo, P., Rifkin, R., Mukherjee, S., Yeang, C. H., & Angelo, M. ... Golub, T. R. (2001). Multiclass cancer diagnosis using tumor gene expression signatures. Proceedings of the National Academy of Sciences of the United States of America, 98(26), 15149–15154. doi:10.1073/pnas.211566398

Rangel, C., Angus, J., Ghahramani, Z., Lioumi, M., Sotheran, E., Gaiba, A., ... Falciani, F. (2004). Modeling T-cell activation using gene expression profiling and state-space models. *Bioinformatics (Oxford, England), 20*(9), 1361–1372. doi:10.1093/bioinformatics/bth093 PubMed

Rigden, D. J., Fernández-Suárez, X. M., & Galperin, M. Y. (2016). The 2016 database issue of Nucleic Acids Research and an updated molecular biology database collection. *Nucleic Acids Research, 44*(D1), D1–D6. doi:10.1093/nar/gkv1356 PubMed

Roy, M., Chakraborty, S., Mali, K., Chatterjee, S., Banerjee, S., & Chakraborty, A. ... Roy, K. (2017). Biomedical image enhancement based on modified Cuckoo Search and morphology. 2017 8th Annual Industrial Automation and Electromechanical Engineering Conference (IEMECON), 230–235. 10.1109/IEMECON.2017.8079595

Roy, M., Chakraborty, S., Mali, K., Chatterjee, S., Banerjee, S., & Mitra, S. ... Bhattacharjee, A. (2018). Cellular image processing using morphological analysis. 2017 IEEE 8th Annual Ubiquitous Computing, Electronics and Mobile Communication Conference, UEMCON 2017, 2018–Janua. 10.1109/UEMCON.2017.8249037

Roy, M., Chakraborty, S., Mali, K., Mitra, S., Mondal, I., & Dawn, R. ... Chatterjee, S. (2019). A dual layer image encryption using polymerase chain reaction amplification and dna encryption. 2019 International Conference on Opto-Electronics and Applied Optics, Optronix 2019. doi:10.1109/OPTRONIX.2019.8862350

Roy, M., Mali, K., Chatterjee, S., Chakraborty, S., Debnath, R., & Sen, S. (2019). A Study on the Applications of the Biomedical Image Encryption Methods for Secured Computer Aided Diagnostics. 2019 Amity International Conference on Artificial Intelligence (AICAI), 881–886. doi:10.1109/AICAI.2019.8701382

Sarddar, D., Chakraborty, S., & Roy, M. (2015). An Efficient Approach to Calculate Dynamic Time Quantum in Round Robin Algorithm for Efficient Load Balancing. *International Journal of Computers and Applications*, *123*(14), 48–52. doi:10.5120/ijca2015905701

Seal, A., Chakraborty, S., & Mali, K. (2017). A new and resilient image encryption technique based on pixel manipulation, value transformation and visual transformation utilizing single–Level haar wavelet transform. In Advances in Intelligent Systems and Computing (Vol. 458). doi:10.1007/978-981-10-2035-3_61

Shamir, R., Maron-Katz, A., Tanay, A., Linhart, C., Steinfeld, I., Sharan, R., ... Elkon, R. (2005). EXPANDER - An integrative program suite for microarray data analysis. *BMC Bioinformatics*, *6*(1), 232. doi:10.1186/1471-2105-6-232 PubMed

Shi, Q., Harris, L. N., Lu, X., Li, X., Hwang, J., Gentleman, R., ... Miron, A. (2006). Declining plasma fibrinogen alpha fragment identifies HER2-positive breast cancer patients and reverts to normal levels after surgery. *Journal of Proteome Research*, *5*(11), 2947–2955. doi:10.1021/pr060099u PubMed

Shipp, M. A., Ross, K. N., Tamayo, P., Weng, A. P., Aguiar, R. C. T., Gaasenbeek, M., ... Golub, T. R. (2002). Diffuse large B-cell lymphoma outcome prediction by gene-expression profiling and supervised machine learning. *Nature Medicine*, *8*(1), 68–74. doi:10.1038/nm0102-68 PubMed

Sill, M., Kaiser, S., Benner, A., & Kopp-schneider, A. (2011). Robust biclustering by sparse singular value decomposition incorporating stability selection. *Bioinformatics (Oxford, England)*, *27*(15), 2089–2097. doi:10.1093/bioinformatics/btr322 PubMed

Singh, D., Febbo, P. G., Ross, K., Jackson, D. G., Manola, J., Ladd, C., ... Sellers, W. R. (2002). Gene expression correlates of clinical prostate cancer behavior. *Cancer Cell*, *1*(2), 203–209. doi:10.1016/S1535-6108(02)00030-2 PubMed

Song, Y., Zhang, C., Lee, J., Wang, F., Xiang, S., & Zhang, D. (2009). Semi-supervised discriminative classification with application to tumorous tissues segmentation of MR brain images. *Pattern Analysis & Applications*, *12*(2), 99–115. doi:10.1007/s10044-008-0104-3

Sotiriou, C., Neo, S.-Y.-Y., McShane, L. M., Korn, E. L., Long, P. M., & Jazaeri, A. ... Liu, E. T. (2003). Breast cancer classification and prognosis based on gene expression profiles from a population-based study. Proceedings of the National Academy of Sciences of the United States of America, 100(18), 10393–10398. doi:10.1073/pnas.1732912100

Spellman, P. T., Sherlock, G., Zhang, M. Q., Iyer, V. R., Anders, K., Eisen, M. B., ... Futcher, B. (1998). Comprehensive Identification of Cell Cycle-regulated Genes of the Yeast Saccharomyces cerevisiae by Microarray Hybridization. *Molecular Biology of the Cell*, *9*(12), 3273–3297. doi:10.1091/mbc.9.12.3273 PubMed

Staal, J., Abràmoff, M. D., Niemeijer, M., Viergever, M. A., & Van Ginneken, B. (2004). Ridge-Based Vessel Segmentation in Color Images of the Retina. *IEEE Transactions on Medical Imaging*, *23*(4), 501–509. doi:10.1109/TMI.2004.825627 PubMed

Sun, W., Tseng, T. L. B., Zhang, J., & Qian, W. (2016). Computerized breast cancer analysis system using three stage semi-supervised learning method. *Computer Methods and Programs in Biomedicine*, *135*, 77–88. doi:10.1016/j.cmpb.2016.07.017 PubMed

Tan, P., Dowe, D., & Dix, T. (2007). Building Classification Models from Microarray Data with Tree-Based Classification Algorithms. In AI 2007 (pp. 589–598). Advances in Artificial Intelligence. doi:10.1007/978-3-540-76928-6_60

Tanay, A., Sharan, R., & Shamir, R. (2002). Discovering statistically significant biclusters in gene expression data. *Bioinformatics (Oxford, England)*, *18*(Suppl 1), S136–S144. doi:10.1093/bioinformatics/18.suppl_1.S136 PubMed

Tang, C., Zhang, L., Zhang, A., & Ramanathan, M. (2001). Interrelated two-way clustering: An unsupervised approach for gene expression data analysis. Proceedings - 2nd Annual IEEE International Symposium on Bioinformatics and Bioengineering, BIBE 2001, 41–48. 10.1109/BIBE.2001.974410

Tavazoie, S., Hughes, J. D., Campbell, M. J., Cho, R. J., & Church, G. M. (1999). Systematic determination of genetic network architecture. *Nature Genetics*, *22*(3), 281–285. doi:10.1038/10343 PubMed

van 't Veer, L. J., Dai, H., van de Vijver, M. J., He, Y. D., Hart, A. A. M., Mao, M., ... Friend, S. H. (2002). Gene expression profiling predicts clinical outcome of breast cancer. *Nature*, *415*(6871), 530–536. doi:10.1038/415530a PubMed

van Uitert, M., Meuleman, W., & Wessels, L. (2008). Biclustering sparse binary genomic data. Journal of Computational Biology : A Journal of Computational Molecular Cell Biology, 15(10), 1329–1345. doi:10.1089/cmb.2008.0066

Wang, S., Chaovalitwongse, W., & Babuska, R. (2012). Machine Learning Algorithms in Bipedal Robot Control. *IEEE Transactions on Systems, Man and Cybernetics. Part C, Applications and Reviews*, *42*(5), 728–743. doi:10.1109/TSMCC.2012.2186565

Wang, X., Peng, Y., Lu, L., Lu, Z., Bagheri, M., & Summers, R. M. (2017). ChestX-ray8: Hospital-scale Chest X-ray Database and Benchmarks on Weakly-Supervised Classification and Localization of Common Thorax Diseases. doi:10.1109/CVPR.2017.369

West, M., Blanchette, C., Dressman, H., Huang, E., Ishida, S., & Spang, R. ... Nevins, J. R. (2001). Predicting the clinical status of human breast cancer by using gene expression profiles. Proceedings of the National Academy of Sciences of the United States of America, 98(20), 11462–11467. doi:10.1073/pnas.201162998

Wingender, E. (2000). TRANSFAC: An integrated system for gene expression regulation. *Nucleic Acids Research*, *28*(1), 316–319. doi:10.1093/nar/28.1.316 PubMed

Winzeck, S., Hakim, A., McKinley, R., Pinto, J. A. A. D. S. R., Alves, V., Silva, C., ... Reyes, M. (2018). ISLES 2016 and 2017-benchmarking ischemic stroke lesion outcome prediction based on multispectral MRI. *Frontiers in Neurology*, *9*(SEP), 679. doi:10.3389/fneur.2018.00679 PubMed

Xu, X. Q., Leow, C. K., Lu, X., Zhang, X., Liu, J. S., Wong, W. H., ... Leung, H. C. E. (2004). Molecular classification of liver cirrhosis in a rat model by proteomics and bioinformatics. *Proteomics*, *4*(10), 3235–3245. doi:10.1002/pmic.200400839 PubMed

Yang, J., Wang, H., Wang, W., & Yu, P. (2003). Enhanced biclustering on expression data. Proceedings - 3rd IEEE Symposium on BioInformatics and BioEngineering, BIBE 2003, 321–327. 10.1109/BIBE.2003.1188969

Zhang, H., Yu, C.-Y., & Singer, B. (2003). Cell and tumor classification using gene expression data: Construction of forests. *Proceedings of the National Academy of Sciences of the United States of America*, *100*(7), 4168–4172. doi:10.1073/pnas.0230559100 PubMed

Zhang, H. H., Ahn, J., Lin, X., & Park, C. (2006). Gene selection using support vector machines with non-convex penalty. *Bioinformatics (Oxford, England)*, *22*(1), 88–95. doi:10.1093/bioinformatics/bti736 PubMed

Zhang, X., Lu, X., Shi, Q., Xu, X. Q., Leung, H. C. E., Harris, L. N., ... Wong, W. H. (2006). Recursive SVM feature selection and sample classification for mass-spectrometry and microarray data. *BMC Bioinformatics*, *7*(1), 197. doi:10.1186/1471-2105-7-197 PubMed

KEY TERMS AND DEFINITIONS

Artificial Intelligence: It is the ability of the machines to mimic the human intelligence and act accordingly.

Big Data Analysis: It is the process of analyzing huge amount of varied data to explore hidden relation from the dataset.

Biological Data Analysis: Study of the data which are acquired from the biological sources to interpret and find some hidden information.

Biomedical Image Analysis: Study of the biomedical images of various modalities using digital image processing techniques to detect and diagnose different diseases and help the medical investigation.

Data Mining: It is the process of determining hidden patterns from the dataset using various methods like machine learning, statistics, etc.

Intelligent Computing: It generally refers to the ability of a system to gather some knowledge from the data or the experiments.

Machine Learning: It is the ability of a system to learn or adapt something automatically from the environment, that is, experiments performed or the data being shown to the system and can make some decision in the unknown environment without any human intervention.

Performance Evaluation: Evaluate the performance of any method or algorithm in terms of some parameters (need not to be always quantitative).

Chapter 4
An Advanced Approach to Detect Edges of Digital Images for Image Segmentation

Shouvik Chakraborty

https://orcid.org/0000-0002-3427-7492

University of Kalyani, India

ABSTRACT

Image segmentation has been an active topic of research for many years. Edges characterize boundaries, and therefore, detection of edges is a problem of fundamental importance in image processing. Edge detection in images significantly reduces the amount of data and filters out useless information while preserving the important structural properties in an image. Edges carry significant information about the image structure and shape, which is useful in various applications related with computer vision. In many applications, the edge detection is used as a pre-processing step. Edge detection is highly beneficial in automated cell counting, structural analysis of the image, automated object detection, shape analysis, optical character recognition, etc. Different filters are developed to find the gradients and detect edges. In this chapter, a new filter (kernel) is proposed, and the compass operator is applied on it to detect edges more efficiently. The results are compared with some of the previously proposed filters both qualitatively and quantitatively.

DOI: 10.4018/978-1-7998-2736-8.ch004

INTRODUCTION

The problem of image segmentation is well-known and addressed by many scientists because it plays an important role in the various applications based on the image analysis and the computer vision systems. But, still it is considered being one of the most difficult and challenging tasks in image processing and object recognition, and determines the quality of final results of the image analysis. In the domain of image processing (Acharya & Ray, 2005; Bhabatosh, 2011; Gonzalez & Woods, 2008; Hore et al., 2016; Hore, Chatterjee, Chakraborty, & Shaw, n.d.) and image analysis (Al-amri, Kalyankar, & D., 2010; Huang, Wu, & Fan, 2003; Mansoor et al., 2015; Rampun et al., 2019), the interpretation is frequently required and dependent on the difference between foreground and the background. When the human visual system is mimicked by the computer algorithms, several problems may arise. Segmentation is process that divides an image into its various constituent regions or separately highlight different objects. The number of segments or the depth of the hierarchical division is dependent on the subject. That is, segmentation process must stop when the desired segments are achieved or the constituting of objects are separated (Chakraborty, Roy, & Hore, 2016; Palus, n.d.). The process of segmentation must be carefully performed to avoid over or under segmentation related problems (Barnard, Duygulu, Guru, Gabbur, & Forsyth, 2003; Gao, Mas, Kerle, & Pacheco, 2011).

Edge detection is one of the most primitive tools and frequently used in many of the image processing applications to generate some useful information from the images and often used as the pre-processing step in feature extraction and object recognition (Lyu, Fu, Hu, & Liu, 2019; Madireddy et al., 2019). The edge detection have been used by different real life applications like object recognition (Shin, Goldgof, & Bowyer, 2001), target tracking (Boumediene, Ouamri, & Dahnoun, 2007; Etienne-Cummings, Spiegel, Mueller, & Zhang, 1997; Ould-Dris, Ganoun, & Canals, 2006), segmentation (Kaganami & Beiji, 2009; Xiaohan et al., 1992), structural analysis (Kanitkar, Bharti, & Hivarkar, 2011; Luo, Higgs, & Kowalik, 1996), data compression (Deepu & Lian, 2015; Hsu, 1993), biomedical image analysis (Chakraborty, Mali, Banerjee, et al., 2018; Chakraborty, Mali, Chatterjee, Anand, et al., 2018; S. Chakraborty, Mali, Chatterjee, Banerjee, Roy, et al., 2018; Chakraborty, Mali, Chatterjee, Banerjee, Sah, et al., 2018; Chakraborty, Chatterjee, Ashour, Mali, & Dey, 2017; Chakraborty et al., 2018; Chakraborty, Chatterjee, Das, & Mali, 2020; Shouvik Chakraborty & Mali, 2018; Shouvik Chakraborty, Mali, Chatterjee, Banerjee, Mazumdar, Debnath, et al., 2017; Chakraborty, Mali, Chatterjee, Banerjee, Roy, Dutta, et al., 2017; Liu et al., 2014; Pacelli, Loriga, Taccini, & Paradiso, 2006; Roy et al., 2018), cryptographic analysis (Chakraborty, Seal, Roy, & Mali, 2016; Mali, Chakraborty, & Roy, 2015; Mali, Chakraborty, Seal, & Roy,

2015; Roy, Chakraborty, et al., 2019; Roy, Mali, et al., 2019; Seal, Chakraborty, & Mali, 2017) and also help for pattern matching and reconstruction, such as image reconstruction and so on. Edge detection is an active area of research as it facilitates higher level image analysis. In image processing and computer vision, the edge detection methods are focused to find the different sharp changes in the intensity in the image so that some essence of the physical and geometrical features of objects can be extracted. In general, three broad steps associated with the Edge detection process and the steps are as follows:

1. **Filtering:** Images are recovered from the unwanted corruption caused by noise such as salt and pepper noise, impulse noise and Gaussian noise etc.
2. **Enhancement:** It emphasizes pixels where there is a considerable fluctuation in the local intensity and is typically performed by computing the gradient magnitude.
3. **Detection:** The gradient value can be non-zero for several locations in an image. But the interesting point to be remember is that a point with a non-zero gradient value need not to be necessarily an edge.

In the context of edge detection, image kernel plays a significant role (Zhang, Liu, Liu, Li, & Ye, 2019). A kernel is a (usually) small matrix of numbers that is used in image convolutions. Differently sized kernels containing different patterns of numbers give rise to different results under convolution. For instance, Figure 1 shows a 3×3 kernel that implements a mean filter.

Figure 1. Structure of an image Kernel (Values may vary)

Set of coordinates

1	1	1
1	1	1
1	1	1

(-1,-1)	(-1,0)	(-1,1)
(0,-1)	(0,0)	(0,1)
(1,-1)	(1,0)	(1,1)

LITERATURE REVIEW

In the previous research, many algorithms were developed to perform the edge detection. Many kernels for edge detection have been proposed by many researchesrs. There are various kernels are available for example, sobel's filter, canny filter, prewitt filter, Robert's filter, Laplacian of Gaussian e.t.c. Anna Fabijańska ("Variance filter for edge detection and edge-based image segmentation - IEEE Conference Publication," n.d.) proposed a technique which is based on the Variance Filter for edge detection to segment an image. Variance filter is used to detect the location of an edge. Metaheuristic algorithms (S. Chakraborty & Bhowmik, 2015; Chakraborty & Bhowmik, 2013, 2015; Chakraborty, Chatterjee, Dey, Ashour, Ashour, et al., 2017; Shouvik Chakraborty et al., 2019; Shouvik Chakraborty, Seal, & Roy, 2015) are frequently used to solve various optimization (Datta et al., 2017; Sarddar, Chakraborty, & Roy, 2015) problems and the application of the metaheuristic algorithms in the edge detection is observed in (Nhat-Duc, Nguyen, & Tran, 2018). Sobel Gradient filter is integrated with K-means and used to extract the edges in (Siswantoro, Prabuwono, Abdullah, & Idrus, n.d.). The impact of the choice of the size of the kernel window on the edge detection process is discussed in (Chakraborty, Chatterjee, Dey, Ashour, & Shi, 2017; M. Roy et al., 2017). In (Hore et al., 2015), authors proposed a new edge detection mask and applied for the microscopic image segmentation. In (Jamil et al., 2019), authors proposed an melanoma segmentation method using biomedical image analysis. In (Halder, Bhattacharya, & Kundu, 2018), authors presented an edge detection method which is based on the Richardson's Extrapolation Formula (Richardson, 1911; Richardson & Gaunt, 1927). The Richardson's Extrapolation Formula is used to find the edge strength in the proposed method. A new method for edge detection is proposed in (Yin, Lu, Gong, Jiang, & Yao, 2019) which is based on dual parity morphological gradients. This method is used to segment infrared images to spot the porcelain insulators. Sometimes, poor edges may not be always traced by the conventional methods. To overcome this problem, a fuzzy multi-threshold inference method is designed in (Song, Gao, Li, Luo, & Peng, 2019). To reduce the impact of the noise, an improved sigma filter is used in this work. A Bi-Directional Cascade Network based edge detection method is proposed in (He, Zhang, Yang, Shan, & Huang, n.d.) to identify and extract edges in different scales. Some of the well-known filters for edge detection are given in figure 2 to figure 4.

Image segmentation is still a very challenging domain of research and the application domain of the image segmentation is large enough to further develop the image segmentation techniques and methods. There is no such algorithm which can be treated as a generalized method and can be used universally for different types of images and therefore it is a difficult and interesting problem to solve. (Chen, 2010).

Figure 2. Sobel's mask

$$
G_x=
\begin{array}{|c|c|c|}
\hline
-1 & 0 & +1 \\
\hline
-2 & 0 & +2 \\
\hline
-1 & 0 & +1 \\
\hline
\end{array}
\qquad
G_y=
\begin{array}{|c|c|c|}
\hline
+1 & +2 & +1 \\
\hline
0 & 0 & 0 \\
\hline
-1 & -2 & -1 \\
\hline
\end{array}
$$

Figure 3. Prewitt Mask

$$
G_x=
\begin{array}{|c|c|c|}
\hline
-1 & 0 & +1 \\
\hline
-1 & 0 & +1 \\
\hline
-1 & 0 & +1 \\
\hline
\end{array}
\qquad
G_y=
\begin{array}{|c|c|c|}
\hline
+1 & +1 & +1 \\
\hline
0 & 0 & 0 \\
\hline
-1 & -1 & -1 \\
\hline
\end{array}
$$

Figure 4. Robert's Mask

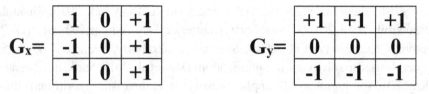

$$
G_x=
\begin{array}{|c|c|}
\hline
+1 & 0 \\
\hline
0 & -1 \\
\hline
\end{array}
\qquad
G_y=
\begin{array}{|c|c|}
\hline
0 & +1 \\
\hline
-1 & 0 \\
\hline
\end{array}
$$

FOUNDATION OF OUR SYSTEM

To detect edges, the underlying algorithm must be capable to find the sharp changes in the intensity. It can be accomplished using first-order or second order derivatives. In this section, the foundation of the proposed systems is discussed.

Image Gradient

An image gradient is a directional fluctuation in the intensity or color in an image. Image gradients are very useful and frequently used to extract information from images. An edge in a continuous region can be detected by finding the continuous one-dimensional gradient G(x,y). If the gradient is found to be sufficiently large and crosses some predetermined threshold value, then it can be concluded that an edge is present. The gradient along can be computed with the help of equation 1.

$$G(x,y) = \frac{\partial F(x,y)}{\partial x} + \frac{\partial F(x,y)}{\partial y} \tag{1}$$

In case of the discrete domain then the row gradient will be computed using $G_R(j,k)$ and column gradient will be computed using $G_C(j,k)$. The amplitude of the spatial can be computed using equation 2.

$$G(j,k) = \left[\left[G_R(j,k) \right]^2 + \left[G_C(j,k) \right]^2 \right]^{\frac{1}{2}} \tag{2}$$

For ease and efficiency in computation, the gradient amplitude can be expressed and approximated by using the magnitudes. The equation 3 can be used for this purpose.

$$G(j,k) = \left| G_R(j,k) \right| + \left| G_C(j,k) \right| \tag{3}$$

The direction of the spatial gradient can be expressed using equation 4.

$$, (j,k) = \arctan\left(\frac{G_C(j,k)}{G_R(j,k)} \right) \tag{4}$$

Gradient Operators

To obtain gradient of an image requires computing partial derivatives at every pixel location in the image. But digital approximation of the gradient is required because of the digital images.

$$G_x = \frac{\partial F(x,y)}{\partial x} = F(x+1,y) - F(x,y) \tag{5a}$$

$$G_y = \frac{\partial F(x,y)}{\partial y} = F(x,y+1) - F(x,y) \tag{5b}$$

The equation (5a) and (5b) can be implemented by applying the 1D filters as given in figure 5.

Figure 5. 1D Cross Filter

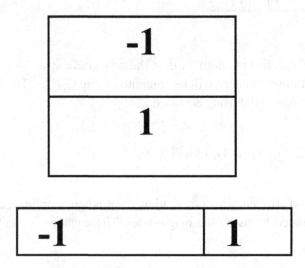

When there is a need to compute the diagonal edge direction then 2D mask is required. Roberts cross-gradient operators is one of the oldest approach in 2D filtering. The Roberts operator can be implemented using equation 6a and 6b. The pixel map is given in figure 6.

The prewitt operator can be implemented using equation 7a and 7b.

$$G_x = (z_7 + z_8 + z_9) - (z_1 + z_2 + z_3) \tag{7a}$$

$$G_x = (z_3 + z_6 + z_9) - (z_1 + z_4 + z_7) \tag{7b}$$

The sobel operator can be implemented using equation 8a and 8b.

$$G_x = (z_7 + 2z_8 + z_9) - (z_1 + 2z_2 + z_3) \tag{8a}$$

$$G_x = (z_3 + 2z_6 + z_9) - (z_1 + 2z_4 + z_7) \tag{8b}$$

Filter

To detect the edges, a 4x4 kernel is used which is combination of the high-pass and the low-pass filters. The high pass filter is generally suppress the low frequency components and allows to pass the high frequency components. The operation of

Figure 6. 3x3 Image pixel map

$$G_x = z_9 - z_5 \qquad\qquad (6a)$$

$$G_y = z_8 - z_6 \qquad\qquad (6b)$$

Z_1	Z_2	Z_3
Z_4	Z_5	Z_6
Z_7	Z_8	Z_9

the low-pass filter is exactly opposite of the high-pass filter i.e. it allows to pass the low frequency components (Marwa et al., 2019).

PROPOSED APPROACH

The masks discussed above are used to obtain the gradient components Gx and Gy. These two components are used to compute edge strength and direction. Two 4x4 kernels are developed in this work to detect edges. The following filters which are given in figure 7, are used to construct our convolution kernels.

Convolution kernels are developed using equation 9a and 9b.

$$G_x = hpfltr*lpfltr \qquad\qquad (9a)$$

$$G_x = lpfltr'*hpfltr' \qquad\qquad (9b)$$

Figure 7. Proposed high pass and low pass filter

Low-pass filter:

1	2	1	2

High-pass filter

-1
0
0
1

Where, hpfltr stands for the High-pass filter, jpfltr stands for the Low-pass filter, hpfltr' is the transpose of the High-pass filter, jpfltr' is the transpose of Low-pass filter.

The following convolution kernels which are given in figure 8 and figure 9 can be obtained using equation 9a and 9b respectively. These convolution kernels can be implemented by using equation 10a and equation 10b.

$$G_x = (2z_1 + z_2 + 2z_3 + z_4) - (2z_{13} + z_{14} + 2z_{15} + z_{16}) \tag{10a}$$

$$G_y = (2z_1 + z_5 + 2z_9 + z_{13}) - (2z_4 + z_8 + 2z_{12} + z_{16}) \tag{10b}$$

The corresponding pixel map is given in figure 10.

Figure 8. Proposed kernel for X direction

$$Gx =$$

1	2	1	2
0	0	0	0
0	0	0	0
-1	-2	-1	-2

Figure 9. Proposed kernel for Y direction

$$Gy =$$

1	0	0	-1
2	0	0	-2
1	0	0	-1
2	0	0	-2

Figure 10. 4x4 Image pixel map

Z_1	Z_2	Z_3	Z_4
Z_5	Z_6	Z_7	Z_8
Z_9	Z_{10}	Z_{11}	Z_{12}
Z_{13}	Z_{14}	Z_{15}	Z_{16}

The gradient magnitude can be computed using equation 11.

$$\text{Gradient} = \sqrt{(G_x^2 + G_y^2)} \qquad (11)$$

The proposed kernel can be convolved throughout the image using equation 12a and 12b. Equation 12a can be used to find the gradient in the X direction and similarly, equation 12b can be used find the gradient magnitude in the Y direction.

GradX=(Gx(1,1)*Img(i,j)+Gx(1,2)*Img(i,j+1)+Gx(1,3)*Img(i,j+2)+Gx(1,4)*Img(i,j+3)+Gx(2,1)*Img(i+1,j)+Gx(2,2)*Img(i+1,j+1)+Gx(2,3)*Img(i+1,j+2)+Gx(2,4)*Img(i+1,j+3)+Gx(3,1)*Img(i+2,j)+Gx(3,2)*Img(i+2,j+1)+Gx(3,3)*Img(i+2,j+2)+Gx(3,4)*Img(i+2,j+3)+Gx(4,1)*Img(i+3,j)+Gx(4,2)*Img(i+3,j+1)+Gx(4,3)*Img(i+3,j+2)+Gx(4,4)*Img(i+3,j+3))   (12a)

GradY=(Gy(1,1)*Img(i,j)+Gy(1,2)*Img(i,j+1)+Gy(1,3)*Img(i,j+2)+Gy(1,4)*Img(i,j+3)+Gy(2,1)*Img(i+1,j)+Gy(2,2)*Img(i+1,j+1)+Gy(2,3)*Img(i+1,j+2)+Gy(2,4)*Img(i+1,j+3)+Gy(3,1)*Img(i+2,j)+Gy(3,2)*Img(i+2,j+1)+Gy(3,3)*Img(i+2,j+2)+Gy(3,4)*Img(i+2,j+3)+Gy(4,1)*Img(i+3,j)+Gy(4,2)*Img(i+3,j+1)+Gy(4,3)*Img(i+3,j+2)+Gy(4,4)*Img(i+3,j+3))   (12b)

The above discussion is on the basics of the proposed kernel. Now the compass operator is applied on the proposed kernel to detect edges in different directions. The kernel for X direction i.e. Gx is rotated anti-clockwise whereas the kernel for the Y direction i.e. Gy is rotated clockwise. The kernels after applying the compass operator can be observed from figure 11 and figure 12. Figure 11 shows the various kernels which are obtained after applying the compass operator on Gx in the anti-clockwise direction. Figure 12 shows the various kernels which are obtained after applying the compass operator on Gy in the clockwise direction.

RESULTS AND DISCUSSION

The Berkley benchmark dataset ("UC Berkeley Computer Vision Group - Reorganization," n.d.) is used to study the proposed method and to compare the obtained results with some other standard methods. 12 images are used along with the ground truth edge detections. The images are particularly selected to avoid possible vagueness by only including images that indubitably portray one or two object/s in the foreground that vary from its surroundings by either texture, intensity or other low level cues. The experiments are conducted using Matlab 2014, which is popular software used for digital image processing mathematical computations. Figure 13 -17 shows the comparative results of different edge detection techniques with the proposed method. Table 1 shows the overall comparative result of 12 images while Figure 18 shows the results of all 12 images under test where Original Image, Human Segmentation, and other edge detected images are visible. Some standard performance metrics are used for the evaluation purpose example pratt score, F-Measure etc. The validation measures are given below.

Figure 11. All 12 kernels after applying compass operator on Gx (anti-clockwise rotation):

1	2	1	2
0	0	0	0
0	0	0	0
-1	-2	-1	-2

2	1	2	0
1	0	0	0
0	0	0	-2
0	-1	-2	-1

1	2	0	0
2	0	0	-2
1	0	0	-1
0	0	-1	-2

2	0	0	-2
1	0	0	-1
2	0	0	-2
1	0	0	-1

0	0	-2	-1
2	0	0	-2
1	0	0	-1
2	1	0	0

0	-2	-1	-2
0	0	0	-1
2	0	0	0
1	2	1	0

-2	-1	-2	-1
0	0	0	0
0	0	0	0
2	1	2	1

-1	-2	-1	0
-2	0	0	0
0	0	0	1
0	2	1	2

-2	-1	0	0
-1	0	0	1
-2	0	0	2
0	0	2	1

-1	0	0	1
-2	0	0	2
-1	0	0	1
-2	0	0	2

0	0	1	2
-1	0	0	1
-2	0	0	2
-1	-2	0	0

0	2	1	0
0	0	0	0
-1	0	0	2
-2	-1	-2	1

Figure 12. All 12 kernels after applying compass operator on Gy (clockwise rotation)

1	0	0	-1
2	0	0	-2
1	0	0	-1
2	0	0	-2

2	1	0	0
1	0	0	-1
2	0	0	-2
0	0	-2	-1

1	2	1	0
2	0	0	0
0	0	0	-1
0	-2	-1	-2

2	1	2	1
0	0	0	0
0	0	0	0
-2	-1	-2	-1

0	2	1	2
0	0	0	1
-1	0	0	0
-1	-2	-1	0

0	0	2	1
-2	0	0	2
-1	0	0	1
-2	-1	0	0

-2	0	0	2
-1	0	0	1
-2	0	0	2
-1	0	0	1

-1	-2	0	0
-2	0	0	2
-1	0	0	1
0	0	1	2

-2	-1	-2	0
-1	0	0	0
0	0	0	2
0	1	2	1

-1	-2	-1	-2
0	0	0	0
0	0	0	0
1	2	1	2

0	-1	-2	-1
0	0	0	-2
1	0	0	0
2	1	2	0

0	0	-1	-2
1	0	0	-1
2	0	0	-2
1	2	0	0

1. Pratt Score: Pratt score is also known as the Pratt figure of merit. It is one of the well-known matrices to validate the segmentation performance and the efficiency is already proven (Tleis & Ipskamp Printing, n.d.). Pratt score is an important measure to check the output segmentation by comparing with the ground truth segmentation images. Pratt score is defined in equation 13.

$$\Pr attScore = \frac{1}{\max(E_D, E_A)} \sum_{j=1}^{E_D} \frac{1}{1 + \alpha d^2(j)} \tag{13}$$

where, E_D is the number of points present in the detected edge and E_A is the number of points present in the actual edge in the ground truth image. α is the scaling factor and $d(j)$ is the distance between the computed edge points and the actual edge points.

2. F-Measure: F-Measure is a validation metric that considers the precision and recall into its consideration. It is defined in equation 14.

$$F - Measure = 2 \times \frac{\Pr ecision \times \Re call}{\Pr ecision + \Re call} \tag{14}$$

3. Precision: The precision is defined in equation 15.

$$\Pr ecision = \frac{Number\,of\,correctly\,\det ected\,po\operatorname{int}s}{Total\,\det ected\,po\operatorname{int}s} \tag{15}$$

4. Recall: The recall is also known as the sensitivity and it is defined in equation 16.

$$\Re call = \frac{Number\,of\,correctly\,\det ected\,po\operatorname{int}s}{Total\,number\,of\,correct\,po\operatorname{int}s} \tag{16}$$

5. Accuracy: Accuracy is defined in equation 17.

$$Accuracy = \frac{True\,Positives + True\,Negetives}{Total\,number\,of\,positive\,and\,negetive\,po\operatorname{int}s} \tag{17}$$

6. False alarm count: It is the number of false positive detected. It is defined in equation 18.

$$FAC = \frac{False\,Positives}{True\,Negetives + False\,Positives} \tag{18}$$

7. Specificity: Specificity is defined as the ratio between total number of correctly detected negative points and the total number of the negative points. It is defined in equation 19.

$$Specificity = \frac{Correctly\,\det ected\,negetive\,po\operatorname{int} s}{Total\,number\,of\,negetive\,po\operatorname{int} s} \tag{19}$$

Figure 13. Comparison of the pratt score

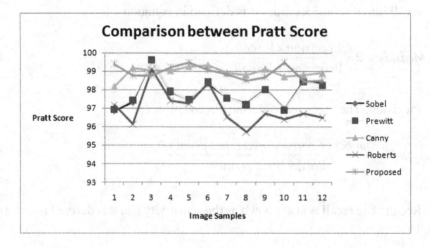

Figure 14. Comparison of the F-measure score

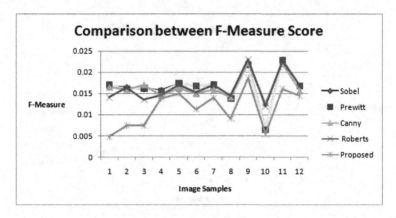

Figure 15. Comparison of the accuracy value

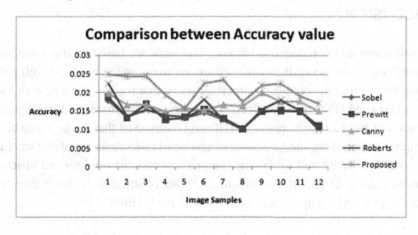

Figure 16. Comparison between false alarm count

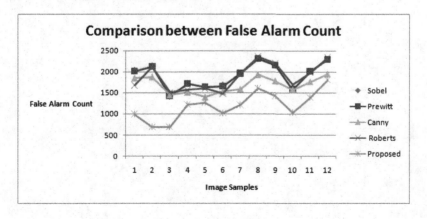

Figure 17. Comparison between specificity

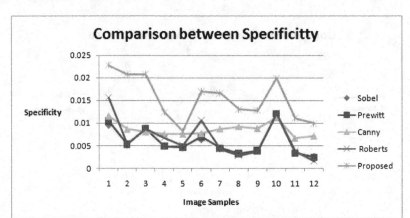

CONCLUSION

The evaluations and comparisons made in this work are based on the quantitative measures (i.e. various validation parameters as mentioned above) as well visual interpretation. From the obtained numerical and visual results, it can be concluded that the proposed filter is very effective for edge enhancement and the detection purposes. For the 12 images under test, it can be observed that the performance of the proposed method is quite satisfactory in terms of false alarm count and increases pratt score, specificity and some other parameters and can be deployed in several real life scenarios. Depending on the image, value of some of the parameters may vary but the overall result is better than most of the traditional filters.

Figure 18. (A) Original Image (B) Human Segmented (C) Sobel (D) Prewitt (E) Canny (F) Roberts (G) Proposed

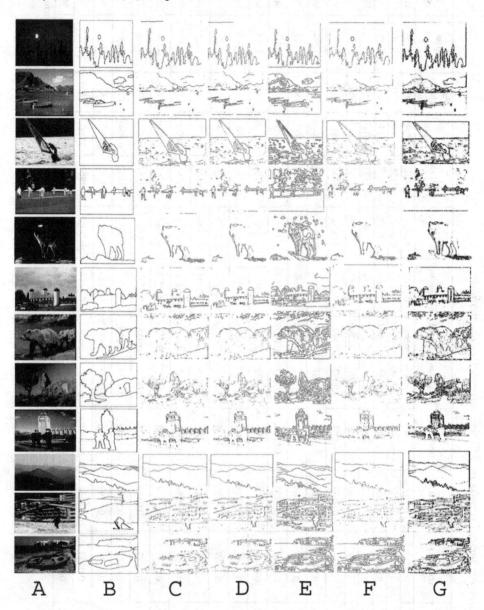

Table 1. Comparative numerical results of different edge detection methods

Image	Method	Accuracy	Sensitivity	Specificity	Precision	Recall	F-Measure	G-Mean	TP Rate	TN Rate	False Alarm Count	Miss Count	Pratt Score
238011	sobel	0.0178	0.907	0.0095	0.0085	0.907	0.0168	0.0928	0.907	0.0095	2041	975	96.8611
	prewitt	0.0187	0.9155	0.0104	0.0086	0.9155	0.017	0.0974	0.9155	0.0104	2008	978	96.9553
	canny	0.0197	0.8901	0.0116	0.0083	0.8901	0.0165	0.1017	0.8901	0.0116	1854	1315	98.1837
	roberts	0.0224	0.7577	0.0156	0.0071	0.7577	0.0141	0.1086	0.7577	0.0156	1682	704	97.1605
	proposed	0.0249	0.2563	0.0228	0.0024	0.2563	0.0048	0.0764	0.2563	0.0228	995	2346	99.3887
68077	sobel	0.0133	0.9433	0.0051	0.0083	0.9433	0.0164	0.0692	0.9433	0.0051	2142	1272	97.3211
	prewitt	0.0132	0.9194	0.0053	0.0081	0.9194	0.016	0.0695	0.9194	0.0053	2119	1294	97.4349
	canny	0.0166	0.9164	0.0087	0.0081	0.9164	0.016	0.0893	0.9164	0.0087	1881	3169	99.198
	roberts	0.0135	0.9373	0.0054	0.0082	0.9373	0.0163	0.071	0.9373	0.0054	2125	744	96.1167
	proposed	0.0243	0.3774	0.0208	0.0037	0.3774	0.0074	0.0887	0.3774	0.0208	692	4744	98.7729
62096	sobel	0.0168	0.8275	0.0089	0.0081	0.8275	0.016	0.0858	0.8275	0.0089	1417	1645	99.5888
	prewitt	0.0168	0.8356	0.0088	0.0082	0.8356	0.0162	0.0858	0.8356	0.0088	1424	1602	99.5996
	canny	0.0166	0.8841	0.0081	0.0086	0.8841	0.0171	0.0846	0.8841	0.0081	1448	3815	99.0464
	roberts	0.0153	0.6954	0.0087	0.0068	0.6954	0.0135	0.0776	0.6954	0.0087	1502	1285	99.0876
	proposed	0.0243	0.3774	0.0208	0.0037	0.3774	0.0074	0.0887	0.3774	0.0208	692	4744	98.7729
368016	sobel	0.0127	0.9557	0.0049	0.0079	0.9557	0.0157	0.0685	0.9557	0.0049	1720	1016	97.8506
	prewitt	0.0127	0.9462	0.0049	0.0078	0.9462	0.0155	0.0683	0.9462	0.0049	1716	1039	97.9163
	canny	0.0148	0.8797	0.0076	0.0073	0.8797	0.0145	0.082	0.8797	0.0076	1512	3813	99.0463
	roberts	0.0139	0.8861	0.0067	0.0073	0.8861	0.0146	0.0769	0.8861	0.0067	1569	661	97.4014
	proposed	0.0192	0.8418	0.0124	0.007	0.8418	0.0139	0.1021	0.8418	0.0124	1218	2999	99.2279

continued on following page

Table X. Continued

Image	Method	Accuracy	Sensitivity	Specificity	Precision	Recall	F-Measure	G-Mean	TP Rate	TN Rate	False Alarm Count	Miss Count	Pratt Score
42078	sobel	0.0132	0.957	0.0045	0.0087	0.957	0.0173	0.0656	0.957	0.0045	1642	770	97.4755
	prewitt	0.0133	0.957	0.0047	0.0087	0.957	0.0173	0.0667	0.957	0.0047	1640	769	97.4784
	canny	0.0157	0.894	0.0076	0.0082	0.894	0.0162	0.0824	0.894	0.0076	1400	2913	99.2733
	roberts	0.0135	0.9398	0.005	0.0086	0.9398	0.017	0.0687	0.9398	0.005	1601	621	97.2304
	proposed	0.0157	0.8972	0.0082	0.0076	0.8972	0.015	0.086	0.8972	0.0082	1270	2074	99.4723
97017	sobel	0.0146	0.8997	0.0063	0.0085	0.8997	0.0168	0.0752	0.8997	0.0063	1688	1182	98.3346
	prewitt	0.0154	0.9025	0.007	0.0085	0.9025	0.0168	0.0796	0.9025	0.007	1658	1192	98.439
	canny	0.0152	0.7994	0.0078	0.0075	0.7994	0.015	0.079	0.7994	0.0078	1524	2605	99.3481
	roberts	0.0181	0.8162	0.0106	0.0077	0.8162	0.0153	0.093	0.8162	0.0106	1476	952	98.3433
	proposed	0.0224	0.5961	0.017	0.0057	0.5961	0.0113	0.1006	0.5961	0.017	1016	3578	99.066
100075	sobel	0.0128	0.9371	0.0043	0.0086	0.9371	0.017	0.0636	0.9371	0.0043	1963	1164	97.5519
	prewitt	0.013	0.9371	0.0045	0.0086	0.9371	0.017	0.0649	0.9371	0.0045	1961	1167	97.5644
	canny	0.0166	0.8714	0.0088	0.008	0.8714	0.0159	0.0873	0.8714	0.0088	1588	4298	98.9195
	roberts	0.0126	0.9314	0.0042	0.0085	0.9314	0.0169	0.0622	0.9314	0.0042	1960	719	96.5072
	proposed	0.0234	0.76	0.0166	0.0071	0.76	0.014	0.1124	0.76	0.0166	1215	4570	98.8409
295087	sobel	0.0103	0.911	0.0034	0.007	0.911	0.0138	0.0553	0.911	0.0034	2307	1424	97.2433
	prewitt	0.0102	0.911	0.0033	0.007	0.911	0.0138	0.0549	0.911	0.0033	2306	1411	97.2148
	canny	0.0163	0.9349	0.0093	0.0072	0.9349	0.0142	0.0932	0.9349	0.0093	1932	4683	98.8123
	roberts	0.0101	0.9589	0.0028	0.0073	0.9589	0.0145	0.0516	0.9589	0.0028	2358	828	95.7048
	proposed	0.0174	0.5925	0.013	0.0046	0.5925	0.0091	0.0876	0.5925	0.013	1610	5795	98.5107

continued on following page

Table X. Continued

Image	Method	Accuracy	Sensitivity	Specificity	Precision	Recall	F-Measure	G-Mean	TP Rate	TN Rate	False Alarm Count	Miss Count	Pratt Score
368078	sobel	0.0149	0.9154	0.004	0.011	0.9154	0.0218	0.0604	0.9154	0.004	2149	1573	98.0291
	prewitt	0.0148	0.9089	0.0039	0.011	0.9089	0.0217	0.0595	0.9089	0.0039	2153	1567	98.0037
	canny	0.0199	0.9262	0.0089	0.0112	0.9262	0.0222	0.0906	0.9262	0.0089	1784	3450	99.1265
	roberts	0.0154	0.9675	0.0038	0.0117	0.9675	0.023	0.0608	0.9675	0.0038	2199	1081	96.7148
	proposed	0.0219	0.7701	0.0128	0.0094	0.7701	0.0186	0.0992	0.7701	0.0128	1432	5010	98.6957
55067	sobel	0.0151	0.4316	0.012	0.0033	0.4316	0.0065	0.072	0.4316	0.012	1581	496	96.9542
	prewitt	0.0151	0.4316	0.012	0.0033	0.4316	0.0065	0.0719	0.4316	0.012	1586	486	96.9174
	canny	0.0176	0.8561	0.0113	0.0064	0.8561	0.0128	0.0984	0.8561	0.0113	1579	1227	98.7255
	roberts	0.018	0.8035	0.0121	0.006	0.8035	0.012	0.0986	0.8035	0.0121	1697	381	96.3823
	proposed	0.0224	0.3579	0.0199	0.0027	0.3579	0.0054	0.0844	0.3579	0.0199	1035	1789	99.4836
61086	sobel	0.0149	0.9507	0.0034	0.0116	0.9507	0.0229	0.0566	0.9507	0.0034	2020	1611	98.4805
	prewitt	0.0149	0.9465	0.0034	0.0116	0.9465	0.0228	0.0567	0.9465	0.0034	2015	1581	98.4206
	canny	0.0177	0.9079	0.0067	0.0111	0.9079	0.022	0.078	0.9079	0.0067	1771	4755	98.8041
	roberts	0.0152	0.9358	0.0038	0.0114	0.9358	0.0226	0.0598	0.9358	0.0038	1986	837	96.7151
	proposed	0.019	0.6617	0.0111	0.0082	0.6617	0.0161	0.0857	0.6617	0.0111	1399	6004	98.4625
118020	sobel	0.011	0.9731	0.0026	0.0085	0.9731	0.0168	0.0501	0.9731	0.0026	2299	1857	98.3215
	prewitt	0.011	0.9731	0.0025	0.0085	0.9731	0.0168	0.0498	0.9731	0.0025	2297	1822	98.2412
	canny	0.015	0.9012	0.0072	0.0079	0.9012	0.0157	0.0805	0.9012	0.0072	1954	4328	98.9055
	roberts	0.0101	0.979	0.0016	0.0085	0.979	0.0169	0.0393	0.979	0.0016	2344	1145	96.4922
	proposed	0.0171	0.8293	0.0099	0.0073	0.8293	0.0145	0.0907	0.8293	0.0099	1815	5811	98.4942

REFERENCES

Acharya, T., & Ray, A. (2005). *Image processing: principles and applications*. Retrieved from https://books.google.co.in/books?hl=en&lr=&id=smBw4-xvfrIC &oi=fnd&pg=PR7&dq=T.+Acharya+and+A.+K.+Ray.+"Image+Processing+ Principles+and+Applications",John+Wiley+%26+Sons+Inc.,+2005&ots=FYH Y6GxTCK&sig=20KnAwOoxANLmjLAzwVLIuGbbsE

Al-amri, S. S., Kalyankar, N. V., & D., K. S. (2010). *Image Segmentation by Using Threshold Techniques*. Retrieved from https://arxiv.org/abs/1005.4020

Barnard, K., Duygulu, P., Guru, R., Gabbur, P., & Forsyth, D. (2003). The effects of segmentation and feature choice in a translation model of object recognition. *Proceedings of the IEEE Computer Society Conference on Computer Vision and Pattern Recognition*, 2. 10.1109/CVPR.2003.1211532

Bhabatosh, C. (2011). *Digital image processing and analysis*. Retrieved from https://books.google.co.in/books?hl=en&lr=&id=3xGLVyEc_SIC&oi=fnd &pg=PR15&dq=B.+Chanda+.,+D.+Majumder.+"Digital+Image+Processi ng+and+Analysis",+Prentice+Hall,+2003&ots=wB9CT70GS6&sig=Jfxd_ ocNHBoBIt4POLvYw6mSHZM

Boumediene, M., Ouamri, A., & Dahnoun, N. (2007). Lane boundary detection and tracking using NNF and HMM approaches. *IEEE Intelligent Vehicles Symposium, Proceedings*, 1107–1111. 10.1109/IVS.2007.4290265

Chakraborty, S., & Bhowmik, S. (2013). Job Shop Scheduling using Simulated Annealing. *First International Conference on Computation and Communication Advancement, 1*(1), 69–73. Retrieved from https://scholar.google.co.in/citations?u ser=8lhQFaYAAAAJ&hl=en

Chakraborty, S., & Bhowmik, S. (2015). An Efficient Approach to Job Shop Scheduling Problem using Simulated Annealing. *International Journal of Hybrid Information Technology, 8*(11), 273–284. doi:10.14257/ijhit.2015.8.11.23

Chakraborty, S., & Bhowmik, S. (2015). Blending roulette wheel selection with simulated annealing for job shop scheduling problem. *Michael Faraday IET International Summit 2015, 100*(7). doi:10.1049/cp.2015.1696

Chakraborty, S., Chatterjee, S., Ashour, A. S., Mali, K., & Dey, N. (2017). Intelligent Computing in Medical Imaging: A Study. In N. Dey (Ed.), *Advancements in Applied Metaheuristic Computing* (pp. 143–163). doi:10.4018/978-1-5225-4151-6.ch006

Chakraborty, S., Chatterjee, S., Chatterjee, A., Mali, K., Goswami, S., & Sen, S. (2018). Automated Breast Cancer Identification by analyzing Histology Slides using Metaheuristic Supported Supervised Classification coupled with Bag-of-Features. *2018 Fourth International Conference on Research in Computational Intelligence and Communication Networks (ICRCICN)*, 81–86. 10.1109/ICRCICN.2018.8718736

Chakraborty, S., Chatterjee, S., Das, A., & Mali, K. (2020). *Penalized Fuzzy C-Means Enabled Hybrid Region Growing in Segmenting Medical Images*. doi:10.1007/978-981-13-8930-6_3

Chakraborty, S., Chatterjee, S., Dey, N., Ashour, A. S., Ashour, A. S., Shi, F., & Mali, K. (2017). Modified cuckoo search algorithm in microscopic image segmentation of hippocampus. *Microscopy Research and Technique*, *80*(10), 1051–1072. doi:10.1002/jemt.22900 PMID:28557041

Chakraborty, S., Chatterjee, S., Dey, N., Ashour, A. S., & Shi, F. (2017). Gradient approximation in retinal blood vessel segmentation. *2017 4th IEEE Uttar Pradesh Section International Conference on Electrical, Computer and Electronics (UPCON)*, 618–623. 10.1109/UPCON.2017.8251120

Chakraborty, S., & Mali, K. (2018). Application of Multiobjective Optimization Techniques in Biomedical Image Segmentation—A Study. In Multi-Objective Optimization (pp. 181–194). doi:10.1007/978-981-13-1471-1_8

Chakraborty, S., Mali, K., Banerjee, S., Roy, K., Saha, D., Chatterjee, S., … Majumder, S. (2018). Bag-of-features based classification of dermoscopic images. *2017 4th International Conference on Opto-Electronics and Applied Optics, Optronix 2017, 2018–Janua*. 10.1109/OPTRONIX.2017.8349977

Chakraborty, S., Mali, K., Chatterjee, S., Anand, S., Basu, A., Banerjee, S., … Bhattacharya, A. (2018). Image based skin disease detection using hybrid neural network coupled bag-of-features. *2017 IEEE 8th Annual Ubiquitous Computing, Electronics and Mobile Communication Conference, UEMCON 2017, 2018–Janua*. 10.1109/UEMCON.2017.8249038

Chakraborty, S., Mali, K., Chatterjee, S., Banerjee, S., Mazumdar, K. G., Debnath, M., … Roy, K. (2017). Detection of skin disease using metaheuristic supported artificial neural networks. *2017 8th Annual Industrial Automation and Electromechanical Engineering Conference (IEMECON)*, 224–229. 10.1109/IEMECON.2017.8079594

Chakraborty, S., Mali, K., Chatterjee, S., Banerjee, S., Roy, K., Deb, K., … Prasad, N. (2018). An integrated method for automated biomedical image segmentation. *2017 4th International Conference on Opto-Electronics and Applied Optics, Optronix 2017, 2018–Janua*. 10.1109/OPTRONIX.2017.8349978

112

Chakraborty, S., Mali, K., Chatterjee, S., Banerjee, S., Roy, K., Dutta, N., ... Mazumdar, S. (2017). Dermatological effect of UV rays owing to ozone layer depletion. *2017 4th International Conference on Opto-Electronics and Applied Optics (Optronix)*, 1–6. 10.1109/OPTRONIX.2017.8349975

Chakraborty, S., Mali, K., Chatterjee, S., Banerjee, S., Sah, A., Pathak, S., ... Roy, D. (2018). Bio-medical image enhancement using hybrid metaheuristic coupled soft computing tools. *2017 IEEE 8th Annual Ubiquitous Computing, Electronics and Mobile Communication Conference, UEMCON 2017, 2018–Janua*. 10.1109/UEMCON.2017.8249036

Chakraborty, S., Raman, A., Sen, S., Mali, K., Chatterjee, S., & Hachimi, H. (2019). Contrast Optimization using Elitist Metaheuristic Optimization and Gradient Approximation for Biomedical Image Enhancement. *2019 Amity International Conference on Artificial Intelligence (AICAI)*, 712–717. 10.1109/AICAI.2019.8701367

Chakraborty, S., Roy, M., & Hore, S. (2016). A Study on Different Edge Detection Techniques in Digital Image Processing. In Feature Detectors and Motion Detection in Video Processing (pp. 100–122). doi:10.4018/978-1-5225-1025-3.ch005

Chakraborty, S., Seal, A., & Roy, M. (2015). An Elitist Model for Obtaining Alignment of Multiple Sequences using Genetic Algorithm. *2nd National Conference NCETAS 2015, 4*(9), 61–67.

Chakraborty, S., Seal, A., Roy, M., & Mali, K. (2016). A novel lossless image encryption method using DNA substitution and chaotic logistic map. *International Journal of Security and Its Applications, 10*(2), 205–216. doi:10.14257/ijsia.2016.10.2.19

Chen, T. (2010). An adaptive image segmentation method using region growing. *ICCET 2010 - 2010 International Conference on Computer Engineering and Technology, Proceedings, 7*. 10.1109/ICCET.2010.5485360

Datta, S., Chakraborty, S., Mali, K., Banejiee, S., Roy, K., Chatterjee, S., ... Bhattacharjee, S. (2017). Optimal usage of pessimistic association rules in cost effective decision making. *2017 4th International Conference on Opto-Electronics and Applied Optics (Optronix)*, 1–5. 10.1109/OPTRONIX.2017.8349976

Deepu, C. J., & Lian, Y. (2015). A Joint QRS detection and data compression scheme for wearable sensors. *IEEE Transactions on Biomedical Engineering, 62*(1), 165–175. doi:10.1109/TBME.2014.2342879 PMID:25073164

Etienne-Cummings, R., Van der Spiegel, J., Mueller, P., & Zhang, M. (1997). Foveated visual tracking chip. *Digest of Technical Papers - IEEE International Solid-State Circuits Conference, 40*, 38–39. doi:10.1109/isscc.1997.585566

Gao, Y., Mas, J. F., Kerle, N., & Pacheco, J. A. N. (2011). Optimal region growing segmentation and its effect on classification accuracy. *International Journal of Remote Sensing, 32*(13), 3747–3763. doi:10.1080/01431161003777189

Gonzalez, R. C., & Woods, R. E. (2008). Digital image processing. Prentice Hall.

Halder, A., Bhattacharya, P., & Kundu, A. (2018). Edge detection method using richardson's extrapolation formula. In Advances in Intelligent Systems and Computing (Vol. 758, pp. 727–733). doi:10.1007/978-981-13-0514-6_69

He, J., Zhang, S., Yang, M., Shan, Y., & Huang, T. (n.d.). *Bi-Directional Cascade Network for Perceptual Edge Detection*. Retrieved from https://www.pkuvmc.com/dataset.html

Hore, S., Chakraborty, S., Chatterjee, S., Dey, N., Ashour, A. S., & Van Chung, L., … - Nhuong Le, D. (2016). An Integrated Interactive Technique for Image Segmentation using Stack based Seeded Region Growing and Thresholding. *Iranian Journal of Electrical and Computer Engineering, 6*(6), 2773–2780. doi:10.11591/ijece.v6i6.11801

Hore, S., Chakroborty, S., Ashour, A. S., Dey, N., Ashour, A. S., Sifaki-Pistolla, D., … Chaudhuri, S. R. B. (2015). Finding Contours of Hippocampus Brain Cell Using Microscopic Image Analysis. *Journal of Advanced Microscopy Research, 10*(2), 93–103. doi:10.1166/jamr.2015.1245

Hore, S., Chatterjee, S., Chakraborty, S., & Shaw, R. K. (n.d.). *Analysis of Different Feature Description Algorithm in object Recognition*. doi:10.4018/978-1-5225-1025-3.ch004

Hsu, H.-S. (1993). Moment-preserving edge detection and its application to image data compression. *Optical Engineering (Redondo Beach, Calif.), 32*(7), 1596. doi:10.1117/12.139804

Huang, H., Wu, B., & Fan, J. (2003). Analysis to the Relationship of Classification Accuracy, Segmentation Scale, Image Resolution. *International Geoscience and Remote Sensing Symposium (IGARSS), 6*, 3671–3673. 10.1109/IGARSS.2003.1295233

Jamil, U., Sajid, A., Hussain, M., Aldabbas, O., Alam, A., & Shafiq, M. U. (2019). Melanoma segmentation using bio-medical image analysis for smarter mobile healthcare. *Journal of Ambient Intelligence and Humanized Computing, 10*(10), 4099–4120. doi:10.100712652-019-01218-0

Kaganami, H. G., & Beiji, Z. (2009). Region-based segmentation versus edge detection. *IIH-MSP 2009 - 2009 5th International Conference on Intelligent Information Hiding and Multimedia Signal Processing*, 1217–1221. 10.1109/IIH-MSP.2009.13

Kanitkar, A., Bharti, B., & Hivarkar, U. N. (2011). Vision based preceding vehicle detection using self shadows and structural edge features. *ICIIP 2011 - Proceedings: 2011 International Conference on Image Information Processing*. 10.1109/ICIIP.2011.6108922

Liu, S., Liu, S., Cai, W., Pujol, S., Kikinis, R., & Feng, D. (2014). Early diagnosis of Alzheimer's disease with deep learning. *2014 IEEE 11th International Symposium on Biomedical Imaging (ISBI)*, 1015–1018. 10.1109/ISBI.2014.6868045

Luo, Y., Higgs, W. G., & Kowalik, W. S. (1996). Edge detection and stratigraphic analysis using 3D seismic data. *1996 SEG Annual Meeting*, 324–327. 10.1190/1.1826632

Lyu, H., Fu, H., Hu, X., & Liu, L. (2019, August 26). Esnet. *Edge-Based Segmentation Network for Real-Time Semantic Segmentation in Traffic Scenes, 1855–1859.* doi:10.1109/icip.2019.8803132

Madireddy, S., Chung, D.-W., Loeffler, T., Sankaranarayanan, S. K. R. S., Seidman, D. N., Balaprakash, P., & Heinonen, O. (2019). *Phase Segmentation in Atom-Probe Tomography Using Deep Learning-Based Edge Detection*. Retrieved from https://arxiv.org/abs/1904.05433

Mali, K., Chakraborty, S., & Roy, M. (2015). A Study on Statistical Analysis and Security Evaluation Parameters in Image Encryption. *International Journal for Scientific Research & Development, 3*, 2321–0613. Retrieved from www.ijsrd.com

Mali, K., Chakraborty, S., Seal, A., & Roy, M. (2015). An Efficient Image Cryptographic Algorithm based on Frequency Domain using Haar Wavelet Transform. *International Journal of Security and Its Applications, 9*(12), 279–288. doi:10.14257/ijsia.2015.9.12.26

Mansoor, A., Bagci, U., Foster, B., Xu, Z., Papadakis, G. Z., Folio, L. R., ... Mollura, D. J. (2015). Segmentation and image analysis of abnormal lungs at CT: Current approaches, challenges, and future trends. *Radiographics*, *35*(4), 1056–1076. doi:10.1148/rg.2015140232 PMID:26172351

Marwa, F., Elhadj Youssef, W., Machhout, M., Petit, P., Baron, C., Guillermin, R., & Lasaygues, P. (2019). Automatic recognition processing in ultrasound computed tomography of bone. In N. V. Ruiter & B. C. Byram (Eds.), *Medical Imaging 2019: Ultrasonic Imaging and Tomography* (p. 39)., doi:10.1117/12.2506473

Nhat-Duc, H., Nguyen, Q. L., & Tran, V. D. (2018). Automatic recognition of asphalt pavement cracks using metaheuristic optimized edge detection algorithms and convolution neural network. *Automation in Construction*, *94*, 203–213. doi:10.1016/j.autcon.2018.07.008

Ould-Dris, N., Ganoun, A., & Canals, R. (2006). Improved object tracking with camshift algorithm. *ICASSP, IEEE International Conference on Acoustics, Speech and Signal Processing - Proceedings, 2*. 10.1109/icassp.2006.1660428

Pacelli, M., Loriga, G., Taccini, N., & Paradiso, R. (2006). Sensing Fabrics for Monitoring Physiological and Biomechanical Variables: E-textile solutions. *2006 3rd IEEE/EMBS International Summer School on Medical Devices and Biosensors*, 1–4. doi:10.1109/ISSMDBS.2006.360082

Palus, H. (n.d.). *Color Image Segmentation*. doi:10.1201/9781420009781.ch5

Rampun, A., López-Linares, K., Morrow, P. J., Scotney, B. W., Wang, H., Ocaña, I. G., ... Macía, I. (2019). Breast pectoral muscle segmentation in mammograms using a modified holistically-nested edge detection network. *Medical Image Analysis*, *57*, 1–17. doi:10.1016/j.media.2019.06.007 PMID:31254729

Richardson, L. F. (1911). The Approximate Arithmetical Solution by Finite Differences of Physical Problems Involving Differential Equations, with an Application to the Stresses in a Masonry Dam. *Philosophical Transactions of the Royal Society A: Mathematical, Physical and Engineering Sciences, 210*(459–470), 307–357. doi:10.1098/rsta.1911.0009

Richardson, L. F., & Gaunt, J. A. (1927). The Deferred Approach to the Limit. Part I. Single Lattice. Part II. Interpenetrating Lattices. *Philosophical Transactions of the Royal Society A: Mathematical, Physical and Engineering Sciences, 226*(636–646), 299–361. doi:10.1098/rsta.1927.0008

Roy, M., Chakraborty, S., Mali, K., Chatterjee, S., Banerjee, S., Chakraborty, A., … Roy, K. (2017). Biomedical image enhancement based on modified Cuckoo Search and morphology. *2017 8th Industrial Automation and Electromechanical Engineering Conference, IEMECON 2017.* 10.1109/IEMECON.2017.8079595

Roy, M., Chakraborty, S., Mali, K., Chatterjee, S., Banerjee, S., Mitra, S., … Bhattacharjee, A. (2018). Cellular image processing using morphological analysis. *2017 IEEE 8th Annual Ubiquitous Computing, Electronics and Mobile Communication Conference, UEMCON 2017, 2018–Janua.* 10.1109/UEMCON.2017.8249037

Roy, M., Chakraborty, S., Mali, K., Mitra, S., Mondal, I., Dawn, R., … Chatterjee, S. (2019). A dual layer image encryption using polymerase chain reaction amplification and dna encryption. *2019 International Conference on Opto-Electronics and Applied Optics, Optronix 2019.* 10.1109/OPTRONIX.2019.8862350

Roy, M., Mali, K., Chatterjee, S., Chakraborty, S., Debnath, R., & Sen, S. (2019). A Study on the Applications of the Biomedical Image Encryption Methods for Secured Computer Aided Diagnostics. *2019 Amity International Conference on Artificial Intelligence (AICAI)*, 881–886. 10.1109/AICAI.2019.8701382

Sarddar, D., Chakraborty, S., & Roy, M. (2015). An Efficient Approach to Calculate Dynamic Time Quantum in Round Robin Algorithm for Efficient Load Balancing. *International Journal of Computers and Applications, 123*(14), 48–52. doi:10.5120/ijca2015905701

Seal, A., Chakraborty, S., & Mali, K. (2017). A new and resilient image encryption technique based on pixel manipulation, value transformation and visual transformation utilizing single–Level haar wavelet transform. In Advances in Intelligent Systems and Computing (Vol. 458). doi:10.1007/978-981-10-2035-3_61

Shin, M. C., Goldgof, D. B., & Bowyer, K. W. (2001). Comparison of edge detector performance through use in an object recognition task. *Computer Vision and Image Understanding, 84*(1), 160–178. doi:10.1006/cviu.2001.0932

Siswantoro, J., Prabuwono, A. S., Abdullah, A., & Idrus, B. (n.d.). *Automatic Image Segmentation using Sobel Operator and k-Means Clustering: A Case Study in Volume Measurement System for Food Products.* Academic Press.

Song, W., Gao, X., Li, J., Luo, L., & Peng, J. (2019). Weak image edge detection based on improved fuzzy inference. In M. Pu, X. Feng, Y. Jiang, X. Li, X. Ma, & B. Kippelen (Eds.), *9th International Symposium on Advanced Optical Manufacturing and Testing Technologies: Optoelectronic Materials and Devices for Sensing and Imaging* (p. 66). 10.1117/12.2506668

Tleis, M. (n.d.). *Image analysis for gene expression based phenotype characterization in yeast cells*. Ipskamp Printing.

UC Berkeley Computer Vision Group - Reorganization. (n.d.). Retrieved November 10, 2019, from https://www2.eecs.berkeley.edu/Research/Projects/CS/vision/grouping/

Variance filter for edge detection and edge-based image segmentation. (n.d.). Retrieved November 8, 2019, from https://ieeexplore.ieee.org/abstract/document/5960309

Xiaohan, Y., Ylä-Jääski, J., Huttunen, O., Vehkomäki, T., Sipilä, O., & Katila, T. (1992). Image segmentation combining region growing and edge detection. *Proceedings - International Conference on Pattern Recognition, 3*, 481–484. 10.1109/ICPR.1992.202029

Yin, J., Lu, Y., Gong, Z., Jiang, Y., & Yao, J. (2019). Edge Detection of High-Voltage Porcelain Insulators in Infrared Image Using Dual Parity Morphological Gradients. *IEEE Access: Practical Innovations, Open Solutions, 7*, 32728–32734. doi:10.1109/ACCESS.2019.2900658

Zhang, L., Liu, L., Liu, Li, & Ye. (2019). Edge Detection Algorithm of a Symmetric Difference Kernel SAR Image Based on the GAN Network Model. *Symmetry, 11*(4), 557. doi:10.3390ym11040557

KEY TERMS AND DEFINITIONS

Edge Detection: Edge detection is a process to determine the contours of various objects in an image.

Image Analysis: It is the process by which useful information are extracted from an image and interpreted for further application.

Image Gradient: Image gradient represent a change in the image intensity or color in a specific direction.

Image Segmentation: Image segmentation is a method to individually identify each constituting segments in an image.

Kernel: Kernel is generally a small matrix which used to apply different types effects on the image.

Object Detection: It is a method to locate and detect different objects from digital images and digital videos.

Validation Measures: These are some parameters which are used to validate a segmentation procedure.

Chapter 5
Fusion Approach–Based Horticulture Plant Diseases Identification Using Image Processing

Balakrishna K.
Maharaja Institute of Technology, India

ABSTRACT

Plant disease is the major threat to the productivity of the plants. Identification of the plant diseases is the key to prevent the losses in the productivity and quality of the yield. It is a very challenging task to identify diseases detection on the plant for sustainable agriculture, where it requires a tremendous amount of work, expertise in the plant disease, and also requires excessive processing time. Hence, image processing is used here for detection of diseases in multi-horticulture plants such as alternaria alternata, anthracnose, bacterial blight, and cercospora leaf spot and also addition with the healthy leaves. In the first stage, the leaf is classified as healthy or unhealthy using the KNN approach. In the second stage, they classify the unhealthy leaf using PNN, SVM, and the KNN approach. The features are like GLCM, Gabor, and color are used for classification purposes. Experimentation is conducted on the authors own dataset of 820 healthy and unhealthy leaves. The experimentation reveals that the fusion approach with PNN and SVM classifier outperforms KNN methods.

DOI: 10.4018/978-1-7998-2736-8.ch005

INTRODUCTION

Indian economy is majorly depends upon the Agriculture with around 70% of the population earning their livelihood directly or indirectly from this sector as per the 2011 census (Government of India, 2017). Presently, India ranks second worldwide in horticulture farm produce. The economic contribution of agriculture to India's GDP (Gross Domestic Product) is steadily declining with the country's broad-based economic growth. Still, agriculture is demographically the broadest economic sector and plays a significant role in the overall socio-economic fabric of India (Government of India, 2017). Agriculture is a critical sector as it plays major part in the development of the Indian economy and food security for the vast population of the country. As India is a rain fed area, agriculture majorly depends on the climatic conditions, and due to the adverse effect of nature like excessive or deficit rainfall, extremely hot or dry weather which affects the growth stages of a plant, which will impact on the crop productivity. Current agriculture modernization practice has opened a new avenue due to the globalization and liberalization policies of this country (Pradnya A Joshi, 2015). Even though many farmers try to follow the modern agricultural practice they fail to achieve higher productivity due to various reasons. A special attention for development planning in the field of agriculture is needed which will eventually help the sector to sustain, hence a sustainable agriculture would be the choice.

Horticulture crops grown mainly for the purpose of food, materials, comfort and beauty i.e., flowers, fruits, vegetables and plants for ornament and fancy. These crops are continuously under the intervention of plants parasites and pests due to various pathogens attack. During the growth period of this plant it is attacked by a number of diseases from bacteria, fungal and virus. Bacteria grow by decaying the organic matter in soil and multiply themselves in the tissues of the plant and Fungi looks like thread vegetative growth, in the presence of moisture they germinate spores and produce infection as both of these are microorganisms. Virus diseases cause a streaking of the stem, which will kill the growing conditions that affect the growth of the plants (Mahlein, 2016). Some of the major diseases affecting the growth of the Alternaria Alternata, Anthracnose, Bacterial Blight and Cercospora Leaf Spot and also addition with the healthy leaves. From all these diseases lead to a reduction in productivity and downward in the profit to the farmer (Joshi, 2015)

Typically, detection of diseases in the plant leaves has been carried with the experience by farmer's i.e. visual inspection of the cultivators and they apply some fertilizers or pesticides to overcome from that disease. The potential of detecting different diseases in the plant is desirable, where in the growth stages of plants may be affected simultaneously by many pathogens, such as bacteria, fungal and viruses (Mahlein, 2016). Nowadays, automatic detection of diseases attracts researchers from the different domains due to its benefit in monitoring large field and the consistency which it can provide (Gavhale and Gawande, 2016). A modern approach for detecting and analysis of leaf diseases are lacking to reach the expectation level. Even though using various detection, extraction and classification techniques in image processing are available but they have not been applied and proven on some of these vegetable plants under various conditions. Further farmer needs a better detection model to identify the different diseases affecting from the pathogens and measures to cure that disease so the application of pesticides, etc can be in precise quantity.

In this paper, a new approach is proposed for detection and classification of plant diseases appearing in the leaves based on Image processing where feature extraction, classification and some measure to cure the diseases is suggested. Example taken here is the Tomato plant, by considering six classifications of tomato leaves including one class of healthy leaf and five classes of unhealthy leaves, such as Alternaria Alternata, Anthracnose, Bacterial Blight and Cercospora Leaf Spot and also addition with the healthy leaves are selected, which are majorly affecting the growth stages of the plant such as reduction of photosynthesis rate, the water content in the leaves, etc,. Therefore farmers require relatively a new approach looking for easy, rapid, often inexpensive and reliable model for the detection of these diseases in early stages is of great realistic and precise amount of inputs to cure unhealthy plant.

LITERATURE SURVEY

To analyze the work of state-of-art, here discussed relevant work done so far in horticulture plant leaves diseases identification and classification using an image processing.

(Balakrishna, & Rao,, 2019) worked on identification and classification of tomato plant leaves diseases such as Verticilium wilt, Powdery mildew, Leaf miners, Septoria leaf spot and Spidermites. For the experiment purpose collected around 600 images of datasets from the farm fields. In the initial stage, leaves are classified for healthy and unhealthy, where if the leaf is healthy no further processing is carried. For the unhealthy leaf, specific diseases classification processing is carried with GLCM features, Sobel edge detection, Morphological operation and Gabor filter. Finally, the classifications are done using KNN and PNN classifiers. The result shows the accuracy ranging between 78 to 91%.

(Khirade and Patil, 2015) worked on identification and classification of horticulture plant leaves diseases such as Alternaria Alternata, Anthracnose, Bacterial Blight and Cercospora Leaf Spot. For the experiment purpose collected around 400 images of datasets from the Google database. In the initial stages applied the preprocessing for the datasets like color conversion and image smoothing filter, segmentation done using otsu method, k-means clustering and RGB to HIS model, features are extracted like color, texture, morphology for diseases detection. Finally all this features are extracted applied to the neural network like BPNN and SVM classifiers for the classification purposes. The result shows the accuracy ranging around 90%.

(Kaur, Pandey and Goel, 2019) studied on various plant diseases such as fungal (molds, rust, mildew, rots, cankers, spots and wilts), bacterial (soft spot, spot and wilt) and viral (mottling, distortion and dwarfing). For diseases detection system is first trained and then tested for the accuracy purpose. The general flow of training phase is carried with acquisition, preprocessing, segmentation, feature extraction and classification stages. Different classifiers are studied with respect to supervised and unsupervised method for horticulture plants. The results are discussed by varying classifiers and training – testing ratio.

(Dhingra, Kumar and Joshi, 2018) done comprehensive study of diseases recognition and classification of plant leaf using a digital image processing. Discussed horticulture plant leaf diseases recognition approach using an different segmentation techniques such as Region based segmentation, Watershed segmentation, Edge based approaches, K-means segmentation, Histogram Thresholding and Neural networks approaches. Here authors precisely discussed about the advantages and disadvantages applying different segmentation techniques. Finally, concluded to design model with minimizing training time, complex computation and avoid over segmentation.

(Sharif et al., 2018) worked on hybrid method for detection and classification of citrus plants diseases such as anthracnose, black spot, canker, scab, greening, and melanose. The proposed method consists of two phases, first detection of lesion spot on the citrus leaves and then classification of citrus diseases. The lesion spots are extracted by an optimized weighted segmentation method for enhanced images, then the color, texture, PCA score, entropy, skewness based covariance vector and geometric features are extracted and fused. For the classification purpose used Multi-Class Support Vector Machine (M-SVM) and performance shows between 89 to 90.4% for own datasets and image gallery dataset.

Several state-of-the-art from the above detection and classifier models, developed a KNN, SVM, BPNN, K-means, Color based strategy and hyperspectral imaging to detect and classify the diseases. But still lack in achieving the better performance for the identification and classification of multi horticulture leaves diseases do not have a great consideration so far.

PROPOSED METHOD

In proposed method, we propose a two-stage classification system.

In initial stage, the given input image is classified as two class problem which includes healthy or unhealthy based. Here we used GLCM features and KNN classifiers for the purpose of classification. During second stage classification, if the output of the pervious stage is classified as unhealthy which is called as infected leaf image. Further classification of infected leaf image into specified diseases includes Pre-Processing using sobel edge detection, Gabor feature extraction, PNN, KNN and SVM for classification. Figure 1 shows the working principle of proposed system.

Figure 1. Working Flowchart of the Proposed Model

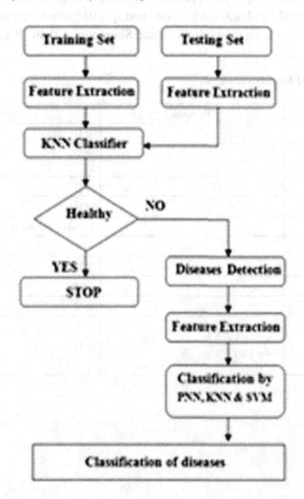

123

1. Leaf classification

For given input leaf image, GLCM (Gray level Co-occurrence Matrix) features are extracted and fed into KNN (K-nearest neighbor) classifier to find healthy or unhealthy leafs. Below section gives a brief description of both the methods.

A. GLCM

GLCM is a statistical method of extracting texture features considering the spatial relationship of pixels from the leaf images. It defines the various texture features measured based on the probability matrix to extract the features from the leaf images. In this work, we consider the four important features such as contrast, correlation, energy and homogeneity. GLCM function characterizes texture by calculating how often pairs of pixels with intensity value *j* and specific values in a specified spatial relationship value *k* in an image (Suresh and Shunmuganathan, 2012).

Table 1. GLCM features formula

Feature	Formula	Range
Entropy		[0 1]
Inverse Difference Moment		[-1 1]
Dissimilarity		[0 1]
Mean		[0 1]
Contrast		[0 (Size (GLCM, 1) – 1) ^ 2]
Variance		[-1 1]
Standard Deviation		[0 1]
Correlation		[-1 1]
Energy		[0 1]
Homogeneity	$\sum_{j,k} \dfrac{p(j,k)}{1+\lvert j-k\rvert}$	[0 1]

KNN

In pattern recognition, the KNN algorithm classifies objects based on the neighbor training samples in the feature space and measures the distance between the query scenario and the set of scenario in the data-sets. The image is classified by a majority vote of its neighbors, with an image being allocating to the most common class of its K nearest neighbor (Taman et al., 2014). The classification algorithm is as follows

1. Calculate the GLCM value of the input image.
2. Calculate the spatial features of image using equation.
3. Fuse all features.
4. Apply KNN classifier to find the class.

Infected Leaf Classification

If output from the previous is an unhealthy leaf, and then it is called has infected leaf, the infected leaf classification includes following stages Preprocessing, Gabor filter and Classification. Brief introduction for each stage is given below.

Pre-Processing

In an initial stage of the collected infected leaf images, the noise will be removed using a median filter. Later, the color space transformation used to create an independent transformation structure that defines the color space conversion i.e. RGB to HSV color format (Chernov, Alander and Bochko, 2015). As a hue, saturation and value varies from 0 to 1.0 i.e.

$$H = \begin{cases} 0 & \dfrac{60(G-B)}{S} & ifV = R \\[2ex] 180 + & \dfrac{60(B-R)}{S} & ifV = G \\[2ex] 240 + & \dfrac{60(R-G)}{S} & ifV = B \end{cases}$$

$$S = \dfrac{255(V - \min(R,G,B))}{V} \quad ifV \neq 0, 0\, otherwise$$

$$V = \max(R,G,B)$$

Sobel Edge Detection

Leaf Image Detection step is used to simplify the representation of an image and easier to analyze the region of interest. Sobel Edge detection is applied for the 'V' component as it gives more information compare to other components. It works by calculating the gradient of image intensity at each pixel within the image to detect the presence of gradient discontinuity (ElhamJasim Mohammad et al., 2014). This has been done with measuring magnitude [M] and direction angle [θ] given by

$$M = \sqrt{\left(\Delta x\right)^2 + \left(\Delta y\right)^2}$$

$$\theta = \arctan\left(\frac{\Delta y}{\Delta x}\right)$$

Here identify the green colored pixels in the image, based on the specified threshold value that is computed for these pixels. The RGB component value assigned to zero, if the intensity of the green color pixel in the image is lesser than the defined computed value. Green pixels are masked and masked pixels are removed. This will reduce the processing time because green colored pixels represent the healthy area of leaf and they do not add any valuable weight to the result.

Morphological Operation

The basic morphological operations are dilation and erosion, applied to structuring the element in the pixels of the image to describe the neighborhood. In dilation (add pixels) and erosion (remove pixels) for structuring element is applied to all pixels of an image to test whether the element fits or hits the neighborhood element, where an image will get brighter with flat disk shaped structuring element. The bright pixel surrounded by dark pixel grows in size and dark pixel surrounded by bright pixel shrink in size. Small dark pixels will get disappear with filling neighbor intensity value and the small bright pixel will become large spot (Shevaani Garg and Suman Thapar, 2012). So proposed method in feature extraction derives the informative data from the image related to dimensionality reduction of data by extracting only infected part and reduces a large amount of memory and computation power.

$$\text{ero}^g \left(f(x)\right) = \text{Min}\ \{f(y) - g(x - y): y\ \hat{I}\ E\}$$

$$\text{dil}^g \left(f(x)\right) = \text{Max}\ \{f(y) + g(x - y): y\ \hat{I}\ E\}$$

Gabor Filter

In our proposed model, we have used Gabor features for representation of diseases recognition in unhealthy leaf. Gabor features have been used for capturing local information in both spatial and frequency domain of the leaf image, as contrasting to other comprehensive techniques such as Fourier and Wavelet transform. One of the tasks of an approach is dealing with the joint uncertainty in space and frequency domains compact. Suggestive frequency based analysis cannot be localized without bound. An impressive mathematical property of Gabor functions is that they diminish the joint uncertainty in space and frequency and produce the compact optimum between localizing the scrutiny in spatial and frequency domains. Estimation of stroke directions in the different scale and orientation can be achieved with the property of Gabor filter. Also, the filtering output is robust to several noises because information from all pixels in the kernel is used by Gabor filter (Chaki, Parekh and Bhattacharya, 2015). Gabor filter is band pass filter which has both orientations elective and frequency selective properties and has an optimal joint resolution in both spatial and frequency domains (Wicaksono and Wahono, 2015). By applying properly tuned Gabor filters to an unhealthy tomato leaf image, local information about the leaf can be extracted in detail. The unhealthy tomato leaf analysis is accomplished by applying a bank of scale and orientations elective Gabor filters to an image (Khan et al., 2014).

$$f(a, b, \omega, \theta, \sigma_a, \sigma_b) = \frac{1}{2\pi \ \sigma_a \ \sigma_b} \exp$$

$$\left[\frac{-1}{2} \left(\left(\left(\frac{a}{\sigma_a} \right)^2 + \left(\frac{b}{\sigma_b} \right)^2 \right) + j(a\cos + b\sin) \right) \right]$$

where

σ = Spatial spread: $\omega = (2\pi f)$ Frequency: θ = Orientation.

Image Segmentation

The segmentation done for pre-processed images using various methods like otsu methods and K-means clustering. Segmentation using the boundary and spot detection algorithm helps to find the infected part of the leaf. Otsu method calculates the threshold level of leaf greenness to find the infected leaf area. Then the green pixels is masked and removed if the green pixel intensities are less than the computed threshold.

Classification

For the purpose of classification we have used both the classifiers KNN and PNN. In previous section we given introduction of KNN, here we have given introduction to PNN and SVM classification.

PNN

PNN is forward feed network with three layers and derived from the radial basis neural network function, which consists of several layers of nodes. PNN uses similar to probability density function to calculate each test vector (S. Deepa and V. Subbiah Bharathi, 2013). . In the first layer, it contains input, output and hidden nodes respectively, the vectors will be normalized prior to input to the network. In the second layer, the input is fully connected to the hidden layer for pattern classification. Each hidden node calculates the dot product of the input vector with a test vector subtracts 1 from it and divides the result by the standard deviation squared (Premalatha V, Valarmathy S and Sumithra M. G, 2015). The output layer has a node for each pattern classification.

$$ RBF = \left[\frac{(y_j - 1)}{\sigma^2} \right] \quad y_j = X \times \omega_j $$

where ω_j = weight vector; X = Sample

In the third layer pattern connected to the summation layer depends on the contribution of each class and sum up to produce a probabilistic value for each hidden node is sent to the output layer and the highest values wins. Finally, a complete transfer function picks the maximum probabilities and fed 1 to count for the respective class and remaining class will be retained with the previous count.

SVM

SVM works by mapping data to a high-dimensional feature space so that data points are categorized, even when the data are not in linear stage. The wider the margin between the two categories, the better the model will be at predicting the category for new records. The margin is not very wide, and the model is said to be over fitted. A small amount of misclassification can be accepted in order to widen the margin.

EXPERIMENTATION

Data-Set Collection

In this work created an own database with 620 data-sets of different tomato leaves images were collected in a farmland using the digital camera of 1080×1920 pixels. To maintain standardization in a collection of all images followed steps i.e. all images captured by plugging the leaf from the plant and place that on a white drawing sheet to maintain similar background. Captured the images in sunny condition but avoided the shadow and maintained a distance of length 2 meters from the images. The images are rescaled to 256×256 for the processing shown below. The large intra-class variability and the small inter-class variability make this dataset very challenging.

RESULTS

We conducted experimentation by varying training samples. In this work, the experimentation is conducted on two stages. In the first stage, we identify the healthy or unhealthy leaf images using KNN algorithm. If the leaf images are healthy then the process will be stop else if leaf image is infected means the further process has been carried to identify the particular diseases. A total of 620 leaves images were selected in the first phase, out of which 88 were healthy and remaining 532 were infected leaves images.

Figure 2. Snapshot of a working model

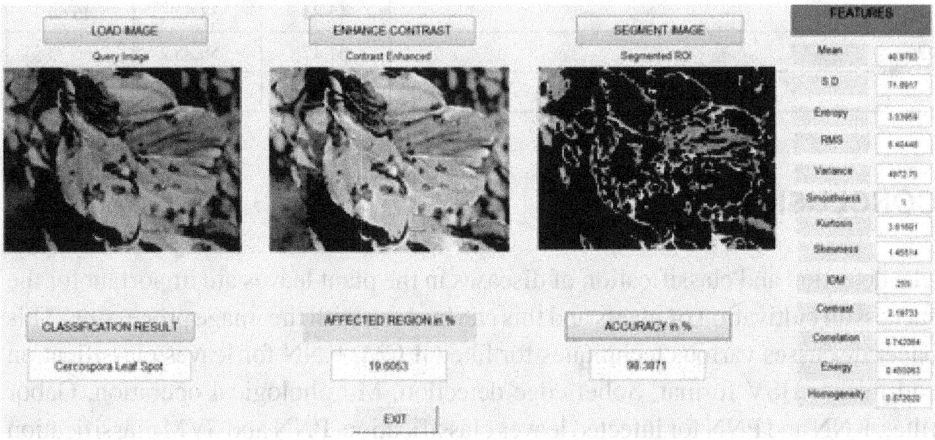

For evaluation of the first stage, we used Precision and Recall measures; precision shows a result of 422 out of 500 images for infected leaves and 78 out of 100 images for healthy leaves, so 78 healthy and 422 infected tomato leaves were recalled for further analysis. Table 2 shows the results of Precision and Recall

In the second stage, we have used PNN and KNN classifier for the experimentation. Table 3 shows the results of PNN classifiers under varying training & testing samples. By analyzing the above tables, we achieved good accuracy when compare out other existing methods.

$$\text{Precision} = \frac{Total\ numbers\ of\ correctly\ detected\ leaves}{Total\ numbers\ of\ detected\ leaves}$$

$$\text{Recall} = \frac{Total\ numbers\ of\ correctly\ detected\ leaves}{Total\ numbers\ of\ expected\ leaves}$$

Table 2. Precision and Recall result

	Diseases Leaves	Healthy Leaves
Precision	431/532	78/88
Recall	431/431	78/78

Table 3. PNN Classification results with Varying Training Data-Set

Training Percentage	PNN	KNN	SVM
20	45.84	38.67	46.64
30	64.47	56.85	66.73
50	92.49	72.85	91.47

CONCLUSION

The detection and classification of diseases in the plant leaves are important for the successful cultivation of plants and this can be done with the image processing. This paper discusses various techniques for like GLCM, KNN for leaves classification and further HSV format, Sobel edge detection, Morphological operation, Gabor filter, KNN and PNN for infected leaves classification, PNN and SVM classification performance better compared to KNN. In future work app-based model can be build for the real time analysis by users in their farm field to identify specific diseases.

REFERENCES

Balakrishna, K., & Rao, M. (2019). Tomato Plant Leaves Disease Classification Using KNN and PNN. *International Journal of Computer Vision and Image Processing*, *9*(1), 51–63. doi:10.4018/IJCVIP.2019010104

Chaki, Parekh, & Bhattacharya. (2015). *Plant leaf recognition using texture and shape features with neural classifiers*. Academic Press.

Chernov, Alander, & Bochko. (2015). *Integer-based accurate conversion between RGB and HSV color spaces*. Elsevier.

Deepa & Bharathi.(2013). Textural feature extraction and classification of mammogram image using CCCM and PNN. *IOSR-JCE, 10*, 7-13.

Dhingra, Kumar, & Joshi. (2018). Study of digital image processing techniques for leaf disease detection and classification. *Multimedia Tools and Application, 77*(15), 19951-20000.

Garg & Thapar. (2012). Feature extraction using Morphological Operations on finger print images. *IJCBR*.

Gavhale & Gawande. (2016). An overview of the research on plant leaves disease detection using image processing techniques. *IOSR-JCE, 16*, 10-16.

Government of India. (2017). State of Indian agriculture 2015-16. Ministry of Agriculture and Farmers Welfare.

Government of India. (2017). *Biology of Solanum lycopersicum*. Ministry of Environment, Forestry and Climate change and Indian Institute of Vegetable Research.

Joshi. (2015). Challenges of agriculture economy of India. *ICIEE, 5*, 211-218.

Kaur, Pandey, & Goel. (2019). Plants Diseases Identification and Classification through Leaf Images: A Survey. *Archives of Computational Methods in Engineering, 26*(2), 507-530.

Khan, S., Hussian, M., Aboalsamh, H., & Bebis, G. (2015). *A comparison of different Gabor feature extraction approaches for mass classification in mammography*. CrossMark.

Khirade & Patil. (2015). Plant Disease Detection using Image Processing. ICCCCA, 768-771.

Mahlein. (2016). Plant diseases detection by imaging sensors – Parallels and specific demands for precision agriculture and plant phenotyping. American Pathological Society.

Mohammad, Kadhim, Hamad, & Helyel. (2014). Study Sobel edge detection effect on the image edges using MATLAB. *IJIRSET, 2*, 10408-10415.

Premalatha, V., Valarmathy, S., & Sumithra, M. G. (2015). Diseases identification in cotton plants using spatial FCM and PNN classifier. *IJIRCCE, 2*, 3195 – 3201.

Sharif, Khan, Iqbal, Azam, Lali, & Javed. (2018). Detection and Classification of citrus diseases in a griculture based on optimized weighted segmentation and feature selection. *Computers and Electronics in Agriculture, 150*, 220-234.

Suresh & Shunmuganathan. (2012). An efficient texture classification system based on Gray Level Co-Occurrence Matrix. *IJCSITS, 2*, 793-798.

Taman, Rosid, Karis, Hasim, & Abidin. (2014). Classification system for wood recognition using K-Nearest neighbor with optimized features from binary gravitational algorithm. *ICRET*.

Wicaksono & Wahono. (2015). Color and texture feature extraction using gabor filter – Local binary pattern for image segmentation with fuzzy C – means. *JIS*.

Chapter 6
A Generalized Overview of the Biomedical Image Processing From the Big Data Perspective

Mousomi Roy
University of Kalyani, India

ABSTRACT

Computer-aided biomedical data and image analysis is one of the inevitable parts for today's world. A huge dependency can be observed on the computer-aided diagnostic systems to detect and diagnose a disease accurately and within the stipulated amount of time. Big data analysis strategies involve several advanced methods to process big data, such as biomedical images, efficiently and fast. In this work biomedical image analysis techniques from the perception of the big data analytics are studied. Big data and machine learning-based biomedical image analysis is helpful to achieve high accuracy results by maintaining the time constraints. It is also helpful in telemedicine and remote diagnostics where the physical distance of the patient and the domain experts is not a problem. This work can also be helpful in future developments in this domain and also helpful in improving present techniques for biomedical data analysis.

INTRODUCTION

Computer aided Diagnostic systems have changed the face of the biomedical data analysis. In general manual investigations are sometimes error prone and time consuming due to the inherent limitations of the human experts (Robb & Hanson, 1990; R. A. Shaikh, Li, Khan, & Memon, 2016). Therefore computer aided

DOI: 10.4018/978-1-7998-2736-8.ch006

Diagnostic methods are very useful to detect various diseases accurately and within the stipulated amount of time (Doi, 2007). Accuracy and time is very precious from the perspective of the diagnostic industry because it is directly associated with the health of the patients. There is no provision to compromise with the accuracy and the precision of the obtained results because it can leads to the wrong treatment which can be harmful for the patients (Doi, 2007; Kohn & Furuie, 1991). Computer aided diagnostic systems have changed the face of the biomedical data analysis. In general manual investigations are sometimes error prone and time consuming due to the inherent limitations of the human experts (Shah et al., 2018). Therefore computer aided Diagnostic methods are very useful to detect various diseases accurately and within the stipulated amount of time. Accuracy and time is very precious from the perspective of the diagnostic industry because it is directly associated with the health of the patients. There is no provision to compromise with the accuracy and the precision of the obtained results because it can leads to the wrong treatment which can be harmful for the patients (Bischof et al., 1999; Dolatabadi, Khadem, & Asl, 2017).

Manual investigation of the biomedical data generally takes considerable amount of time. Moreover various hidden patterns are may not be discoverable by the human experts all the time because of the inherent limitations of the humans (Endsley & Kiris, 1995; Podgurski et al., 2003). In general amount of data which is generated in the medical industry is quite huge and may be very difficult to be processed by the digital systems with limited resources (Breton, Medina, & Montagnat, 2003; Lim, De Heras Ciechomski, Sarni, & Thalmann, 2003). Generally the type of data is not homogeneous in nature. The speed off the data generation is quite high. To handle all these constraints, some efficient data processing methods are required to effectively process data in real time. Big data analytics is one of the major advancements in the field of data science that helps to process data in real time. Real time data processing also demands intelligent algorithms that can efficiently understand the acquired data, remove noises and interpret the data by considering the inconsistencies which can be present sometime (Ilyasova, Kupriyanov, Paringer, & Kirsh, 2018; Luo, Wu, Gopukumar, & Zhao, 2016; Nair & Ganesh, 2016; Neshatpour et al., 2016; Tchagna Kouanou et al., 2018). Big data handling methods are therefore required to overcome all these barriers. Big Data Analytics has several applications including market research, healthcare, agriculture, weather prediction, satellite data analysis etc (Murdoch & Detsky, 2013; Sin & Muthu, 2015).

Biomedical data produced from different sources like pathological Labs, hospital and nursing homes, different sensors, pharmaceutical sources etc. Show the source of Biomedical data generation is quite heterogeneous which is a big problem to analyze the data with conventional algorithms. Biomedical images can be acquired from different sources with various modalities like X-Ray, MRI, computed tomography, positron emission tomography, ultrasonic imaging, microscopic imaging etc. Several high quality images can be generated from all these methods which are needs to be interpreted correctly to accurately diagnose the disease (Rangayyan, 2004; Shekhar, Walimbe, & Plishker, 2013). The images can be monitored remotely by the physicians. So is very hectic and practically infeasible process to study all these pictures manually and generate the results precisely within a short period of time. Artificial intelligence and machine learning algorithms are helpful in this context. these methods are designed to learn complex models which is helpful in understanding the structure of the acquired data and also useful in exploring various hidden patterns from the data (Dwivedi, Bali, Naguib, & Nassar, 2007; "M-Health," 2006, "US6829378B2 - Remote medical image analysis - Google Patents," n.d.). In this article, biomedical image analysis based on big data and artificial intelligence is presented. this work explores different approaches to process biomedical images where, biomedical images are considered as big data. It is necessary to study the recent developments in this domain to find out the drawbacks of the existing systems and the scope of further development.

Different stages which are involved in the biomedical data processing are data acquisition, storage, processing, interpretation etc. and it is very challenging to process huge amount of biomedical data and extract some meaningful information, correlation, patterns etc. from the acquired biomedical image data or other biomedical data which can be beneficial in interpreting the condition of a patient. Error or incorrect results are not affordable because diagnostics is the basis of any treatment and it is directly related with the health of the patient. Wrong diagnosis can leads to the wrong treatment and sometimes it is life threatening. Biomedical data are sometime used to forecast some future conditions of a patient. Therefore, it is necessary to analyse a biomedical image or any other biomedical data accurately. Moreover, if an automated method takes a lot of time to improve its accuracy then the corresponding method may not be suitable for real life applications because time is precious in case of diagnosis. Early diagnosis helps to start the appropriate treatment at earliest which can save millions of life. Conventional and manual data analysis methods are not highly reliable because manual investigations are error prone and time consuming. Due to the inherent problems of human associated with the manual investigation, automated diagnostic methods are preferred in various occasions. Due the advancement in technology, the conventional biomedical image acquisition devices are improved and can produce high quality images. Moreover, portable versions of the conventional biomedical imaging devices and different handheld devices like smartphones are frequently used to capture biomedical images and communicate instantly to a remote processing node. The volume of the generated medical image data is considerably large and difficult to handle by the conventional methods of data and image processing. Moreover, conventional data analysis methods takes huge amount of time to handle large amount of biomedical data. To overcome the drawbacks of the conventional data analysis methods, some methods are developed to process huge amount of data i.e. big data which are based on artificial intelligence. This article will be helpful for understanding the current trend in the biomedical image analysis based on big data analytics and recent advancements in the computer aided diagnostics.

RECENT DEVELOPMENTS

In most of the situations, the biomedical data is obtained from different patients in various formats. Sophisticated hardwires and transmission mechanisms are required to store and transmit biomedical images in real time (Chakraborty, Chatterjee, Ashour, Mali, & Dey, 2017; Chakraborty & Mali, 2018). To manage and process biomedical images efficiently, some architectures are developed which are based on big data analysis, artificial Intelligence and machine learning.

Artificial intelligence based systems are frequently used in various medical applications. In modern days artificial intelligence becomes inevitable for automated and fast diagnosis. In medical applications, artificial intelligence based systems are highly beneficial to make accurate decisions, prediction, classification, data analysis etc (Nahar, Imam, Tickle, Shawkat Ali, & Chen, 2012; Shukla, Lakhmani, & Agarwal, 2016). Till date, artificial intelligence based diagnostic systems are not efficient enough to replace the human experts in the diagnostic process (King, 2018) but certainly, intelligent systems become helping hand of the physicians and in some of the cases, intelligent systems can rectify the human errors which is beneficial in accurate decision making process (Dilsizian & Siegel, 2014; Jiang et al., 2017; Mayo & Leung, 2018; Miller & Brown, 2018; Pesapane, Volonté, Codari, & Sardanelli, 2018). There are lots of paper can be found in the literature which are focused on Big Data Analytics and machine learning to solve by medical image analysis problem efficiently, among which some of the articles are discussed in brief below.

In (Guo et al., 2018), authors proposed a biomedical image classification system based on hadoop and mapreduce systems. The total architecture is divided into some pipeline stages where feature extraction (Chakraborty, Roy, & Hore, 2016; S. Hore, Chatterjee, Chakraborty, & Shaw, 2016), clustering and classification task are divided into the stages of the pipeline. The concept of an additional Momentum is proposed in this work. Authors also compare the several influencing parameters and analyze various factors which is crucial in the classification process. They also tried to establish the optimal values for the learning rate and Momentum factor so that a good prediction accuracy can be achieved within a reasonable amount of time. The proposed architecture is tested on the breast cancer dataset. Authors also illustrated the dependency of the training time on the size of the data. In (Meng, Pratx, & Xing, 2011), a mapreduce based image reconstruction technique is proposed. The proposed method is developed for four dimensional computerized tomography images and cone beam computerized tomography images. The experiment is performed in the Cloud Computing environment and authors demonstrated the usefulness of the mapreduce framework to analyze the medical images.

A cloud computing based images analysis method is proposed in (Huo et al., 2018). It can exploit the benefits of the high-performance computing environments to process and interpret the images faster.

Cloud Computing based biomedical image segmentation framework is proposed in (Zhang, Xing, Liu, & Yang, n.d.). This work is based on Apache spark cloud computing framework. The proposed approach is applied for the skeletal muscle cell image segmentation. It is a distributed approach where skeletal muscle cell images can be segmented 10 times faster than the conventional approach. Moreover, authors proposed a new region selection method which is based on hierarchical tree. The total workload is equivalent distributed on the available module of the Apache Spark framework. Azure based biomedical image classification Framework is proposed in (Roychowdhury & Bihis, 2016). This method exploits the benefits of the cloud computing architecture with the machine learning models for biomedical image analysis. A workflow is demonstrated in this work which is suitable for various machine learning applications for example classification, regression, learning etc. The efficiency of the proposed method is proved by applying the proposed method on 18 biomedical image data sets and observed near about 8% improvement in comparison with the existing works.

Now it is necessary to measure the quality of the input data and the obtained results. To assess the quality of the data, threshold based approaches not very suitable because it has been found experimentally that these kind of approaches are not capable to find the discrepancies in the data or result accurately due to lack of its domain knowledge. Due to this inherent problem associated with the thresholding based approaches, some solutions are designed which are based on semantic web. One of the major problems associated with the solutions which are based on the traditional semantic web is that, these methods you are not very useful to handle large amount of data with precision and sometimes these algorithms completely fail in real life scenarios. to solve this problem, a hadoop and mapreduce based solution is proposed in (Bonner et al., 2015). The proposed method is equipped with optimal joining techniques, efficient data caching methods etc. The efficiency of the algorithm is proven by comparing with some standard existing methods.

Some other interesting works are available in the literature which are focused to solve biomedical image analysis problem from the perspective of big data analysis. For example, in (Mavandadi et al., 2012), authors proposed a biomedical image analysis framework which is based on digital gaming. It is a mathematical architecture where, advantages of digital gaming are explored and applied to solve the biomedical image analysis problem which has a great impact on the telemedicine and telediagnostics.

In (Farahmand et al., 2016), authors proposed and big data based biomedical image analysis architecture where the problem of the huge resource requirement by the conventional biomedical image analysis procedures is addressed. In this work, a hardware acceleration method is proposed which is based on it FPGA. The proposed work is based on the machine learning algorithms and Big Data Analytics which is implemented using the mapreduce architecture. The experimental results Prove the efficiency of proposed method.

Application of big data and machine learning algorithms to support radiology and to assist radiologist, can be found in (Syeda-Mahmood, 2018). A clear picture about the mapreduce Framework with big data analysis can be obtained from. In this work, the recent trend of medical image analysis and clinical data analysis based on big data structures and artificial intelligence are discussed in detail. Moreover a future direction is given that can be helpful for further research.

GENERAL OUTLINE FOR BIOMEDICAL IMAGE ANALYSIS USING BIG-DATA FRAMEWORKS

Biomedical image analysis plays a vital role in understanding the functions of internal organs. It is a reliable method to get the internal details without taking any surgical measure (Bauer, Wiest, Nolte, & Reyes, 2013; Sridevi & Sundaresan, 2013). Therefore the underlying architecture to analyze the biomedical images should be very strong and efficient on which one can rely. As discussed earlier, big data analysis plays a vital role in biomedical image analysis. Therefore it is necessary to design a biomedical image analysis algorithm in such a way so that it can be implemented and executed in a distributed environment with parallel computational power. In this part of the article, a conceptual overview of the big Data architecture based biomedical image analysis is presented along with the generalized sequence of operations.

One of the prime objective of the big data management is that, data quality assurance and easy accessibility of the data for analysis and interpretation (Qiu, Wu, Ding, Xu, & Feng, 2016; Sivarajah, Kamal, Irani, & Weerakkody, 2017). Therefore, the analytical workflow plays a vital role in big data based clinical data management including biomedical data analysis.

Biomedical Image Acquisition

The major source of biomedical images are the human body and the body of the other animals. Different modalities like ultrasound, computerized tomography, positron emission tomography, microscopic imaging, magnetic resonance imaging, X-Ray etc. are used to capture the images from different parts of the body and sometimes, same body part is examined with the help of various modalities to uncover important information depending on the suspected disease (Robb & Hanson, 1990; Tangherlini, Merla, & Romani, 2006). With the advancement of the technology, different image acquisition procedures can produce high quality images for clear study and interpretation of the disease or body part. In general, the size of the captured biomedical images are considerably large and therefore difficult to process. If the disease is on the skin, then digital camera can be used to capture the images. Moreover, a simple mobile phone can be used to capture and transmit the acquired images to the cloud or in some distributed big data environments and the analysis can be performed in real time (Basu, Schlangen, Meinhardt-Wollweber, & Roth, 2015; Du et al., 2016; Pan, Lankenau, Welzel, Birngruber, & Engelhardt, 1996).

Biomedical Image Selection

It is necessary to filter important images from the acquired images. Here the term 'important' is dependent on the application. 'Important' images may be good quality images, image of a region of interest, images which are captured within a specific time period or in a particular instance etc (Khapli & Bhalachandra, 2008; Taquet & Labit, 2012). In general, the selection is performed by the automated algorithms but in some occasions, experts use semi-automatic algorithms (Hore, Chakraborty, et al., 2016). The main advantage of using the semi-automated algorithms is that, it allows human interaction. It is sometimes required to achieve more precision in the results. Moreover, the region of interests can be chosen accurately and physicians can manually interact with the system. It is somewhat flexible and useful in some scenarios (Chakraborty, Chatterjee, Dey, Ashour, & Shi, 2017; Chevaillier et al., 2008; Chklovskii, Vitaladevuni, & Scheffer, 2010; Lee et al., 2003).

Biomedical Image Cleaning

Cleaning is one of the most important step in biomedical image preprocessing. In most of the cases, various biomedical images are inherently noisy. Some of the modalities have affinity towards noise. Noise can be generated due various factors (Chakraborty, Mali, Chatterjee, Banerjee, Sah, et al., 2018; M. Roy et al., 2018). For example, the quality of the image acquisition device has a great impact on the quality of the captured images. Some foreign articles may degrade the quality of the captured image (Duan, Gao, Tang, & Yao, 2019; Roy et al., 2017). The quality of the image is highly dependent on the subject under test i.e. the patient's body or the sample being examined. Noisy images are one of major reason behind the failure of the automated image analysis algorithms (Chakraborty et al., 2019; Yu, Gao, & Li, 2016). Noise in the biomedical images can leads to various problems like wrong prediction, misclassification, incorrect segmentation etc (Chakraborty, Chatterjee, Dey, et al., 2017; Chakraborty, Chatterjee, Das, & Mali, 2020; Hore et al., 2015). which leads to wrong diagnosis that can be life threatening in some occasions. Therefore, image cleaning with noise removal is necessary and in most of the scenarios, unavoidable for perfect diagnosis and better results.

Biomedical Image Annotation

Annotation is a process to add some metadata to the images. In real world, lots of biomedical images are captured, organized and processed regularly. The time required to organize the image is considerable in case of large number of images. In some scenarios, there is a need to get the information about a group of biomedical images at once (Gadermayr, Klinkhammer, Boor, & Merhof, 2016). This task can be performed manually but it can be easily understood that manual solution is very expensive in terms of time and effort. Annotation for biomedical images is sometimes essential to improve the search capabilities. A biomedical image can be annotated manually for example one can manually assign the class to the images. But manual annotation is not preferable because it is very hectic and time consuming for a human being. Machine learning based solutions are frequently used which can mimic the human annotation to some extent.

Categorization of the Images

Categorization of the biomedical images is sometimes essential to send it to the next stages. In general, the categorization is performed by the automated methods. It can be done on the basis of annotation or some other features can be used.

MODELLING AND TRANSLATION OF THE BIOMEDICAL IMAGES

This stage uses mathematical tools for modeling or translating the biomedical images. Mathematical models are applied on the images by using some computational algorithms. Modelling and translation is necessary in some occasions for efficient and meaningful processing. Moreover, modelling and translation is helpful in reducing the computational cost. Depending on the images, the modelling and translation methods can be chosen. For example, dimensions of an image can be manipulated as per requirements (Zhang, Xia, Xie, Fulham, & Feng, 2018).

Biomedical Image Classification

This stage involves the automated classification of the biomedical images based on some characteristics or features. Automated classification can be performed in various ways (Chakraborty, Chatterjee, Chatterjee, Mali, Goswami, et al., 2018). Broadly, the task of classification can be divided into two categories. First is supervised classification and second one is unsupervised classification. Apart from these two categories, there are some other types of classification methods are available (Chakraborty, Mali, Chatterjee, Banerjee, Roy, Dutta, et al., 2018; Shouvik Chakraborty, Mali, Banerjee, et al., 2017; Chakraborty, Mali, Chatterjee, Anand, et al., 2017). For example, semi-supervised classification. If the class labels are known earlier, then it is possible to train the system using machine learning methods so that the system can learn a model based on the training samples (Gutman et al., 2016). The learned model can be can be tested on the unknown samples (unknown to the model i.e. the classification framework is completely unaware about these samples). It is necessary before the deployment of the classification framework in the real life scenarios, to ensure the reliability of the classification method. In case of unsupervised classification methods, there is no need of training samples with known class labels. The unsupervised classification methods can adapt the environment and try to find out the class of the samples by analyzing the obtained features or by analyzing some patterns (Shaikh, Kollerathu, & Krishnamurthi, 2019). This type of learning is basically helpful when the data is not annotated properly or not labelled properly.

Semi supervised classification take both labelled and unlabeled images. In general, the amount of labelled images is quite small compared with the labelled images. There is some assumptions like continuity, cluster, manifold etc. among which at least one needs to be satisfied (Papernot, Abadi, Erlingsson, Goodfellow, & Talwar, 2016). Semi supervised learning may not work appropriately all the time. Sometimes semi supervised learning based methods fails and sometimes it works well. Actually it depends on the scenario and should not be applied blindly. Beside some of the failures, if the semi supervised algorithms are applied properly, it has been observed that it is working well than the unsupervised algorithms (Li et al., 2016). Some other types of classification methods are observed like reinforcement learning period reinforcement learning is basically a machine learning based method where the data labels for the labels for the images are not present at the time of training but some agents called reinforcement agents are used to decide what to do in a specific condition (Maicas, Carneiro, Bradley, Nascimento, & Reid, 2017).

Machine learning algorithms deals with big data for training the classification model. Big data itself is not sufficient for any kind of decision or prediction purposes unless or until some useful information can be extracted from the big data. But the machine learning algorithms and not solely dependent on the big data. Huge amount of data sometimes increases the classification accuracy but sometimes it also decreases the classification accuracy due to over fitting or some such type of problems. Now to perform the classification in the big data environment the conventional algorithms may not be suitable always. Therefore deep learning based methods and other modern machine learning approaches are frequently used in recent days to handle big data efficiently.

Prediction and Decision Making from Big-Data Using Machine Learning

As discussed above, computer-aided biomedical image analysis requires application specific prediction and decision making capability in some occasions. To get better accuracy, deep learning methods frequently used in recent days which includes convolutional neural network and other deep learning tools to extract and mine data from the big data efficiently. With the advent of deep learning methods, the quality of the disease diagnosis and prediction from the biomedical images is improved. Moreover, it can solve some Complex computational problems related with prediction and decision making very efficiently and can study a large number of images very fast so that the reports can be generated within the stipulated amount of time (Chakraborty, Mali, Chatterjee, Banerjee, Roy, Deb, et al., 2018; Gallo, Anayiotos, & Morbiducci, 2015). Metaheuristic methods (Chakraborty & Bhowmik, 2015a, 2015b, Chakraborty & Bhowmik, 2013, 2015; Chakraborty, Seal, & Roy, 2015) are frequently used to optimize the machine learning models. Sometimes prediction methods fails due to development features and redundant features. It is necessary to extract meaningful and diagnostically relevant features and information which can be used to train the model as well as to get better predicted results. Here the term better means precise results with high accuracy which can be achieved within reasonable amount of time. Deep learning based medical image analysis methods are highly efficient and can extract semantic information from an image which are beneficial in understanding an image. Prediction can help in various ways like it can alert a patient before some serious health issues. Intelligent predictions can also help physicians to analyze symptoms and predict the future consequences and continue the treatment accordingly. Convolutional Neural Networks have to compute and adjust a large number of parameters (Sabuncu, Neuroinformatics, & 2015, n.d.).

To do so, the training dataset should be sufficient enough and the dataset should be efficiently explored otherwise the learned model may not be powerful enough for real life applications where the incoming data is completely unknown to the model (Chakraborty, Mali, Chatterjee, Banerjee, et al., 2017). So, big data helps the convolutional neural network in acquiring sufficient knowledge about the underlying images. Moreover, the convolutional neural networks are helpful in extracting useful information from the big data and prediction. Therefore, the application of deep learning methods in big data mining (Datta et al., 2018) and prediction is very useful in biomedical image analysis (Dua & Acharya, 2016).

The result of the prediction and decision making systems must be validated before the deployment in the real world. A model should be tested and validated rigorously using various validation techniques. The procedure must be generalized i.e. not biased towards any specific samples of the dataset, environment or any other factors (Muhlert, Sethi, & Cipolotti, 2015). So, the generalizability is one of the very important criteria to apply any machine learning based biomedical image analysis algorithms for real life applications. There are several methods that can be used for the validation purposes like cross validation, bootstrap method etc. The classification model must be chosen in such a way so that the chosen model is the most difficult, complex and general and its complexity and generalize nature is reduced gradually depending on the problem. In this way the correct validation model can be chosen. Moreover, the error distribution must be studied carefully to clearly understand and choose or create an effective validation method.

Compression of the Biomedical Images

Compression is one of the most important steps in biomedical image analysis under bigdata architectures. Compression helps to reduce the complexity and the processing time of the biomedical image processing algorithms and helps the big data frameworks to efficiently handle the biomedical images. Compression allows faster analysis of the biomedical images in a computationally cheaper way (Matejek, Haehn, Lekschas, Mitzenmacher, & Pfister, 2017). Specifically, it is helpful in real time biomedical image analysis systems where the underlying bigdata framework has to process continuous incoming biomedical images. This step is also helpful in storing, transmitting and managing the biomedical images by the big data architectures. In general, the compression methods can be classified in two ways. First one is known as the lossy compression where the actual biomedical image cannot be reconstructed from the corresponding compressed image i.e. some information will be permanently lost during the reconstruction. Another type of compression scheme is known as the lossless compression. In this type, the original image can be reconstructed from the corresponding compressed image without losing any information. The amount of compression is very low in case of lossless compression (Ahn, Bui, & Shin, 2019). So, in most of the applications, lossy compression is preferred due to its high compression ratio. Although, in some applications of biomedical image analysis, lossy compression cannot be used because every information is important and therefore loss of information is not permitted. In those cases, only lossless compression can be applied.

Storage and Transmission

Storage and transmission of the bigdata is one of the major concerns while processing biomedical images. Conventional database systems with relational model is not efficient enough to handle bigdata. Some different models like NoSQL are often used to handle the bigdata. Biomedical images demands large amount of storage space. In general, local storages are not used because local storages are not suitable for information sharing at large scale (Marimuthu, Bialkowski, & Abbosh, 2016). Moreover, the cost of locally establishing a large amount of storage space of is quite huge. That is why, the cloud based infrastructures are very popular (Sarddar, Chakraborty, & Roy, 2015). Cloud based bigdata handling facilities are very flexible in terms of cost and establishment aspects. Users can pay for their used amount of infrastructure. Moreover, there is nothing to bother about the hardware costs and maintenance. It also allows efficient data and information sharing which helps in telemedicine. Hypervisors in the cloud computing environment allows several hosts to access the dynamic virtual resources remotely (Azar, Makhoul, Barhamgi, & Couturier, 2019).

Transmission of the bigdata can be performed in both wired and wireless media. With the increase in IoT, biomedical images can be captured by many handheld devices like a mobile phone. Therefore in case of Biomedical image analysis, it does not only depend on the wired communication but it also depends on the wireless communications (Krolopp et al., 2016). Many devices directly transfer the captured medical images to an another node for processing or storage. Bigdata transmission is an another challenge because it involves various issues like spectrum efficiency, capacity of the medium, design specifications etc. Some advanced transmission methods are developed to transmit big data efficiently. For example, in some cases multiple antennas are used for bigdata transmission. Some other bigdata transmission methods are use of extreme bandwidth for transmission, channel adaptive and cognitive radio transmission etc. To test the performance of a method for bigdata transmission, some suitable metrices are required. Moreover, in case of biomedical image transmission, only channel based mattresses are not sufficient to judge the quality of the transmission. Some data oriented evaluation metrics are also required to correctly analyse the transmission quality. Some of the commonly used performance metrics are amount of transmission time, utilisation of bandwidth, maximum entropy throughput etc. Therefore, the transmission method as well as the evaluation method should be carefully chosen for biomedical image transmission and sharing.

DISCUSSION

Developments in the biobiomedical imaging technologies increases the challenges for the biomedical image analysis and management algorithms. Various modalities and smart devices produce large amount of image data and therefore efficient algorithms are required to interpret and analyse the acquired biomedical images in a cost effective manner. The data can be structured or unstructured. In this article, generalized aspects of the biomedical image handling using bigdata architectures are presented. With the help of bigdata architectures, artificial intelligence and machine learning algorithms, different stages of biomedical image analysis like image acquisition, preprocessing and quality enhancement, classification, transmission etc. can be automatically performed. Bigdata architectures like hadoop, spark etc. are frequently used to manage and process continuous incoming flow of the biomedical images which are generated from various devices. With the development of the IoT, the amount of the smart devices are increasing day by day. Although, a large amount of data is difficult to process but, it is helpful for the machine learning algorithms specifically deep learning algorithms. Hyperparameters of a deep learning model can be efficiently tuned with a large number of training samples. Moreover, a dataset with rich variety of biomedical images can be helpful in understanding the reliability of a model. The model can be validated with a good number of testing samples which increases the faith on the model for real life deployment. In bigdata environment, parallelism plays a vital role. Both model parallelism and data parallelism needs to be achieved for optimal performance. Spark architecture use the concept of resilient distributed dataset and it is behind the optimization power of the spark architecture. Apart from these issues, another major issue is the format of the biomedical images. In general, DICOM (Digital Imaging and COMmunications) format is used to store and transmit biomedical image data. This format is preferred over the standard image representations because the DICOM for keep the patients' data secured which is very essential from the perspective of the patients' confidentiality because security and integrity of the patients' personal data is very important and many methods are available to secure the biomedical images in distributed environments (Chakraborty, Seal, Roy, & Mali, 2016; Mali, Chakraborty, & Roy, 2015; Mali, Chakraborty, Seal, & Roy, 2015; Roy, Chakraborty, Mali, Banerjee, et al., 2020; Mousomi Roy, Chakraborty, et al., 2019; Roy, Chakraborty, Mali, Swarnakar, et al.,

2020; Mousomi Roy, Mali, et al., 2019; A. Seal, Chakraborty, & Mali, 2017; Seal, Chakraborty, & Mali, 2017). Therefore, DICOM protocol is used to communicate among the hospitals and the other processing nodes. Smart devices like mobile phones generally capture images in general image formats and capable to transmit these images as it is. So, the underlying bigdata architectures should be capable to handle various type of data.

CONCLUSION

In this article, biomedical image analysis, which is one of the trending and important topics, is discussed from the perspective of bigdata analytics. Different stages of biomedical image analysis is discussed in detail and the need of the bigdata analytics is highlighted for every step. Due to advancement in the technology, the quantity and quality of the biomedical images are increasing day by day. Not only conventional biomedical image acquisition tools, smart devices like smart phones, watches etc. and can be communicated to a remote host in real time with the help of IoT. Therefore it is necessary to have some efficient methods which can handle these biomedical images efficiently and can generate results by processing and interpreting these images. From the discussion of this article, it is clear that the Big Data Analytics and its related methods are quite helpful for analyzing biomedical images in real time and perform certain task within stipulated amount of time. Sophisticated architectures along with efficient algorithms are required to develop to support the ever increasing need of the biomedical imaging industry. There is a lot of scope of research to improve the current bigdata architectures and develop new frameworks which are specifically optimized to handle biomedical image data. IoT and could computing technologies makes the data sharing easier. Moreover, the infrastructural constraints are removed by the cloud computing environment. Therefore, research must be carried on this domain to enhance the quality of the biomedical image analysis and reduce the computational complexity and time.

ACKNOWLEDGMENT

Author is highly grateful to the editors of this book to prepare this chapter.

REFERENCES

Ahn, S., Bui, T. D., & Shin, J. (2019, Apr.). Compression and intensity modules for brain MRI segmentation. Proceedings - International Symposium on Biomedical Imaging, 719–722. 10.1109/ISBI.2019.8759272

Azar, J., Makhoul, A., Barhamgi, M., & Couturier, R. (2019). An energy efficient IoT data compression approach for edge machine learning. *Future Generation Computer Systems*, *96*, 168–175. doi:10.1016/j.future.2019.02.005

Basu, C., Schlangen, S., Meinhardt-Wollweber, M., & Roth, B. (2015). Light source design for spectral tuning in biomedical imaging. *Journal of Medical Imaging (Bellingham, Wash.)*, *2*(4), 44501. doi:10.1117/1.JMI.2.4.044501 PubMed

Bauer, S., Wiest, R., Nolte, L. P., & Reyes, M. (2013, July 7). A survey of MRI-based medical image analysis for brain tumor studies. *Physics in Medicine and Biology*, *58*(13), R97–R129. doi:10.1088/0031-9155/58/13/R97 PubMed

Bischof, L. M., Talbot, H., Breen, E., Lovell, D., Chan, D., Stone, G., ... Caffin, R. (1999, July 8). Automated melanoma diagnosis system. doi:10.1117/12.351632

Bonner, S., McGough, A. S., Kureshi, I., Brennan, J., Theodoropoulos, G., & Moss, L. ... Antoniou, G. (2015). Data quality assessment and anomaly detection via map/reduce and linked data: A case study in the medical domain. 2015 IEEE International Conference on Big Data (Big Data), 737–746. doi:10.1109/BigData.2015.7363818

Breton, V., Medina, R., & Montagnat, J. (2003). DataGrid, prototype of a biomedical grid. *Methods of Information in Medicine*, *42*(2), 143–147. doi:10.1055/s-0038-1634325 PubMed

Chakraborty, S., & Bhowmik, S. (2013). Job Shop Scheduling using Simulated Annealing. First International Conference on Computation and Communication Advancement, 1(1), 69–73. Retrieved from https://scholar.google.co.in/citations?user=8lhQFaYAAAAJ&hl=en

Chakraborty, S., & Bhowmik, S. (2015). An Efficient Approach to Job Shop Scheduling Problem using Simulated Annealing. *International Journal of Hybrid Information Technology*, *8*(11), 273–284. doi:10.14257/ijhit.2015.8.11.23

Chakraborty, S., & Bhowmik, S. (2015a). Blending roulette wheel selection with simulated annealing for job shop scheduling problem. Michael Faraday IET International Summit 2015, 100(). doi:10.1049/cp.2015.1696

Chakraborty, S., & Bhowmik, S. (2015b). Blending roulette wheel selection with Simulated Annealing for Job Shop Scheduling Problem. IET Conference Publications, 2015(CP683). doi:10.1049/cp.2015.1696

Chakraborty, S., Chatterjee, S., Ashour, A. S., Mali, K., & Dey, N. (2017). Intelligent Computing in Medical Imaging: A Study. In N. Dey (Ed.), *Advancements in Applied Metaheuristic Computing* (pp. 143–163)., doi:10.4018/978-1-5225-4151-6.ch006

Chakraborty, S., Chatterjee, S., Chatterjee, A., Mali, K., Goswami, S., & Sen, S. (2018). Automated Breast Cancer Identification by analyzing Histology Slides using Metaheuristic Supported Supervised Classification coupled with Bag-of-Features. 2018 Fourth International Conference on Research in Computational Intelligence and Communication Networks (ICRCICN), 81–86. doi:10.1109/ICRCICN.2018.8718736

Chakraborty, S., Chatterjee, S., Das, A., & Mali, K. (2020). Penalized Fuzzy C-Means Enabled Hybrid Region Growing in Segmenting Medical Images. doi:10.1007/978-981-13-8930-6_3

Chakraborty, S., Chatterjee, S., Dey, N., Ashour, A. S., Ashour, A. S., Shi, F., & Mali, K. (2017). Modified cuckoo search algorithm in microscopic image segmentation of hippocampus. *Microscopy Research and Technique*, *80*(May), 1–22. doi:10.1002/jemt.22900 PubMed

Chakraborty, S., Chatterjee, S., Dey, N., Ashour, A. S., & Shi, F. (2017). Gradient approximation in retinal blood vessel segmentation. 2017 4th IEEE Uttar Pradesh Section International Conference on Electrical, Computer and Electronics (UPCON), 618–623. 10.1109/UPCON.2017.8251120

Chakraborty, S., & Mali, K. (2018). Application of Multiobjective Optimization Techniques in Biomedical Image Segmentation—A Study. In Multi-Objective Optimization (pp. 181–194). doi:10.1007/978-981-13-1471-1_8

Chakraborty, S., Mali, K., Banerjee, S., Roy, K., Saha, D., & Chatterjee, S. … Majumder, S. (2017). Bag-of-features based classification of dermoscopic images. 2017 4th International Conference on Opto-Electronics and Applied Optics (Optronix), 1–6. 10.1109/OPTRONIX.2017.8349977

Chakraborty, S., Mali, K., Chatterjee, S., Anand, S., Basu, A., & Banerjee, S., … Bhattacharya, A. (2017). Image based skin disease detection using hybrid neural network coupled bag-of-features. 2017 IEEE 8th Annual Ubiquitous Computing, Electronics and Mobile Communication Conference (UEMCON), 242–246. 10.1109/UEMCON.2017.8249038

Chakraborty, S., Mali, K., Chatterjee, S., Banerjee, S., Mazumdar, K. G., & Debnath, M. ... Roy, K. (2017). Detection of skin disease using metaheuristic supported artificial neural networks. 2017 8th Annual Industrial Automation and Electromechanical Engineering Conference (IEMECON), 224–229. 10.1109/IEMECON.2017.8079594

Chakraborty, S., Mali, K., Chatterjee, S., Banerjee, S., Roy, K., & Deb, K. ... Prasad, N. (2018). An integrated method for automated biomedical image segmentation. 2017 4th International Conference on Opto-Electronics and Applied Optics, Optronix 2017, 2018–Janua. 10.1109/OPTRONIX.2017.8349978

Chakraborty, S., Mali, K., Chatterjee, S., Banerjee, S., Roy, K., & Dutta, N. ... Mazumdar, S. (2018). Dermatological effect of UV rays owing to ozone layer depletion. 2017 4th International Conference on Opto-Electronics and Applied Optics, Optronix 2017, 2018–Janua. 10.1109/OPTRONIX.2017.8349975

Chakraborty, S., Mali, K., Chatterjee, S., Banerjee, S., Sah, A., & Pathak, S. ... Roy, D. (2018). Bio-medical image enhancement using hybrid metaheuristic coupled soft computing tools. 2017 IEEE 8th Annual Ubiquitous Computing, Electronics and Mobile Communication Conference, UEMCON 2017, 2018–Janua. 10.1109/UEMCON.2017.8249036

Chakraborty, S., Raman, A., Sen, S., Mali, K., Chatterjee, S., & Hachimi, H. (2019). Contrast Optimization using Elitist Metaheuristic Optimization and Gradient Approximation for Biomedical Image Enhancement. 2019 Amity International Conference on Artificial Intelligence (AICAI), 712–717. doi:10.1109/AICAI.2019.8701367

Chakraborty, S., Roy, M., & Hore, S. (2016). *A study on different edge detection techniques in digital image processing*. Feature Detectors and Motion Detection in Video Processing; doi:10.4018/978-1-5225-1025-3.ch005

Chakraborty, S., Seal, A., & Roy, M. (2015). An Elitist Model for Obtaining Alignment of Multiple Sequences using Genetic Algorithm. *2nd National Conference NCETAS 2015*, 4(9), 61–67.

Chakraborty, S., Seal, A., Roy, M., & Mali, K. (2016). A novel lossless image encryption method using DNA substitution and chaotic logistic map. *International Journal of Security and Its Applications*, 10(2), 205–216. doi:10.14257/ijsia.2016.10.2.19

Chevaillier, B., Ponvianne, Y., Collette, J. L., Mandry, D., Claudon, M., & Pietquin, O. (2008). Functional semi-automated segmentation of renal DCE-MRI sequences. ICASSP, IEEE International Conference on Acoustics, Speech and Signal Processing - Proceedings, 525–528. 10.1109/ICASSP.2008.4517662

Chklovskii, D. B., Vitaladevuni, S., & Scheffer, L. K. (2010, October). Semi-automated reconstruction of neural circuits using electron microscopy. *Current Opinion in Neurobiology*, *20*(5), 667–675. doi:10.1016/j.conb.2010.08.002 PubMed

Datta, S., Chakraborty, S., Mali, K., Baneijee, S., Roy, K., & Chatterjee, S. … Bhattacharjee, S. (2018). Optimal usage of pessimistic association rules in cost effective decision making. 2017 4th International Conference on Opto-Electronics and Applied Optics, Optronix 2017, 2018–Janua. 10.1109/OPTRONIX.2017.8349976

Davari Dolatabadi, A., Khadem, S. E. Z., & Asl, B. M. (2017). Automated diagnosis of coronary artery disease (CAD) patients using optimized SVM. *Computer Methods and Programs in Biomedicine*, *138*, 117–126. doi:10.1016/j.cmpb.2016.10.011 PubMed

Dilsizian, S. E., & Siegel, E. L. (2014). Artificial intelligence in medicine and cardiac imaging: Harnessing big data and advanced computing to provide personalized medical diagnosis and treatment. *Current Cardiology Reports*, *16*(1), 441. doi:10.1007/s11886-013-0441-8 PubMed

Doi, K. (2007). Computer-aided diagnosis in medical imaging: Historical review, current status and future potential. *Computerized Medical Imaging and Graphics*, *31*(4–5), 198–211. doi:10.1016/j.compmedimag.2007.02.002 PubMed

Du, Y., Liu, C.-H., Lei, L., Singh, M., Li, J., Hicks, M. J., … Mohan, C. (2016). Rapid, noninvasive quantitation of skin disease in systemic sclerosis using optical coherence elastography. *Journal of Biomedical Optics*, *21*(4), 46002. doi:10.1117/1. JBO.21.4.046002 PubMed

Dua, S., & Acharya, R. (2016). Data Mining in Biomedical Imaging, Signaling, and Systems. Retrieved from https://books.google.co.in/books?hl=en&lr=&id=lB 7OBQAAQBAJ&oi=fnd&pg=PP1&dq=prediction+and+decision+making+in+b iomedical+imaging&ots=e98FQYAzA0&sig=SDIFF_hM4gAgYhwgJf-uzcTIa0A

Duan, T., Gao, F., Tang, Y., & Yao, J. (2019). Application of mathematical morphological filter for noise reduction in photoacoustic imaging. In A. A. Oraevsky & L. V. Wang (Eds.), Photons Plus Ultrasound: Imaging and Sensing 2019 (p. 187)., doi:10.1117/12.2512176.

Dwivedi, A. N., Bali, R. K., Naguib, R. N. G., & Nassar, N. S. (2007). *The Efficacy of the M-Health Paradigm* (pp. 15–32). Incorporating Technological, Organisational and Managerial Perspectives. In M-Health; doi:10.1007/0-387-26559-7_2

Endsley, M. R., & Kiris, E. O. (1995). The Out-of-the-Loop Performance Problem and Level of Control in Automation. *Human Factors, 37*(2), 381–394. doi:10.1518/001872095779064555

Farahmand, F., Rafatirad, S., Neshatpour, K., Koohi, A., Joshi, R., Sasan, A., & Homayoun, H. (2016). Big biomedical image processing hardware acceleration: A case study for K-means and image filtering. doi:10.1109/ISCAS.2016.7527445

Gadermayr, M., Klinkhammer, B. M., Boor, P., & Merhof, D. (2016). Do we need large annotated training data for detection applications in biomedical imaging? A case study in renal glomeruli detection. Lecture Notes in Computer Science (Including Subseries Lecture Notes in Artificial Intelligence and Lecture Notes in Bioinformatics), 10019 LNCS, 18–26. doi:10.1007/978-3-319-47157-0_3

Gallo, D., Anayiotos, A., & Morbiducci, U. (2015, June 11). The Evolution of Computational Hemodynamics as a Clinical Tool in Decision Making, Patient Specific Treatment and Clinical Management. Part II. *Annals of Biomedical Engineering, 43*(6), 1273–1274. doi:10.1007/s10439-015-1338-z PubMed

Guo, S., Zhang, Y., Wu, Q., Niu, L., Zhang, W., & Li, S. (2018). The Performance Evaluation of a Distributed Image Classification Pipeline Based on Hadoop and MapReduce with Initial Application to Medical Images. *Journal of Medical Imaging and Health Informatics, 8*(1), 78–83. doi:10.1166/jmihi.2018.2236

Gutman, D., Codella, N. C. F., Celebi, E., Helba, B., Marchetti, M., Mishra, N., & Halpern, A. (2016). Skin Lesion Analysis toward Melanoma Detection: A Challenge at the International Symposium on Biomedical Imaging (ISBI) 2016, hosted by the International Skin Imaging Collaboration (ISIC). Retrieved from https://arxiv.org/abs/1605.01397

Hore, S., Chakraborty, S., Chatterjee, S., Dey, N., Ashour, A. S., Van Chung, L., & Le, D.-N. (2016). An integrated interactive technique for image segmentation using stack based seeded region growing and thresholding. *Iranian Journal of Electrical and Computer Engineering, 6*(6). doi:10.11591/ijece.v6i6.11801

Hore, S., Chakroborty, S., Ashour, A. S., Dey, N., Ashour, A. S., Sifaki-Pistolla, D., ... Chaudhuri, S. R. B. (2015). Finding Contours of Hippocampus Brain Cell Using Microscopic Image Analysis. *Journal of Advanced Microscopy Research, 10*(2), 93–103. doi:10.1166/jamr.2015.1245

Hore, S., Chatterjee, S., Chakraborty, S., & Shaw, R. K. (2016). *Analysis of different feature description algorithm in object recognition.* Feature Detectors and Motion Detection in Video Processing; doi:10.4018/978-1-5225-1025-3.ch004

Huo, Y., Blaber, J., Damon, S. M., Boyd, B. D., Bao, S., Parvathaneni, P., ... Landman, B. A. (2018, June 1). Towards Portable Large-Scale Image Processing with High-Performance Computing. *Journal of Digital Imaging*, *31*(3), 304–314. doi:10.1007/s10278-018-0080-0 PubMed

Ilyasova, N., Kupriyanov, A., Paringer, R., & Kirsh, D. (2018). Particular Use of BIG DATA in Medical Diagnostic Tasks. *Pattern Recognition and Image Analysis*, *28*(1), 114–121. doi:10.1134/S1054661818010066

Jiang, F., Jiang, Y., Zhi, H., Dong, Y., Li, H., Ma, S., . . . Wang, Y. (2017, December 1). Artificial intelligence in healthcare: Past, present and future. Stroke and Vascular Neurology, 2(4), 230–243. doi:10.1136vn-2017-000101

Khapli, V. R., & Bhalachandra, A. S. (2008). CBIR system for biomedical images: challenges and open issues. IET Conference on Wireless, Mobile and Multimedia Networks, 85–88. doi:10.1049/cp:20080150

King, B. F. Jr. (2018, March 1). Artificial Intelligence and Radiology: What Will the Future Hold? *Journal of the American College of Radiology*, *15*(3), 501–503. doi:10.1016/j.jacr.2017.11.017 PubMed

Kohn, A. F., & Furuie, S. S. (1991). Safely in Medical Signal Analysis. *IEEE Engineering in Medicine and Biology Magazine*, *10*(4), 56. doi:10.1109/51.107170 PubMed

Krolopp, Á., Csákányi, A., Haluszka, D., Csáti, D., Vass, L., Kolonics, A., ... Szipőcs, R. (2016). Handheld nonlinear microscope system comprising a 2 MHz repetition rate, mode-locked Yb-fiber laser for in vivo biomedical imaging. *Biomedical Optics Express*, *7*(9), 3531. doi:10.1364/BOE.7.003531 PubMed

Lee, J. M., Yoon, U., Nam, S. H., Kim, J. H., Kim, I. Y., & Kim, S. I. (2003). Evaluation of automated and semi-automated skull-stripping algorithms using similarity index and segmentation error. *Computers in Biology and Medicine*, *33*(6), 495–507. doi:10.1016/S0010-4825(03)00022-2 PubMed

Li, Q., Feng, B., Xie, L., Liang, P., Zhang, H., & Wang, T. (2016). A cross-modality learning approach for vessel segmentation in retinal images. *IEEE Transactions on Medical Imaging*, *35*(1), 109–118. doi:10.1109/TMI.2015.2457891 PubMed

Lim, I. S., De Heras Ciechomski, P., Sarni, S., & Thalmann, D. (2003). Planar arrangement of high-dimensional biomedical data sets by Isomap coordinates. *Proceedings of the IEEE Symposium on Computer-Based Medical Systems*, 50–55. 10.1109/cbms.2003.1212766

Luo, J., Wu, M., Gopukumar, D., & Zhao, Y. (2016). Big Data Application in Biomedical Research and Health Care: A Literature Review. Biomedical Informatics Insights, 8. doi:10.4137/bii.s31559

Maicas, G., Carneiro, G., Bradley, A. P., Nascimento, J. C., & Reid, I. (2017). Deep reinforcement learning for active breast lesion detection from DCE-MRI. Lecture Notes in Computer Science (Including Subseries Lecture Notes in Artificial Intelligence and Lecture Notes in Bioinformatics), 10435 LNCS, 665–673. doi:10.1007/978-3-319-66179-7_76

Mali, K., Chakraborty, S., & Roy, M. (2015). A Study on Statistical Analysis and Security Evaluation Parameters in Image Encryption. *International Journal for Scientific Research & Development*, *3*, 2321–0613. Retrieved from www.ijsrd.com

Mali, K., Chakraborty, S., Seal, A., & Roy, M. (2015). An Efficient Image Cryptographic Algorithm based on Frequency Domain using Haar Wavelet Transform. *International Journal of Security and Its Applications*, *9*(12), 279–288. doi:10.14257/ijsia.2015.9.12.26

Marimuthu, J., Bialkowski, K. S., & Abbosh, A. M. (2016). Software-defined radar for medical imaging. *IEEE Transactions on Microwave Theory and Techniques*, *64*(2), 643–652. doi:10.1109/TMTT.2015.2511013

Matejek, B., Haehn, D., Lekschas, F., Mitzenmacher, M., & Pfister, H. (2017). Compresso: Efficient compression of segmentation data for connectomics. Lecture Notes in Computer Science (Including Subseries Lecture Notes in Artificial Intelligence and Lecture Notes in Bioinformatics), 10433 LNCS, 781–788. doi:10.1007/978-3-319-66182-7_89

Mavandadi, S., Feng, S., Yu, F., Dimitrov, S., Yu, R., & Ozcan, A. (2012). BioGames: A Platform for Crowd-Sourced Biomedical Image Analysis and Telediagnosis. *Games for Health Journal*, *1*(5), 373–376. doi:10.1089/g4h.2012.0054 PubMed

Mayo, R. C., & Leung, J. (2018, May 1). Artificial intelligence and deep learning – Radiology's next frontier? *Clinical Imaging*, *49*, 87–88. doi:10.1016/j.clinimag.2017.11.007 PubMed

Meng, B., Pratx, G., & Xing, L. (2011). Ultrafast and scalable cone-beam CT reconstruction using MapReduce in a cloud computing environment. *Medical Physics*, *38*(12), 6603–6609. doi:10.1118/1.3660200 PubMed

Miller, D. D., & Brown, E. W. (2018, February 1). Artificial Intelligence in Medical Practice: The Question to the Answer? *The American Journal of Medicine*, *131*(2), 129–133. doi:10.1016/j.amjmed.2017.10.035 PubMed

Muhlert, N., Sethi, V., Cipolotti, L., Haroon, H., Parker, G. J. M., Yousry, T., ... Chard, D. (2015). The grey matter correlates of impaired decision-making in multiple sclerosis. *Journal of Neurology, Neurosurgery, and Psychiatry*, *86*(5), 530–536. doi:10.1136/jnnp-2014-308169 PubMed

Murdoch, T. B., & Detsky, A. S. (2013, April 3). The inevitable application of big data to health care. *Journal of the American Medical Association*, *309*(13), 1351–1352. doi:10.1001/jama.2013.393 PubMed

Nahar, J., Imam, T., Tickle, K. S., Shawkat Ali, A. B. M., & Chen, Y. P. P. (2012). Computational intelligence for microarray data and biomedical image analysis for the early diagnosis of breast cancer. *Expert Systems with Applications*, *39*(16), 12371–12377. doi:10.1016/j.eswa.2012.04.045

Nair, S. S. K., & Ganesh, N. (2016). An exploratory study on big data processing: A case study from a biomedical informatics. 2016 3rd MEC International Conference on Big Data and Smart City, ICBDSC 2016, 30–33. 10.1109/ICBDSC.2016.7460338

Neshatpour, K., Koohi, A., Farahmand, F., Joshi, R., Rafatirad, S., Sasan, A., & Homayoun, H. (2016). Big biomedical image processing hardware acceleration: A case study for K-means and image filtering. Proceedings - IEEE International Symposium on Circuits and Systems, 2016–July, 1134–1137. doi:10.1109/ISCAS.2016.7527445

Pan, Y., Lankenau, E., Welzel, J., Birngruber, R., & Engelhardt, R. (1996). Optical coherence - Gated imaging of biological tissues. *IEEE Journal of Selected Topics in Quantum Electronics*, *2*(4), 1029–1034. doi:10.1109/2944.577332

Papernot, N., Abadi, M., Erlingsson, Ú., Goodfellow, I., & Talwar, K. (2016). Semi-supervised Knowledge Transfer for Deep Learning from Private Training Data. Retrieved from https://arxiv.org/abs/1610.05755

Pesapane, F., Volonté, C., Codari, M., & Sardanelli, F. (2018, October 1). Artificial intelligence as a medical device in radiology: Ethical and regulatory issues in Europe and the United States. *Insights Into Imaging*, *9*(5), 745–753. doi:10.1007/s13244-018-0645-y PubMed

Podgurski, A., Leon, D., Francis, P., Masri, W., Minch, M., Sun, J., & Wang, B. (2003). Automated support for classifying software failure reports. Proceedings - International Conference on Software Engineering, 465–475. doi:10.1109/ICSE.2003.1201224

Qiu, J., Wu, Q., Ding, G., Xu, Y., & Feng, S. (2016, December 1). A survey of machine learning for big data processing. *EURASIP Journal on Advances in Signal Processing*, *2016*. doi:10.118613634-016-0355-x

Rangayyan, R. (2004). Biomedical image analysis. Retrieved from https://content. taylorfrancis.com/books/download?dac=C2009-0-00397-8&isbn=978042920909 3&format=googlePreviewPdf

Robb, R. A., & Hanson, D. P. (1990). ANALYZE: A software system for biomedical image analysis. Proceedings of the First Conference on Visualization in Biomedical Computing, 507–518. doi:10.1109/VBC.1990.109363

Roy, M., Chakraborty, S., Mali, K., Banerjee, A., Ghosh, K., & Chatterjee, S. (2020). Biomedical Image Security Using Matrix Manipulation and DNA Encryption. Advances in Intelligent Systems and Computing, 1065, 49–60. doi:10.1007/978-981-15-0361-0_4

Roy, M., Chakraborty, S., Mali, K., Chatterjee, S., Banerjee, S., & Chakraborty, A. ... Roy, K. (2017). Biomedical image enhancement based on modified Cuckoo Search and morphology. 2017 8th Industrial Automation and Electromechanical Engineering Conference, IEMECON 2017. 10.1109/IEMECON.2017.8079595

Roy, M., Chakraborty, S., Mali, K., Chatterjee, S., Banerjee, S., & Mitra, S. ... Bhattacharjee, A. (2018). Cellular image processing using morphological analysis. 2017 IEEE 8th Annual Ubiquitous Computing, Electronics and Mobile Communication Conference, UEMCON 2017, 2018–Janua. 10.1109/UEMCON.2017.8249037

Roy, M., Chakraborty, S., Mali, K., Mitra, S., Mondal, I., & Dawn, R. ... Chatterjee, S. (2019). A dual layer image encryption using polymerase chain reaction amplification and dna encryption. 2019 International Conference on Opto-Electronics and Applied Optics, Optronix 2019. doi:10.1109/OPTRONIX.2019.8862350

Roy, M., Chakraborty, S., Mali, K., Swarnakar, R., Ghosh, K., Banerjee, A., & Chatterjee, S. (2020). Data Security Techniques Based on DNA Encryption. Advances in Intelligent Systems and Computing, 1065, 239–249. doi:10.1007/978-981-15-0361-0_19

Roy, M., Mali, K., Chatterjee, S., Chakraborty, S., Debnath, R., & Sen, S. (2019). A Study on the Applications of the Biomedical Image Encryption Methods for Secured Computer Aided Diagnostics. 2019 Amity International Conference on Artificial Intelligence (AICAI), 881–886. doi:10.1109/AICAI.2019.8701382

Roychowdhury, S., & Bihis, M. (2016). AG-MIC: Azure-Based Generalized Flow for Medical Image Classification. *IEEE Access : Practical Innovations, Open Solutions*, 4, 5243–5257. doi:10.1109/ACCESS.2016.2605641

Sabuncu, M., & Neuroinformatics, E. K. (2015). Clinical prediction from structural brain MRI scans: a large-scale empirical study. Springer. Retrieved from https://link.springer.com/article/10.1007/s12021-014-9238-1

Sarddar, D., Chakraborty, S., & Roy, M. (2015). An Efficient Approach to Calculate Dynamic Time Quantum in Round Robin Algorithm for Efficient Load Balancing. *International Journal of Computers and Applications*, *123*(14), 48–52. doi:10.5120/ijca2015905701

Seal, A., Chakraborty, S., & Mali, K. (2017). A new and resilient image encryption technique based on pixel manipulation, value transformation and visual transformation utilizing single–Level haar wavelet transform. In Advances in Intelligent Systems and Computing (Vol. 458). doi:10.1007/978-981-10-2035-3_61

Seal, A., Chakraborty, S., & Mali, K. (2017). A New and Resilient Image Encryption Technique Based on Pixel Manipulation (pp. 603–611). Value Transformation and Visual Transformation Utilizing Single–Level Haar Wavelet Transform. In Proceedings of the First International Conference on Intelligent Computing and Communication; doi:10.1007/978-981-10-2035-3_61.

Shah, A., Lynch, S., Niemeijer, M., Amelon, R., Clarida, W., & Folk, J. … Abramoff, M. D. (2018). Susceptibility to misdiagnosis of adversarial images by deep learning based retinal image analysis algorithms. Proceedings - International Symposium on Biomedical Imaging, 2018–April, 1454–1457. 10.1109/ISBI.2018.8363846

Shaikh, M., Kollerathu, V. A., & Krishnamurthi, G. (2019). Recurrent attention mechanism networks for enhanced classification of biomedical images. Proceedings - International Symposium on Biomedical Imaging, 2019–April, 1260–1264. doi:10.1109/ISBI.2019.8759214

Shaikh, R. A., Li, J. P., Khan, A., & Memon, I. (2016). Biomedical image processing and analysis using Markov Random Fields. 2015 12th International Computer Conference on Wavelet Active Media Technology and Information Processing, ICCWAMTIP 2015, 179–183. 10.1109/ICCWAMTIP.2015.7493970

Shekhar, R., Walimbe, V., & Plishker, W. (2013). Medical image processing. In Handbook of Signal Processing Systems: Second Edition (pp. 349–379). doi:10.1007/978-1-4614-6859-2_12

Shukla, S., Lakhmani, A., & Agarwal, A. K. (2016). Approaches of artificial intelligence in biomedical image processing: A leading tool between computer vision & biological vision. Proceedings - 2016 International Conference on Advances in Computing, Communication and Automation, ICACCA 2016. doi:10.1109/ICACCA.2016.7578900

Sin, K., & Muthu, L. (2015). Application of big data in education data mining and learning analytics-A literature review. ICTACT, 4.

Sivarajah, U., Kamal, M. M., Irani, Z., & Weerakkody, V. (2017). Critical analysis of Big Data challenges and analytical methods. *Journal of Business Research*, *70*, 263–286. doi:10.1016/j.jbusres.2016.08.001

Sridevi, S., & Sundaresan, M. (2013). Survey of image segmentation algorithms on ultrasound medical images. Proceedings of the 2013 International Conference on Pattern Recognition, Informatics and Mobile Engineering, PRIME 2013, 215–220. doi:10.1109/ICPRIME.2013.6496475

Syeda-Mahmood, T. (2018). Role of Big Data and Machine Learning in Diagnostic Decision Support in Radiology. *Journal of the American College of Radiology*, *15*(3), 569–576. doi:10.1016/j.jacr.2018.01.028 PubMed

Tangherlini, A., Merla, A., & Romani, G. L. (2006). Field-warp registration for biomedical high-resolution thermal infrared images. Annual International Conference of the IEEE Engineering in Medicine and Biology - Proceedings, 961–964. doi:10.1109/IEMBS.2006.260664

Taquet, J., & Labit, C. (2012). Hierarchical oriented predictions for resolution scalable lossless and near-lossless compression of CT and MRI biomedical images. *IEEE Transactions on Image Processing*, *21*(5), 2641–2652. doi:10.1109/TIP.2012.2186147 PubMed

Tchagna Kouanou, A., Tchiotsop, D., Kengne, R., Zephirin, D. T., Adele Armele, N. M., & Tchinda, R. (2018, January 1). An optimal big data workflow for biomedical image analysis. Informatics in Medicine Unlocked, 11, 68–74. doi:10.1016/j.imu.2018.05.001

US6829378B2 - Remote medical image analysis - Google Patents. (n.d.). Retrieved December 27, 2019, from https://patents.google.com/patent/US6829378B2/en

Yu, H., Gao, J., & Li, A. (2016). Probability-based non-local means filter for speckle noise suppression in optical coherence tomography images. *Optics Letters*, *41*(5), 994. doi:10.1364/OL.41.000994 PubMed

Zhang, J., Xia, Y., Xie, Y., Fulham, M., & Feng, D. D. (2018). Classification of Medical Images in the Biomedical Literature by Jointly Using Deep and Handcrafted Visual Features. *IEEE Journal of Biomedical and Health Informatics*, *22*(5), 1521–1530. doi:10.1109/JBHI.2017.2775662 PubMed

Zhang, Z., Xing, F., Liu, F., & Yang, L. (n.d.). High Throughput Automatic Muscle Image Segmentation Using Cloud Computing and Multi-core Programming. Academic Press.

KEY TERMS AND DEFINITIONS

Artificial Intelligence: It is the method of mimicking the human intelligence by the machines.

Automated Clinical Investigation: It is method of clinical investigations where automated machines and software are engaged for investigation purpose.

Big Data: Extremely large set of data which is used to extract some meaningful information.

Biomedical Image Analysis: Method to analyse biomedical images manually or automatically.

Computer-Aided Diagnostics: It is the system that assists a doctor in diagnosis by analyzing the medical data.

Data Analysis: Data analysis is the collection of data processing techniques to extract meaningful information, which is beneficial to support different decision-making tasks.

Data Interpretation: Making sensible information from the processed data.

Machine Learning: It is an application of the artificial intelligence in which machines can automatically learn and solve problems using the learned experience.

Chapter 7
Image Fusion Techniques for Different Multimodality Medical Images Based on Various Conventional and Hybrid Algorithms for Disease Analysis

Rajalingam B.
Priyadarshini College of Engineering and Technology, India

Priya R.
Annamalai University, India

Bhavani R.
Annamalai University, India

Santhoshkumar R.
Annamalai University, India

ABSTRACT

Image fusion is the process of combining two or more images to form a single fused image, which can provide more reliable and accurate information. Over the last few decades, medical imaging plays an important role in a large number of healthcare applications including diagnosis, treatment, etc. The different modalities of medical images contain complementary information of human organs and tissues, which help the physicians to diagnose the diseases. The multimodality medical images can

DOI: 10.4018/978-1-7998-2736-8.ch007

provide limited information. These multimodality medical images cannot provide comprehensive and accurate information. This chapter proposed and examines some of the hybrid multimodality medical image fusion methods and discusses the most essential advantages and disadvantages of these methods. The hybrid multimodal medical image fusion algorithms are used to improve the quality of fused multimodality medical image. An experimental result of proposed hybrid fusion techniques provides the fused multimodal medical images of highest quality, shortest processing time, and best visualization.

BACKGROUND AND MOTIVATION

Medical imaging, diagnostics, and treatment planning are in a transition phase. Modern medicine relies on information provided in the form of images. Transverse slices of the human body obtained from different modalities like Computed Tomography (CT), Magnetic Resonance Imaging (MRI), Positron Emission Tomography (PET), Single Photon Emission Computed Tomography (SPECT), etc are widely used for the evaluation of the patients' health status. Different imaging reveals different information about the same anatomy and hence provides complimentary information to the clinicians. Medical imaging technology has undergone tremendous improvement over the last decades. Many modalities are now able to provide three-dimensional and four-dimensional information (i.e.) 3D imaging over time. The ways the images are presented and interpreted are also being changed. Even though 3D- and 4D-visualization techniques are used for an increasing number of applications, the cross-sectional 2D slice images are still predominantly used in radiology.

For proper diagnosis, medical images need to provide two important and interrelated pieces of information to radiologists: exactly what is going on and precisely where in the body. Anatomic imaging technologies like MRI and CT clearly show the morphological features like size and shape, but no information on proliferation or inflammation are provided. Using CT image alone it is difficult to determine whether the suspicious mass is a malignant tumour or fibrosis. The functional imaging technologies like SPECT and PET use radio labeled glucose or monoclonal antibodies to give the necessary information on the cellular activity, but it they cannot provide the anatomical details needed for exact localization. From the functional information alone, it is difficult to locate exactly whether the metastatic hot spot is in the muscle or the nearby bone. Radiologists need both anatomic and functional data to make a definitive diagnosis. High-quality digital displays are emerging from radiology reading rooms into interventional settings and even into portable devices. Instead of looking at X-Ray films and side-by-side CT slice images on a back-lit panel in the operating room, surgeons can now visualise live interventional imaging. Gone are the days where the medical images provided by different modalities were considered as separate sources of information, integrated only in the minds of the physician. Accurate diagnosis and treatment planning is possible by integrating the medical images obtained using different imaging techniques. The recent advancement in the medical imaging technology and the development of image processing algorithms provide new means of visualisation. Merging of multiple imaging data of the same patient, acquired at different times and by different modalities, is termed as multimodal fusion. Bringing together anatomical and functional information with sensitivity and specificity gives the true value of multimodal fusion imaging. Merging together the images obtained from different modalities without any artefacts is the focus of this dissertation.

MEDICAL IMAGING MODALITIES

Medical imaging is the technique of creating visual representations of the interior of a body for clinical analysis and medical intervention. It seeks to reveal the internal structures hidden by the skin and bones, as well as to diagnose and treat disease. Medical images are acquired in various bands of the electromagnetic spectrum. The various modalities used in medical imaging are presented in this chapter. The basic principles of CT, MRI, PET and SPECT imaging are described. The background information of the various imaging systems, the physics behind it are presented.

1. Computed Tomography (CT)
    ◦   The drawback of the conventional X-ray is that it is not possible to differentiate soft tissue structures from radiographic images and also unable to resolve spatial structures along the direction of X-ray.
    ◦   The above mentioned drawbacks can be eliminated by using another imaging technology called as computed tomography.
    ◦   In CT a planar slice of the body is defined and x-rays are passed through the slice.
    ◦   The acquisition time is four minutes for a single section which is a time consuming process.
    ◦   But nowadays advanced CT scanners are used with minimum acquisition time of milliseconds.
    ◦   Also provides frozen images for moving organs like heart and lungs.
    ◦   Reconstruction of the image is done by a method called as back projection of each filtered projection into an array of detectors. Figure 1(a) shows the CT scan machine. Neurocyticercosis disease affected CT image is shown in Figure 1(b).

Figure 1. (a) Neurocyticercosis (b) CT – Scan Machine disease affected CT image (Courtesy: A Wizyweb creation)

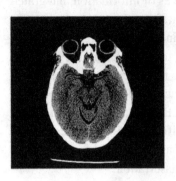 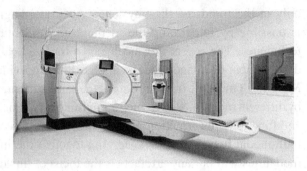

2. Magnetic Resonance Imaging (MRI)
   ◦ The fast development of medical imaging techniques allows the medical images for the applications of image guided surgery, surgical simulation, neuroscience studies and therapeutically developed usages.
   ◦ To overcome the difficulties in diagnose the clinical images, segmentation process of digital imaging is employed which provides increase in diagnostic efficiency.
   ◦ MRI is a well known non-invasive medical imaging technique based on the nuclear magnetic resonance phenomenon.
   ◦ Even if the qualitative image analysis is sufficient for the diagnosis of some diseases, quantitative analysis is also needed for many applications.
   ◦ Processing of MR image is a challenging problem due to its complexity and the absence of capturing the deformations in each structure of the anatomy.
   ◦ Conventional MRI relies on a difference in the weighted average of spectral and temporal information from tissue to tissue to make diagnosis.
   ◦ The intensity of MR image is of human tissue is homogeneous and the structure of each tissue is connected, but it is difficult to separate the adjacent tissue due to the small intensity changes and smoothed boundaries between tissues. Metastatic bronchogenic carcinoma disease affected MRI image is shown in Figure 2 (a) and MRI image scanner is illustrated in Figure 2(b).

Figure 2. (a) Metastatic bronchogenic (b) MRI - Scan Machine carcinoma affected MRI image (Courtesy: Independent Imaging)

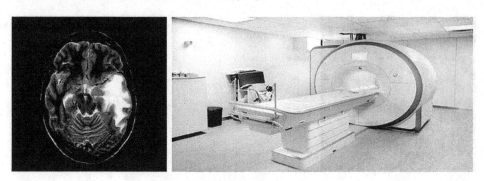

3.   Positron Emission Tomography (PET)

- ◦ PET is a nuclear medicine, functional imaging technique that produces a three-dimensional image of functional processes in the body.
- ◦ The model uses a set of gamma rays generated indirectly by a positron-emitting radionuclide (tracer), which is introduced into the body on a biologically active molecule.
- ◦ The 3-Dimension images produced from the scanner are reconstructed using computer aided process.
- ◦ In the advanced PET scanner machine, it is done by a CT X-ray scan provided in the same scanning device.
- ◦ A biological molecule which is same as glucose called as Fluoro Deoxy Glucose (FDG) is preferred for the indication of metabolic activity of the tissue in a tracer of the PET scanner.
- ◦ This tracer is used to explore the availability of cancer metastasis in the human body.
- ◦ Many other tracers are also used in PET scanners to evaluate the concentration of the tissue of other molecules. Figure 3 (a) shows the PET image scanner and the PET image acquired from the scanner is given in the Figure 3 (b).

Figure 3. (a) Astrocytoma disease (b) PET-Scan Machine affected PET Image (Courtesy: Scranton Gillette Communications)

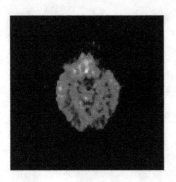 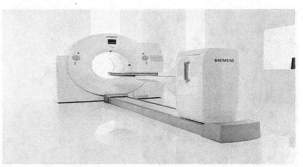

4. Single-Photon Emission Computed Tomography (SPECT or SPET)
   ○ SPECT is a special type of imaging technique which uses gamma rays.
   ○ It is similar to conventional nuclear medicine planar imaging using a gamma camera.
   ○ The specialty of SPECT is its ability to produce 3- dimensional images.
   ○ It produces cross-sectional slices of the tissue images, but it can be altered as per our requirements.
   ○ The SPECT scanning technique needs a supply of gamma-emitting radioisotope into the body of the patient, normally through the injection.
   ○ The radioisotope is a simple soluble dissolved ion, such as a radioisotope of gallium.
   ○ SPECT scan monitors the biological activity level at each place in the 3-D region to be analyzed.
   ○ The amount of blood flow can be indicated by the radionuclide in the capillaries of the imaged regions.
   ○ The SPECT image of a patient is captured by using a gamma camera tube from various angles.
   ○ A computer based process is applied, then convert the image into 3-dimensional image.
   ○ Then this data is manipulated into slices along any selected angle of the body, similar to those obtained with CT and MRI. Alzheimer's disease affected SPECT is shown in Figure 4 (a) and the SPECT scanning machine is shown in Figure 4 (b).

Figure 4. (a) Alzheimer's disease (b) SPECT – Scan Machine affected SPECT Image (Courtesy: Siemens Healthcare Private Limited)

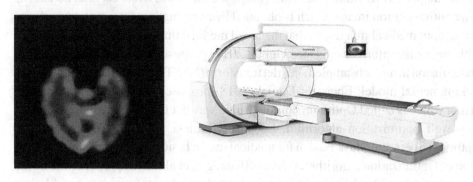

Figure 5. Categories of Multimodality Medical Images

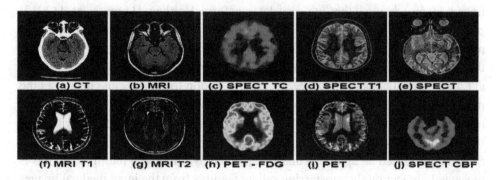

i.   *MRI T1* – T1-weighted
ii. *MRI T2* – T2-weighted
iii. *PET FDG* – Positron Emission Tomography with **Fluorine-18 Deoxyglucose**
iv. *SPECT T1* – Single Photon Emission Computed Tomography with **Thallium-201**
v.   *SPECT TC* – Single Photon Emission Computed Tomography with perfusion agent **Tc99m-HM-PAO**
vi. *SPECT CBF* – Single Photon Emission Computed Tomography with Cerebral Blood Flow; Perfusion

RELATED WORK FOR MEDICAL IMAGE FUSION

Alex pappachen James, et al (2014) provides a factual listing of methods and summarizes the broad scientific challenges faced in the field of medical image fusion. C. Karthikeyan, et al (2016) proposed the method for fusion of multimodality medical images using dual tree complex wavelet transform and self organizing feature map. C. T. Kavitha, et al (2015) proposed the fast discrete curvelet transform to a multiresolution image which is obtained by applying integer wavelet transform to the input medical images, so that the fused medical image will give all the details with clear edge information. Deep Gupta (2017) proposed the CT and MR medical image fusion in nonsubsampled shearlet transform (NSST) domain using the adaptive spiking neural model. Ebenezer Daniel (2018) proposed a homomorphic wavelet fusion which is called Optimum homomorphic wavelet fusion using hybrid genetic grey wolf optimization algorithm. Ebenezer Daniela, et al (2013) proposed an Optimum Spectrum Mask Fusion for medical image fusion using conventional Gray Wolves Optimization algorithm. Gaurav Bhatnagar, et al (2013) proposed the novel framework for medical image fusion based on framelet transform, it is considering the characteristics of human visual system. H.S. Bhadauria, et al (2018) proposed a noise reduction method for both CT and MRI medical images which fuses the images by processing it through curvelet transform. Haithem Hermessi, et al (2017) proposed a fusion method for CT and MR medical images based on convolutional neural network in the shearlet domain. Hamid Reza Shahdoosti, et al (2018) proposed the tetrolet transform for multimodal medical image fusion. Heba M. El-Hoseny, et al (2015) investigates some of medical image fusion techniques and discusses the most important advantages and disadvantages of these techniques to develop hybrid techniques that enhance the fused image quality. Jiao Du, et al (2015) describes and reviews the methods in the field of multimodal medical image fusion. Jiao Du, et al (2016) proposed an approach union Laplacian pyramid with multiple features is presented for accurately transferring salient features from the input medical images into a single fused image. Jing-jing Zonga, et al (2017) proposed a new fusion scheme for multimodal medical images based on sparse representation of classified image patches. Jingming Xi, et al (2018) proposed a multimodal medical image fusion algorithm combined with sparse representation and pulse coupling neural network for clinical treatment analysis. Jyoti Agarwal, et al (2015) proposed a hybrid multimodal medical fusion technique using curvelet and wavelet transform used in disease diagnosis. K.N. Narasimha Murthy, et al (2016) proposed the novel method for the medical image fusion Shearlet Transform is applied on multimodality medical image by using the Singular Value Decomposition to improve the information content of the medical images. Kai-jian Xia, et al (2018) proposed a novel fusion scheme for multi-modal medical images that utilizes both the features of the multi-scale transformation and deep convolutional neural network. Kavitha C.T, et al (2014) proposed new approach for medical image fusion based on the hybrid intelligence system. Lu Tang, et al (2017) proposed new multimodal medical image fusion method based on discrete Tchebichef moments and pulse coupled neural network to overcome the aforementioned problems. Meenu Manchanda, et al (2016) proposed a novel method of multimodal medical image fusion using fuzzy-transform. Niu Ling, et al (2016) proposed a novel fusion technique for medical images based on shearlet transform and compressive sensing model. Padma Ganasala, et al (2015) proposed a novel medical image fusion technique for utilizing feature motivated adaptive PCNN in NSST domain for fusion of anatomical multimodality medical images. Patil Hanmant Venkatrao (2018) presents a model, named holoentropywhale fusion (HWFusion), for the image fusion using multimodality medical images. P. Shanmugam Gomathi, et al(2016) proposed an image fusion technique for the fusion of multimodal medical images is proposed based on Non-Subsampled Contourlet Transform. Rajalingam, et al. (2017)a proposed an efficient multimodal therapeutic image fusion approach based on both traditional and hybrid fusion techniques are evaluated using several quality metrics. Rajalingam, et al. (2017)b Proposed a novel multimodal medicinal image fusion approach based on hybrid fusion techniques. Magnetic resonance imaging, positron emission tomography and single photon emission computed tomography are the input multimodal therapeutic brain images and the curvelet transform with neural network techniques are applied to fuse the multimodal medical image. Rajalingam, et al. (2018)a proposed a novel neuro-fuzzy hybrid multimodal medical image fusion technique to improve the quality of fused multimodality medical image. Rajalingam, et al. (2018)b proposed an efficient multimodal medical image fusion approach based on deep learning convolutional neural networks (CNN) for fusion process. Rajalingam, et al. (2018)c proposed work combines the guided image filtering and pulse coupled neural network for fusion process. Rajalingam, et al. (2018)d proposed an efficient hybrid multimodal medical image fusion approach based on combining the Transform technique with pulse coupled neural network fusion rule. The proposed work combines the discrete cosine harmonic wavelet transform (DCHWT) and pulse coupled neural network (PCNN) for fusion process. Rajalingam, et al. (2018)e Review the improvement of multimodality medical image fusion based on combined transform techniques, it is systematically reviewed in this paper. Rajalingam, et al. (2018)f proposed and examines some of the hybrid multimodality medical image fusion methods and discusses the most essential advantages and disadvantages of these methods to develop hybrid multimodal image fusion algorithms that improve the feature of merged multimodality therapeutic image. Rajalingam, et al. (2018)i proposed the hybrid multimodality medical image fusion methods and discusses the most essential advantages and disadvantages of these methods. It has been exposed that the best multimodality medical image fusion technique implemented was the (AWT-NSST) hybrid algorithm Rajalingam, et al. (2018)j proposed research work presents the feature based fusion algorithms in transforms domain to combine the relevant and complementary spectral features of two modalities Rajalingam, et al. (2019)a proposed the method for multimodal medical image fusion using the hybrid (NSST-

DFRWT) fusion algorithm. Rajalingam, et al. (2019)b proposed method combination of discrete fractional wavelet transform (DFRWT) with dual tree complex wavelet transform (DTCWT) based hybrid fusion technique for multimodality medical images. Rajalingam, et al. (2019)c proposed the combination of NSCT with DTCWT hybrid fusion algorithm. The hybrid fusion algorithm is verified through a simulation experiment on different multimodality images. Rajalingam, et al. (2019)d a novel method has been proposed for multimodal medical image fusion using combination of Non-subsampled contourlet transform (NSCT) with Non-subsampled shearlet transform (NSST) hybrid fusion algorithm. Qamar Nawaz, et al (2016) proposed a novel Quaternion Discrete Fourier Transform algorithm for the fusion of multimodal color medical images. Richa Srivastava, et al (2016) proposed a multimodal medical image fusion technique based on curvelet transform. S. Chavan, et al (2017) proposed a novel approach to nonsubsampled rotated complex wavelet transform based multimodality medical image fusion used for the analysis of the lesions for the diagnostic purpose and post treatment review of neurocysticercosis S. Chavan, et al (2017) proposed the feature based multimodality medical image fusion is based on Rotated Wavelet Transform technique is used for better visualization of lesions and calcification. Sharma Dileepkumar Ramlal, et al (2018) proposed a novel medical fusion algorithm for non-subsampled shearlet transform which is based on simplified model of pulse coupled neural network. Shuaiqi Liu, et al (2015) proposed the combined the complex shearlet with the feature of guided filtering for a medical image fusion. Shutao Li, et al (2013) proposed method is based on a novel guided filtering-based weighted average technique is to make full use of spatial consistency for fusion of the base and detail layers. Shutao Li, et al (2016) provides a comprehensive survey of the state of the art pixel-level image fusion methods. Sneha Singh, et al (2015) proposed a new fusion algorithm for the CT and MR medical images that utilizes both the features of the non-subsampled shearlet transform and spiking neural network. Sreeja, et.al (2018) proposed to fuse together, texture enhanced and edge enhanced images of the input image in order to obtain significant enhancement in the output image. The algorithm is tested in low contrast medical images. Udhaya Suriya, et al (2016) proposed an innovative image fusion technique for the detection of brain tumors. Fusing images obtained from MRI and PET can accurately access the tumor response. Vikrant Bhateja, et al (2015) proposed the two level multimodal fusion frameworks using the cascaded combination of stationary wavelet transform and non sub-sampled Contourlet transform domains for images acquired using two distinct medical imaging sensor modalities. Wenda Zhao, et al (2017) proposed an effective variation model for multimodality medical image fusion and denoising based on Sequential Filter and Adaptive Fractional Order Total Variation. Xiaojun Xua (2016) proposed a multimodal medical image fusion based on discrete fractional wavelet transform. Xiao-Qing Luo, et al (2016) proposed the novel method for contextual information based multimodality medical image fusion using contourlet domain. Xin Jin, et al(2018) proposed a novel two-level multimodal medical image fusion scheme, which is based on non-subsampled shearlet transform and simplified pulse coupled neural networks is used in the hue-saturation-value color space. Xingbin Liu, et al (2018) proposed a novel multimodality medical image fusion algorithm which involves gradient minimization smoothing filter and pulse coupled neural network. Xingbin Liu, et al (2018) proposed the full advantages of structure tensor and nonsubsampled shearlet transform to effectively extract geometric features a novel unified optimization model is used for fusing the multimodality medical images. Xingbin Liu, et al (2017) proposed a novel multi-modality medical image fusion algorithm exploiting a moving frame based decomposition framework and the nonsubsampled shearlet transform. Xinzheng Xu, et al (2016) proposed a method to fuse multimodal medical images using the adaptive pulse-coupled neural networks, which was optimized by the quantum-behaved particle swarm optimization algorithm. Yong Yang, et al (2018) proposed a novel multimodal medical image fusion method based on structural patch decomposition and fuzzy logic technology. Zhaodong Liu, et al(2014) proposed an efficient multimodal medical image fusion approach based on compressive sensing is presented to fuse CT and MRI multimodal medical images.

Figure 6. General block diagram of medical image fusion system

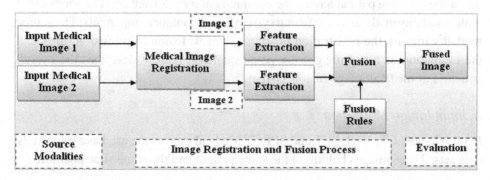

DATASET DESCRIPTIONS

The sample study sets used in the experimentation are obtained from online databases. Website: http://www.med.harvard.edu (Whole Brain Atlas Harvard Medical School), Website: https://radiopaedia.org (Radipaedio). In this research work used some of the disease affected multimodal medical images taken for the experimental work. The experimented diseases are follows.

i. Neurocyticercosis
ii. Neoplastic Disease
   ◦ Astrocytoma
   ◦ Anaplastic Astrocytoma
   ◦ Metastatic Brochogenic Carcinoma
iii. Degenerative disease
   ◦ Alzhimer's Disease
   ◦ Mild Alzheimer's disease

Proposed Research Work

This chapter experiment the some of the conventional and hybrid fusion algorithms for different types of input medical images. Existing methods require the potential to get superior quality images. To enhance the visual quality of the output the proposed algorithm is used to combine the two domain algorithms. Before fusion process the two level conversions on source images are applied. These outcomes give best quality, superior handling of curved shapes and improved characterization of input images.

1. Generalized Medical Image Fusion Scheme

The generalized diagram of medical image fusion consists of different input image modalities of same patient having the complementary information. The generalized multi-modality medical image fusion system has four major components: The source modality images, the registration of source images, fusion using fusion rules, and the evaluation of fused images for visual quality. Figure 8 describes the overall structure of medical image fusion system.

a. Input Image Modalities

In this chapter, CT, MRI, PET and SPECT Medical images are used as a pilot study data sets. These images belong to the same patient and the same slice positions.

b. Medical Image Registration

Second stage of the fusion process registration of source modality images and aligns them such that anatomical structures coincide with each other. It is a very crucial step in image fusion because the effectiveness of fusion process completely depends on the proper image registration. It involves voxel alignment of one modality image with another. The source images are co-registered using registration algorithm. The medical image registration is a trivial problem due to non-similarity of the representations in the input modalities. The acquisition process and devices are different, so the source images vary in orientation, structural presentations, and spatial resolution. In this method, input mages are observed by overlapping on each other in all three views (sagittal, axial and coronal) and simple geometric transformation techniques which include scaling, rotation, panning, shifting, etc. are applied to bring them into voxel alignment. This image registration process helps to achieve perfect fusion of anatomical structures from both Input modalities

c. Fusion Process

The features are selected in the spectral domain. Source modality images are decomposed into the spectral domain using one of the selected transforms. Anatomical structures in both the modalities may be differently localized or orientated. The physics behind the acquisition of both input modalities are different which result in variations of spatial resolution and size. But, these images carry rich and complementary information which needs to be combined. These fused images present better visual quality compared to input modalities, and hence, the radiologist can interpret them with ease. The fused images also provide better visualization of abnormalities compared to source images. Proposed algorithm features are combined using appropriate fusion rules which are designed considering human visual system.

d. Evaluation

The proposed fusion techniques are tested on various sample study sets. The details of study sets, the processing system, and evaluation of algorithms are in this research work. The performance and effectiveness of the proposed algorithms are evaluated based on the visual quality of the fused images. The fused images are evaluated using subjective (qualitative) evaluation with the help of expert radiologists and by estimating fusion metrics as objective (quantitative) evaluation. The criteria for subjective evaluation and various fusion parameters used to estimate objective evaluation are also defined in this work. Multimodality medical image fusion algorithms are evaluated using quantitative evaluation method which is a challenging task due to unavailability of ground truth. The values of the parameters vary as the study set changes. Large number of metrics provides different assessment of algorithms. However, the selection of fusion metrics is the choice of fusion application. The visual quality is tested using such fusion metrics. Some of the fusion metrics/parameters used in this research work is presented below. These parameters are very useful in validation of quality of fused images objectively.

i. Fusion Factor (FusFac)

The similarity of fused image with source images can be measured using Fusion Factor (FusFac). It gives estimation of the content being imparted to the fused image by source images. It is calculated based on mutual information estimation using equation (1). Here, $MI_{A,B}$ means the mutual information between image A and image B which is calculated with the help of equation (2). Here, p(.) is probability distribution function. Greater value of *FusFac* means the better quality of the fused image.

$$MI_{A,B} = \sum_{i,j} p_{A,B}(i,j) \log \frac{p_{A,B}(i,j)}{p_A(i)_B(j)} \tag{1}$$

$$FusFac = MI_{input1,Fus} + MI_{input2,Fus} \tag{2}$$

ii. Fusion Symmetry (FusSym)

Another similarity measure is fusion symmetry (FusSym) which indicates the closeness of fused image with respect to source images. It is estimated using mutual information between source images and fused image. It is computed using equation (3). The fused image is visually better, if the value of FusSym is smaller.

$$FusSym = abs(\frac{MI_{Input1,Fus}}{MI_{Input1,Fus} + MI_{Input2,Fus}} - 0.5) \tag{3}$$

iii. Image Quality Index (IQI)

Wang et al. presented image quality index (IQI) which is measure of similarities between source images and fused image. It is computed using equation (4). Here, μ and σ stands for mean and standard deviation, respectively. The value of IQI should be close to one for representing better quality of fused image.

$$IQI(A,B) = \frac{2\sigma_{A,B}.2\mu_A\mu_B}{(\sigma_A^2 + \sigma_B^2)(\mu_A^2 + \mu_B^2)} \tag{4}$$

iv. Edge Quality Measure ($EQ_{a,b}^f$)

The edges are important in medical image analysis. The proposed system is using edge related feature to generate fused image. The fusion metric 'Edge Quality Measure ($EQ_{a,b}^f$) is an estimate of preserving edges in the fused image. The edge quality measure is calculated using equation (5). Here, EI (edge index) and Sxy (window) are estimated using equations (6) and (7), respectively. The fused image f is reconstructed from two source images a and b. The value zero of $EQ_{a,b}^f$ represents the loss of edge information, whereas one indicates that edge information is preserved in the fused image.

$$EQ_{a,b}^f = \frac{EI}{S_{xy}}$$ (5)

$$EI = \sum_{x=0}^{N-1}\sum_{y=0}^{M-1} EQ_{a,f}(x,y)w_a + EQ_{b,f}(x,y)w_b$$ (6)

$$S_{xy} = \sum_{i=0}^{N-1}\sum_{j=0}^{M-1} w_a(i,j) + w_b(i,j)$$ (7)

v. mean Structural Similarity Index Measure (mSSIM)

The parameter 'mean structural similarity index measure (mSSIM)' indicates structural similarities between the fused image and source images. The mSSIM is computed using equation (8) and equation (9). Here, μ_m is mean intensity and σ_m is standard deviation. The iterative parameters, C1 = 6:50 and C2 = 58:52, are constants. The similarities are retained in the fused images, if mSSIM approaches to value one.

$$SSIM(i,j) = \frac{(2\mu_i\mu_j + C_1)(2\sigma_i\sigma_j + C_2)}{(\mu_i^2 + \mu_j^2 + C_1)(\sigma_i^2 + \sigma_j^2) + C_2)}$$ (8)

$$mSSIM(i,j) = \frac{1}{M}\sum_{k=1}^{M} SSIM(i_k, j_k)$$ (9)

vi. Cross Entropy (CEn)

The cross entropy is a measure of dis-similarity between the source images and the fused image. The relative quality of the fused image with respect to source images is estimated using the parameter called cross entropy (CEn) which is estimated using equation (10). Here, A and B are two source images, p(.) is probability distribution function, and N is highest gray value in an image. The fused image is of better quality, if CEn has lower value.

$$CEn(A,B) = \sum_{i=0}^{N-1} P_A(i) \log_2 \frac{P_A(i)}{P_B(i)} \tag{10}$$

vii. Correlation Coefficient (Rcorr)

The correlation coefficient (*Rcorr*) represents the closeness of fused image with source modalities. It is computed using equation (11). Here, f_s is source image and f_{fus} is fused image. The fused image and source images will be similar, if *Rcorr* is close to value `one'.

$$Rcor(i,j) = \frac{2\sum_{i=0}^{M-1}\sum_{j=0}^{N-1} f_s(i,j).f_{fus}(i,j)}{\sum_{i=0}^{M-1}\sum_{j=0}^{N-1}|f_s(i,j)|^2 + \sum_{i=0}^{M-1}\sum_{j=0}^{N-1}|f_{fus}(i,j)|^2} \tag{11}$$

2. Traditional Multimodal Medical Image Fusion Techniques

This paper implements different traditional image fusion algorithms for different types of multimodality medical images as shown in Figure 7.

a. Principal Component Analysis Method

The PCA is a mathematical tool which transforms several correlated variables into several interrelated variables. It generates a new set of axes which are orthogonal. The first principal component is taken along the direction of maximum variance. The second principal component is taken in the subspace perpendicular to the first principal component. This method is suitable for multi-spectral images like panchromatic images.

174

Figure 7. Traditional image fusion techniques

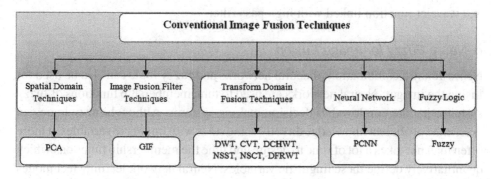

b. Transform Based Image Fusion Techniques

Wavelet transform process is a multi-resolution analysis that gives the image variation at various wavelet scales. A wavelet is an attenuated and oscillating function with integration as zero. In image processing always get the discrete signal that is mostly obtained by the pixel intensity values. So to process discrete pixel intensity value of an image, DWT is preferred a wavelet transform wavelet transform in which the wavelets or the input function is discretely sampled. Com-pared to other wavelet transformation, the advantage of DWT over Fourier transform or any other transform is that of temporal resolution. Other transforms only capture the location details, but DWT captures the information of frequency and location. The estimation of the wavelet transform of an image comprises recursive filtering and sub-sampling. The decomposition of the image gives three detail high-level sub-images. These detail high-level images are denoted as LH (presence of horizontal data in high frequency), HL (presence of vertical data in high frequency) and HH (presence of diagonal data in high frequency). The wavelet transform also yields single approximation image represented as LL that is low-level sub-image, which is sensitive to human eyes. In

Figure 8. Three Level of DWT decomposition of a signal

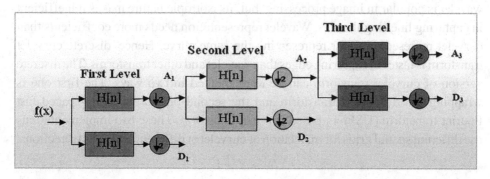

DWT implementation scaling function is related to smooth filters or low pass filters and wavelet function linked with high pass filter.

c. Neuro Fuzzy for Image Fusion

Neuro-fuzzy a combination of neural networks and fuzzy logic can also be used for fusing the images. Neural networks are used to tune membership functions of fuzzy systems that are employed as decision making systems. Although fuzzy logic can determine proficient knowledge directly using rules with linguistic variables, it more often than not takes a lot of time to design and tune the membership functions which quantitatively define these linguistic variables. Neural network learning techniques can computerize this process and significantly reduce progress time and cost while recovering performance. To prevail over the problem of facts acquisition, neural networks are extended to automatically extract fuzzy rules from numerical data.

d. Curvelet Transform Techniques

In the current research topic ridgelet transform is one of the new powerful transform techniques. Ridgelet transform is anisotropic in nature and can efficiently capture the global straight line singularities. However, in real medical images, global straight line is not so common. To handle this situation, the whole multimodal medical image is partitioned into small sub multimodality medical images. This partitioning is done in a manner so that the curves and edge lines appear just as a straight line. Ridgelet transform is then applied on each sub medical image. This block-based ridgelet transform is the basic concept of first generation curvelet transform. The theoretical idea of first generation curvelet is easy to understand, but, its implementation in discrete domain is difficult. Also, it is not quite popular because of its dependency on ridgelet transform whose geometry is very unclear. Discrete version of curvelet transform, which is based on frequency partition. This version of curvelet transform is efficient for representing curves and edges. Unlike wavelet transform, curvelet transform is localised in scale, position and orientation. Due to these properties, curvelet transform can give efficient results for medical image fusion. The traditional wavelet is popular in image processing, but, its isotropic nature makes it inefficient in capturing line singularities. Wavelet representation needs more coefficients than curvelet representation for representing the same curve. Hence, discrete curvelet transform is faster in capturing edges than wavelet and other transforms. The discrete version of curvelet transform can be implemented in two ways. The first one is wrapping-based curvelet transform and the second one is unequally-spaced fast Fourier transform (USFFT)-based curvelet transform. These two implementations use different spatial grids for translation of curvelet at different scales and directions.

e. Non-Subsampled Contourlet Transform (NSCT)

The NSCT is based on the theory of Contourlet Transform (CT) which achieves better results in image processing in geometric transformations. The contourlet transform is a shift variant because it contains both down-samplers and up-samplers in the Laplacian Pyramid (LP) and Directional Filter Bank (DFB) stages. NSCT is a shift invariant, multi-scale and multi-directional transform which has a very vibrant implementation. It is obtained by using the Non-subsampled Pyramid Filter Bank (NSP or NSPFB) and the Non-subsampled Directional Filter Bank (NSDFB).

f. Non subsampled shearlet transform (NSST)

The NSST is a newly established multi-scale geometric analysis tool, which is superior at capturing multidimensional geometry and is optimally well-organized in medical images representation. In the implementation procedure of NSST, nonsubsampled Laplacian pyramid is adopted to realize multi-scale factorization and shearing filters are used to complete multi-orientation factorization. As a result, the NSST has not only shift invariance property but also a more flexible directional selectivity than other geometric analysis tools. The original multimodal medical image can be decomposed into a low-frequency sub-image and several high-frequency sub-images.

g. Discrete Fractional Wavelet Transforms (DFRWT)

The DWT can provide better spatial and spectral localization of image information; it has no shift invariant property because of the down-sampling operation. Thus, the fused image of the DWT method cannot efficiently preserve the salient features of the input images and produce pseudo-Gibbs effect. A step is added to the DFRWT multimodal medical image fusion method. The input multimodality medical images are first decomposed into low-frequency subbands and a sequence of high-frequency subbands in different scales and orientations and in different p orders. Then, at each position in the transformed sub-bands, the coefficients of both the low-and high-frequency bands are performed with a certain fusion rule. Finally, the fused image is obtained by applying inverse DFRWT transform on the fused sub-bands. From analysis of the previous steps, the decomposition coefficients are a variety of different p orders; the fusion effects are different. This characteristic adds additional flexibility for the DFRWT fusion method and enhances the selection space for the fusion results. In the wavelet medical image fusion method, because of different decomposition coefficients feature in the low-and high-frequency bands, the LF- and HF-subbands are fused using the different combinations of fusion rules. However, in low p order, the decomposition a coefficient of the DFRWT in each subband has the same histogram distribution and shows the same non-sparse characteristics; hence, the authors use identical fusion rule in the LF- and HF-subbands.

h. Image Fusion with Guided Filtering

Currently, in medical image processing energetic research topic is edge preserving filter technique. Image processing has several edge preserving smoothing filtering techniques such as guided filter, weighted least squares and bilateral filter. Among the several filter techniques the guided image filter is giving better results and less execution time for fusion process. This image fusion filter method is based on a local linear form, creating it eligible for other image processing methods such as image matting, up-sampling and colorization. A multi-level representation is utilized by average smoothing filter. Subsequently, based on weighted average fusion technique, the guided image filter fuses the bottom and feature layers of multi-modal medical images.

3. Hybrid Multimodal Medical Image Fusion Techniques

Traditional medical image fusion techniques lack the ability to get high-quality images. So, there is a bad need to use hybrid fusion techniques to achieve this objective. The basic idea of the hybrid technique is to combine the guided image filter fusion technique with neural network fusion techniques to improve the performance and increase fused image quality. Another possibility is applying two stage transformations on input images before fusion process. These transformations provide better characterization of input images, better handling of curved shapes and higher quality for fused details. The overall advantages of the hybrid techniques are improving the visual quality of the images, and decreasing image artifacts and noise. Figure 9a, 9b shows dataset 1 of original MRI and PET images. Each image size is 256*256, 356*356 and 512*512 dimensions. Figure 8 to 17 illustrates the schematic diagram of the proposed hybrid multimodal medical image fusion techniques.

a. Proposed Hybrid Multimodal Image Fusion Algorithm (NSST-PCA)

Step 1: Take the two input multimodal medical images.

Step 2: Resize both images into 512 x 512 dimensions.

Step 3: Decompose the each input multimodal medical image using shearlet transform.

Step 4: Compute the low and high frequency of Shearlet transform.

Step 5: Fuse the selected low and high frequency of the subband coefficients.

Step 6: Apply the PCA fusion rule

Step 7: Finally take the Inverse shearlet transform (IST) to reconstruct the multimodal medical image.

Step 8: Perform the image reconstruction and get the final fused multimodal medical image.

Figure 9. Overall structure of proposed hybrid fusion Algorithm (NSST-PCA)

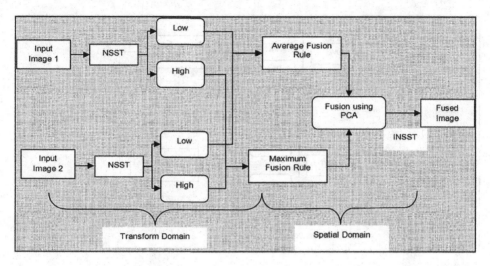

b. Proposed Hybrid Multimodal Image Fusion Algorithm (DWT-DCHWT)

Step 1: Obtain the wavelet coefficients of the two source multimodal medical images.

Step 2: Alter the wavelet coefficient matrices into column vectors.

Step 3: Compute the covariance matrix using these vectors such that each matrix has first column vector obtained through first image and second column vector obtained through second image will give us four sets of covariance matrices.

Step 4: Form the eigen values K and eigen vectors E of the covariance matrices.

Step 5: Divide the first 2D image into rows and link them together in a chain form to have a 1D row vector R.

Step 6: Divide the second 2D image into columns and link them together in a chain form to have a 1D column vector C.

Step 7: Do this for both approximate and detail coefficients of both the images.

Step 8: Apply inverse DWT and DCHWT on both source images separately and then apply averaging operation on the vectors. .

Step 9: Fused output multimodal medical image is displayed.

Figure 10. Overall structure of proposed hybrid fusion Algorithm (DWT-DCHWT)

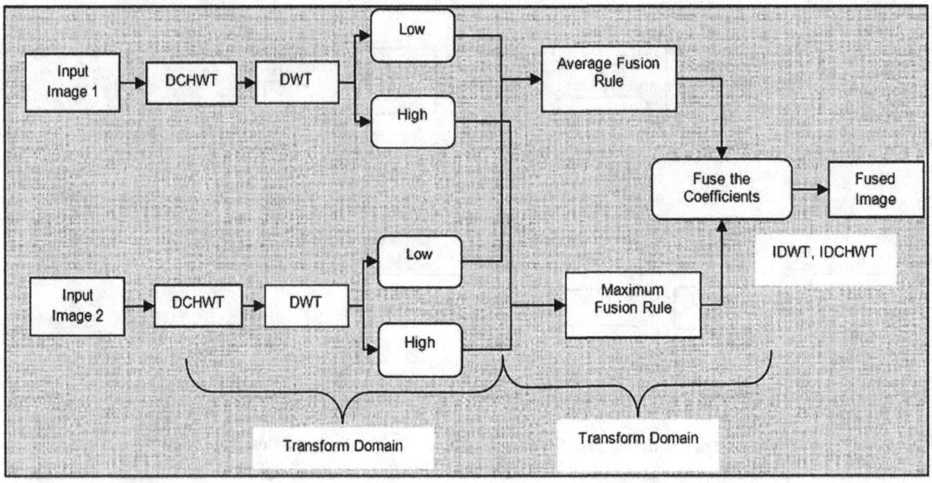

c. Proposed Hybrid Multimodal Image Fusion Algorithm (NSCT- CVT)

Step 1: Take the two input multimodal medical images.

Step 2: Resize both images into 512 x 512 dimensions.

Step 3: NSCT is applied on the both input images to obtain lowpass subband coefficients and high pass directional subband coefficients at each scale and each direction. NSPFB and NSDFB are used to complete multiscale decomposition and multi-direction decomposition.

Step 4: The transformed coefficients are performed with fusion rules to select NSCT coefficients of the fused image.

Step 5: Then, apply cuevelet transform maximum selection, minimum selection and simple average fusion rules.

Step 6: The fused image is constructed by performing an inverse NSCT to the selected coefficients

Step 7: Now apply the inverse curvelet transform (ICVT) to reconstruct the multimodal medical image.

Step 8: Fused final output multimodal medical image is displayed.

Figure 11. Overall structure of proposed hybrid fusion Algorithm (NSCT-CVT)

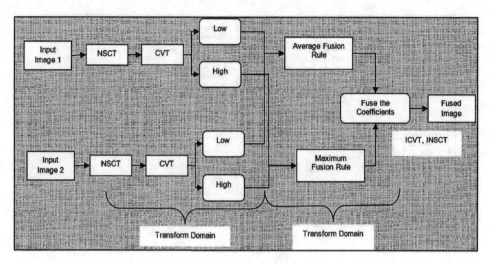

d. Proposed Hybrid Multimodal Image Fusion Algorithm (DTCWT – NSST)

Step 1: Get the two input images.

Step 2: Input images resized into 256 x 256.

Step3: Multimodal Medical Images are decomposed by dual tree complex wavelet transform into complex coefficient sets. For both the coefficient sets, thresholds are calculated for each decomposition level.

Step 4: Absolute difference of all wavelet coefficients from their corresponding threshold are calculated.

Step 5: Source images are decomposed based on NSST fusion rule

Step 6: Calculating low pass and high pass subband coefficients using NSST

Step7: Absolute differences of corresponding coefficients of both the input medical images are compared and the coefficient having larger value of absolute difference from the threshold is selected, to form coefficient set of the fused image.

Figure 12. Overall structure of proposed hybrid fusion Algorithm (DTCWT-NSST)

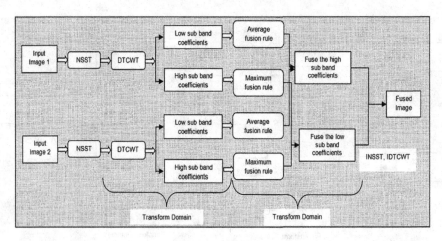

e. Proposed Hybrid Multimodal Image Fusion Algorithm (NSST-NSCT)

Step 1: Get the two input images.

Step 2: Input images resize into 256 x 256.

Step 3: Compute the high pass and low pass subband coefficients of the NSCT spectral domain.

Step 4: Merge the low pass and high pass sub band frequency coefficients.

Step 5: Apply the NSST fusion rule in the subbands coefficients.

Step 6: Each input images are decomposed by contourlet transform.

Step 7: Apply the inverse NSCT and inverse NSST to get the final output image.

Figure 13. Overall structure of proposed hybrid fusion Algorithm (NSST-NSCT)

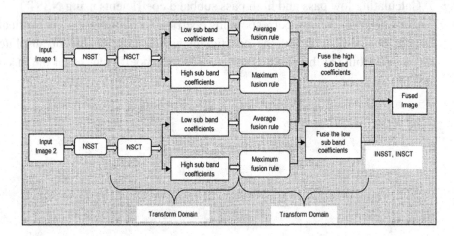

f. Proposed Hybrid Multimodal Image Fusion Algorithm (DFRWT-DTCWT)

Step 1: Get the two input images.

Step 2: Input images resized into 256 x 256.

Step 3: Obtain highpass directional subband coefficients and lowpass sub and coefficients of input images at each scale and each direction by DFRWT.

Step 4: Multimodal Medical Images are decomposed by dual tree complex wavelet transform into complex coefficient sets. For both the coefficient sets, thresholds are calculated for each decomposition level.

Step 5: Absolute difference of all wavelet coefficients from their corresponding threshold is calculated.

Step 6: Absolute differences of corresponding coefficients of both the input medical image are compared and the coefficient having larger value of absolute difference from the threshold is selected, to form coefficient set of the output image.

Step 7: Finally, inverse DFRWT and inverse DTCWT is applied on the fused coefficient set to obtain the final outcome.

Figure 14. Overall structure of proposed hybrid fusion Algorithm (DFRWT-DTCWT)

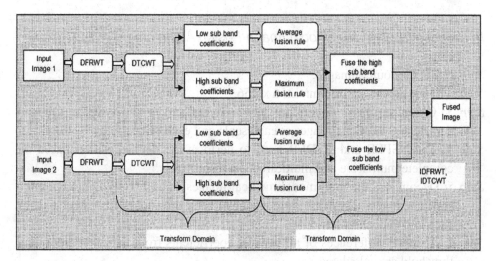

g. Proposed Hybrid Multimodal Image Fusion Algorithm (NSCT-DFRWT)

Step 1: Get the two input images.

Step 2: Input images are resized into 256 x 256.

Step 3: Compute the subaband coefficients of the NSCT and fuse the coefficients.

Step 4: Apply the fusion rule based on DFRWT spectral domain algorithm

Step 5: Each input images are decomposed by contourlet transform.

Step 6: Finally, apply the inverse NSCT and inverse DFRWT to get the output image.

Figure 15. Overall structure of proposed hybrid fusion Algorithm (NSCT-DFRWT)

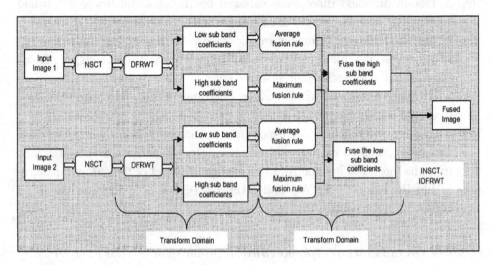

h. Proposed Hybrid Multimodal Image Fusion Algorithm (NSCT-DTCWT)

Step 1: Get the source images.

Step 2: Input images resized into 256 x 256.

Step 3: Obtain highpass directional subband coefficients and lowpass subband coefficients of Input images at each scale and each direction by NSCT.

Step 4: The NSPFB and NSDFB used to perform the decomposition based on complete multiscale and multidirection respectively.

Step 5: Decompose the multimodal medical images using DTCWT into complex coefficient sets. For both the coefficient sets, thresholds are calculated for each decomposition level.

Step 6: Absolute differences of all wavelet coefficients from their corresponding threshold are calculated.

Step 7: Absolute differences of corresponding coefficients of both the source modalites are compared and the coefficient having larger value of absolute difference from the threshold is selected, to form coefficient set of the fused image.

Step 8: Finally, IDTCWT and INSCT are applying on the combined coefficient set to obtain the final output image.

Figure 16. Overall structure of proposed hybrid fusion Algorithm (NSCT-DTCWT)

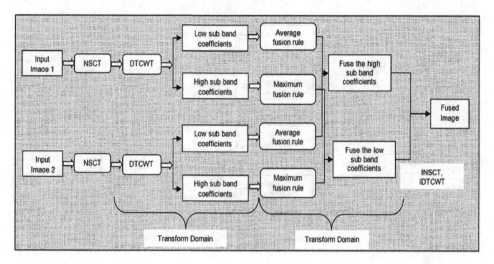

i. Proposed Hybrid Multimodal Medical Image Fusion Algorithm (NSST-DFRWT)

Step 1: Take the two input multimodal medical images.

Step 2: Resize both images into 256 x 256 dimensions.

Step 3: Compute the low and high frequency of Shearlet transform coefficients.

Step 4: Fuse the selected low and high frequency of the subband coefficients.

Step 5: Apply the discrete fractional wavelet transform maximum and minimum fusion rule in the lowpass and highpass subbands coefficients

Step 6: Decompose the each input multimodal medical image using shearlet transform.

Step 7: Finally take the Inverse shearlet transform (IST) to reconstruct the multimodal medical image.

Step 8: Then, apply the inverse DFRWT to reconstruct the fused image.

Step 9: Perform the image reconstruction and get the final fused multimodal medical image

EXPERIMENTAL RESULTS AND DISCUSSIONS

The implementations are based on two stages. Firstly, the conventional fusion algorithms are applied to datasets of CT/MRI, MRI/PET and MRI/SPECT images and evaluated using all metrics mentioned in the previous section. The implementation is executed in MATLAB R2015b on windows 10 laptop with Intel Core I5 Processor,

Figure 17. Overall structure of proposed hybrid fusion Algorithm (NSST-DFRWT)

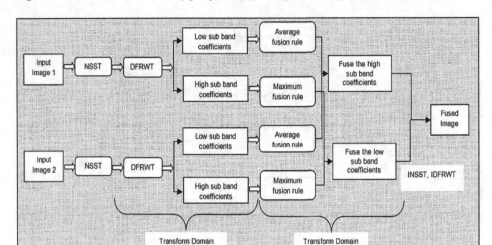

4.0 GB RAM and 500 GB Hard Disk. Table 1 shows the experimental results of the different traditional medical image fusion algorithms on set 1. The proposed hybrid fusion algorithms (PCA – NSST, DCHW – DWT, NSC – CVT, NSS – DFRWT, NSCT – DFRWT, DTCWT – NSST, NSST – NSCT, DFRWT – DTCWT and NSCT – DTCWT) compared with existing conventional algorithms (PCA, DWT, GIF, CVT, DTCWT, NSCT and NSST). The proposed hybrid algorithms are evaluated based on qualitative and quantitative performance parameter analysis. The visual quality of the fused image is estimated based on performance evaluation metrics.

Figure 18. Experimental results for Hybrid Algorithm (NSCT-DFRWT)

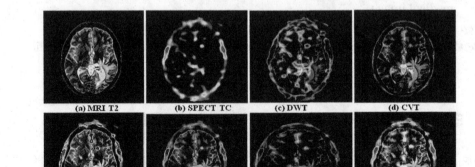

Figure 19. Experimental results for Hybrid Algorithm (NSST-DTCWT)

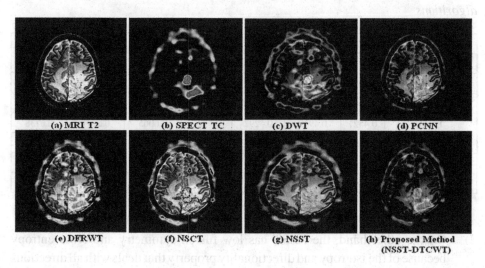

Figure 20. Experimental results for Hybrid Algorithm (DFRWT-DTCWT)

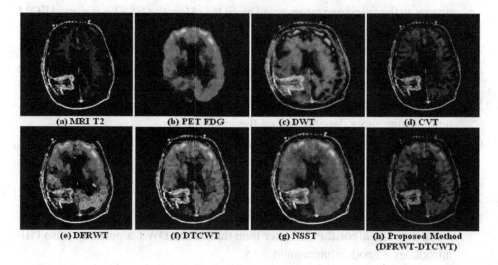

From the previous table, it is clear that:

1) The NSST fusion algorithm introduces the highest fusion factor, image quality index, edge quality measure and correlation coefficients values because of the isotropy and directionality property that enhances the representation of curves and edges leading to fused images with much details and much more clearness. Also, NSCT fusion has fusion factor, image quality index, edge quality measure and correlation coefficients values than the other algorithms.

187

Table 1. Performance Metrics obtained for different traditional medical image fusion algorithms

Metrics	PCA	DWT	GIF	CVT	DTCWT	NSCT	NSST
Fus Fac	1.5201	1.8513	2.4322	1.3769	3.2723	2.5658	3.3452
Fus Sym	1.8053	1.5602	1.2845	1.4049	1.1988	1.0342	1.1075
IQI	0.4061	0.49281	0.5745	0.5835	0.6154	0.6574	0.6937
EQM	0.4521	0.4919	0.5292	0.5721	0.6065	0.6191	0.6738
mSSIM	0.4391	0.4917	0.7667	0.7487	0.7376	0.7936	0.7639
CE_n	2.7102	2.3127	2.3389	2.5698	1.7246	1.5389	1.5821
R_{Corr}	0.4691	0.5042	0.5736	0.5556	0.6158	0.6487	0.6836

2) On the other hand, the NSST has low fusion symmetry and cross entropy because of the isotropy and directionality property that deals with all directions collectively leading to loss of clarity.

3) The CVT and DWT achieve the best edge information transferred from source images to the fused one represented by EQM. Also, the NSST has a good EQM value.

4) In the fusion process, a new image of new properties is produced. So, perfect similarities between the input images and the fused one are not preferred. The NSST and NSCT present lower similarities with input images.

5) The GIF and DTCWT have the highest fusion factor with input images representing more dependency on the input images.

6) The GIF achieves the highest mSSIM between the input and the fused images. The NSST and NSCT have the highest correlation between the input and fused images represented in the universal image quality index.

7) All algorithms introduce good entropy results.

8) Visual inspection ensures that the overall enhancement in the fused images using curvelet algorithm is better than that of the DWT algorithm. Also GIF introduces a good enhancement.

In summary:

❖ The NSST has a superior performance followed by the NSCT except for Fus sym and cross entropy that reduces purity of view in the case of the NSST algorithm.

❖ NSCT fusion has a better performance than the other algorithms except for the processing time that is very long.

❖ NSCT has a good performance with fusion factor, entropy, and image quality index.

❖ PCA and DWT have the worst performance compared to the other algorithms.

❖ Increasing the number of pixels of the input images increases the processing time, dataset 1. On the other hand, lower size images decrease the time, dataset 1.

❖ We could make use of hybrid transforms that combine advantages of all algorithms.

Figure 21. Performance comparative analysis for Traditional algorithms

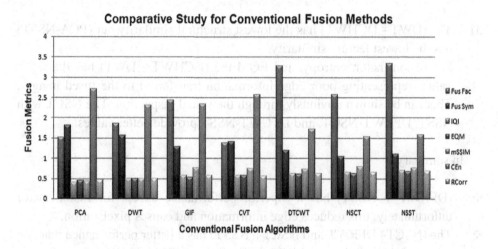

Comparative Study for Conventional Fusion Methods

Secondly, the hybrid fusion algorithms are applied to datasets of CT, MRI, PET and SPECT images and evaluated. Nine combination techniques are implemented in this section: (PCA – NSST, DCHW – DWT, NSC – CVT, NSS – DFRWT, NSCT – DFRWT, DTCWT – NSST, NSST – NSCT, DFRWT – DTCWT and NSCT – DTCWT). These combinations are studied and evaluated to obtain optimum fusion technique that achieves as much advantages as possible. Table 2 shows the experimental results of the hybrid fusion algorithms on set 1.

From the previous table, it is clear that:

1) The (DFRWT-NSST) hybrid fusion technique introduces the highest image quality index, mSSIm, and R_{corr} values. Also the (NSCT- DFRWT) hybrid technique has better performance than the other hybrid techniques.

2) All hybrid techniques provide IQI, EQM, mSSIM, entropy correlation coefficient values close to 1.

Table 2. Performance Metrics obtained for different hybrid fusion algorithms

Metrics	PCA - NSST	DCHWT - DWT	NSCT - CVT	NSST - DFRWT	NSCT -DFRWT	DTCWT – NSST	NSST - NSCT	DFRWT -DTCWT	NSCT -DTCWT
Fus Fac	4.1213	4.9873	4.9153	5.8515	6.5346	4.0191	4.8991	5.4821	4.8991
Fus Sym	0.1391	0.3076	0.2063	0.1802	0.1627	0.1542	0.1173	0.2824	0.1173
IQI	0.9982	0.8172	1.0150	1.0184	0.8621	0.9012	0.9201	1.1045	0.8901
EQM	0.8982	0.8062	0.8765	0.8848	0.9012	0.9312	0.8793	0.9483	0.8793
mSSIM	0.8264	0.8216	0.8732	0.9395	0.8127	0.8512	0.9997	0.8605	0.8997
CE_n	0.9015	0.6891	0.9231	0.9011	0.6590	0.6981	0.7054	0.8879	0.7054
R_{Corr}	0.8917	0.7281	0.9151	0.9422	0.8856	0.8912	0.9256	0.9128	0.8818

3) The (DWT - DCHWT) has the lowest structural similarity but (PCA-NSST) has the lowest feature similarity.

4) For fusion factor, entropy, and EQM the (DCHWT - DWT) has the worst values representing poor edge information transferred to the fused images. This can be shown obviously through the visual inspection. The NSCT with NSST, DFRWT-NSCT, and DTCWT-NSST provide better values.

In summary

❖ (DFRWT + NSST) has a superior performance except for fusion factor unfortunately; this reduces edge information and causes pixelization.

❖ The (NSCT+DFRWT and NSCT+ NSST) has a better performance than the other hybrid techniques with the fusion factor, EQM and IQI values.

Figure 22. Performance comparative analysis for Hybrid algorithms

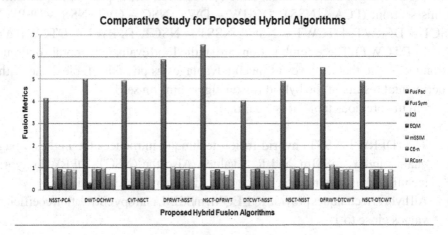

CONCLUSION

This paper examines the performance of both the traditional and hybrid multimodal medical image fusion techniques using some evaluation metrics. It has been exposed that the best multimodality medical image fusion technique implemented was the hybrid algorithm. This hybrid fusion algorithm gives a better performance compared to traditional algorithms. Compared with existing techniques the proposed experimental result gives the better processing performance in both qualitative and quantitative evaluation criteria. It gives much more image details, higher image quality, and a better visual inspection. All these advantages make it a good choice for several applications such as medical disease analysis for an accurate treatment.

REFERENCES

Agarwal & Bedi. (2015). Implementation of hybrid image fusion technique for feature enhancement in medical diagnosis. *Human-centric Computing and Information Sciences*, *5*(3).

Bhadauria, H. S., & Dewal, M. L. (2013). Medical image denoising using adaptive fusion of curvelet transform and total variation. *Computers & Electrical Engineering*, *39*(5), 1451–1460. doi:10.1016/j.compeleceng.2012.04.003

Bhateja, V., Patel, H., Krishn, A., Sahu, A., & Lay-Ekuakille, A. (2015). Multimodal Medical Image Sensor Fusion Framework Using Cascade of Wavelet and Contourlet Transform Domains. *IEEE Sensors Journal*, *15*(12), 6783–6790. doi:10.1109/JSEN.2015.2465935

Bhatnagar, G., Wua, Q. M. J., & Liu, Z. (2013). Human visual system inspired multi-modal medical image fusion framework. *Expert Systems with Applications*, *40*(5), 1708–1720. doi:10.1016/j.eswa.2012.09.011

Chavan, S., Pawar, A., & Talbar, S. (2017). Multimodality Medical Image Fusion using Rotated Wavelet Transform. *Advances in Intelligent Systems Research*, *37*, 627–635. doi:10.2991/iccasp-16.2017.89

Chavan, S. S., Mahajan, A., Talbar, S. N., Desai, S., Thakur, M., & D'cruz, A. (2017). Nonsubsampled rotated complex wavelet transform (NSRCxWT) for medical image fusion related to clinical aspects in neurocysticercosis. *Computers in Biology and Medicine, Elsevier*, *81*, 64–78. doi:10.1016/j.compbiomed.2016.12.006 PMID:28013026

Daniel, E. (2018). Optimum Wavelet Based Homomorphic Medical Image Fusion Using Hybrid Genetic – Grey Wolf Optimization Algorithm. *IEEE Sensors Journal, 18*(16), 1558–1748. doi:10.1109/JSEN.2018.2822712

Daniela, E., Anithaa, J., Kamaleshwaran, K.K., & Rani, I. (2017). Optimum spectrum mask based medical image fusion using Gray Wolf Optimization. Biomedical Signal Processing and Control, 34, 36 – 43.

Du, Li, Lu, & Xiao. (2015). An Overview of Multi-Modal Medical Image Fusion Algorithm in NSST Domain. *Journal of Digital Imaging*.

Du, J., Li, W., Xiao, B., & Nawaz, Q. (2016). Union Laplacian pyramid with multiple features for medical image fusion. *Neurocomputing, 194*, 326–339. doi:10.1016/j.neucom.2016.02.047

El-Hoseny, El-Rabaie, Elrahman, & El-Samie. (2017) Medical Image Fusion Techniques Based on Combined Discrete Transform Domains. In *34th National Radio Science Conference*. Port Said, Egypt: Arab Academy for Science, Technology & Maritime Transport, IEEE.

Gomathi, P. S., & Kalaavathi, B. (2016). Multimodal Medical Image Fusion in Non-Subsampled Contourlet Transform Domain. *Circuits and Systems, 7*(08), 1598–1610. doi:10.4236/cs.2016.78139

Gupta, D. (2017). Nonsubsampled shearlet domain fusion techniques for CT–MR neurological images using improved biological inspired neural model. *Biocybernetics and Biomedical Engineering*.

Harvard Medical School. (n.d.). Retrieved from http://www.med.harvard.edu

Hermessi, H., Mourali, O., & Zagrouba, E. (2018). *Convolutional neural network-based multimodal image fusion via similarity learning in the shearlet domain. In Neural Computing and Applications*. Springer.

James & Dasarathy. (2014). Medical image fusion: A survey of the state of the art. *Information Fusion, 19*, 4 – 19.

Jin, C., & Hou, J. Zhou, & Yao. (2018). Multimodal Sensor Medical Image Fusion Based on Nonsubsampled Shearlet Transform and S-PCNNs in HSV Space. In Signal Processing. Elsevier.

Jing-jing, Z., & Qiu, T. (2017). Medical image fusion based on sparse representation of classified image patches. *Biomedical Signal Processing and Control, Elsevier, 34*, 195–205. doi:10.1016/j.bspc.2017.02.005

Karthikeyan, C., & Ramadoss, B. (2016). Comparative Analysis of Similarity Measure Performance for Multimodality Image Fusion using DTCWT and SOFM with Various Medical Image Fusion Techniques. *Indian Journal of Science and Technology, 9*(22). doi:10.17485/ijst/2016/v9i22/95298

Kavitha, C. T., & Chellamuthu, C. (2014). Medical image fusion based on hybrid intelligence. *Applied Soft Computing, Elsevier, 20,* 83–94. doi:10.1016/j.asoc.2013.10.034

Kavitha, C. T., & Chellamuthu, C. (2015). Fusion of SPECT and MRI images using integer wavelet transform in combination with curvelet transform. *Imaging Science Journal, 63*(1), 17–23. doi:10.1179/1743131X14Y.0000000092

Li, S., Kang, X., Fang, L., Hu, J., & Yin, H. (2016). *Pixel-level image fusion: A survey of the state of the art. In Information Fusion.* Elsevier.

Li, S., Kang, X., & Hu, J. (2013). Image Fusion with Guided Filtering. *IEEE Transactions on Image Processing, 22*(7), 2864–2875. doi:10.1109/TIP.2013.2244222 PMID:23372084

Ling, N., & Duan, M.-X. (2016). Fusion for Medical Images based on Shearlet Transform and Compressive Sensing Model, *International Journal of Signal Processing, Image Processing and Pattern Recognition, 9*(4), 1–10. doi:10.14257/ijsip.2016.9.4.01

Liu, S., Shi, M., Zhu, Z., & Zhao, J. (2015). *Image fusion based on complex-shearlet domain with guided filtering. In Multidim Syst Sign Process.* Springer.

Liu, X., Mei, W., & Du, H. (2016). Multimodality medical image fusion algorithm based on gradient minimization smoothing filter and pulse coupled neural network. *Biomedical Signal Processing and Control, Elsevier, 30,* 140–148. doi:10.1016/j.bspc.2016.06.013

Liu, X., Mei, W., & Du, H. (2017). *Structure tensor and nonsubsampled shearlet transform based algorithm for CT and MRI image fusion. In Neurocomputing.* Elsevier.

Liu, X., Mei, W., & Du, H. (2018). Multi-modality medical image fusion based on image decomposition framework and nonsubsampled shearlet transform. *Biomedical Signal Processing and Control, Elsevier, 40,* 43–350. doi:10.1016/j.bspc.2017.10.001

Liu, Z., Yin, H., Chai, Y., & Yang, S. X. (2014). A Novel Approach for Multimodal Medical Image Fusion. *Expert Systems with Applications, 41*(16), 7425–7435. doi:10.1016/j.eswa.2014.05.043

Luo, X.-Q., Zhang, Z.-C., Zhang, B.-C., & Wu, X.-J. (2016). Contextual Information Driven Multi-modal Medical Image Fusion. *IETE Technical Review*.

Manchanda, M., & Sharma, R. (2016). A novel method of multimodal medical image fusion using fuzzy transform. *J. Visual Communication and Image Representation, Elsevier, 40*, 197–217. doi:10.1016/j.jvcir.2016.06.021

Narasimha Murthy, K. N., & Kusuma, J. (2015). Fusion of Medical Image Using STSVD. *Proceedings of the 5th International Conference on Frontiers in Intelligent Computing: Theory and Applications*, 69-79.

Nawaz, Xiao, Hamid, & Jiao. (2016). Multi-modal Color Medical Image Fusion Using Quaternion Discrete Fourier Transform. *Sens Imaging, 17*(7).

Radiopaedia. (n.d.). Retrieved from https://radiopaedia.org

Rajalingam, B., & Priya, R. (2017a). Multimodality Medical Image Fusion Based on Hybrid Fusion Techniques. *International Journal of Engineering and Manufacturing Science, 7*(1), 1–6.

Rajalingam, B., & Priya, R. (2017b). A Novel approach for Multimodal Medical Image Fusion using Hybrid Fusion Algorithms for Disease Analysis. *International Journal of Pure and Applied Mathematics, 117*(15), 599–619.

Rajalingam, B., & Priya, R. (2018a). Hybrid Multimodality Medical Image Fusion Technique for Feature Enhancement in Medical Diagnosis. *International Journal of Engineering Science Invention, 2*, 52–60.

Rajalingam, B., & Priya, R. (2018b). Combining Multi-Modality Medical Image Fusion Based on Hybrid Intelligence for Disease Identification. *International Journal of Advanced Research Trends in Engineering and Technology, 5*(12), 862–870.

Rajalingam, B., & Priya, R. (2018c). Hybrid Multimodality Medical Image Fusion based on Guided Image Filter with Pulse Coupled Neural Network. *International Journal of Scientific Research in Science, Engineering and Technology, 5*(3), 86–100.

Rajalingam, B., & Priya, R. (2018d). Multimodal Medical Image Fusion based on Deep Learning Neural Network for Clinical Treatment Analysis. *International Journal of Chemtech Research, 11*(06), 160–176.

Rajalingam, B., & Priya, R. (2018e). Review of Multimodality Medical Image Fusion Using Combined Transform Techniques for Clinical Application. *International Journal of Scientific Research in Computer Science Applications and Management Studies, 7*(3).

Rajalingam, B., & Priya, R. (2018f). Multimodal Medical Image Fusion Using Various Hybrid Fusion Techniques For clinical Treatment Analysis. *Smart Construction Research*, 2(2), 1–20.

Rajalingam, B., & Priya, R. (2018g). Enhancement of Hybrid Multimodal Medical Image Fusion Techniques for Clinical Disease Analysis. *International Journal of Computer Vision and Image Processing, IGI Global Publisher*, 8(3), 17–40. doi:10.4018/IJCVIP.2018070102

Rajalingam, B., Priya, R., & Bhavani, R. (2018h). Comparative Analysis for Various Traditional and Hybrid Multimodal Medical Image Fusion Techniques for Clinical Treatment Analysis. In Image Segmentation: A Guide to Image Mining. ICSES Publisher.

Rajalingam, B., Priya, R., & Bhavani, R. (2019a). Hybrid Multimodality Medical Image Fusion Using Various Fusion Techniques with Quantitative and Qualitative Analysis. In Advanced Classification Techniques for Healthcare Analysis. IGI Global.

Rajalingam, B., Priya, R., & Bhavani, R. (2019b). Hybrid Multimodal Medical Image Fusion Algorithms for Astrocytoma Disease Analysis. *Emerging Technologies in Computer Engineering: Microservices in Big Data Analytics, ICETCE 2019. Communications in Computer and Information Science, Springer*, 985, 336–348. doi:10.1007/978-981-13-8300-7_28

Rajalingam, B., Priya, R., & Bhavani, R. (2019c). *Hybrid Multimodal Medical Image Fusion Using Combination of Transform Techniques for Disease Analysis. Procedia Computer Science, 152*, 150–157.

Rajalingam, B., Priya, R., & Bhavani, R. (2019d). Multimodal Medical Image Fusion Using Hybrid Fusion Techniques for Neoplastic and Alzhimers's Disease Analysis. *Journal of Computational and Theoretical Nanoscience, 16*(4), 1–12. doi:10.1166/jctn.2019.8038

Ramlal, S. D., Sachdeva, J., Ahuja, C. K., & Khandelwal, N. (2018). *Multimodal medical image fusion using non-subsampled shearlet transform and pulse coupled neural network incorporated with morphological gradient. In Signal, Image and Video Processing*. Springer.

Shahdoosti & Mehrabi. (2018). *Multimodal Image Fusion Using Sparse Representation Classification in Tetrolet Domain. In Digital Signal Processing*. Elsevier.

Singh, Gupta, Anand, & Kumar. (2015). Nonsubsampled shearlet based CT and MR medical image fusion using biologically inspired spiking neural network. Biomedical Signal Processing and Control, 18, 91 – 101.

Sreeja & Hariharan. (2018). *An improved feature based image fusion technique for enhancement of liver lesions. In Biocybernetics and Biomedical Engineering.* Elsevier.

Srivastava, R., Prakash, O., & Khare, A. (2016). Local energy-based multimodal medical image fusion in curvelet domain. *IET Computer Vision, 10*(6), 513–527. doi:10.1049/iet-cvi.2015.0251

Suriya & Rangarajan. (2016). Brain tumour detection using discrete wavelet transform based medical image fusion. *Biomedical Research.*

Tang, L., Qian, J., Li, L., Hu, J., & Wu, X. (2017). Multimodal Medical Image Fusion Based on Discrete Tchebichef Moments and Pulse Coupled Neural Network, *Wiley Periodicals. Inc, 27,* 57–65.

Venkatrao, P. H., & Damodar, S. S. (2018). WFusion: Holoentropy and SP-Whale optimisation-based fusion model for magnetic resonance imaging multimodal image fusion. *IET Image Processing, 12*(4), 572–581. doi:10.1049/iet-ipr.2017.0573

Xi, J., Chen, Y., Chen, A., & Chen, Y. (2018). *Medical Image Fusion Based on Sparse Representation and PCNN in NSCT Domain. In Computational and Mathematical Methods in Medicine.* Hindawi.

Xia, K., Yin, H., & Wang, J. (2018). A novel improved deep convolutional neural network model for medical image fusion. In Cluster Computing. Springer.

Xu, X., Shan, D., Wang, G., & Jiang, X. (2016). *Multimodal medical image fusion using PCNN optimized by the QPSO algorithm. In Applied Soft Computing.* Elsevier.

Xua, X., Wang, Y., & Chen, S. (2016). Medical image fusion using discrete fractional wavelet transform. *Biomedical Signal Processing and Control, Elsevier, 27,* 103–111. doi:10.1016/j.bspc.2016.02.008

Yang, Wu, Huang, Fang, Lin, & Que. (n.d.). Multimodal Medical Image Fusion Based on Fuzzy Discrimination with Structural Patch Decomposition. *Journal of Biomedical and Health Informatics,* 2168 – 2194

Yang, Y., Que, Y., Huang, S., & Lin, P. (2016). Multimodal Sensor Medical Image Fusion Based on Type-2 Fuzzy Logic in NSCT Domain. *IEEE Sensors Journal, 16*(10), b3735–b3745. doi:10.1109/JSEN.2016.2533864

Zhao, W., & Lu, H. (2017). Medical Image Fusion and Denoising with Alternating Sequential Filter and Adaptive Fractional Order Total Variation. *IEEE Transactions on Instrumentation and Measurement, 66*(9), 2283–2293. doi:10.1109/TIM.2017.2700198

Chapter 8
An Overview of Biomedical Image Analysis From the Deep Learning Perspective

Shouvik Chakraborty
(iD) https://orcid.org/0000-0002-3427-7492
University of Kalyani, India

Kalyani Mali
University of Kalyani, India

ABSTRACT

Biomedical image analysis methods are gradually shifting towards computer-aided solutions from manual investigations to save time and improve the quality of the diagnosis. Deep learning-assisted biomedical image analysis is one of the major and active research areas. Several researchers are working in this domain because deep learning-assisted computer-aided diagnostic solutions are well known for their efficiency. In this chapter, a comprehensive overview of the deep learning-assisted biomedical image analysis methods is presented. This chapter can be helpful for the researchers to understand the recent developments and drawbacks of the present systems. The discussion is made from the perspective of the computer vision, pattern recognition, and artificial intelligence. This chapter can help to get future research directions to exploit the blessings of deep learning techniques for biomedical image analysis.

DOI: 10.4018/978-1-7998-2736-8.ch008

INTRODUCTION

Biomedical imaging is one of the most important tools which is being used to analyze and diagnose different diseases over a long period of time (Hore et al., 2016). Physicians examines the images to understand the source, type etc. of a disease. Several modalities of the biomedical images are available which are used to diagnose different types of diseases. For example, X-Ray, computed tomography scan (CT-Scan), magnetic resonance imaging (MRI), positron emission tomography (PET), microscopy, ultrasound etc (Alheejawi et al., 2020). In general, biomedical images are studied and interpreted by the physicians or radiologists. Due to the huge variations of the diseases, it may be sometimes difficult for the humans to analyze the images appropriately. Moreover, inherent limitations of the humans prevent the experts to explore the hidden patterns from the biomedical images. To reduce the human effort and the inherent errors, manual investigations can be replaced to some extent with the computer assisted diagnosis. The machine learning methods causes a significant advancement in the domain of computer assisted diagnosis and helps in the growth of this field. Machine learning methods coupled with the image processing techniques make the computer assisted diagnosis more powerful and reliable (Greenspan, Van Ginneken, & Summers, 2016).

Artificial intelligence is one of the revolutionary technologies which has a great impact in our everyday life. Machine learning and other advanced computational techniques (Chakraborty & Bhowmik, 2015; Chakraborty & Bhowmik, 2013, 2015; Chakraborty, Seal, & Roy, 2015; Roy, Chakraborty, Mali, Chatterjee, Banerjee, Chakraborty, et al., 2017) based image analysis techniques are very useful to automate the image analysis process. Machine learning methods are used in different stages of image analysis to reduce the human intervention as well as to improve the quality of the results. It is possible to discover various hidden patterns and relationships among the pixels using machine learning techniques (Madabhushi & Lee, 2016). Many times, a human being cannot explore various hidden information from the images which are necessary in various applications of computer vision and image processing like automated object detection (Chakraborty, Chatterjee, Dey, Ashour, & Shi, 2017; Chakraborty, Mali, Chatterjee, Anand, Basu, Banerjee, et al., 2017; Chakraborty, Mali, Chatterjee, Banerjee, Mazumdar, Debnath, et al., 2017), image security (S. Chakraborty, Seal, Roy, & Mali, 2016; Mali, Chakraborty, & Roy, 2015; Mali, Chakraborty, Seal, & Roy, 2015; Roy, Chakraborty, Mali, Banerjee, et al., 2020; Roy, Chakraborty, et al., 2019; Roy, Chakraborty, Mali, Swarnakar, et al., 2020; Roy, Mali, et al., 2019; Seal, Chakraborty, & Mali, 2017) etc.. Machine learning has several applications in various disciplines including manufacturing process, biomedical image analysis, surveillance, space research, bioinformatics, natural language processing and many more. Deep learning is one of the major contributions in artificial intelligence which is frequently used in various disciplines (Lee et al., 2017). Application of the deep learning based artificial intelligence methods in different domains increases the reliability of the automated systems. The efficiency of the deep learning methods makes it suitable to be applied in different domains where high accuracy is required and computational time is restricted. Biomedical image analysis is one of the important domains where the processing time is stipulated and error in the diagnostic outcome can be very costly and dangerous. Deep learning assisted artificial intelligence methods are very useful for this. In recent years, biomedical image analysis becomes a prominent field where deep learning techniques are frequently applied (Chakraborty, Mali, Chatterjee, Banerjee, Roy, Dutta, et al., 2017).

Deep learning allows a neural architecture to learn various complex mathematical models efficiently. It is helpful in accurate data analysis and prediction. The power of deep learning frameworks is well established for different applications. Deep learning frameworks can be efficiently applied for both linear and nonlinear datasets (Lopez, Giro-I-Nieto, Burdick, & Marques, 2017). Several layers are used in the deep learning frameworks which makes the deep learning frameworks powerful enough to efficiently model complex nonlinear functions. Deep learning methods learn a model from a training dataset and that is why deep learning methods belong to supervised category. Deep learning networks are inspired from the Artificial Neural Networks with multiple layers of neurons. After appropriate training, deep learning methods can be effectively applied on some real life scenarios with some unseen data. Deep learning frameworks has a great generalization capabilities which makes it suitable for practical deployment. The application domain of the deep learning frameworks are ever increasing. The root of the deep learning methods can be found long back. With the advancement in the technology, the amount and the quality of the generated data is increasing day by day (Komura & Ishikawa, 2018). To process such a huge amount of data using standard conventional methods is very difficult. Deep learning methods are very useful in learning a model with huge amount of data precisely, which can be efficiently applied on some new unseen data. It is possible due to the inherent capability of the deep learning methods of modelling complex mathematical functions using deep or several layers of computational blocks. For appropriate training, it is necessary to have sufficient amount of training data in hand. Small amount of data restricts deep learning methods from appropriate learning and the model may lacks the generalization power which makes it unsuitable for real life applications (Razzak, Naz, & Zaib, 2018).

Biomedical image analysis domain is exploiting the benefits of machine learning methods since long time (Chakraborty, Mali, Banerjee, et al., 2018; Chakraborty, Mali, Chatterjee, et al., 2018). With the progress in the biomedical imaging technology, it is possible to acquire high quality images of various body parts. To analyze and extract useful information from the multidimensional and high quality biomedical images, it is necessary to have a good number of layers in the neural architecture. Computer vision and image analysis applications required to process large amount of images for different applications like classification, object detection, recognition etc. Deep learning brings a revolution in the field of computer vision and object detection (Chakraborty, Chatterjee, Chatterjee, et al., 2018). Computer assisted diagnosis and image analysis methods are highly dependent on the deep learning methods for analysis and interpretation. There are several research works are reported in the literature where deep learning frameworks are used for computer assisted diagnosis (Chakraborty et al., 2019). In this article, a comprehensive overview of the computer assisted biomedical image analysis methods are presented from the perspective of the deep learning. The main focus of this paper is the recent developments in the field of biomedical image analysis from the perspective of the deep learning frameworks. This article studies deep learning assisted biomedical image analysis problem and tries to find out the recent developments and existing challenges in the field.

Apart from the deep learning based biomedical image analysis methods, a brief overview and technical concept about the deep learning frameworks is provided so that, readers of this article can easily understand the underlying concepts of the deep learning methods and deep learning assisted biomedical image analysis methods (Roy, Chakraborty, Mali, Chatterjee, Banerjee, Mitra, et al., 2017). Dataset plays a vital role in the biomedical image analysis. Hence, a brief discussion about some of the biomedical image datasets is included. It will help in understanding a dataset and reproducing certain works. As discussed earlier, deep learning based methods give desired performance if the dataset is rich enough. Therefore, it is necessary to carefully choose the dataset before any experiment related with deep learning supported biomedical image analysis. Deep learning based image analysis methods are no exception and must be careful in selecting a dataset and determining a suitable division for the training and testing purposes. In-depth understanding of the deep learning environment and it's influencing parameters, can help in maximum exploitation of the advantages of the deep learning methods in biomedical image analysis domain.

Machine learning algorithms depends of the features that can be extracted from an image. It is necessary to extract significant features from an image to obtain reliable results from the underlying framework (Chakraborty, Roy, & Hore, 2016; Chakraborty, Chatterjee, Das, & Mali, 2020; Hore, Chatterjee, Chakraborty, & Shaw, 2016)s. Most of the machine learning based biomedical image analysis frameworks depends on the pivotal features (which are extracted initially) to start with. Typically, meaningful and significant features are defined and designed by the human experts. The advantage of this is that it reduces the dependency on the artificial intelligence which is often found to be a better choice in certain circumstances because artificial intelligence and computer vision cannot surpass the efficiency and interpretation power of the human intelligence and human vision for various instances truly, till date. But the problem which is associated with this approach is that persons without having the domain knowledge may found the machine learning models difficult because of their lack in the domain knowledge and the features and their mathematical modeling can seems to be black box for them (Chen, Shi, Zhang, Wu, & Guizani, 2017). Deep learning methods can overcome these problems by taking the responsibility of the feature representation inside it (Chakraborty, Chatterjee, Ashour, Mali, & Dey, 2017; Chakraborty & Mali, 2018). It can efficiently perform the feature extraction and representation so that the overhead of feature analysis can be transferred to the deep learning framework. It makes the thing easy for a layman who does not have the domain knowledge. There is no need to understand the biomedical features which are designed by the domain experts. Deep learning methods can take care of it.

FOUNDATION AND BACKGROUND

In this section, some of the basic concepts about the machine learning methods are discussed and then the deep learning architecture is briefly discussed. Machine learning methods are the basis of deep learning frameworks and therefore it is necessary to understand the basic machine learning concepts for better understanding of the deep learning methods.

In case of supervised learning, the training data is available to train the classifier. The main goal is to make the model knowledgeable by showing some samples along with their corresponding classes. Amount of error is to be reduced during training session (Chakraborty, Chatterjee, Dey, Ashour, Ashour, et al., 2017; Hore et al., 2015). But it doesn't mean that more you train more you gain. Actually, deep learning methods require a large amount of training samples. The training algorithms must be carefully designed so that the problem of overfiting can be avoided. In case of unsupervised learning methods, no test data is provided for training. Instead of that, the algorithm tries to find out some patterns from the dataset and tries to identify different regions or clusters. Clustering is performed based on some characteristics like RGB values of a pixel in an image. Deep learning based frameworks are suitable for both supervised and unsupervised learning. Although supervised and semi-supervised learning methods are frequently used, there are some other learning methods like semi-supervised learning, reinforcement learning etc. are used in various occasions. In semi-supervised learning method, a small amount of labelled data is used along with a large number of unlabeled data (Basu, Basu, Banerjee, &

Mooney, 2002). Semi-supervised learning resides somewhere between the supervised and the unsupervised learning. Reinforcement learning tries to maximize the profit in a particular situation by taking certain actions. These topics are is not directly included in the current topic of discussion. Here, the sole focus is on the deep learning methods and their applications in the biomedical image analysis.

As discussed earlier, deep learning based methods works if the number of data set is significantly large. Moreover, the success of the deep learning methods depends on the underlying hardware architectures and resources. Deep learning methods can perform well, if sufficient computational resources like powerful processor (i.e. powerful CPU or sometimes a Graphics processing unit) and memory. Deep learning is basically an improvement over the conventional neural network. The basic structural difference can be observed from figure 1 (Nielsen, 2015). Deep learning frameworks can explore the hierarchical relationship among the features using the several hidden layers (Xie, Xing, Kong, Su, & Yang, 2015).

Convolutional neural networks are one of the most important deep learning approach for image analysis. Confuse neural networks are also consists of multiple layers which is similar like several artificial neural networks. The main difference between the convolutional neural network and an artificial neural network you that in case of convolutional neural network the layers are different than an artificial neural network (O'Shea & Nash, 2015). A convolutional neural network is basically consists of convolutional layer, pooling layers and fully connected layers. The prime task of the convolutional layer is to learn the weights of convolutional kernels which can be used to perform convolution on a certain image. Before the era of convolutional neural networks, these kernels have to be designed manually before applying the learning algorithm. But in case of convolutional neural network these weights can be learnt automatically by the learning algorithm itself. The kernels are convolved over an image (Santos, Xiang, & Zhou, 2015). In this operation the corresponding values of both the matrices are simply multiplied and the corresponding killer value is stored inside the matrix called feature map. This method works well for the two-dimensional images but in case of three dimensional image the same process is repeated for the separate channels and the resultant values are simply added to generate a two dimensional feature map. An example of this convolution method is given in Figure 2 where a two dimensional image is considered.

In convolutional neural network, the constituting elements of a kernel are used as the weights of a particular network. Now the number of rows and columns in a feature map can be significantly large. Now it is necessary to reduce the number of rows and columns in the feature map to reduce the overhead. The pooling of the takes the responsibility of reducing the number of columns and rows of the feature map. The reduction process can be performed by taking a small part from the feature map and map it to a single value which can be computed by taking the average, the maximum, or by any other methods. The name of the layer is decided on the basis of the procedure by which the feature map is reduced. For example if the feature map is reduced by taking the average then the layer can be called as average pooling layer. One important point can be noted about the pooling layer is that there is no parameter required to be learned in this layer.

Figure 1. Difference between Artificial Neural Network and Deep Learning networks (a) Schematic diagram of an Artificial Neural Network (b) Schematic diagram of a Deep Learning Network

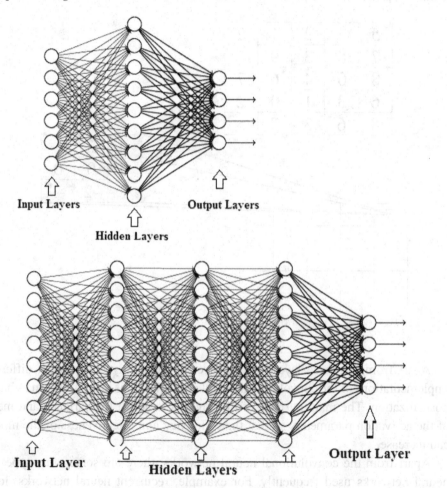

In some of the convolutional neural network implementations, the pooling layer is considered with the convolution layer i.e. The pooling layer is not considered as A separate layer. The last layer which is the fully connected layer is somewhat similar with the general from of the layers in a normal artificial neural network architectures. Activation maps of the fully connected layer is frequently used to efficiently represent the input images (Vu, Adel, Gupta, & Schütze, 2016).

Figure 2. Illustration of the convolution operation: At the top a 5 x 5 image is considered which is convolved with a 3 x 3 kernel (at the middle) and the resulting feature map (for a single pixel only) is given at the bottom.

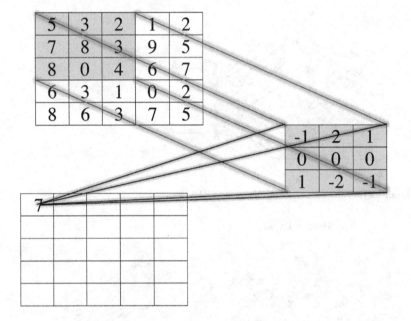

Apart from the three layers a new layer is frequently observed in different implementations of the convolutional neural networks. This layer is known as batch normalization. The main purpose of this layer is to adjust the variance and mean of the activation parameters so that the efficiency and effectiveness of the model can increase.

Apart from the convolutional neural networks, there are some other types of neural networks used frequently. For example, recurrent neural networks, long short-term memory network which is nothing but a modification of the recurrent neural network etc. Some neural networks like autoencoders, generative adversarial networks can also be used for unsupervised learning.

Convolutional neural networks can be used in case of Biomedical image analysis in different ways, for example, it can be used as a feature Extractor where the activations are considered as the features. If the number of available data is not sufficient enough to train a convolutional neural network then updating network can be considered. In this case the network is already trained with some data and it is fine-tuned by using some part of the sample data which are available. This method allows to employ convolutional neural network in such cases where the data limitation is a problem. In most of the cases, the network architecture of the convolutional neural network is decided based on the available data in hand. But it is only possible if the number of the amount of data which is available in hand is sufficiently large. Sometimes, if the training data is not sufficient then the convolutional neural network can also be used to extract the feature only. But in this case the main problem is or we can say the main concern is the representation of power of the convolutional neural network. In general, the representational power is better for those convolutional neural networks which are trained using a large amount of data. In computer vision and pattern recognition, There are several deep learning frameworks (like Tensorflow ("TensorFlow," n.d.), PyTorch ("PyTorch," n.d.), Keras ("Home - Keras Documentation," n.d.), Caffe ("Caffe | Deep Learning Framework," n.d.; Jia et al., 2014), Torch ("Torch | Scientific computing for LuaJIT.," n.d.) and many more) are available which can be directly employed on the defect these deep learning frameworks are highly, efficient and effective to perform different experiments.

APPLICATION OF DEEP LEARNING IN BIOMEDICAL IMAGE ANALYSIS

In this part, some of the recent advancements in the field of biomedical image analysis is discussed. Different approaches to solve different problems can be found in the literature which are based on the deep learning.

In medical image analysis, one of the important components is the localization of the region of interest. It is necessary in many occasions to determine the region of interest from a biomedical image for efficient and fast analysis of the disease. Detection of the appropriate region is also important in preliminary screening of a disease. Image segmentation (Chakraborty, Mali, Chatterjee, Banerjee, Roy, Deb, et al., 2017) is an another important task from the biomedical image analysis point of view. Image segmentation is frequently required to process, analyze and extract significant information from different modalities of the biomedical images. Segmentation helps us in separating a biomedical image into different meaningful regions which is helpful in analyzing and mine important information from various parts of a biomedical image using various data mining algorithms (Datta et al., 2017;

Sarddar, Chakraborty, & Roy, 2015). An another important and useful operation in biomedical image analysis is image registration. In this task, a source image is aligned with the target image. Deep learning based methods has white application in medical Image registration. Classification is an another fundamental task to detect different diseases automatically. Artificial neural network and deep learning based methods for automatic classification are studied from a long time. The invention of the convolutional neural network has revolutionized the classification task. Now convolutional neural networks has the ability to detect the features and use those features for the classification purposes. Also deep learning methods can work on the extracted features and can efficiently learn a model which is based on those features and the model can be used to classify different biomedical images automatically. In this section, some recent developments in the field of Biomedical image analysis are discussed in brief. Table 1 gives a brief overview about some of the deep learning based biomedical images analysis methods.

An application of the deep convolutional network can be observed in automated cell detection and proposed in (F. Liu & Yang, 2017). Cell detection is an important task and often required in various applications of the automated biomedical image analysis. To test the proposed algorithm, authors used two datasets One is a set of 24 images neuroendocrine tissue microarray and Second one is a set of 16 images of lung cancer. The proposed method outperformed various other individual cell detection methods. Deep learning based age related macular degeneration detection method is illustrated in (Burlina, Freund, Joshi, Wolfson, & Bressler, 2016). The method is tested on the AREDS (Age-Related Eye Disease Study) ("National Eye Institute (NEI) Age-Related Eye Disease Study (AREDS)," n.d.) dataset. In an another approach (Xu et al., 2018), deep learning is used to detect bone lesions for multiple myeloma. In this work, a three dimensional investigating method is proposed that analyze the features of the positron emission tomographic image and computerized tomographic image. Two different convolutional neural networks are used to process the images. The proposed method is tested on simulated 68 Ga-Pentixafor ("Definition of gallium Ga 68-pentixafor - NCI Drug Dictionary - National Cancer Institute," n.d.) PET and CT scan images. The experimental results shows that the proposed method out performs some of the standard machine learning methods. In (Sugimori & Kawakami, 2019), authors proposed a method to detect some anatomical structure from the brain MRI images so that an automated algorithm can draw a standard line. The proposed work the experimented on 1200 MRI images which are collected from the Hokkaido University Hospital. The images in the dataset is acquired from 585 male patients and 615 female patients. Experiments prove that the proposed method can perform the desired task with a high rate of accuracy. Detection of different parts from an microscopic images is very important from the diagnostic point of view. This problem is addressed in (Wollmann et al., 2019). Here, a deep learning based method is proposed to detect small particles from fluorescence microscopic images. A domain

adapted Deconvolution Network is used to perform the task. The proposed method is useful to detect particles with different shape and sizes. Moreover, the proposed method is also beneficial in detecting small particles with varied signal-to-noise ratio. The experiments established that performance of the proposed system is quite high. The experiments are performed on the data set provided by the ISBI particle tracking challenge (Chenouard et al., 2014). Deep convolutional neural network based lung nodule segmentation method is proposed in (Amorim, de Moraes, da Silva, & Pedrini, 2019). This method is applied on LIDC-IDRI dataset (Hancock & Magnan, 2016) and found to very effective in reducing false alarm count. The segmentation results are high enough compared to the segmentation results performed by the domain experts. An application of the deep convolutional neural networks in image segmentation can be found in (Y. Liu et al., 2019). In this work, authors used two deep convolutional neural networks to segment shoulder joints from MRI images. The proposed algorithm outperforms various advanced image segmentation algorithms. The experiment is performed on the MRI images of the 50 groups of the patients. The images are collected from Harvard Medical School / Massachusetts General Hospital. Deep convolutional neural network based image registration can be observed in (Blendowski & Heinrich, 2019). In this work a two-step hybrid approach is used to accomplish the task to estimate the motion of the large lungs. DIRLab benchmark dataset (Castillo et al., 2013) is used for the experiments. Deep learning based a liver cancer classification method is proposed in (Sun et al., 2019). The classification of the liver cancer is performed using the histopathology images. The proposed method can be useful in such situations where a huge number of annotated histopathological images are not available. The experiments are performed on the 462 histopathological slides which are collected from the Cancer Genome Atlas ("The Cancer Genome Atlas Program - National Cancer Institute," n.d.). A novel fused convolutional neural network based biomedical image classification framework is proposed in (Pang, Du, Orgun, & Yu, 2019). The experiments are performed on the ImageCLEFmed dataset ("ImageCLEFmedical I ImageCLEF / LifeCLEF - Multimedia Retrieval in CLEF," n.d.). Experiments show a promising result compared with some other standard classification algorithms.

There are various applications of the deep learning frameworks on biomedical image analysis can be found in the literature. There are lots of developments can be observed in the domain of deep learning assisted biomedical image analysis and many scientists are still working in this domain. Some recent reviews on different domains of the deep learning assisted biomedical image analysis can be found in (Anwar et al., 2018; Carneiro, Zheng, Xing, & Yang, 2017; Hu et al., 2018; Litjens

Table 1. A brief overview about some of the deep learning based biomedical images analysis methods

Reference	Problem and the approach	Dataset
(F. Liu & Yang, 2017)	Automated cell detection using deep convolutional network.	Two datasets are used: One is a set of 24 images neuroendocrine tissue microarray and Second one is a set of 16 images of lung cancer.
(Burlina et al., 2016)	Deep learning based age related macular degeneration detection	AREDS (Age-Related Eye Disease Study) ("National Eye Institute (NEI) Age-Related Eye Disease Study (AREDS)," n.d.) dataset.
(Xu et al., 2018)	Deep learning based bone lesions detection for multiple myeloma	Simulated 68 Ga-Pentixafor ("Definition of gallium Ga 68-pentixafor - NCI Drug Dictionary - National Cancer Institute," n.d.) PET and CT scan images
(Sugimori & Kawakami, 2019)	A method to detect some anatomical structure from the brain MRI images so that an automated algorithm can draw a standard line	1200 MRI images which are collected from the Hokkaido University Hospital
(Wollmann et al., 2019)	A deep learning based method to detect small particles from fluorescence microscopic images	ISBI particle tracking challenge (Chenouard et al., 2014).
(Amorim et al., 2019)	Deep convolutional neural network based lung nodule segmentation.	LIDC-IDRI dataset (Hancock & Magnan, 2016)
(Y. Liu et al., 2019)	Two deep convolutional neural networks are used to segment shoulder joints from MRI images	MRI images of the 50 groups of the patients collected from Harvard Medical School / Massachusetts General Hospital
(Blendowski & Heinrich, 2019)	A two-step hybrid approach is used to accomplish the task to estimate the motion of the large lungs	DIRLab benchmark dataset (Castillo et al., 2013).
(Sun et al., 2019)	Histopathological image based liver cancer classification.	462 histopathological slides which are collected from the Cancer Genome Atlas ("The Cancer Genome Atlas Program - National Cancer Institute," n.d.).
(Pang et al., 2019)	Biomedical image classification using fused convolutional neural network.	("ImageCLEFmedical | ImageCLEF / LifeCLEF - Multimedia Retrieval in CLEF," n.d.)

et al., 2017; Y. Liu et al., 2019; Moen et al., 2019; Xing, Xie, Su, Liu, & Yang, 2018; Zhang, Zhong, Deng, Tang, & Li, 2019).

CONCLUSION

Biomedical Image Analysis is one of the inevitable part in the modern healthcare industry. Computer assisted analysis is highly beneficial in diagnosing several diseases from biomedical images without any intervention of the experts. Recent development in computer vision and machine learning and makes the analysis of the biomedical images easier and precise so that it can be helpful in healthcare industry. Several hidden patterns, relations among various segments etc. can be discovered by the computer assisted automated methods which can be used for classification, prediction and other jobs. Deep learning based methods are proven to be highly beneficial in analyzing and diagnosing various diseases from biomedical images. It is necessary to predict the state of the disease in advance. Deep learning based models are also proven to be highly useful in various other healthcare applications. In this work, a brief overview of the deep learning methods and their application in biomedical image analysis is presented. Several aspects and issues related with computerized biomedical image analysis with the help of deep learning is discussed. Various challenges and future directions of the deep learning based biomedical image analysis is illuminated. This article can be used to gather some knowledge about the recent trends and developments in the deep learning based biomedical image analysis techniques for the future development of the deep learning assisted biomedical image analysis.

REFERENCES

Alheejawi, S., Mandal, M., Xu, H., Lu, C., Berendt, R., & Jha, N. (2020). Deep learning-based histopathological image analysis for automated detection and staging of melanoma. In Deep Learning Techniques for Biomedical and Health Informatics (pp. 237–265). doi:10.1016/B978-0-12-819061-6.00010-0

Amorim, P. H. J., de Moraes, T. F., da Silva, J. V. L., & Pedrini, H. (2019). Lung Nodule Segmentation Based on Convolutional Neural Networks Using Multi-orientation and Patchwise Mechanisms. Lecture Notes in Computational Vision and Biomechanics, 34, 286–295. doi:10.1007/978-3-030-32040-9_30

Anwar, S. M., Majid, M., Qayyum, A., Awais, M., Alnowami, M., & Khan, M. K. (2018, November 1). Medical Image Analysis using Convolutional Neural Networks: A Review. *Journal of Medical Systems*, *42*(11), 1–13. doi:10.1007/s10916-018-1088-1 PubMed

Basu, S., Basu, S., Banerjee, A., & Mooney, R. (2002). Semi-supervised Clustering by Seeding. In Proceedings of 19th International Conference on Machine Learning (ICML-2002). Retrieved from http://citeseerx.ist.psu.edu/viewdoc/summary?doi=10.1.1.7.9416

Blendowski, M., & Heinrich, M. P. (2019). Combining MRF-based deformable registration and deep binary 3D-CNN descriptors for large lung motion estimation in COPD patients. *International Journal of Computer Assisted Radiology and Surgery*, *14*(1), 43–52. doi:10.1007/s11548-018-1888-2 PubMed

Burlina, P., Freund, D. E., Joshi, N., Wolfson, Y., & Bressler, N. M. (2016). Detection of age-related macular degeneration via deep learning. Proceedings - International Symposium on Biomedical Imaging, 184–188. doi:10.1109/ISBI.2016.7493240

Caffe | Deep Learning Framework. (n.d.). Retrieved February 16, 2020, from https://caffe.berkeleyvision.org/

Carneiro, G., Zheng, Y., Xing, F., & Yang, L. (2017). Review of deep learning methods in mammography, cardiovascular, and microscopy image analysis. In Advances in Computer Vision and Pattern Recognition (pp. 11–32). doi:10.1007/978-3-319-42999-1_2

Castillo, R., Castillo, E., Fuentes, D., Ahmad, M., Wood, A. M., Ludwig, M. S., & Guerrero, T. (2013). A reference dataset for deformable image registration spatial accuracy evaluation using the COPDgene study archive. *Physics in Medicine and Biology*, *58*(9), 2861–2877. doi:10.1088/0031-9155/58/9/2861 PubMed

Chakraborty, S., & Bhowmik, S. (2013). Job Shop Scheduling using Simulated Annealing. First International Conference on Computation and Communication Advancement, 1(1), 69–73. Retrieved from https://scholar.google.co.in/citations?user=8lhQFaYAAAAJ&hl=en

Chakraborty, S., & Bhowmik, S. (2015). An Efficient Approach to Job Shop Scheduling Problem using Simulated Annealing. *International Journal of Hybrid Information Technology*, *8*(11), 273–284. doi:10.14257/ijhit.2015.8.11.23

Chakraborty, S., & Bhowmik, S. (2015). Blending roulette wheel selection with simulated annealing for job shop scheduling problem. Michael Faraday IET International Summit 2015, 100(7). doi:10.1049/cp.2015.1696

Chakraborty, S., Chatterjee, S., Ashour, A. S., Mali, K., & Dey, N. (2017). Intelligent Computing in Medical Imaging: A Study. In N. Dey (Ed.), *Advancements in Applied Metaheuristic Computing* (pp. 143–163)., doi:10.4018/978-1-5225-4151-6.ch006

Chakraborty, S., Chatterjee, S., Chatterjee, A., Mali, K., Goswami, S., & Sen, S. (2018). Automated Breast Cancer Identification by analyzing Histology Slides using Metaheuristic Supported Supervised Classification coupled with Bag-of-Features. 2018 Fourth International Conference on Research in Computational Intelligence and Communication Networks (ICRCICN), 81–86. doi:10.1109/ICRCICN.2018.8718736

Chakraborty, S., Chatterjee, S., Das, A., & Mali, K. (2020). Penalized Fuzzy C-Means Enabled Hybrid Region Growing in Segmenting Medical Images. doi:10.1007/978-981-13-8930-6_3

Chakraborty, S., Chatterjee, S., Dey, N., Ashour, A. S., Ashour, A. S., Shi, F., & Mali, K. (2017). Modified cuckoo search algorithm in microscopic image segmentation of hippocampus. *Microscopy Research and Technique, 80*(10), 1051–1072. doi:10.1002/jemt.22900 PubMed

Chakraborty, S., Chatterjee, S., Dey, N., Ashour, A. S., & Shi, F. (2017). Gradient approximation in retinal blood vessel segmentation. 2017 4th IEEE Uttar Pradesh Section International Conference on Electrical, Computer and Electronics (UPCON), 618–623. 10.1109/UPCON.2017.8251120

Chakraborty, S., & Mali, K. (2018). Application of Multiobjective Optimization Techniques in Biomedical Image Segmentation—A Study. In Multi-Objective Optimization (pp. 181–194). doi:10.1007/978-981-13-1471-1_8

Chakraborty, S., Mali, K., Banerjee, S., Roy, K., Saha, D., & Chatterjee, S. ... Majumder, S. (2018). Bag-of-features based classification of dermoscopic images. 2017 4th International Conference on Opto-Electronics and Applied Optics, Optronix 2017, 2018–Janua. 10.1109/OPTRONIX.2017.8349977

Chakraborty, S., Mali, K., Chatterjee, S., Anand, S., Basu, A., & Banerjee, S., ... Bhattacharya, A. (2017). Image based skin disease detection using hybrid neural network coupled bag-of-features. 2017 IEEE 8th Annual Ubiquitous Computing, Electronics and Mobile Communication Conference (UEMCON), 242–246. 10.1109/UEMCON.2017.8249038

Chakraborty, S., Mali, K., Chatterjee, S., Banerjee, S., Mazumdar, K. G., & Debnath, M. ... Roy, K. (2017). Detection of skin disease using metaheuristic supported artificial neural networks. 2017 8th Annual Industrial Automation and Electromechanical Engineering Conference (IEMECON), 224–229. 10.1109/IEMECON.2017.8079594

Chakraborty, S., Mali, K., Chatterjee, S., Banerjee, S., Roy, K., & Deb, K. ... Prasad, N. (2017). An integrated method for automated biomedical image segmentation. 2017 4th International Conference on Opto-Electronics and Applied Optics (Optronix), 1–5. 10.1109/OPTRONIX.2017.8349978

Chakraborty, S., Mali, K., Chatterjee, S., Banerjee, S., Roy, K., & Dutta, N. ... Mazumdar, S. (2017). Dermatological effect of UV rays owing to ozone layer depletion. 2017 4th International Conference on Opto-Electronics and Applied Optics (Optronix), 1–6. 10.1109/OPTRONIX.2017.8349975

Chakraborty, S., Mali, K., Chatterjee, S., Banerjee, S., Sah, A., & Pathak, S. ... Roy, D. (2018). Bio-medical image enhancement using hybrid metaheuristic coupled soft computing tools. 2017 IEEE 8th Annual Ubiquitous Computing, Electronics and Mobile Communication Conference, UEMCON 2017, 2018–Janua. 10.1109/UEMCON.2017.8249036

Chakraborty, S., Raman, A., Sen, S., Mali, K., Chatterjee, S., & Hachimi, H. (2019). Contrast Optimization using Elitist Metaheuristic Optimization and Gradient Approximation for Biomedical Image Enhancement. 2019 Amity International Conference on Artificial Intelligence (AICAI), 712–717. doi:10.1109/AICAI.2019.8701367

Chakraborty, S., Roy, M., & Hore, S. (2016). *A study on different edge detection techniques in digital image processing*. Feature Detectors and Motion Detection in Video.Processing; doi:10.4018/978-1-5225-1025-3.ch005

Chakraborty, S., Seal, A., & Roy, M. (2015). An Elitist Model for Obtaining Alignment of Multiple Sequences using Genetic Algorithm. *2nd National Conference NCETAS 2015*, 4(9), 61–67.

Chakraborty, S., Seal, A., Roy, M., & Mali, K. (2016). A novel lossless image encryption method using DNA substitution and chaotic logistic map. *International Journal of Security and Its Applications*, 10(2), 205–216. doi:10.14257/ijsia.2016.10.2.19

Chen, M., Shi, X., Zhang, Y., Wu, D., & Guizani, M. (2017). Deep Features Learning for Medical Image Analysis with Convolutional Autoencoder Neural Network. IEEE Transactions on Big Data, 1–1. doi:10.1109/tbdata.2017.2717439

Chenouard, N., Smal, I., De Chaumont, F., Maška, M., Sbalzarini, I. F., Gong, Y., ... Meijering, E. (2014). Objective comparison of particle tracking methods. *Nature Methods*, 11(3), 281–289. doi:10.1038/nmeth.2808 PubMed

Datta, S., Chakraborty, S., Mali, K., Baneijee, S., Roy, K., & Chatterjee, S. ... Bhattacharjee, S. (2017). Optimal usage of pessimistic association rules in cost effective decision making. 2017 4th International Conference on Opto-Electronics and Applied Optics (Optronix), 1–5. 10.1109/OPTRONIX.2017.8349976

Definition of gallium Ga 68-pentixafor - NCI Drug Dictionary - National Cancer Institute. (n.d.). Retrieved February 14, 2020, from https://www.cancer.gov/ publications/dictionaries/cancer-drug/def/gallium-ga-68-pentixafor

dos Santos, C. N., Xiang, B., & Zhou, B. (2015). Classifying Relations by Ranking with Convolutional Neural Networks. ACL-IJCNLP 2015 - 53rd Annual Meeting of the Association for Computational Linguistics and the 7th International Joint Conference on Natural Language Processing of the Asian Federation of Natural Language Processing, Proceedings of the Conference, 1, 626–634. Retrieved from https://arxiv.org/abs/1504.06580

Greenspan, H., Van Ginneken, B., & Summers, R. M. (2016, May 1). Guest Editorial Deep Learning in Medical Imaging: Overview and Future Promise of an Exciting New Technique. *IEEE Transactions on Medical Imaging*, *35*(5), 1153–1159. doi:10.1109/TMI.2016.2553401

Hancock, M. C., & Magnan, J. F. (2016). Lung nodule malignancy classification using only radiologist-quantified image features as inputs to statistical learning algorithms: Probing the Lung Image Database Consortium dataset with two statistical learning methods. *Journal of Medical Imaging (Bellingham, Wash.)*, *3*(4), 44504. doi:10.1117/1.JMI.3.4.044504 PubMed

Home - Keras Documentation. (n.d.). Retrieved February 16, 2020, from https:// keras.io/

Hore, S., Chakraborty, S., Chatterjee, S., Dey, N., Ashour, A. S., & Van Chung, L., ... - Nhuong Le, D. (2016). An Integrated Interactive Technique for Image Segmentation using Stack based Seeded Region Growing and Thresholding. *Iranian Journal of Electrical and Computer Engineering*, *6*(6), 2773–2780. doi:10.11591/ ijece.v6i6.11801

Hore, S., Chakroborty, S., Ashour, A. S., Dey, N., Ashour, A. S., Sifaki-Pistolla, D., ... Chaudhuri, S. R. B. (2015). Finding Contours of Hippocampus Brain Cell Using Microscopic Image Analysis. *Journal of Advanced Microscopy Research*, *10*(2), 93–103. doi:10.1166/jamr.2015.1245

Hore, S., Chatterjee, S., Chakraborty, S., & Shaw, R. K. (2016). *Analysis of different feature description algorithm in object recognition*. Feature Detectors and Motion Detection in Video Processing; doi:10.4018/978-1-5225-1025-3.ch004

Hu, Z., Tang, J., Wang, Z., Zhang, K., Zhang, L., & Sun, Q. (2018). Deep learning for image-based cancer detection and diagnosis: A survey. *Pattern Recognition*, *83*, 134–149. doi:10.1016/j.patcog.2018.05.014

ImageCLEFmedical | ImageCLEF / LifeCLEF - Multimedia Retrieval in CLEF. (n.d.). Retrieved November 20, 2019, from https://www.imageclef.org/2019/medical

Jia, Y., Shelhamer, E., Donahue, J., Karayev, S., Long, J., & Girshick, R. … Darrell, T. (2014). Caffe: Convolutional architecture for fast feature embedding. MM 2014 - Proceedings of the 2014 ACM Conference on Multimedia, 675–678. 10.1145/2647868.2654889

Komura, D., & Ishikawa, S. (2018, January 1). Machine Learning Methods for Histopathological Image Analysis. *Computational and Structural Biotechnology Journal*, *16*, 34–42. doi:10.1016/j.csbj.2018.01.001 PubMed

Lee, C. S., Tyring, A. J., Deruyter, N. P., Wu, Y., Rokem, A., & Lee, A. Y. (2017). Deep-learning based, automated segmentation of macular edema in optical coherence tomography. *Biomedical Optics Express*, *8*(7), 3440. doi:10.1364/BOE.8.003440 PubMed

Litjens, G., Kooi, T., Bejnordi, B. E., Setio, A. A. A., Ciompi, F., Ghafoorian, M., … Sánchez, C. I. (2017, December 1). A survey on deep learning in medical image analysis. *Medical Image Analysis*, *42*, 60–88. doi:10.1016/j.media.2017.07.005 PubMed

Liu, F., & Yang, L. (2017). A novel cell detection method using deep convolutional neural network and maximum-weight independent set. In Advances in Computer Vision and Pattern Recognition (pp. 63–72). doi:10.1007/978-3-319-42999-1_5

Liu, Y., Wang, R., Jin, R., Sun, D., Xu, H., & Dong, C. (2019). Shoulder joint image segmentation based on joint convolutional neural networks. ACM International Conference Proceeding Series, 236–241. doi:10.1145/3366194.3366235

Madabhushi, A., & Lee, G. (2016, October 1). Image analysis and machine learning in digital pathology: Challenges and opportunities. *Medical Image Analysis*, *33*, 170–175. doi:10.1016/j.media.2016.06.037 PubMed

Mali, K., Chakraborty, S., & Roy, M. (2015). A Study on Statistical Analysis and Security Evaluation Parameters in Image Encryption. *International Journal for Scientific Research & Development*, *3*, 2321–0613. Retrieved from www.ijsrd.com

Mali, K., Chakraborty, S., Seal, A., & Roy, M. (2015). An Efficient Image Cryptographic Algorithm based on Frequency Domain using Haar Wavelet Transform. *International Journal of Security and Its Applications, 9*(12), 279–288. doi:10.14257/ijsia.2015.9.12.26

Moen, E., Bannon, D., Kudo, T., Graf, W., Covert, M., & Van Valen, D. (2019, December 1). Deep learning for cellular image analysis. *Nature Methods, 16*(12), 1233–1246. doi:10.1038/s41592-019-0403-1 PubMed

National Eye Institute (NEI) Age-Related Eye Disease Study (AREDS). (n.d.). Retrieved February 14, 2020, from https://www.ncbi.nlm.nih.gov/projects/gap/cgi-bin/study.cgi?study_id=phs000001.v2.p1&phv=173&phd=1552&pha=2856&pht=371&phvf=&phdf=0&phaf=&phtf=&dssp=1&temp=1

Nielsen, M. A. (2015). *Neural Networks and Deep Learning*. Determination Press.

O'Shea, K., & Nash, R. (2015). An Introduction to Convolutional Neural Networks. Retrieved from https://arxiv.org/abs/1511.08458

Pang, S., Du, A., Orgun, M. A., & Yu, Z. (2019). A novel fused convolutional neural network for biomedical image classification. *Medical & Biological Engineering & Computing, 57*(1), 107–121. doi:10.1007/s11517-018-1819-y PubMed

PyTorch. (n.d.). Retrieved February 16, 2020, from https://pytorch.org/

Razzak, M. I., Naz, S., & Zaib, A. (2018). Deep learning for medical image processing: Overview, challenges and the future. In Lecture Notes in Computational Vision and Biomechanics (Vol. 26, pp. 323–350). doi:10.1007/978-3-319-65981-7_12

Romero Lopez, A. Giro-I-Nieto, X., Burdick, J., & Marques, O. (2017). Skin lesion classification from dermoscopic images using deep learning techniques. Proceedings of the 13th IASTED International Conference on Biomedical Engineering, BioMed 2017, 49–54. doi:10.2316/P.2017.852-053

Roy, M., Chakraborty, S., Mali, K., Banerjee, A., Ghosh, K., & Chatterjee, S. (2020). Biomedical Image Security Using Matrix Manipulation and DNA Encryption. Advances in Intelligent Systems and Computing, 1065, 49–60. doi:10.1007/978-981-15-0361-0_4

Roy, M., Chakraborty, S., Mali, K., Chatterjee, S., Banerjee, S., & Chakraborty, A. ... Roy, K. (2017). Biomedical image enhancement based on modified Cuckoo Search and morphology. 2017 8th Annual Industrial Automation and Electromechanical Engineering Conference (IEMECON), 230–235. 10.1109/IEMECON.2017.8079595

Roy, M., Chakraborty, S., Mali, K., Chatterjee, S., Banerjee, S., & Mitra, S., ... Bhattacharjee, A. (2017). Cellular image processing using morphological analysis. 2017 IEEE 8th Annual Ubiquitous Computing, Electronics and Mobile Communication Conference (UEMCON), 237–241. 10.1109/UEMCON.2017.8249037

Roy, M., Chakraborty, S., Mali, K., Mitra, S., Mondal, I., & Dawn, R. ... Chatterjee, S. (2019). A dual layer image encryption using polymerase chain reaction amplification and dna encryption. 2019 International Conference on Opto-Electronics and Applied Optics, Optronix 2019. doi:10.1109/OPTRONIX.2019.8862350

Roy, M., Chakraborty, S., Mali, K., Swarnakar, R., Ghosh, K., Banerjee, A., & Chatterjee, S. (2020). Data Security Techniques Based on DNA Encryption. Advances in Intelligent Systems and Computing, 1065, 239–249. doi:10.1007/978-981-15-0361-0_19

Roy, M., Mali, K., Chatterjee, S., Chakraborty, S., Debnath, R., & Sen, S. (2019). A Study on the Applications of the Biomedical Image Encryption Methods for Secured Computer Aided Diagnostics. 2019 Amity International Conference on Artificial Intelligence (AICAI), 881–886. doi:10.1109/AICAI.2019.8701382

Sarddar, D., Chakraborty, S., & Roy, M. (2015). An Efficient Approach to Calculate Dynamic Time Quantum in Round Robin Algorithm for Efficient Load Balancing. *International Journal of Computers and Applications*, *123*(14), 48–52. doi:10.5120/ijca2015905701

Seal, A., Chakraborty, S., & Mali, K. (2017). A new and resilient image encryption technique based on pixel manipulation, value transformation and visual transformation utilizing single–Level haar wavelet transform. In Advances in Intelligent Systems and Computing (Vol. 458). doi:10.1007/978-981-10-2035-3_61

Sugimori, H., & Kawakami, M. (2019). Automatic Detection of a Standard Line for Brain Magnetic Resonance Imaging Using Deep Learning. Applied Sciences (Basel, Switzerland), 9(18), 3849. doi:10.3390/app9183849

Sun, C., Xu, A., Liu, D., Xiong, Z., Zhao, F., & Ding, W. (2019). Deep Learning-Based Classification of Liver Cancer Histopathology Images Using Only Global Labels. IEEE Journal of Biomedical and Health Informatics, 1–1. doi:10.1109/JBHI.2019.2949837

TensorFlow. (n.d.). Retrieved February 16, 2020, from https://www.tensorflow.org/

The Cancer Genome Atlas Program - National Cancer Institute. (n.d.). Retrieved February 16, 2020, from https://www.cancer.gov/about-nci/organization/ccg/research/structural-genomics/tcga

Torch | Scientific computing for LuaJIT. (n.d.). Retrieved February 16, 2020, from http://torch.ch/

Vu, N. T., Adel, H., Gupta, P., & Schütze, H. (2016). Combining Recurrent and Convolutional Neural Networks for Relation Classification. *2016 Conference of the North American Chapter of the Association for Computational Linguistics: Human Language Technologies, NAACL HLT 2016 - Proceedings of the Conference,* 534–539. Retrieved from https://arxiv.org/abs/1605.07333

Wollmann, T., Ritter, C., Dohrke, J. N., Lee, J. Y., Bartenschlager, R., & Rohr, K. (2019). Detnet: Deep neural network for particle detection in fluorescence microscopy images. *Proceedings - International Symposium on Biomedical Imaging,* 517–520. 10.1109/ISBI.2019.8759234

Xie, Y., Xing, F., Kong, X., Su, H., & Yang, L. (2015). Beyond classification: Structured regression for robust cell detection using convolutional neural network. *Lecture Notes in Computer Science (Including Subseries Lecture Notes in Artificial Intelligence and Lecture Notes in Bioinformatics),* 9351, 358–365. doi:10.1007/978-3-319-24574-4_43

Xing, F., Xie, Y., Su, H., Liu, F., & Yang, L. (2018). Deep Learning in Microscopy Image Analysis: A Survey. *IEEE Transactions on Neural Networks and Learning Systems, 29*(10), 4550–4568. doi:10.1109/TNNLS.2017.2766168 PubMed

Xu, L., Tetteh, G., Lipkova, J., Zhao, Y., Li, H., Christ, P., ... Menze, B. H. (2018). ... Menze, B. H. (2018). Automated Whole-Body Bone Lesion Detection for Multiple Myeloma on 68 Ga-Pentixafor PET/CT Imaging Using Deep Learning Methods. *Contrast Media & Molecular Imaging, 2018,* 1–11. doi:10.1155/2018/2391925 PubMed

Zhang, P., Zhong, Y., Deng, Y., Tang, X., & Li, X. (2019). A Survey on Deep Learning of Small Sample in Biomedical Image Analysis. Retrieved from https://arxiv.org/abs/1908.00473

KEY TERMS AND DEFINITIONS

Artificial Intelligence: It is the method of mimicking the human intelligence by the machines.

Artificial Neural Networks: It mimics animal neural networks and useful in taking some action by observing some example instead of being explicitly programmed.

Big Data: Extremely large set of data which is used to extract some meaningful information.

Biomedical Image Analysis: Study of the biomedical images of various modalities using digital image processing techniques to detect and diagnose different diseases and help the medical investigation.

Computer-Aided Diagnostics: It is the system that assists a doctor in diagnosis by analyzing the medical data.

Deep Learning: A category of machine learning methods which is inspired by the artificial neural networks,

Feature Extraction: Extracting or deriving some useful information from the initially obtained data.

Machine Learning: It is an application of the artificial intelligence in which machines can automatically learn and solve problems using the learned experience.

Chapter 9
Segmentation-Free Word Spotting in Handwritten Documents Using Scale Space Co-HoG Feature Descriptors

Prabhakar C. J.
Kuvempu University, India

ABSTRACT

In this chapter, the author present a segmentation-free-based word spotting method for handwritten documents using Scale Space co-occurrence histograms of oriented gradients (Co-HOG) feature descriptor. The chapter begin with introduction to word spotting, its challenges, and applications. It is followed by review of the existing techniques for word spotting in handwritten documents. The literature survey reveals that segmentation-based word spotting methods usually need a layout analysis step for word segmentation, and any segmentation errors can affect the subsequent word representations and matching steps. Hence, in order to overcome the drawbacks of segmentation-based methods, the author proposed segmentation-free word spotting using Scale Space Co-HOG feature descriptor. The proposed method is evaluated using mean Average Precision (mAP) through experimentation conducted on popular datasets such as GW and IAM. The performance of the proposed method is compared with existing state-of-the-segmentation and segmentation-free methods, and there is a considerable increase in accuracy.

DOI: 10.4018/978-1-7998-2736-8.ch009

INTRODUCTION

There is a huge amount of information in libraries and institutions all over the world in the form of books, documents and in other conventional methods. We need to be digitized in order to preserve and for efficient searching and browsing of information for different applications. In order to create digital libraries, thousands of digitized documents have to be transcribed (George, N, et al., 2006). Optical Character Recognition (OCR) is first used to transcribe documents where image-based documents are converted into ASCII format through automatic recognition. The automatic recognition by OCR system achieves best performance for modern high-quality printed documents with simple layouts and known fonts. The performance of OCR is very poor for handwritten text due to various challenges posed by handwritten text such as unconstrained writing styles, open vocabulary and paper degradation such as stains, ancient fonts, and faded ink.

To overcome the aforementioned limitations of OCR, the Document Image Analysis (DIA) community has developed a technique called as word spotting. Word spotting is a technique for recognition and retrieval of words in any form of document images. Word spotting can be defined as process aimed at locating and retrieving a particular word from a document image collection. The main objective of word spotting systems is to propose methods that show high accuracy, high speed and work on any language with minimum preprocessing steps. A word spotting method requires a collection of documents/document corpus and an input element is a query word. The output of word spotting method is spotting and retrieval of documents or sub images that are similar to the query word. Figure 1 illustrates a general architecture of word spotting method where the whole procedure is divided in an offline and an online phase. In the offline stage, a set of features are extracted from either word images, or text lines or whole document pages which are then represented by feature vectors. In the online phase, a user formulates a query either by selecting an actual example from the collection or by typing an ASCII text word. Then matching process is applied to these representations in order to obtain a similarity score which yields a ranking list of results according to their similarity with the query.

CHALLENGES POSED BY WORD SPOTTING PROBLEM

The word spotting in handwritten documents is not completely solved due to various challenges posed by handwritten documents and the challenges involved in handwritten documents are:

Figure 1. General architecture of word spotting (Courtesy: Giotis et al., 2017)

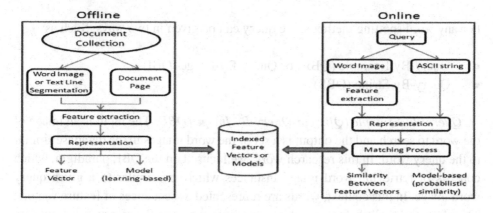

- Either historical or modern Handwritten documents suffer from variability in writing style, not only for different authors but also for documents of the same writer.
- The handwritten words may be skewed, characters may be slanted, non-text content such as symbols may be present and letters may be broken or connected in a cursive manner
- Degradations such as missing data, non-stationary noise due to illumination changes, low contrast, and warping effects, which directly affect the segmentation and feature extraction stages of a word spotting method.

APPLICATIONS OF WORD SPOTTING

There are a variety of applications of word spotting in handwritten documents such as:

- Searching and browsing historical handwritten documents collections written by a single or several authors. Retrieval of documents with a given word in company/organization files. Retrieval of keywords in hospital care reports.
- Helps human transcribers in identifying words in degraded documents
- Sorting of mails based on significant words like urgent, cancellation and complain
- Identification of figures and their corresponding captions. Word spotting in geographical maps.

QUERY FORMAT

For any word spotting methods, the query can be given in two ways. Such as:

- Query-By-Example (QBE) or Query-By-Image (QBI)
- Query-By-String (QBS)

Query-By-Example (QBE) or Query-By-Image (QBI): The input is an image of the word to search and the output is a set of the word images in the database similar to the query word. In this research work, we focused on the QBE paradigm, which consists of retrieving word image instances which are similar to a given query word image. In this context, words are represented as sequences of feature vectors. Therefore, the quality of the matching directly depends on the measure of similarity between such sequences.

Query-By-String (QBS): The input is text string. Character models are learned in advance and at runtime, the character models are combined to form words and probability of each word is evaluated. This approach is more complicated than query-by-example because word models are needed to be created even though no samples of that word exist in the training set and also faced similar drawbacks of OCR systems.

LITERATURE SURVEY ON HANDWRITTEN WORD SPOTTING

The literature survey reveals that a lot of techniques have been developed to spot and retrieve words in handwritten documents collections/documents corpus. In this section, we briefly discuss the word spotting methods proposed by various researchers for handwritten documents. There are two main approaches for handwritten word spotting such as template-based and learning-based approaches. In the template-based methods, query word image is compared with set of word images in the dataset and images with the highest similarity is retrieved. These methods do not need a training step and are not appropriate where labeled data are not available. The drawback is that for each query, only a restricted number of word images are retrievable. Learning-based approaches train a statistical model by applying statistical learning methods and then word images are retrieved and spotted based on the built scoring model.

Generally, word spotting methods have followed a well-defined process. Initially, document images are segmented into words based on layout analysis of documents. Then, the segmented word images are represented as sequences of features such as geometric features (Marti et al., 2001), profile based features (Rath et al., 2003;

Larvenko et al., 2004), local gradient features (Rodriguez et al., 2008) and other forms. Finally, similarity measures are used to compare the feature of query word image and set of word images presented in the dataset, using popular similarity measures such as Euclidean distance, Hausdorff distance, Dynamic Time Warping (DTW) and Hidden Markov Models (HMM). Finally, retrieved word images are ranked according to this similarity.

Word spotting was initially proposed by Jones et al. (1995) for spotting and retrieving speech file in the field of speech processing. This procedure was later adopted by several researchers in the field of printed and handwritten documents for the purpose of spotting and retrieving words. Manmatha et al. (1999) have introduced the concept of word spotting in printed and handwritten as an alternative to OCR based results. Rath et al. (2003) proposed spotting method for handwritten words in noisy historical documents where segmentation is done in order to segment word images and word images are preprocessed followed by extraction of 1-dimensional features, which are used to train the probabilistic classifier, finally, similarity measure is used to estimate similarity between word images. Rothfeder et al. (2003) have proposed to find correspondences between points of interest in two word images and utilizes these correspondences to measure the similarities between the images.

Zhang et al. (2004) have proposed word spotting technique based on gradient based binary features can offer higher accuracy and much faster speed than DTW matching of profile features. Srihari et al. (2005) indexed documents using global word image features such as stroke width and slant. Word gaps are used to measure the similarities between the spotted words and a set of prototypes from known writers. Srihari et al. (2006) developed a word spotting system that retrieves the candidate words from the documents and ranks them based on global word shape features. Rath et al. (2007) proposed an approach which involves grouping word images into clusters of similar words by using both K-means and agglomerative clustering techniques. They construct an index automatically that links words to the locations of occurrence which helps to spot the words easily. Rodriguez et al. (2008) proposed a method that relaxes the segmentation problem by requiring only segmentation at the text line level.

Louloudis et al. (2009) proposed a segmentation of the page to detect significant text regions. The represented queries are in the form of a descriptor based on the density of the image patches. Then, a sliding window search is performed over the significant regions of the documents using refined template-based matching. A probabilistic representation for learning based word spotting in a multi-writer text is proposed by Rodriguez et al. (2009). The query and the dataset word images are represented as sequences of feature vectors extracted using a sliding window in the writing direction and they are modeled using statistical models.

Unsupervised writer adaptation for unlabeled data has been successfully used for word spotting method proposed by Rodrguez-Serrano et al. (2010) based on statistical adaption of the initial universal codebook to each document. Rodriguez-Serrano et al. (2010) proposed an unsupervised handwritten word spotting using semi-continuous hidden Markov model to separate the word model parameters into a codebook of shapes and a set of word-specific parameters. An HMM-based method which learns character models for word spotting in handwritten documents is proposed by Fischer et al. (2010). Initially, text lines of the document are represented by a sequence of nine geometrical features which is obtained by a sliding window of one-pixel width from left to right over the image. The character models are trained in offline using labeled text line images. Then, a text line model is created as a sequence of letter models according to the transcription.

Kesidis et al. (2011) extracted pixel density of zones and projection profile features and computes the Euclidean distance between word images, and refines the search procedure by user feedback. A template free word spotting method for handwritten documents was described by Frinken et al. (2011) which is derived from the neural network based system. The word spotting is done using a modification of the Connectionist Temporal Classification (CTC) token passing algorithm in conjunction with a recurrent neural network. Rusinol et al. (2011) have proposed a word spotting method for handwritten documents using SIFT descriptor. The drawback of this technique is that directly matching local key points is computationally expensive when dealing with large datasets.

Rodriguez-Serrano et al. (2012) proposed a model-based similarity between vector sequences of handwritten word images with semi-continuous Gaussian mixture HMMs. The work of Shekhar et al. (2013) avoids segmentation by representing regions with a fixed length SIFT descriptor. Khurshid et al. (2012) have proposed a word spotting method for scanned documents using a sequence of sub-patterns. The connected components algorithm is used to transform a word pattern into a sequence of sub-patterns. Each sub-pattern is represented by a sequence of feature vectors. Then, modified Edit distance is used to perform a segmentation-driven string matching and to compute the Segmentation Driven Edit (SDE) distance between the words.

The segmentation-free method for word spotting in handwritten documents proposed by Zhang et al. (2013) based on heat kernel signatures (HKS) descriptors are extracted from a local patch centered at each keypoint. Kessentini et al. (2013) proposed a novel system for segmentation free and lexicon free word spotting and regular expression detection in handwritten documents using filler model which allows accelerating the decoding process. Huang et al. (2013) proposed contextual word model for keyword spotting in off-line Chinese handwritten documents by combining a character classifier and the geometric context as well as linguistic context.

They conducted experiments on handwriting database CASIA-HWDB demonstrate the effectiveness of the proposed method and justify the benefits of geometric and linguistic contexts. A template-free word spotting method for handwritten documents was proposed by Almazan et al. (2013) for multi-writer handwritten documents, which uses attributes-based approach for the pyramidal histogram of characters. This embeds the handwritten words in a more discriminative space, where the similarity between words is independent of the writing style. have proposed to combine SIFT descriptor with Hidden Markov Models (HMM) in a patch-based segmentation free word spotting. Zhang et al. (2013) have proposed segmentation free word spotting based on Heat Kernel Signature (HKS) descriptor. HKS descriptors are extracted from a local patch centered at each key point detected by the SIFT key point detector on the document pages and the query image.

Wshah et al. (2014) proposed a statistical script independent line based word spotting method for offline handwritten documents based on hidden Markov models by comparing filler models and background models for the representation of background and non-keyword text. An unsupervised Exemplar SVM framework for segmentation free word spotting method proposed by Almazan et al. (2014) using a grid of HOG descriptors for documents representation. Then, a sliding window is used to locate the document regions that are most similar to the query. Coherent learning segmentation based Arabic handwritten word spotting system proposed by Khayyat et al. (2014) which can adapt to the nature of Arabic handwriting and the system recognizes Pieces of Arabic Words (PAWs).

The keypoint matching based methods have drawback i.e. an alignment between the keypoint sets has to be computed. In order to avoid exhaustively matching all keypoint pairs, the bag-of-features technique was adopted as the Bag-of-Visual-Words (BoVW). Thontadari et al. (2017) have proposed a segmentation-based word spotting method for handwritten documents using Bag of Visual Words (BoVW) framework based on curvature features. The curvature feature is scalar value describes the geometrical shape of the strokes and requires less memory space to store. In (Rusinol, M., 2011) a bag-of-features word spotting method is presented. It is based on gradient-based SIFT (Scale Invariant Feature Transform) descriptors. In order to create a visual vocabulary, descriptors are calculated on a dense grid over the training corpus and clustered with the k-means algorithm. Each document is divided into overlapping patches and for each patch a bag-of-features statistic is created. Descriptors are quantized with respect to the visual vocabulary. Patches similar to a query image can now be retrieved by evaluating a distance measure between the feature representations. One main drawback of BoVW models is that they do not take into account the spatial distribution of the features. In order to add spatial information to the order less BoVW model, Lazebnik et al. proposed the Spatial Pyramid Matching (SPM) method which takes into account the visual word distribution over the fixed-size patch by creating a pyramid of spatial bins. In Rusinol et al. (2015), and Sudholt et al. (2015) densely extracted SIFT descriptors are used in a Bag-of-Features approach. The quantized descriptors are aggregated into a Spatial Pyramid to form a holistic word image descriptor which can then be used in a simple nearest neighbor approach for word spotting.

An efficient segmentation free word spotting method for the historical document is proposed by Rusinol et al. (2015). They used a patch-based framework of the bag-of-visual-words model powered by SIFT descriptors. By projecting the patch descriptors to a topic space with the latent semantic analysis technique and compressing the descriptors with the product quantization method efficiently index the document information both in terms of memory and time. Based on inkball character models, Howe (2015) proposed a word spotting method using synthetic models composed of individual characters. Ghosh et al. (2015) proposed a segmentation-free query by string word spotting method based on a Pyramidal Histogram of Characters (PHOC) are learned using linear SVMs along with the PHOC labels of the corresponding strings.

Line-level keyword spotting method proposed by Toselli et al. (2016) on the basis of frame-level word posterior probabilities of a full-fledged handwritten text recognizer based on hidden Markov models and N-gram language models. A template-based learning-free word spotting method proposed by Dey et al. (2016) by combining the Local Binary Pattern (LBP) histograms and spatial sampling. One of the main advantages is its independence from the actual representation formalism as well as the underlying language of the document. However, template-based word spotting does not generalize well to different writing styles. Sfikas et al. (2017) have proposed semi supervised segmentation-based keyword spotting based on probabilistic interpretation of Canonical Correlation Analysis (CCA), using Expectation Maximization (EM). Segmentation-free word spotting method for multi-write handwritten documents based on Radial Line Fourier (RLF) descriptor is proposed by Hast et al. (2017). RLF is a short-length feature vector of 32 dimensions, that adheres to the property that the handwritten words across different documents are indeed similar.

Convolutional neural networks (CNN) have been increasingly used for word spotting recently due to success in other fields of computer vision. CNN comes under category of learning-based methods, recently, researchers are moving towards utilizing neural networks for keyword spotting. In order to define word image description and word to word matching, convolutional neural networks (CNN) that include convolutional layers have been used. The first works for word spotting using CNN was presented in (Sharma et al. 2015), the authors used AlexNet pretrained on the ImageNet database to predict word image classes. The CNN features from the second to last layer are then used in order to perform word spotting. In Zhong et al. (2016), proposed a CNN that accepts pairs of word images has been proposed.

This model directly outputs similarity scores for the input pair. In (Poznanski et al. 2016), the author proposed to customize available CNN architecture which processes fixed sized word images and outputs a Pyramidal Histogram of Characters (PHOC) representation. Each level of the Pyramidal Histogram of Characters (PHOC) is then predicted by an individual MLP. All MLPs, however, make use of a shared convolutional part of the network. In (Wilkinson. 2016), a Residual Network is used in combination with a Soft Positive Negative Triplet Loss in order to learn holistic descriptors for word images. These descriptors are then used as features for training.

Rodriguez et al. (2008) have proposed sliding window based Histogram of Oriented Gradients (HOG) features extraction for word spotting in unconstrained handwritten documents. In sliding window approach, at each position, the window is subdivided into cells, and in each cell, a HOG features are accumulated. Slit style HOG features for handwritten document image word spotting was proposed by Terasawa et al. (2009). Newell et al. (2011) have extended the HOG descriptor to include features at multiple scales for character recognition. Saidani et al. (2015) have proposed a novel approach for Arabic and Latin script identification based on HOG feature descriptors. HOG is first applied at word level based on writing orientation analysis. Then, they are extended to word image partitions to capture fine and discriminating details. The unsupervised segmentation-free HOG based word spotting method was proposed by Almazan et al. (2014). Documents are represented by a grid of HOG descriptors, and a sliding-window approach is used to locate the document regions that are most similar to the query.

The appearance and shape of the local object in an image is represented through the distribution of the local intensity gradient orientation and edge direction without requiring equivalent gradient and edge positions (Carcagni et al., 2015). This orientation analysis is robust to lighting changes since the histogram provides translational invariance. The HOG feature descriptor summarizes the distribution of measurements within the image regions. When extracting HOG features, the orientations of gradients are usually quantized into histogram bins and each bin has an orientation range. A histogram of oriented gradients falling into each bin is computed and then normalized to overcome the illumination variation. The orientation of gradients from all blocks are then concatenated together to form a feature descriptor of the whole image.

HOG feature descriptor captures orientation of only isolated pixels, whereas spatial information of neighboring pixels is ignored. Co-occurrence Histogram of Oriented Gradients (Co-HOG) (Watanabe et al., 2009) feature descriptor is an extension of the original HOG feature descriptor that captures the spatial information of neighboring pixels. Instead of counting the occurrence of the gradient orientation of a single pixel, gradient orientations of two or more neighboring pixels are considered. For each pixel in an image block, the gradient orientations of the pixel pair formed by its neighbor and itself are examined. Co-occurrence Histogram of Oriented Gradients is dominant feature descriptor widely used in object detection because Co-HOG feature descriptor accurately represents significant characteristics of the object structure. At the same time, it is more efficient compared with HOG and therefore more suitable for real-time applications. The pedestrian detection method is proposed by Watanabe et al. (2009) based on extraction of Co-HOG feature descriptors. Ren et al. (2010) have proposed object detection method using Co-HOG features with variable location and variable size blocks which captures the characteristics of object structure. Face recognition using weighted Co-HOG feature descriptor is proposed by Do (2012). The character recognition in natural scenes using Convolutional Co-HOG feature descriptors are proposed by Su et al. (2014) and multilingual scene character recognition using Co-HOG and Convolutional Co-HOG feature descriptors are proposed by Tian et al. (2015). In this chapter, we propose a segmentation-free word spotting method for handwritten document images using Scale Space Co-HOG feature descriptor.

PROPOSED METHOD

The state-of-the-art word spotting methods for handwritten documents can be categorized into two groups, segmentation-based methods and segmentation-free methods. In segmentation-based methods, the sequences of operations are applied to the document images. First, the document is pre-processed based on text layout analysis; the handwritten document is segmented into word images. Then, extract the feature descriptor from the segmented word image. Based on this feature descriptor, a distance measure is used to measure the similarity between the query word image and the segmented word image. Thontadari et al. (2016) have proposed segmentation-based word spotting technique using scale space CO-HoG feature descriptor for handwritten documents. One of the limitations of the segmentation-based word spotting methods is that they usually need a layout analysis step for segments the document into words and they also need to perform segmentation step for select the candidate words. But this segmentation step is not always straight forward and any segmentation errors can affect the subsequent word representations and matching steps. This motivates us to move towards segmentation-free word spotting method.

The segmentation-free approaches overcome the problems associated with poor segmentation results by considering the document image as a whole. The gradient information and local image features have been used in segmentation-free approaches trying to benefit from the scale, rotation invariance and they offer robustness to noise. In segmentation-free methods (Leydier et al., 2004; Gatos et al., 2009), the document images are represented by feature descriptor such as SIFT. Then, sliding window approaches are used to locate the document regions that are most similar to the query word (Rusinol et al.,2015; Shekhar et al., 2012; Rothacker et al., 2013; Zhang et al., 2013). The drawback of SIFT-based word spotting is that they are memory intensive; window size cannot be adapted to the length of the query, relatively slow to compute and match.

In this chapter, we proposed to address word spotting problem by dividing the original document images into a set of non-overlapping local patches. Instead of fixed length patches, we adopted multi-length patch representation (Rusinol et al., 2015), which increases the retrieval performance by taking into account the different possible lengths of the query words. The handwritten words are spotted within the document using these patches. Once a query image is given, the local patches are used to determine the word locations within a given document. These local patches must roughly match the size of the text in the document. To the best of the author's knowledge, there is no approach which uses segmentation-free word spotting using Scale Space Co-HOG feature descriptor for handwritten document images. The proposed approach is made up of three steps. Initially, all the document images of the corpus are represented in multiscale (three scale) and in each scale, CO-HOG feature descriptor is extracted from local patches of the document. In the second step, query model is constructed through patch-based approach, in which query patch is represented using scale space Co-HOG descriptor. Finally, we retrieve the local patches using Nearest Neighbor Search *(NNS)* similarity measure algorithm by computing the similarity between the query patch descriptor and the document patch descriptors of dataset by considering appropriate threshold T. The proposed method avoids an explicit word segmentation and any other word preprocessing steps such as binarization, slant correction, etc.

Scale Space Representation

The holistic shapes such as whole words and simple shapes such as characters contained in a handwritten document are extracted more effectively at coarser scales. The extracted shape features of the whole word at coarser scales are potentially more resistant to variation occurring in a different writing style. At finer scales, it is convenient to extract the local information about image gradient and stroke orientation of the words which is more convenient for word image contour description. Hence, in order to represent word in multi scale, we derive images from original document image, which yields scale space representation of original document image. Integrating scale space representation with Co-HOG feature descriptor helps to extract sufficient information from handwritten word image contour. Hence, in this chapter, we proposed to extract Co-HOG feature descriptor at multiple scales and these feature descriptors are called as Scale Space Co-HOG (SS Co-HOG) feature descriptor.

In order to represent document image in multi scale, we derive images from the original document image based on Gaussian convolution operation. We employed three scale representation of an image and at each scale, we extract Co-HOG features and finally concatenate them to form a feature descriptor.

Let I represent an original image. Then, the scale space representation of I can be defined as

$$L(\sigma, I) = I * G(\sigma),$$

where, $G(\sigma)$ is a Gaussian kernel with variance σ and (*) is convolution operation. The width of the Gaussian kernel is controlled by σ. Larger the value of σ makes the Gaussian kernel G wider and smooth the original image more significant. Hence, using a larger value of σ, the convolve operation gets a coarser scale version of the original image. Therefore, different values of σ indicate different scales. It is verified that the width of the Gaussian kernel σ preserves the similar spatial sampling at three scale parameters such as $\sigma=0$, $\sigma=1$, and $\sigma=2$. Hence, in all the experiments, we derive three images from original document image based on Gaussian convolution operation using these three different values of σ.

CO-HOG Feature Descriptor

After representing document image into multiple scales, for each scale, we split every document image into a set of non-overlapping local patches. In order to cope up with different lengths of query words, we adopted multi-length patch approach (Rusinol et al., 2015) where we use four different length sizes of patches. Employing particular patch size is decided at the query time based on length of query word. Based on experimental observation on the document, resolution of a document, height and width of characters present in the document, we consider the local patch has a dimension of $LP_w \times LP_h$ pixels and patch is densely sampled at each pixel. In order to extract Co-HOG feature descriptor from each local patch, we divide a local patch into an equal sized regular grid of dimension. This parameter is related to the font size, and in our method, experimentally set. For each regular grid in the local patch, we calculate the co-occurrence matrix. We compute co-occurrence matrix over a grid G of size at an offset as follows:

$$K_{x,y}(i,j) = \sum_{p=1}^{N}\sum_{q=1}^{M} \begin{cases} 1, & \text{if } G(p,q) = i \text{ and } G(p+x,q+y) = j \\ 0, & \text{otherwise} \end{cases}, \tag{2}$$

where, $K_{x,y}$ is a square matrix of dimension 8×8. Gradient orientation interval $[0^0, 360^0]$ is divided into $N_{bin}=8$ orientations per 45^0. The co-occurrence matrix expresses the distribution of gradient orientations at a given offset over a grid and combinations of neighbor gradient orientations can express shapes in detail. We extract Co-HOG features from corresponding three patches occurred in three scales and finally concatenating the feature descriptors of corresponding patches of all three scales gives the feature descriptor for the local patch of the original document image.

Retrieval Stage

In order to spot the similar words for a given query word, the query-by-example paradigm is followed, where the user inputs the system a sample image of the word. The Co-HOG feature descriptor is extracted from the query patch which is cropped from the document corresponding to a single patch within a document. We retrieve the local patches using Nearest Neighbor Search (NNS) similarity measure algorithm by computing the similarity between the query patch descriptor (f_q) and the document patch descriptors (f_p) of dataset by considering appropriate threshold T. The NNS similarity measure between query descriptor and document patch descriptor is calculated using following equation:

$$NNS = \sqrt{\sum_{i=1}^{D_{LP}}(f_P(i) - f_q(i))^2} < T, \tag{3}$$

where, *NNS* is the similarity distance computed between two patch descriptors i.e. f_p and f_q and D_{LP} is the dimension of a patch descriptor. The returned region from the documents will be considered as relevant if it overlaps with a query patch by at least 60%. Once the most similar local patches have been retrieved, the regions of the document found which is most similar to patch selected. For each document page image, a 2D voting space is constructed where each retrieved local patch will cast its votes. In our case, we consider each grid dimension of the voting space is same as the local patch. Then, each retrieved local patch casts a vote to the location of the document where its geometric center falls and weighted by the approximate threshold T. Once the most similar local patches have been retrieved, the regions of the document which gather most support have to be found and selected as retrieved locations.

Figure 2. Visualization of the word spotting. (a) query image, (b) sample document from GW dataset (c) spotted local patches where words similar to query words are found

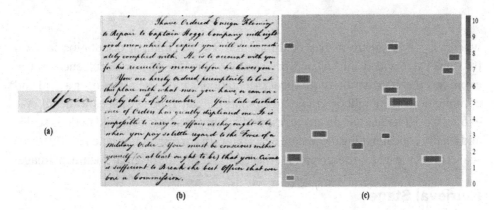

(a)

(b)   (c)

EXPERIMENTAL RESULTS

In this section, we present the performance of the proposed system. First, we present some qualitative results to assess the effectiveness of the method to retrieve visually similar words. Subsequently, we compare the obtained results with other state-of-the-art methods. The proposed method is evaluated on two popular handwritten datasets which are widely used for evaluation of word spotting methods, such as George Washington (GW) dataset (Lavrenko et al., 2004), and IAM dataset (Marti et al., 2002). The Figure 3 shows sample handwritten document images of GW and IAM dataset. The handwriting style in the GW images is less variable and the image quality is quite good, whereas the IAM collection is the most challenging one since the images present severe degradations and the variability in handwriting style is highly noticeable. In our segmentation free approach, a set of patches which are visually similar to the given query are first obtained. Then, a voting scheme aims at finding the locations within the document pages with a high likelihood to find the query word.

Evaluation Metrics

In order to measure the accuracy of proposed word spotting method, we used popular metric Precision (P). Precision gives the fraction of retrieved word instances that are relevant to the query. The Precision (P) is defined as follows:

Figure 3. Sample handwritten document image from GW and IAM dataset

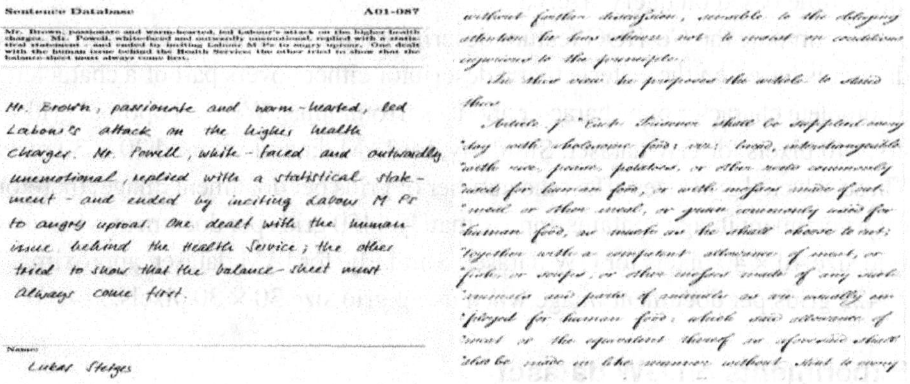
Sentence Database A01-087

Mr. Brown, passionate and warm-hearted, led Labour's attack on the higher health charges. Mr. Powell, white-faced and outwardly unemotional, replied with a statistical statement - and ended by inciting Labour M Ps to angry uproar. One dealt with the human issue behind the Health Service; the other tried to show that the balance-sheet must always come first.

Name: Lukas Stelges

$$P = \frac{\left|\{relavant\ instances\}\right| \cap \left|\{retrieved\ instances\}\right|}{\left|\{retrieved\ instances\}\right|} \tag{4}$$

The mean Average Precision (*mAP*) provides a mean of the average precision for all the query word images and it can be computed as

$$mAP = \frac{\sum_{q=1}^{Q} AveP(q)}{Q}, \tag{5}$$

where, Q is the number of query word images.

Parameters Used

For GW and IAM database, we calculated the line height parameter H in order to define patch size of documents. The line height H has been estimated automatically using projection profile technique of every documents of each database. The text line height H is obtained by calculating the median separation between peaks of the projection profile. After analyzing projection profile of every document of GW database, it is found that the line height H is 80 pixels and similarly for IAM database documents, line height H is 60 pixels. In order to cope up with queries of different lengths, four different sizes of patches are used based on height H of each database. For GW documents, four different patch sizes are 80x80,160x80, 240x80, and 320x80 pixels. Similarly, for IAM dataset documents, four different size patches are 60x60, 120x60, 180x60 and 240x60 pixels. The patch size is determined during query time based on query size.

To compute the Co-HOG feature descriptors, the selection of grid size for each dataset is based on the criteria that a descriptor either covers part of a character, or a complete character or a character and its surroundings. We used optimal grid size 40×40 pixels for GW dataset. Similarly, for IAM dataset we used 30×30 pixels. These selected grid sizes affect the number of grids per document image; therefore, each document image contains approximately 4450 grids per document when using grid size 40×40 pixels for GW dataset. Similarly, for IAM dataset, approximately 19422 grids per document image when using grid size 30×30 pixels.

Experiments on GW dataset

The GW dataset is a historical dataset consists of 20 pages from a collection of English letters written by George Washington and his associates in the year 1755. We have conducted the experiments using 20 pages of GW dataset. Each class of words may occur at least two times per document. Figure 4 demonstrates the qualitative results obtained on one of the documents of GW dataset using our approach for the query word *"your"*. The spotted regions are shown using the red color.

Figure 5 shows qualitative retrieval results of our approach obtained for documents of GW dataset. The first column shows query words and subsequent columns display spotted local patches where words similar to query word are found.

Figure 4. Example of spotting results for the query word "your" in one of documents of GW dataset

234

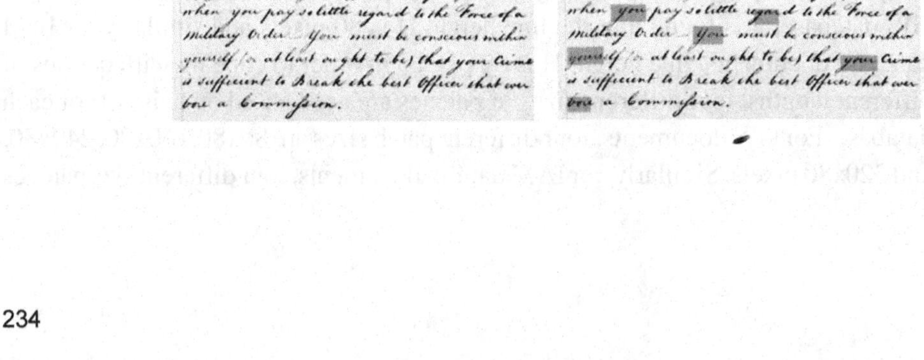

Figure 5. Sample retrieval results: Query word images (first column) and corresponding retrieved word instance patches from GW dataset

The word spotting and retrieval accuracy of the proposed segmentation-free method for handwritten documents is compared with existing segmentation-free and segmentation-based methods which are popular and considered as benchmark word spotting methods for handwritten documents. Table 1 demonstrates quantitative results of our approach obtained on GW dataset and the review of the achieved performances of four state-of-the-art segmentation-free and three segmentation-based methods. We compared the performance of the proposed method with existing segmentation-free methods such as Rothacker et al. (2013), Zhang et al. (2013), Almazan et al. (2014) and Rusinol et al. (2015). Similarly, we considered segmentation based methods such as Rath et al. (2007), Rodriguez et al. (2008), and Almazan et al. (2013) for comparison purpose.

Experimental setup such as dataset size and number of query words are maintained separately for two categories of existing techniques such as segmentation-free and segmentation-based word spotting methods. The dataset set size and number of query words are 20 document pages and 4860 query words(patches) for all the segmentation-free methods. In case of segmentation-based methods, it is necessary to segment document into word images in order to extract and represent word images using feature vector. Hence, documents of dataset must be segmented into words. We segment document images into lines and then into words using robust algorithm proposed by Papavassiliou et al. (2010). The sample results of segmented word images are shown in Figure 5. After segmenting GW documents into words, we have taken subsets of manually labeled 1680 word instances of 28 classes of words from all the 20 pages of scanned handwritten documents (28 *classes* $\times$ 20 *pages* $\times$ 3 *instances* = 1680). Each class of words may occur at least two times per document. For segmentation based methods, we conducted experiments using five-fold cross validation. While performing five-fold cross-validation, we partitioned the dataset into five disjoint subsets and each subset consists of 336 word images (from each class of words we have considered 8 word instances). In the training stage, 1344 word instances are used and remaining 336 word images are used for testing. Hence, for every experiment, we have 336 word images as test samples. The cross-validation process is repeated five times, with each subset used exactly once for validation.

In Table 1, the size of the dataset, the feature descriptors and comparison results of our approach with existing methods are shown. From the Table 1, we can see that proposed system obtains quite reasonable results and considerably outperform the existing segmentation-based and segmentation-fee word spotting methods for GW dataset. The proposed method is evaluated with both fixed length and multi-length patches. The fixed length of 180x60 pixels is used to divide document images into patches and similar size is used for query word patches. The experimental setup is maintained as like in multi-length patches based approach given in the Table 1.

Table 1. The performance comparison of our approach with state-of-the-art segmentation free and segmentation-based methods for GW dataset

Methods	Features	Experimental setup	Segmentation	Learning	Map (%)
Rath et al. (2007)	Word profile	20 pages, 1680 queries	Words	5-fold cross validation	73.71
Rodriguez et al. (2008)	HOG	20 pages, 1680 queries	Words	5-fold cross validation	71.70
Almazan et al. (2013)	SIFT	20 pages, 1680 queries	Words	5-fold cross validation	85.63
Zhang et al. (2013)	SIFT	20 pages, 4860 queries	None	NO	79.35
Rothacker et al. (2013)	SIFT	20 pages, 4860 queries	None	NO	61.10
Almanzan et al. (2014)	HOG	20 pages, 4860 queries	None	NO	80.29
Rusinol et al. (2015)	SIFT	20 pages, 4860 queries	None	NO	61.35
Proposed method (Fixed length patches)	SS CO HOG	20 pages, 4860 queries	None	NO	88.35
Proposed method (Multi-length patches)	SS CO HOG	20 pages, 4860 queries	None	NO	91.30

Figure 6. Example of segmented word images from (a) GW database and (b) IAM database

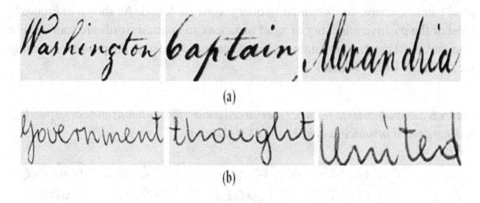

(a)

(b)

The performance of the proposed method for fixed length patches based approach yields lower retrieval accuracy compared to multi-length patches based approach.

Experiments on IAM dataset

The IAM dataset is modern handwritten dataset consists of 1539 pages of handwritten modern English text from the Lancaster-Oslo/Bergen corpus (LOB) (Johansson et al., 1978), written by 657 writers. From this dataset, we have used 5785 query words extracted from the pages of IAM dataset in order to evaluate our approach. The Figure 6 shows word spotting results visually obtained on one of the documents of IAM dataset using our approach for the query word *"British"*. The spotted regions are shown using the red color.

Figure 7. Example of spotting results for the query word "British" in one of the documents of IAM dataset

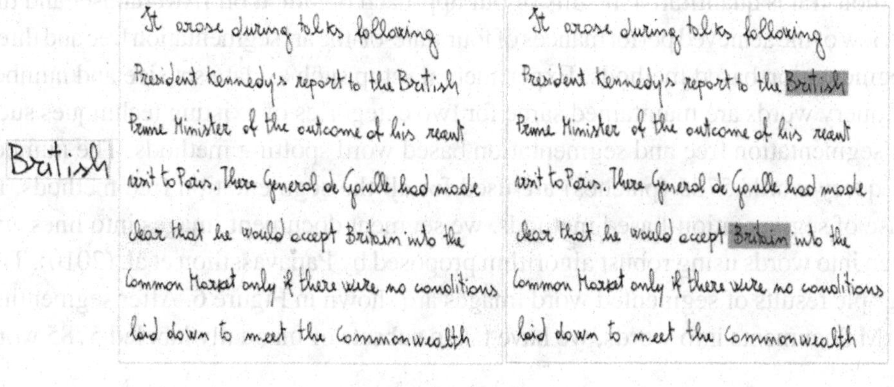

Figure 8 shows the qualitative results of our approach to documents of IAM dataset. The first column shows query words and subsequent columns display spotted local patches where words similar to query word are found. As shown in Figure 8, most of the positive matching of word instances and partial words are spotted. For example, local patches containing "Federation" are spotted as the positive matching for the query word "Federal".

Figure 8. Sample retrieval results: Query word image (first column) and corresponding retrieved word instance patches from IAM dataset

In this section, we present performance comparison of our approach with segmentation-free and segmentation-based methods which are mentioned in the previous section where comparison results on GW database is presented. Table 2 demonstrates quantitative results of our approach obtained on IAM dataset and the review of the achieved performances of four state-of-the art segmentation free and three segmentation based methods. Experimental setup such as data set size and number of query words are maintained same for two categories of existing techniques such as segmentation free and segmentation based word spotting methods. The number of query words 5785 (patches) are used for all the segmentation free methods. In case of segmentation-based methods, we segment document images into lines and then into words using robust algorithm proposed by Papavassiliou et al. (2010). The sample results of segmented word images are shown in Figure 6. After segmenting IAM documents into words, we have taken subsets of manually labeled 5785 word

Table 2. The performance comparison of our approach with state-of-the-art segmentation- free and segmentation-based word spotting methods for IAM dataset

Methods	Features	Experimental setup	Segmentation	Learning	Map (%)
Rath et al. (2007)	Word profile	5785 queries	Words	5-fold cross validation	73.71
Rodriguez et al. (2008)	HOG	5785 queries	Words	5-fold cross validation	71.70
Almazan et al. (2013)	SIFT	5785 queries	Words	5-fold cross validation	85.63
Zhang et al. (2013)	SIFT	5785 queries	None	NO	80.21
Rothacker et al. (2013)	SIFT	5785 queries	None	NO	63.18
Almanzan et al. (2014)	HOG	5785 queries	None	NO	72.16
Rusinol et al. (2015)	SIFT	5785 queries	None	NO	64.29
Proposed method (Fixed length patches)	SS CO HOG	5785 queries	None	NO	86.20
Proposed method (Multi-length patches)	SS CO HOG	5785 queries	None	NO	89.32

instances of scanned handwritten documents. For segmentation based methods, we conducted experiments using five-fold cross validation. While performing five-fold cross-validation, we partitioned the dataset into five disjoint subsets and each subset consists of 1157 word images. In the training stage, 4628 word instances are used and remaining 1157 word images are used for testing. Hence, for every experiment, we have 1157 word images as test samples. The cross-validation process is repeated five times, with each subset used exactly once for validation.

In Table 2, the size of the dataset, the feature descriptors and comparison results of our approach with existing segmentation and segmentation-free methods are shown. It is observed that, compared to existing segmentation based and segmentation free methods, the proposed segmentation free word spotting method yields the highest accuracy. The proposed multi-length patch based approach achieves highest accuracy compared to fixed length (220x80 pixels) patch based approach for our algorithm.

DISCUSSION

The proposed segmentation-free word spotting method spots and retrieves most of the relevant word instances, even if local patches overlap with a query patch by at least 60%. Through experimental results, we found that short queries performed worse than larger ones when using a fixed size of the patch. Therefore, we have used a multi-length patch representation in order to fix this shortcoming. We can see in the results that an important gain in mAP when the patch width is adapted to the query width. It is observed that among four different sizes of patch, only the small patch size configuration performs slightly worse than the fixed length approach. The short queries and substring from longer words are more possible to obtain false positives since we avoided matching the substrings in our method. The Figure 9 shows some examples of false positives.

Based on the experimental results obtained on GW and IAM dataset, we can conclude that our approach efficiently retrieves and localize the handwritten words which are having non uniform illumination, suffering from the noise and written by different writers. The highest accuracy of our approach is due to the extraction of illumination and scale invariant Co-HOG feature descriptor at multi scale representation of word images. Complex objects such as handwritten words are perceived at multiple scales, which encodes the information of the word image at multiple scales. One of the important factors is Co-HOG descriptor which captures the character shape information more precisely and encodes the local spatial information by counting the frequency of co-occurrence of gradient orientation of neighboring pixel pairs. Moreover, Co-HOG descriptor is more robust and discriminative, because it captures the occurrence of edge characteristics of text strokes by exhaustively considering every grid within a word image patch. The Scale Space Co-HOG feature descriptors are robust to illumination variation and invariance to local geometric transformation compared to HOG feature descriptors. Scale space representation dominates more discriminating ability than uniscale, this is due to properties of coarser and finer scale. The coarser scale provides more resistant to variation occurring in a different writing style, and the finer scale provides the local information about image gradient and stroke orientation. The drawback of our approach is its high dimensionality, which has a negative impact on the computational cost. The proposed segmentation free based word spotting method can be employed for industrial applications, such as automatic mail sorting, retrieval of handwritten documents from digital libraries and etc.

CHAPTER SUMMARY

In this chapter, we proposed a segmentation-free based word spotting method for handwritten document images using scale space Co-HOG feature descriptor. We have presented an efficient word spotting method for handwritten document collections that does not involve any segmentation stage. Thus the proposed method presents a clear advantage over segmentation-based methods which are likely to

Figure 9. Examples for some false positives

fail in challenging scenarios. The proposed method yields a very compact, efficient and discriminative representation using SS Co-HOG feature descriptor which is able to efficiently index the document information both in terms of memory and computational cost. By adopting a multi-length patch representation, there is increase in the retrieval performance when querying small words. We have presented a systematic analysis of the proposed method using the popular datasets, in order to assess the configuration which maximizes the word spotting performance. We offered a comprehensive comparison with state-of-the-art segmentation free and segmentation-based word spotting methods, it is observed that, the proposed method achieves the highest accuracy compared to existing segmentation-free and segmentation-based methods for both types of handwritten documents such as historical documents (GW) and modern documents (IAM) which are a single writer and multi writer documents. Based on the experimental results obtained on GW and IAM dataset, we can conclude that our approach efficiently retrieves the handwritten words which are having non uniform illumination, suffering from the noise and written by different writers. The highest accuracy of our approach is due to the extraction of illumination and scale invariant Co-HOG feature descriptor at multi scale representation of multi-length patches.

REFERENCES

Almazan, J., Gordo, A., Fornes, A., & Valveny, E. (2013). Handwritten word spotting with corrected attributes. In *Proceedings of International Conf. on Computer Vision* (pp. 1017-1024). Academic Press.

Almazan, J. Gordo, A. Fornes, A. & Valveny, E. (2014). Segmentation-free word spotting with exemplar SVMs. *Pattern Recognition,* (47), 3967-3978.

Carcagni, P. Del Coco, M. Leo, M. & Distante, C. (2015). Facial expression recognition and histograms of oriented gradients: a comprehensive study. *Springer Plus,* (4), 645.

Dey, S., Nicolaou, A., Llados, J., & Pal, U. (2016). *Local binary pattern for word spotting in handwritten historical. document. In Joint IAPR International Workshops on Statistical Techniques in Pattern Recognition* (pp. 574–583). Structural and Syntactic Pattern Recognition.

Do, T., & Kijak, E. (2012). Face recognition using co-occurrence histograms of oriented gradients. In *37th International Conference on Acoustics, Speech, and Signal Processing* (pp. 1301-1304). 10.1109/ICASSP.2012.6288128

Fischer, A., Keller, A., Frinken, V., & Bunke, H. (2010). HMM-based word spotting in handwritten documents using subword models. In *Proceedings 20th International Conf. on Pattern Recognition* (pp. 3416-3419). 10.1109/ICPR.2010.834

Frinken, V. Fischer, A. & Bunke, H. (2011). A novel word spotting algorithm using bidirectional long short-term memory neural networks. *Artificial Neural Networks in Pattern Recognition*, 185-196.

George, N., & Daniel, L. (2006). Interactive Document Processing and Digital Libraries. In *Proceedings of the Second International Conference on Document Image Analysis for Libraries*. IEEE Computer Society.

Ghosh, S. K., & Valveny, E. (2015). Query by string word spotting based on character bi-gram indexing. In *Proceedings of International Conference on Document Analysis and Recognition* (pp. 881-885). 10.1109/ICDAR.2015.7333888

Giotis, A. P., Sfikas, G., Gatos, B., & Nikou, C. (2017). A survey of document image word spotting techniques. *Pattern Recognition*, *68*, 310–332. doi:10.1016/j.patcog.2017.02.023

Hast, A. & Vats, E. (2017). *Radial Line Fourier Descriptor for Handwritten Word Representation.* arXiv preprint.

Howe, N. R. (2015). Ink ball models for character localization and out-of-vocabulary word spotting. In *Proceedings of International Conf. on Document Analysis and Recognition* (pp. 381-385). Academic Press.

Huang, L. Yin, F. Chen, Q. H. & Liu, C. L. (2013). Keyword spotting in unconstrained handwritten Chinese documents using contextual word model. *Image and Vision Computing,* (31), 958-968.

Jones, G. J., Foote, J. T., Jones, K. S., & Young, S. J. (1995). Video mail retrieval: The effect of word spotting accuracy on precision. In *Proceedings of International Conference on Acoustics, Speech, and Signal Processing* (vol. 1, pp. 309-312). 10.1109/ICASSP.1995.479535

Keaton, P., Greenspan, H., & Goodman, R. (1997). Keyword spotting for cursive document retrieval. *Proceedings of International Workshop on Document Image Analysis,* 74-81. 10.1109/DIA.1997.627095

Kesidis, A. L. Galiotou, E. Gatos, B.& Pratikakis, I. (2011). A word spotting framework for historical machine-printed documents. *International Journal on Document Analysis and Recognition,* (14), 131-144.

Kessentini, Y., Chatelain, C., & Paquet, T. (2013). Word spotting and regular expression detection in handwritten documents. In *Proceedings of International Conference on Document Analysis and Recognition* (pp. 516-520). 10.1109/ICDAR.2013.109

Khayyat, M., Lam, L., & Suen, C. Y. (2014). Learning-based word spotting system for arabic handwritten documents. *Pattern Recognition, 47*(3), 1021–1030. doi:10.1016/j.patcog.2013.08.014

Khurshid, K., Faure, C., & Vincent, N. (2012). Word spotting in historical printed documents using shape and sequence comparisons. *Pattern Recognition, 45*(7), 2598–2609. doi:10.1016/j.patcog.2011.10.013

Kumar, G., & Govindaraju, V. (2014). A Bayesian approach to script independent multilingual keyword spotting. In *Proceedings of International Conf. on Frontiers in Handwriting Recognition* (pp. 357-362). 10.1109/ICFHR.2014.66

Lavrenko, V., Rath, T. M., & Manmatha, R. (2004). Holistic word recognition for handwritten historical documents. In *Proceedings of First International Workshop on Document Image Analysis for Libraries* (pp. 278-287). 10.1109/DIAL.2004.1263256

Lazebnik, S., Schmid, C., & Ponce, J. (2006). Beyond bags of features: spatial pyramid matching for recognizing natural scene 1480 categories. In *Proceedings of the IEEE Computer Society Conference on Computer Vision and Pattern Recognition* (pp. 2169–2178).

Leydier, Y., Le Bourgeois, F., & Emptoz, H. (2005). Omni lingual segmentation-free word spotting for ancient manuscripts indexation. In *Proceedings of IEEE International Conf. on Document Analysis and Recognition* (pp. 533-537). 10.1109/ICDAR.2005.171

Louloudis, G. Gatos, B. Pratikakis, I. & Halatsis, C. (2009). Text line and word segmentation of handwritten documents. *Pattern Recognition,* (42), 3169-3183.

Manmatha, R. & Croft, W. B (1997). Word spotting: Indexing handwritten archives. *Intelligent Multimedia Information Retrieval Collection*, 43-64.

Marti, U. V., & Bunke, H. (2001). Using a statistical language model to improve the performance of an HMM-based cursive handwriting recognition system. *International Journal of Pattern Recognition and Artificial Intelligence, I*(01), 65–90. doi:10.1142/S0218001401000848

Marti, U. V. & Bunke, H. (2002). The IAM-database: An English sentence database for offline handwriting recognition. *International Journal on Document Analysis and Recognition,* (5), 39-46.

Newell, A. J., & Griffin, L. D. (2011). Multiscale histogram of oriented gradient descriptors for robust character recognition. In *Proceedings of International Conference on Document Analysis and Recognition* (pp. 1085-1089). 10.1109/ICDAR.2011.219

Papavassiliou, V., Katsouros, V., & Carayannis, G. (2010). A Morphological Approach for Text-Line Segmentation in Handwritten Documents. In *Proceedings of 15th International Conference on Frontiers in Handwriting Recognition*. 10.1109/ICFHR.2010.11

Poznanski, A., & Wolf, L. (2016). CNN-N-Gram for Handwriting Word Recognition. Proceedings Computer Vision and Pattern Recognition, 2305–2314.

Rath, T. M., & Manmatha, R. (2003). Word image matching using dynamic time warping. In *Proceedings of IEEE International Conference on Computer Vision and Pattern Recognition* (vol. 2, pp. 1-7). 10.1109/CVPR.2003.1211511

Rath, T. M., & Manmatha, R. (2003). Features for word spotting in historical manuscripts. In *Proceedings of International Conf. on Document Analysis and Recognition* (pp. 218-222). 10.1109/ICDAR.2003.1227662

Rath, T. M., & Manmatha, R. (2007). Word spotting for historical documents. *International Journal on Document Analysis and Recognition*, 9(2-4), 139–152. doi:10.100710032-006-0027-8

Ren, H., Heng, C. K., Zheng, W., Liang, L., & Chen, X. (2010). Fast object detection using boosted co-occurrence histograms of oriented gradients. In *Proceedings of IEEE 17th International Conference on Image Processing* (pp. 2705-2708). 10.1109/ICIP.2010.5651963

Rodriguez, J. A., & Perronnin, F. (2008). Local gradient histogram features for word spotting in unconstrained handwritten documents. In *Proceedings of First International Conf. on Frontiers in Handwriting Recognition* (pp. 7-12).

Rodriguez-Serrano, J. A., & Perronnin, F. (2009). Handwritten word-spotting using hidden Markov models and universal vocabularies. *Pattern Recognition*, 42(9), 2106–2116. doi:10.1016/j.patcog.2009.02.005

Rodriguez-Serrano, J. A., & Perronnin, F. (2012). A model-based sequence similarity with application to handwritten word spotting. *IEEE Transactions on Pattern Analysis and Machine Intelligence*, (34), 2108-2120.

Rodriguez-Serrano, J. A. Perronnin, F. Snchez, G. & Llads, J. (2010). Unsupervised writer adaptation of whole-word HMMs with application to word-spotting. *Pattern Recognition Letters*, (31),742-749.

Rothacker, L., Rusinol, M., & Fink, G. (2013). Bag-of-features HMMs for segmentation-free word spotting in handwritten documents. In *Proceedings of International Conferences on Document Analysis and Recognition* (pp.1305-1309). 10.1109/ICDAR.2013.264

Rothfeder, J. L., Feng, S., & Rath, T. M. (2003). Using corner feature correspondences to rank word images by similarity. In *Proceedings of International Workshop on Computer Vision and Pattern Recognition* (vol. 3, pp. 30-30). 10.1109/CVPRW.2003.10021

Rusinol, M., Aldavert, D., Toledo, R., & Llados, J. (2015). Efficient segmentation-free keyword spotting in historical document collections. *Pattern Recognition*, (48), 545-555.

Rusinol, M., Rodriguez-Serrano, A. D., Toledo, R., & Llados, J. (2011). Browsing heterogeneous document collections by a segmentation-free word spotting method. In *Proceedings International Conference on Document Analysis and Recognition* (pp. 63-67). 10.1109/ICDAR.2011.22

Saidani, A., & Echi, A. K. (2015). Pyramid histogram of oriented gradient for machine-printed/handwritten and arabic/latin word discrimination. *Proceedings of International Conf. on Soft Computing and Pattern Recognition (SoC-PaR)*, 267-272.

Sfikas, G., Gatos, B., & Nikou, C. (2017). SEMICCA: A New Semi-Supervised Probabilistic CCA Model for Keyword Spotting. In *Proceedings of International Conf. Image Processing* (pp. 1107-1111). 10.1109/ICIP.2017.8296453

Sharma, A., & Pramod, S. K. (2015). Adapting Off-the-Shelf CNNs for Word Spotting & Recognition. In *Proceedings of the Int. Conf. on Document Analysis and Recognition* (pp. 986–990). 10.1109/ICDAR.2015.7333909

Shekhar, R., & Jawahar, C. V. (2013). Document specific sparse coding for word retrieval. In *Proceedings of International Conf. on Document Analysis and Recognition* (pp. 643-647). 10.1109/ICDAR.2013.132

Srihari, S. N., Srinivasan, H., Babu, P., & Bhole, C. (2006). Handwritten Arabic word spotting using the cedarabic document analysis system. In *Proceedings of Symposium on Document Image Understanding Technology* (pp.123-132). Academic Press.

Srihari, S. N. Srinivasan H. Haung C. & Shetty, S. (2005). Spotting words in Latin, Devanagari and Arabic scripts. *Indian Journal of Artificial Intelligence*, (3), 2-9.

Su, B., Lu, S., Tian, S., Lim, J. H., & Tan, C. L. (2014). Character recognition in natural scenes using convolutional co-occurrence hog. In *Proceedings of the 22nd International Conference on Pattern Recognition* (pp. 2926-2931). 10.1109/ICPR.2014.504

Sudholt, S., & Fink, G. A. (2015). A Modified Isomap Approach to Manifold Learning in Word Spotting. In *Proceedings of the German Conference on Pattern Recognition* (pp. 529–539). 10.1007/978-3-319-24947-6_44

Terasawa, K., & Tanaka, Y. (2009). Slit style HOG feature for document image word spotting. In *Proceedings of International Conference on Document Analysis and Recognition* (pp. 116-120). 10.1109/ICDAR.2009.118

Thontadari & Prabhakar, C. J. (2016). Scale Space Co-Occurrence HOG Features for Word Spotting in Handwritten Document Images. *International Journal of Computer Vision and Image Processing*, (6), 71-86.

Thontadari & Prabhakar, C. J. (2017). Segmentation Based Word Spotting Method for Handwritten Documents. *International Journals of Advanced Research in Computer Science and Software Engineering*, (7), 35-40.

Tian, S., Lu, S., Su, B., & Tan, C. L. (2013). Scene Text Recognition Using Co-occurrence of Histogram of Oriented Gradients. *12th International Conference on Document Analysis and Recognition*, 912-916. 10.1109/ICDAR.2013.186

Toselli, A. H., Vidal, E., Romero, V., & Frinken, V. (2016). HMM word graph-based keyword spotting in handwritten document images. *Information Sciences,* (370), 497-518,

Watanabe, T., Ito, S., & Yokoi, K. (2009). Co-occurrence histograms of oriented gradients for pedestrian detection. In *Advances in Image and Video Technology* (pp. 37–47). Springer Berlin Heidelberg. doi:10.1007/978-3-540-92957-4_4

Wilkinson, T., & Brun, A. (2016). Semantic and Verbatim Word Spotting using Deep Neural Networks. In *Proceedings of the International Conference on Frontiers in Handwriting Recognition* (pp. 307–312). 10.1109/ICFHR.2016.0065

Wshah, S. Kumar, G. & Govindaraju, V. (2014). Statistical script independent word spotting in offline handwritten documents. *Pattern Recognition,* (47), 1039-1050.

Zhang, B., Srihari, S. N., & Huang, C. (2004). Word image retrieval using binary features. In *Proceedings of SPIE Conference on Document Recognition and Retrieval XI* (pp. 45-54), International Society for Optics and Photonics.

Zhang, X., & Tan, C. L. (2013). Segmentation-free keyword spotting for handwritten documents based on heat kernel signature. In *Proceedings of International Conf. on Document Analysis and Recognition* (pp. 827-831). 10.1109/ICDAR.2013.169

Zhong, Z., Pan, W., Jin, L., Mouch'ere, H., & Viard-Gaudin, C. (2016). SpottingNet: Learning the similarity of word images with convolutional neural network for word spotting in handwritten historical documents. In *Proceedings of the 15th International Conference on Frontiers in Handwriting Recognition* (pp. 295–300). 10.1109/ICFHR.2016.0063

Related Readings

To continue IGI Global's long-standing tradition of advancing innovation through emerging research, please find below a compiled list of recommended IGI Global book chapters and journal articles in the areas of artificial intelligence, machine learning, and cognitive science. These related readings will provide additional information and guidance to further enrich your knowledge and assist you with your own research.

Abdolshah, M., Farazmand, N., Mollaaghamirzaei, A., Eshragh, F., & Nezhad, K. G. (2017). Analyzing and Studying the Selection Tests based on their Capabilities in Evaluation of Various Jobs Proficiencies and Abilities. In A. Bhattacharya (Ed.), *Strategic Human Capital Development and Management in Emerging Economies* (pp. 90–109). Hershey, PA: IGI Global. doi:10.4018/978-1-5225-1974-4.ch005

Abuljadail, M. H., Ha, L., Wang, F., & Yang, L. (2015). What Motivates Online Shoppers to "Like" Brands' Facebook Fan Pages? In A. Mesquita & C. Tsai (Eds.), *Human Behavior, Psychology, and Social Interaction in the Digital Era* (pp. 279–293). Hershey, PA: IGI Global. doi:10.4018/978-1-4666-8450-8.ch014

Akbar, S., & Khurana, H. (2017). Chronic Mental Illness in Old Age Homes: An International Perspective. In B. Prasad (Ed.), *Chronic Mental Illness and the Changing Scope of Intervention Strategies, Diagnosis, and Treatment* (pp. 21–39). Hershey, PA: IGI Global. doi:10.4018/978-1-5225-0519-8.ch002

Related Readings

Alcántara-Pilar, J. M., del Barrio-García, S., Crespo-Almendros, E., & Porcu, L. (2015). A Review of Psycho- vs. Socio-Linguistics Theories: An Application to Marketing Research. In J. Alcántara-Pilar, S. del Barrio-García, E. Crespo-Almendros, & L. Porcu (Eds.), *Analyzing the Cultural Diversity of Consumers in the Global Marketplace* (pp. 227–255). Hershey, PA: IGI Global. doi:10.4018/978-1-4666-8262-7.ch011

Alcántara-Pilar, J. M., del Barrio-García, S., Crespo-Almendros, E., & Porcu, L. (2015). The Moderating Role of Language on Perceived Risk and Information-Processing Online. In J. Alcántara-Pilar, S. del Barrio-García, E. Crespo-Almendros, & L. Porcu (Eds.), *Analyzing the Cultural Diversity of Consumers in the Global Marketplace* (pp. 320–345). Hershey, PA: IGI Global. doi:10.4018/978-1-4666-8262-7.ch015

Antonietti, A., Caravita, S. C., Colombo, B., & Simonelli, L. (2015). Blogs' Potentialities in Learning: What Are the Key Variables to Promote Cognitive Empowerment. In A. Mesquita & C. Tsai (Eds.), *Human Behavior, Psychology, and Social Interaction in the Digital Era* (pp. 21–44). Hershey, PA: IGI Global. doi:10.4018/978-1-4666-8450-8.ch002

Antonova, A. (2015). How Social Factors Influence Implicit Knowledge Construction on the Internet. In Z. Jin (Ed.), *Exploring Implicit Cognition: Learning, Memory, and Social Cognitive Processes* (pp. 205–215). Hershey, PA: IGI Global. doi:10.4018/978-1-4666-6599-6.ch010

Araujo, B. H., & Nasseh, I. E. (2017). Understanding the Interdisciplinary Meaning of Beauty to Neuroscience: Designing Beauty to Neuroscience. In R. Zuanon (Ed.), *Projective Processes and Neuroscience in Art and Design* (pp. 103–118). Hershey, PA: IGI Global. doi:10.4018/978-1-5225-0510-5.ch007

Athota, V. S. (2017). Foundations and Future of Well-Being: How Personality Influences Happiness and Well-Being. In S. Háša & R. Brunet-Thornton (Eds.), *Impact of Organizational Trauma on Workplace Behavior and Performance* (pp. 279–294). Hershey, PA: IGI Global. doi:10.4018/978-1-5225-2021-4.ch012

B. N. R., Prasad, B. V., & Tavaragi, M. S. (2017). Legal Aspects of Chronic Mental Illness. In B. Prasad (Ed.), Chronic Mental Illness and the Changing Scope of Intervention Strategies, Diagnosis, and Treatment (pp. 225-235). Hershey, PA: IGI Global. doi:10.4018/978-1-5225-0519-8.ch012

Bandy, J. (2017). Employee Wellness Programs: An International Examination. In F. Topor (Ed.), *Handbook of Research on Individualism and Identity in the Globalized Digital Age* (pp. 359–379). Hershey, PA: IGI Global. doi:10.4018/978-1-5225-0522-8.ch016

Barone, P. A. (2017). Defining and Understanding the Development of Juvenile Delinquency from an Environmental, Sociological, and Theoretical Perspective. In S. Egharevba (Ed.), *Police Brutality, Racial Profiling, and Discrimination in the Criminal Justice System* (pp. 215–238). Hershey, PA: IGI Global. doi:10.4018/978-1-5225-1088-8.ch010

Barratt, J., & Bishop, J. (2015). The Impacts of Alcohol on E-Dating Activity: Increases in Flame Trolling Corresponds with Higher Alcohol Consumption. In J. Bishop (Ed.), *Psychological and Social Implications Surrounding Internet and Gaming Addiction* (pp. 186–197). Hershey, PA: IGI Global. doi:10.4018/978-1-4666-8595-6.ch011

Beard, R. L., & O'Connor, M. K. (2015). Listening to Alzheimer's: The Role of Social Location in Illness Narratives. In C. Dick-Muehlke, R. Li, & M. Orleans (Eds.), *Psychosocial Studies of the Individual's Changing Perspectives in Alzheimer's Disease* (pp. 1–32). Hershey, PA: IGI Global. doi:10.4018/978-1-4666-8478-2.ch001

Bedi, D. (2017). Efficacy of Art Therapy in Treating Patients with Paranoid Schizophrenia. In B. Prasad (Ed.), *Chronic Mental Illness and the Changing Scope of Intervention Strategies, Diagnosis, and Treatment* (pp. 308–320). Hershey, PA: IGI Global. doi:10.4018/978-1-5225-0519-8.ch017

Bermeitinger, C. (2015). Priming. In Z. Jin (Ed.), *Exploring Implicit Cognition: Learning, Memory, and Social Cognitive Processes* (pp. 16–60). Hershey, PA: IGI Global. doi:10.4018/978-1-4666-6599-6.ch002

Bishop, J. (2015). Determining the Risk of Digital Addiction to Adolescent Targets of Internet Trolling: Implications for the UK Legal System. In J. Bishop (Ed.), *Psychological and Social Implications Surrounding Internet and Gaming Addiction* (pp. 31–42). Hershey, PA: IGI Global. doi:10.4018/978-1-4666-8595-6.ch003

Bishop, J. (2015). Using "On-the-Fly Corpus Linguistics" to Systematically Derive Word Definitions Using Inductive Abstraction and Reductionist Correlation Analysis: Considering Seductive and Gratifying Properties of Computer Jargon. In J. Bishop (Ed.), *Psychological and Social Implications Surrounding Internet and Gaming Addiction* (pp. 153–170). Hershey, PA: IGI Global. doi:10.4018/978-1-4666-8595-6.ch009

Boesch, B. (2017). Enabling Creativity: Using Garden Exploration as a Vehicle for Creative Expression and Analysis. In N. Silton (Ed.), *Exploring the Benefits of Creativity in Education, Media, and the Arts* (pp. 117–135). Hershey, PA: IGI Global. doi:10.4018/978-1-5225-0504-4.ch006

Bozoglan, B., & Demirer, V. (2015). The Association between Internet Addiction and Psychosocial Variables. In J. Bishop (Ed.), *Psychological and Social Implications Surrounding Internet and Gaming Addiction* (pp. 171–185). Hershey, PA: IGI Global. doi:10.4018/978-1-4666-8595-6.ch010

Byrd-Poller, L., Farmer, J. L., & Ford, V. (2017). The Role of Leaders in Facilitating Healing After Organizational Trauma. In S. Háša & R. Brunet-Thornton (Eds.), *Impact of Organizational Trauma on Workplace Behavior and Performance* (pp. 318–340). Hershey, PA: IGI Global. doi:10.4018/978-1-5225-2021-4.ch014

Cacho-Elizondo, S., Shahidi, N., & Tossan, V. (2015). Giving Up Smoking Using SMS Messages on your Mobile Phone. In A. Mesquita & C. Tsai (Eds.), *Human Behavior, Psychology, and Social Interaction in the Digital Era* (pp. 72–94). Hershey, PA: IGI Global. doi:10.4018/978-1-4666-8450-8.ch004

Card, S., & Wang, H. (2015). Taking Care to Play: Meaningful Communication in Dementia Care in Chinese Culture. In C. Dick-Muehlke, R. Li, & M. Orleans (Eds.), *Psychosocial Studies of the Individual's Changing Perspectives in Alzheimer's Disease* (pp. 76–103). Hershey, PA: IGI Global. doi:10.4018/978-1-4666-8478-2.ch004

Carrasco, G., & Kinnamon, E. (2017). An Examination of Selfish and Selfless Motives: A Review of the Social Psychological and Behavioral Economics Literature. In R. Ianole (Ed.), *Applied Behavioral Economics Research and Trends* (pp. 93–109). Hershey, PA: IGI Global. doi:10.4018/978-1-5225-1826-6.ch006

Cejka, P., & Mohelska, H. (2017). National Culture Influence on Organisational Trauma: A Conceptual Framework Review. In S. Háša & R. Brunet-Thornton (Eds.), *Impact of Organizational Trauma on Workplace Behavior and Performance* (pp. 162–186). Hershey, PA: IGI Global. doi:10.4018/978-1-5225-2021-4.ch007

Chen, R., Lin, T., & Xie, T. (2015). Towards Intelligent Window Layout Management: The Role of Mental Map. In A. Mesquita & C. Tsai (Eds.), *Human Behavior, Psychology, and Social Interaction in the Digital Era* (pp. 146–161). Hershey, PA: IGI Global. doi:10.4018/978-1-4666-8450-8.ch007

Chuang, S., Lin, S., Chang, T., & Kaewmeesri, R. (2017). Behavioral Intention of Using Social Networking Site: A Comparative Study of Taiwanese and Thai Facebook Users. *International Journal of Technology and Human Interaction, 13*(1), 61–81. doi:10.4018/IJTHI.2017010104

Cialdella, V. T., Lobato, E. J., & Jordan, J. S. (2017). Wild Architecture: Explaining Cognition via Self-Sustaining Systems. In J. Vallverdú, M. Mazzara, M. Talanov, S. Distefano, & R. Lowe (Eds.), *Advanced Research on Biologically Inspired Cognitive Architectures* (pp. 41–62). Hershey, PA: IGI Global. doi:10.4018/978-1-5225-1947-8.ch003

Cleve, R. A., Işık, İ., & Pecanha, V. D. (2017). Sexual Identities in the Workplace: Avoiding Organizational Trauma When Disclosure Occurs – Current Perspectives. In S. Háša & R. Brunet-Thornton (Eds.), *Impact of Organizational Trauma on Workplace Behavior and Performance* (pp. 188–220). Hershey, PA: IGI Global. doi:10.4018/978-1-5225-2021-4.ch008

Contier, A. T., & Torres, L. (2017). Neuroaesthetics: Insights into the Aesthetic Experience of Visual Art. In R. Zuanon (Ed.), *Projective Processes and Neuroscience in Art and Design* (pp. 87–102). Hershey, PA: IGI Global. doi:10.4018/978-1-5225-0510-5.ch006

Crawford, C. M., & Smith, M. S. (2015). Rethinking Bloom's Taxonomy: Implicit Cognitive Vulnerability as an Impetus towards Higher Order Thinking Skills. In Z. Jin (Ed.), *Exploring Implicit Cognition: Learning, Memory, and Social Cognitive Processes* (pp. 86–103). Hershey, PA: IGI Global. doi:10.4018/978-1-4666-6599-6.ch004

de Soir, E., & Kleber, R. (2017). Understanding the Core of Psychological Trauma: Trauma in Contemporary French Theory. In S. Háša & R. Brunet-Thornton (Eds.), *Impact of Organizational Trauma on Workplace Behavior and Performance* (pp. 57–75). Hershey, PA: IGI Global. doi:10.4018/978-1-5225-2021-4.ch003

Delgado, J. J. (2017). How Is the Personality of Facebook Customers?: Cloninger's Psychobiological Model of Temperament as a Predictor of SNSs. In M. Dos Santos (Ed.), *Applying Neuroscience to Business Practice* (pp. 191–229). Hershey, PA: IGI Global. doi:10.4018/978-1-5225-1028-4.ch009

Dentale, F., Vecchione, M., & Barbaranelli, C. (2015). Applying the IAT to Assess Big Five Personality Traits: A Brief Review of Measurement and Validity Issues. In Z. Jin (Ed.), *Exploring Implicit Cognition: Learning, Memory, and Social Cognitive Processes* (pp. 1–15). Hershey, PA: IGI Global. doi:10.4018/978-1-4666-6599-6.ch001

Díez, J. C., & Saiz-Alvarez, J. M. (2016). Leadership in Social Entrepreneurship: Is It Ability or Skill? In J. Saiz-Álvarez (Ed.), *Handbook of Research on Social Entrepreneurship and Solidarity Economics* (pp. 134–153). Hershey, PA: IGI Global. doi:10.4018/978-1-5225-0097-1.ch008

Dikici, A. (2017). Revisiting the Relationships between Turkish Prospective Teachers' Thinking Styles and Behaviors Fostering Creativity. In N. Silton (Ed.), *Exploring the Benefits of Creativity in Education, Media, and the Arts* (pp. 136–157). Hershey, PA: IGI Global. doi:10.4018/978-1-5225-0504-4.ch007

Eapen, V., & Walter, A. (2016). Mind the Gap: Developmental Vulnerability and Mental Health. In R. Gopalan (Ed.), *Handbook of Research on Diagnosing, Treating, and Managing Intellectual Disabilities* (pp. 11–32). Hershey, PA: IGI Global. doi:10.4018/978-1-5225-0089-6.ch002

Fallon, F. (2017). Integrated Information Theory (IIT) and Artificial Consciousness. In J. Vallverdú, M. Mazzara, M. Talanov, S. Distefano, & R. Lowe (Eds.), *Advanced Research on Biologically Inspired Cognitive Architectures* (pp. 1–23). Hershey, PA: IGI Global. doi:10.4018/978-1-5225-1947-8.ch001

Fang, L., & Ha, L. (2015). Do College Students Benefit from Their Social Media Experience?: Social Media Involvement and Its Impact on College Students' Self-Efficacy Perception. In A. Mesquita & C. Tsai (Eds.), *Human Behavior, Psychology, and Social Interaction in the Digital Era* (pp. 259–278). Hershey, PA: IGI Global. doi:10.4018/978-1-4666-8450-8.ch013

Fasko, D. (2017). Creativity in the Schools: Educational Changes Lately? In N. Silton (Ed.), *Exploring the Benefits of Creativity in Education, Media, and the Arts* (pp. 92–116). Hershey, PA: IGI Global. doi:10.4018/978-1-5225-0504-4.ch005

Fazio, S., & Mitchell, D. B. (2015). Self-Preservation in Individuals with Alzheimer's Disease: Empirical Evidence and the Role of the Social Environment. In C. Dick-Muehlke, R. Li, & M. Orleans (Eds.), *Psychosocial Studies of the Individual's Changing Perspectives in Alzheimer's Disease* (pp. 183–207). Hershey, PA: IGI Global. doi:10.4018/978-1-4666-8478-2.ch008

Feitosa-Santana, C. (2017). Understanding How the Mind Works: The Neuroscience of Perception, Behavior, and Creativity. In R. Zuanon (Ed.), *Projective Processes and Neuroscience in Art and Design* (pp. 239–252). Hershey, PA: IGI Global. doi:10.4018/978-1-5225-0510-5.ch014

Ferris, A. (2017). Creativity in the Emerging Adult. In N. Silton (Ed.), *Exploring the Benefits of Creativity in Education, Media, and the Arts* (pp. 26–49). Hershey, PA: IGI Global. doi:10.4018/978-1-5225-0504-4.ch002

Fogliano, F., & Oliveira, H. C. (2017). Neuroesthetics: Perspectives and Reflections. In R. Zuanon (Ed.), *Projective Processes and Neuroscience in Art and Design* (pp. 52–70). Hershey, PA: IGI Global. doi:10.4018/978-1-5225-0510-5.ch004

Folk, J. R., & Eskenazi, M. A. (2017). Eye Movement Behavior and Individual Differences in Word Identification During Reading. In C. Was, F. Sansosti, & B. Morris (Eds.), *Eye-Tracking Technology Applications in Educational Research* (pp. 66–87). Hershey, PA: IGI Global. doi:10.4018/978-1-5225-1005-5.ch004

Franco, M., Ortiz, T. V., Amorim, H. A., & Faber, J. (2017). Can We Induce a Cognitive Representation of a Prosthetic Arm by Means of Crossmodal Stimuli? In R. Zuanon (Ed.), *Projective Processes and Neuroscience in Art and Design* (pp. 182–204). Hershey, PA: IGI Global. doi:10.4018/978-1-5225-0510-5.ch011

G., L. (2017). Psychosocial Intervention Studies for Street Children with Substance Abuse. In B. Prasad (Ed.), *Chronic Mental Illness and the Changing Scope of Intervention Strategies, Diagnosis, and Treatment* (pp. 237-257). Hershey, PA: IGI Global. doi:10.4018/978-1-5225-0519-8.ch013

Gallego, J. (2017). Organizational Trauma and Change Management. In S. Háša & R. Brunet-Thornton (Eds.), *Impact of Organizational Trauma on Workplace Behavior and Performance* (pp. 140–161). Hershey, PA: IGI Global. doi:10.4018/978-1-5225-2021-4.ch006

Galvin, J. E., & Kelleher, M. E. (2015). Dementia and Other Neurocognitive Disorders: An Overview. In C. Dick-Muehlke, R. Li, & M. Orleans (Eds.), *Psychosocial Studies of the Individual's Changing Perspectives in Alzheimer's Disease* (pp. 104–130). Hershey, PA: IGI Global. doi:10.4018/978-1-4666-8478-2.ch005

Gardner, M. K., & Strayer, D. L. (2017). What Cognitive Psychology Can Tell Us About Educational Computer Games. In R. Zheng & M. Gardner (Eds.), *Handbook of Research on Serious Games for Educational Applications* (pp. 1–18). Hershey, PA: IGI Global. doi:10.4018/978-1-5225-0513-6.ch001

Garg, B., Khanna, P., & Khanna, A. (2017). Chronic Mental Illness and the Changing Scope of Intervention Strategies, Diagnosis, and Treatment in Child and Adolescent Population. In B. Prasad (Ed.), *Chronic Mental Illness and the Changing Scope of Intervention Strategies, Diagnosis, and Treatment* (pp. 258–269). Hershey, PA: IGI Global. doi:10.4018/978-1-5225-0519-8.ch014

Giannouli, V. (2017). Creativity and Giftedness: A Study of Attitudes. In N. Silton (Ed.), *Exploring the Benefits of Creativity in Education, Media, and the Arts* (pp. 179–197). Hershey, PA: IGI Global. doi:10.4018/978-1-5225-0504-4.ch009

Gopalan, R. T. (2016). Intellectual Disability: From History to Recent Trends. In R. Gopalan (Ed.), *Handbook of Research on Diagnosing, Treating, and Managing Intellectual Disabilities* (pp. 1–10). Hershey, PA: IGI Global. doi:10.4018/978-1-5225-0089-6.ch001

Hacker, D. J. (2017). The Role of Metacognition in Learning via Serious Games. In R. Zheng & M. Gardner (Eds.), *Handbook of Research on Serious Games for Educational Applications* (pp. 19–40). Hershey, PA: IGI Global. doi:10.4018/978-1-5225-0513-6.ch002

Halder, S., & Mahato, A. (2017). Cognitive Remediation Therapy in Chronic Schizophrenia. In B. Prasad (Ed.), *Chronic Mental Illness and the Changing Scope of Intervention Strategies, Diagnosis, and Treatment* (pp. 292–307). Hershey, PA: IGI Global. doi:10.4018/978-1-5225-0519-8.ch016

Heins, S., Heins, G., & Dick-Muehlke, C. (2015). Steve's Story: Living with Mild Cognitive Impairment. In C. Dick-Muehlke, R. Li, & M. Orleans (Eds.), *Psychosocial Studies of the Individual's Changing Perspectives in Alzheimer's Disease* (pp. 33–60). Hershey, PA: IGI Global. doi:10.4018/978-1-4666-8478-2.ch002

Isik, I. (2017). Organizations and Exposure to Trauma at a Collective Level: The Taxonomy of Potentially Traumatic Events. In S. Háša & R. Brunet-Thornton (Eds.), *Impact of Organizational Trauma on Workplace Behavior and Performance* (pp. 18–56). Hershey, PA: IGI Global. doi:10.4018/978-1-5225-2021-4.ch002

Jančec, L., Vorkapić, S. T., & Vodopivec, J. L. (2015). Hidden Curriculum Determinants in (Pre)School Institutions: Implicit Cognition in Action. In Z. Jin (Ed.), *Exploring Implicit Cognition: Learning, Memory, and Social Cognitive Processes* (pp. 216–242). Hershey, PA: IGI Global. doi:10.4018/978-1-4666-6599-6.ch011

Jerabek, I., & Muoio, D. (2017). The Stress Profile: The Influence of Personal Characteristics on Response to Occupational Trauma. In S. Háša & R. Brunet-Thornton (Eds.), *Impact of Organizational Trauma on Workplace Behavior and Performance* (pp. 77–119). Hershey, PA: IGI Global. doi:10.4018/978-1-5225-2021-4.ch004

Jha, S., Khanna, A., & Khanna, P. (2017). Advanced Intervention Strategies for Suicide in Patients with Chronic Mental Illness. In B. Prasad (Ed.), *Chronic Mental Illness and the Changing Scope of Intervention Strategies, Diagnosis, and Treatment* (pp. 271–291). Hershey, PA: IGI Global. doi:10.4018/978-1-5225-0519-8.ch015

Johard, L., Lippi, V., Safina, L., & Mazzara, M. (2017). Mind and Matter: Why It All Makes Sense. In J. Vallverdú, M. Mazzara, M. Talanov, S. Distefano, & R. Lowe (Eds.), *Advanced Research on Biologically Inspired Cognitive Architectures* (pp. 63–82). Hershey, PA: IGI Global. doi:10.4018/978-1-5225-1947-8.ch004

Kasemsap, K. (2017). Investigating the Roles of Neuroscience and Knowledge Management in Higher Education. In S. Mukerji & P. Tripathi (Eds.), *Handbook of Research on Administration, Policy, and Leadership in Higher Education* (pp. 112–140). Hershey, PA: IGI Global. doi:10.4018/978-1-5225-0672-0.ch006

Kasemsap, K. (2017). Mastering Cognitive Neuroscience and Social Neuroscience Perspectives in the Information Age. In M. Dos Santos (Ed.), *Applying Neuroscience to Business Practice* (pp. 82–113). Hershey, PA: IGI Global. doi:10.4018/978-1-5225-1028-4.ch005

Kaushik, P., & Singh, T. B. (2017). Predictors of Expressed Emotion, Caregiver's Burden, and Quality of Life in Chronic Mental Illness. In B. Prasad (Ed.), *Chronic Mental Illness and the Changing Scope of Intervention Strategies, Diagnosis, and Treatment* (pp. 143–163). Hershey, PA: IGI Global. doi:10.4018/978-1-5225-0519-8.ch008

Keyser, A. K., & Corning, M. (2017). Creative Aging: Stimulating Creativity in Middle and Late Adulthood. In N. Silton (Ed.), *Exploring the Benefits of Creativity in Education, Media, and the Arts* (pp. 50–66). Hershey, PA: IGI Global. doi:10.4018/978-1-5225-0504-4.ch003

Kılıç, B. (2017). An Organizational Trauma Intervention: A Case From Turkey. In S. Háša & R. Brunet-Thornton (Eds.), *Impact of Organizational Trauma on Workplace Behavior and Performance* (pp. 264–277). Hershey, PA: IGI Global. doi:10.4018/978-1-5225-2021-4.ch011

Kirsch, C., Lubart, T., de Vries, H., & Houssemand, C. (2017). Scientific Creativity in Psychology: A Cognitive-Conative Approach. In C. Zhou (Ed.), *Handbook of Research on Creative Problem-Solving Skill Development in Higher Education* (pp. 51–73). Hershey, PA: IGI Global. doi:10.4018/978-1-5225-0643-0.ch003

Kleinmintz, O. M. (2017). Train Yourself to Let Go: The Benefits of Deliberate Practice on Creativity and Its Neural Basis. In N. Silton (Ed.), *Exploring the Benefits of Creativity in Education, Media, and the Arts* (pp. 67–90). Hershey, PA: IGI Global. doi:10.4018/978-1-5225-0504-4.ch004

Kučera, D. (2017). The Potential of Spirituality for the Treatment of Organizational Trauma. In S. Háša & R. Brunet-Thornton (Eds.), *Impact of Organizational Trauma on Workplace Behavior and Performance* (pp. 295–317). Hershey, PA: IGI Global. doi:10.4018/978-1-5225-2021-4.ch013

Kukreti, P., Khanna, P., & Khanna, A. (2017). Chronic Mental Illnesses and Homelessness. In B. Prasad (Ed.), *Chronic Mental Illness and the Changing Scope of Intervention Strategies, Diagnosis, and Treatment* (pp. 1–20). Hershey, PA: IGI Global. doi:10.4018/978-1-5225-0519-8.ch001

Kuss, D. J. (2015). "I Can't Do It by Myself": An IPA of Clients Seeking Psychotherapy for Their MMORPG Addiction. In J. Bishop (Ed.), *Psychological and Social Implications Surrounding Internet and Gaming Addiction* (pp. 78–110). Hershey, PA: IGI Global. doi:10.4018/978-1-4666-8595-6.ch006

Landim, P. D. (2017). Design and Emotion: Contributions to the Emotional Design. In R. Zuanon (Ed.), *Projective Processes and Neuroscience in Art and Design* (pp. 119–136). Hershey, PA: IGI Global. doi:10.4018/978-1-5225-0510-5.ch008

Lebraty, J., & Godé, C. (2015). Assessing the Performance of Decision Support Systems in Military Environment: The 3C Method. In A. Mesquita & C. Tsai (Eds.), *Human Behavior, Psychology, and Social Interaction in the Digital Era* (pp. 45–70). Hershey, PA: IGI Global. doi:10.4018/978-1-4666-8450-8.ch003

Lehenbauer-Baum, M., & Fohringer, M. (2015). Internet Gaming Disorder: A Deeper Look into Addiction vs. High Engagement. In J. Bishop (Ed.), *Psychological and Social Implications Surrounding Internet and Gaming Addiction* (pp. 1–15). Hershey, PA: IGI Global. doi:10.4018/978-1-4666-8595-6.ch001

Lei, M., Liu, W., Gao, Y., & Zhu, T. (2015). Mobile User Behaviors in China. In Z. Yan (Ed.), *Encyclopedia of Mobile Phone Behavior* (pp. 1110–1128). Hershey, PA: IGI Global. doi:10.4018/978-1-4666-8239-9.ch091

Leote, R. (2017). Perceptual Processes and Multisensoriality: Understanding Multimodal Art from Neuroscientific Concepts. In R. Zuanon (Ed.), *Projective Processes and Neuroscience in Art and Design* (pp. 1–14). Hershey, PA: IGI Global. doi:10.4018/978-1-5225-0510-5.ch001

Lin, L., & Lipsmeyer, B. (2015). The Environmental and Technological Factors of Multitasking. In A. Mesquita & C. Tsai (Eds.), *Human Behavior, Psychology, and Social Interaction in the Digital Era* (pp. 1–20). Hershey, PA: IGI Global. doi:10.4018/978-1-4666-8450-8.ch001

Lin, T., Wu, Z., & Chen, Y. (2015). Using High-Frequency Interaction Events to Automatically Classify Cognitive Load. In A. Mesquita & C. Tsai (Eds.), *Human Behavior, Psychology, and Social Interaction in the Digital Era* (pp. 210–228). Hershey, PA: IGI Global. doi:10.4018/978-1-4666-8450-8.ch010

Liu, X., & Zhu, T. (2017). Comparing Online Personality of Americans and Chinese. In I. Management Association (Ed.), *Gaming and Technology Addiction: Breakthroughs in Research and Practice* (pp. 339-351). Hershey, PA: IGI Global. doi:10.4018/978-1-5225-0778-9.ch016

Lopes, M. M. (2017). Inside/Out: Looking Back into the Future. In R. Zuanon (Ed.), *Projective Processes and Neuroscience in Art and Design* (pp. 15–39). Hershey, PA: IGI Global. doi:10.4018/978-1-5225-0510-5.ch002

Lu, Y. Y., & Austrom, M. G. (2015). Disease Awareness, Cognitive Decline, and Communication in Persons with Mild Cognitive Impairment and Caregivers. In C. Dick-Muehlke, R. Li, & M. Orleans (Eds.), *Psychosocial Studies of the Individual's Changing Perspectives in Alzheimer's Disease* (pp. 254–270). Hershey, PA: IGI Global. doi:10.4018/978-1-4666-8478-2.ch011

Lytras, M. D., Raghavan, V., & Damiani, E. (2017). Big Data and Data Analytics Research: From Metaphors to Value Space for Collective Wisdom in Human Decision Making and Smart Machines. *International Journal on Semantic Web and Information Systems*, *13*(1), 1–10. doi:10.4018/IJSWIS.2017010101

M., K., & Boominathan, P. (2016). Assessment and Management of Communication Skills in Individuals with Intellectual Disability: Perspectives in the 21st Century. In R. Gopalan (Ed.), *Handbook of Research on Diagnosing, Treating, and Managing Intellectual Disabilities* (pp. 156-185). Hershey, PA: IGI Global. doi:10.4018/978-1-5225-0089-6.ch009

MacKinlay, E., & Trevitt, C. (2015). Spiritual Factors in the Experience of Alzheimer's Disease and Other Dementias. In C. Dick-Muehlke, R. Li, & M. Orleans (Eds.), *Psychosocial Studies of the Individual's Changing Perspectives in Alzheimer's Disease* (pp. 230–253). Hershey, PA: IGI Global. doi:10.4018/978-1-4666-8478-2.ch010

Mahato, A., & Halder, S. (2017). Disability in Schizophrenia: The Psychosocial and Neurocognitive Perspective. In B. Prasad (Ed.), *Chronic Mental Illness and the Changing Scope of Intervention Strategies, Diagnosis, and Treatment* (pp. 188–202). Hershey, PA: IGI Global. doi:10.4018/978-1-5225-0519-8.ch010

Manthiou, A., Chiang, L. L., & Tang, L. R. (2015). Developing a Successful Facebook Fan Page Based on Costumers' Needs. In A. Mesquita & C. Tsai (Eds.), *Human Behavior, Psychology, and Social Interaction in the Digital Era* (pp. 189–209). Hershey, PA: IGI Global. doi:10.4018/978-1-4666-8450-8.ch009

McCutcheon, J. L. (2017). Emerging Ethical Issues in Police and Public Safety Psychology: Reflections on Mandatory vs. Aspirational Ethics. In C. Mitchell & E. Dorian (Eds.), *Police Psychology and Its Growing Impact on Modern Law Enforcement* (pp. 314–334). Hershey, PA: IGI Global. doi:10.4018/978-1-5225-0813-7.ch016

Menezes, M. (2017). Cells, Organisms, and the Living Brain as New Media for Art: A Pursuit in Art Research. In R. Zuanon (Ed.), *Projective Processes and Neuroscience in Art and Design* (pp. 40–50). Hershey, PA: IGI Global. doi:10.4018/978-1-5225-0510-5.ch003

Mitchell, C. L. (2017). Preemployment Psychological Screening of Police Officer Applicants: Basic Considerations and Recent Advances. In C. Mitchell & E. Dorian (Eds.), *Police Psychology and Its Growing Impact on Modern Law Enforcement* (pp. 28–50). Hershey, PA: IGI Global. doi:10.4018/978-1-5225-0813-7.ch002

Mittlböck, K. (2015). Dangers of Playing with the Virtual Other in Mind: A Psychoanalytical View on Digital Role-Playing Games and the Edge between Facilitating Personality Development and Endangering the Player's Psyche. In J. Bishop (Ed.), *Psychological and Social Implications Surrounding Internet and Gaming Addiction* (pp. 44–61). Hershey, PA: IGI Global. doi:10.4018/978-1-4666-8595-6.ch004

Moraru, A. (2017). Student's Psychological Factors and Metacognitive Skills in Higher Education. In E. Railean, A. Elçi, & A. Elçi (Eds.), *Metacognition and Successful Learning Strategies in Higher Education* (pp. 176–199). Hershey, PA: IGI Global. doi:10.4018/978-1-5225-2218-8.ch009

Morhardt, D., & Spira, M. (2015). Cognitive Decline and the Changing Self in Relationship. In C. Dick-Muehlke, R. Li, & M. Orleans (Eds.), *Psychosocial Studies of the Individual's Changing Perspectives in Alzheimer's Disease* (pp. 61–75). Hershey, PA: IGI Global. doi:10.4018/978-1-4666-8478-2.ch003

Nakamura, D. (2015). Individual Differences in Implicit Learning: Current Problems and Issues for Research. In Z. Jin (Ed.), *Exploring Implicit Cognition: Learning, Memory, and Social Cognitive Processes* (pp. 61–85). Hershey, PA: IGI Global. doi:10.4018/978-1-4666-6599-6.ch003

Navarro, A. B., Díaz-Orueta, U., Martín-Niño, L., & Sánchez-Sánchez, M. E. (2015). Art, Drawing Task Processes, and Identity Awareness: A Case Study on the Retro-Genesis Phenomenon as an Indicator of the Progress of Dementia. In C. Dick-Muehlke, R. Li, & M. Orleans (Eds.), *Psychosocial Studies of the Individual's Changing Perspectives in Alzheimer's Disease* (pp. 208–228). Hershey, PA: IGI Global. doi:10.4018/978-1-4666-8478-2.ch009

Nina, B., & Nadejda, B. (2017). Metacognitive Strategies in Higher Education: Development of Spiritual Intelligence Strategies Within Training of the Academic Staff. In E. Railean, A. Elçi, & A. Elçi (Eds.), *Metacognition and Successful Learning Strategies in Higher Education* (pp. 109–136). Hershey, PA: IGI Global. doi:10.4018/978-1-5225-2218-8.ch006

Norris, S. E., & Porter, T. H. (2017). The Influence of Spirituality in the Workplace and Perceived Organizational Support on Organizational Citizenship Behaviors for Strategic Success. In V. Wang (Ed.), *Encyclopedia of Strategic Leadership and Management* (pp. 1140–1162). Hershey, PA: IGI Global. doi:10.4018/978-1-5225-1049-9.ch080

O'Reilly, A. G., Roche, B., & Cartwright, A. (2015). Function over Form: A Behavioral Approach to Implicit Attitudes. In Z. Jin (Ed.), *Exploring Implicit Cognition: Learning, Memory, and Social Cognitive Processes* (pp. 162–182). Hershey, PA: IGI Global. doi:10.4018/978-1-4666-6599-6.ch008

Pandey, J. M., Mishra, P., Garg, S., & Mshra, B. P. (2017). Chronic Mental Illness and Dumping Patients: A Concern towards Management. In B. Prasad (Ed.), *Chronic Mental Illness and the Changing Scope of Intervention Strategies, Diagnosis, and Treatment* (pp. 40–57). Hershey, PA: IGI Global. doi:10.4018/978-1-5225-0519-8.ch003

Pantos, A. J. (2015). Implicit Social Cognition and Language Attitudes Research. In Z. Jin (Ed.), *Exploring Implicit Cognition: Learning, Memory, and Social Cognitive Processes* (pp. 104–117). Hershey, PA: IGI Global. doi:10.4018/978-1-4666-6599-6.ch005

Park, L. Q., & Busson, B. (2015). The Impact of Decline on Everyday Life in Alzheimer's Disease. In C. Dick-Muehlke, R. Li, & M. Orleans (Eds.), *Psychosocial Studies of the Individual's Changing Perspectives in Alzheimer's Disease* (pp. 327–338). Hershey, PA: IGI Global. doi:10.4018/978-1-4666-8478-2.ch014

Pellas, N. (2015). Unraveling a Progressive Inquiry Script in Persistent Virtual Worlds: Theoretical Foundations and Decision Processes for Constructing a Socio-Cultural Learning Framework. In Z. Jin (Ed.), *Exploring Implicit Cognition: Learning, Memory, and Social Cognitive Processes* (pp. 243–280). Hershey, PA: IGI Global. doi:10.4018/978-1-4666-6599-6.ch012

Pena, P. A., Van den Broucke, S., Sylin, M., Leysen, J., & de Soir, E. (2017). Definitions, Typologies, and Processes Involved in Organizational Trauma: A Literature Review. In S. Háša & R. Brunet-Thornton (Eds.), *Impact of Organizational Trauma on Workplace Behavior and Performance* (pp. 1–17). Hershey, PA: IGI Global. doi:10.4018/978-1-5225-2021-4.ch001

Photiadis, T., & Souleles, N. (2015). A Theoretical Model, Including User-Experience, Aesthetics, and Psychology, in the 3D Design Process. In J. Bishop (Ed.), *Psychological and Social Implications Surrounding Internet and Gaming Addiction* (pp. 139–152). Hershey, PA: IGI Global. doi:10.4018/978-1-4666-8595-6.ch008

Pontes, H. M., & Griffiths, M. D. (2015). New Concepts, Old Known Issues: The DSM-5 and Internet Gaming Disorder and its Assessment. In J. Bishop (Ed.), *Psychological and Social Implications Surrounding Internet and Gaming Addiction* (pp. 16–30). Hershey, PA: IGI Global. doi:10.4018/978-1-4666-8595-6.ch002

Power, G. A. (2015). Changing Perception in Alzheimer's: An Experiential View. In C. Dick-Muehlke, R. Li, & M. Orleans (Eds.), *Psychosocial Studies of the Individual's Changing Perspectives in Alzheimer's Disease* (pp. 271–300). Hershey, PA: IGI Global. doi:10.4018/978-1-4666-8478-2.ch012

R., A., Prasad, B. V., & Kosgi, S. (2017). Psychosocial Intervention Strategies for Patients with Schizophrenia: In Chronic Mental Illness. In B. Prasad (Ed.), *Chronic Mental Illness and the Changing Scope of Intervention Strategies, Diagnosis, and Treatment* (pp. 58-75). Hershey, PA: IGI Global. doi:10.4018/978-1-5225-0519-8.ch004

Reinert, L. (2017). Qualia and Extended Field of Contemporary Design. In R. Zuanon (Ed.), *Projective Processes and Neuroscience in Art and Design* (pp. 138–154). Hershey, PA: IGI Global. doi:10.4018/978-1-5225-0510-5.ch009

Ross, D. B., Exposito, J. A., & Kennedy, T. (2017). Stress and Its Relationship to Leadership and a Healthy Workplace Culture. In V. Bryan & J. Bird (Eds.), *Healthcare Community Synergism between Patients, Practitioners, and Researchers* (pp. 213–246). Hershey, PA: IGI Global. doi:10.4018/978-1-5225-0640-9.ch010

Saberi, M. (2016). Personality-Based Cognitive Design of Characters in Virtual Environments. In J. Turner, M. Nixon, U. Bernardet, & S. DiPaola (Eds.), *Integrating Cognitive Architectures into Virtual Character Design* (pp. 124–150). Hershey, PA: IGI Global. doi:10.4018/978-1-5225-0454-2.ch005

Sharma, R., & Lohan, A. (2016). Psychosocial Interventions for Individuals with Intellectual Disability. In R. Gopalan (Ed.), *Handbook of Research on Diagnosing, Treating, and Managing Intellectual Disabilities* (pp. 262–282). Hershey, PA: IGI Global. doi:10.4018/978-1-5225-0089-6.ch014

Sharon, D. (2015). The Sleep-Wake System and Alzheimer's Disease. In C. Dick-Muehlke, R. Li, & M. Orleans (Eds.), *Psychosocial Studies of the Individual's Changing Perspectives in Alzheimer's Disease* (pp. 339–365). Hershey, PA: IGI Global. doi:10.4018/978-1-4666-8478-2.ch015

Simuth, J. (2017). Psychological Impacts of Downsizing Trauma. In S. Háša & R. Brunet-Thornton (Eds.), *Impact of Organizational Trauma on Workplace Behavior and Performance* (pp. 120–139). Hershey, PA: IGI Global. doi:10.4018/978-1-5225-2021-4.ch005

Sinha, P., Garg, A., Khanna, P., & Khanna, A. (2017). Management of Chronic Mental Illnesses and Substance Use Disorders. In B. Prasad (Ed.), *Chronic Mental Illness and the Changing Scope of Intervention Strategies, Diagnosis, and Treatment* (pp. 101–122). Hershey, PA: IGI Global. doi:10.4018/978-1-5225-0519-8.ch006

Siqueira de Freitas, A. (2017). A Study on the Interface between Arts and Sciences: Neuroesthetics and Cognitive Neuroscience of Art. In R. Zuanon (Ed.), *Projective Processes and Neuroscience in Art and Design* (pp. 71–86). Hershey, PA: IGI Global. doi:10.4018/978-1-5225-0510-5.ch005

Solo, A. M., & Bishop, J. (2015). Avoiding Adverse Consequences from Digital Addiction and Retaliatory Feedback: The Role of the Participation Continuum. In J. Bishop (Ed.), *Psychological and Social Implications Surrounding Internet and Gaming Addiction* (pp. 62–77). Hershey, PA: IGI Global. doi:10.4018/978-1-4666-8595-6.ch005

Soni, S. C. P., & Ahamed, P. C. (2017). Understanding and Management of Caregivers' Stress and Burden of Person with Obsessive Compulsive Disorder. In B. Prasad (Ed.), *Chronic Mental Illness and the Changing Scope of Intervention Strategies, Diagnosis, and Treatment* (pp. 124–142). Hershey, PA: IGI Global. doi:10.4018/978-1-5225-0519-8.ch007

Srivastav, D., & Singh, T. B. (2017). Comorbidity Issues and Treatment in Chronic Mental Illness. In B. Prasad (Ed.), *Chronic Mental Illness and the Changing Scope of Intervention Strategies, Diagnosis, and Treatment* (pp. 77–100). Hershey, PA: IGI Global. doi:10.4018/978-1-5225-0519-8.ch005

Strang, K. D. (2017). Predicting Student Satisfaction and Outcomes in Online Courses Using Learning Activity Indicators. *International Journal of Web-Based Learning and Teaching Technologies, 12*(1), 32–50. doi:10.4018/IJWLTT.2017010103

Svanström, R. (2015). Fragmented Existence: Living Alone with Dementia and a Manifest Care Need. In C. Dick-Muehlke, R. Li, & M. Orleans (Eds.), *Psychosocial Studies of the Individual's Changing Perspectives in Alzheimer's Disease* (pp. 302–326). Hershey, PA: IGI Global. doi:10.4018/978-1-4666-8478-2.ch013

Swiatek, L. (2017). Accessing the Finest Minds: Insights into Creativity from Esteemed Media Professionals. In N. Silton (Ed.), *Exploring the Benefits of Creativity in Education, Media, and the Arts* (pp. 240–263). Hershey, PA: IGI Global. doi:10.4018/978-1-5225-0504-4.ch012

Szymanski, M., & Schindler, E. (2017). Embracing Organizational Trauma: Positive Effects of Death Experiences on Organizational Culture – Three Short Case Studies. In S. Háša & R. Brunet-Thornton (Eds.), *Impact of Organizational Trauma on Workplace Behavior and Performance* (pp. 247–263). Hershey, PA: IGI Global. doi:10.4018/978-1-5225-2021-4.ch010

Tavaragi, M. S. (2017). Chronic Mental Illness in Prisons: Global Scenario. In B. Prasad (Ed.), *Chronic Mental Illness and the Changing Scope of Intervention Strategies, Diagnosis, and Treatment* (pp. 203–224). Hershey, PA: IGI Global. doi:10.4018/978-1-5225-0519-8.ch011

Tavaragi, M. S., & C., S. (2017). Global Burden of Mental Disorders: Quality of Care and Unmet Needs for Treatment of Chronic Mental Illness. In B. Prasad (Ed.), *Chronic Mental Illness and the Changing Scope of Intervention Strategies, Diagnosis, and Treatment* (pp. 164-186). Hershey, PA: IGI Global. doi:10.4018/978-1-5225-0519-8.ch009

Tietze, R. L. (2017). Creativity and the Arts. In N. Silton (Ed.), *Exploring the Benefits of Creativity in Education, Media, and the Arts* (pp. 337–375). Hershey, PA: IGI Global. doi:10.4018/978-1-5225-0504-4.ch016

Toms, G., Lawrence, C., & Clare, L. (2015). Awareness, Self, and the Experience of Dementia: Foundations of a Psychologically Minded Approach. In C. Dick-Muehlke, R. Li, & M. Orleans (Eds.), *Psychosocial Studies of the Individual's Changing Perspectives in Alzheimer's Disease* (pp. 132–158). Hershey, PA: IGI Global. doi:10.4018/978-1-4666-8478-2.ch006

Tran, B. (2017). Impact of Organizational Trauma on Workplace Behavior and Performance: Workplace Bullying Due to (In)Competency. In S. Háša, & R. Brunet-Thornton (Eds.), Impact of Organizational Trauma on Workplace Behavior and Performance (pp. 221-245). Hershey, PA: IGI Global. doi:10.4018/978-1-5225-2021-4.ch009

Tran, B. (2017). Psychological (and Emotional) Architecture: The Values and Benefits of Nature-Based Architecture – Biophilia. In G. Koç, M. Claes, & B. Christiansen (Eds.), *Cultural Influences on Architecture* (pp. 200–230). Hershey, PA: IGI Global. doi:10.4018/978-1-5225-1744-3.ch008

Tran, B. (2017). The Architect of Organizational Psychology: The Geert Hofstede's Dimensions of Cultural (Corporate and Organizational) Identity. In G. Koç, M. Claes, & B. Christiansen (Eds.), *Cultural Influences on Architecture* (pp. 231–258). Hershey, PA: IGI Global. doi:10.4018/978-1-5225-1744-3.ch009

Triberti, S., & Chirico, A. (2017). Healthy Avatars, Healthy People: Care Engagement Through the Shared Experience of Virtual Worlds. In G. Graffigna (Ed.), *Transformative Healthcare Practice through Patient Engagement* (pp. 247–275). Hershey, PA: IGI Global. doi:10.4018/978-1-5225-0663-8.ch010

Tripathi, M. A., & Sridevi, G. (2017). Psychotherapeutic Interventions in Emotional and Behavioural Problems with Adolescents. In B. Prasad (Ed.), *Chronic Mental Illness and the Changing Scope of Intervention Strategies, Diagnosis, and Treatment* (pp. 321–333). Hershey, PA: IGI Global. doi:10.4018/978-1-5225-0519-8.ch018

Trompetter, P. S. (2017). A History of Police Psychology. In C. Mitchell & E. Dorian (Eds.), *Police Psychology and Its Growing Impact on Modern Law Enforcement* (pp. 1–26). Hershey, PA: IGI Global. doi:10.4018/978-1-5225-0813-7.ch001

Valencia, E. (2017). Neuromarketing Step by Step: Based on Scientific Publications. In M. Dos Santos (Ed.), *Applying Neuroscience to Business Practice* (pp. 18–48). Hershey, PA: IGI Global. doi:10.4018/978-1-5225-1028-4.ch002

Valeyeva, N. S., Kupriyanov, R., & Valeyeva, E. R. (2017). Metacognition and Metacognitive Skills: Intellectual Skills Development Technology. In E. Railean, A. Elçi, & A. Elçi (Eds.), *Metacognition and Successful Learning Strategies in Higher Education* (pp. 63–84). Hershey, PA: IGI Global. doi:10.4018/978-1-5225-2218-8.ch004

Vallverdú, J., & Talanov, M. (2017). Naturalizing Consciousness Emergence for AI Implementation Purposes: A Guide to Multilayered Management Systems. In J. Vallverdú, M. Mazzara, M. Talanov, S. Distefano, & R. Lowe (Eds.), *Advanced Research on Biologically Inspired Cognitive Architectures* (pp. 24–40). Hershey, PA: IGI Global. doi:10.4018/978-1-5225-1947-8.ch002

von Kutzleben, M., & Panke-Kochinke, B. (2015). Stable Self-Concepts and Flexible Coping Strategies of People with Dementia Attending Dementia Self-Help Groups in Germany: Results from the Qualitative Longitudinal SEIN Study. In C. Dick-Muehlke, R. Li, & M. Orleans (Eds.), *Psychosocial Studies of the Individual's Changing Perspectives in Alzheimer's Disease* (pp. 159–182). Hershey, PA: IGI Global. doi:10.4018/978-1-4666-8478-2.ch007

Vorkapić, S. T. (2017). Personality and Education: Contemporary Issues in Psychological Science about Personality in Teacher Education. In C. Martin & D. Polly (Eds.), *Handbook of Research on Teacher Education and Professional Development* (pp. 163–186). Hershey, PA: IGI Global. doi:10.4018/978-1-5225-1067-3.ch009

Wagner, C., & Schlough, D. E. (2017). Creativity: A Childhood Essential. In N. Silton (Ed.), *Exploring the Benefits of Creativity in Education, Media, and the Arts* (pp. 1–25). Hershey, PA: IGI Global. doi:10.4018/978-1-5225-0504-4.ch001

Wang, L., Li, C., & Wu, J. (2017). The Status of Research into Intention Recognition. In J. Wu (Ed.), *Improving the Quality of Life for Dementia Patients through Progressive Detection, Treatment, and Care* (pp. 201–221). Hershey, PA: IGI Global. doi:10.4018/978-1-5225-0925-7.ch010

Wehle, M., Weidemann, A., & Boblan, I. W. (2017). Research on Human Cognition for Biologically Inspired Developments: Human-Robot Interaction by Biomimetic AI. In J. Vallverdú, M. Mazzara, M. Talanov, S. Distefano, & R. Lowe (Eds.), *Advanced Research on Biologically Inspired Cognitive Architectures* (pp. 83–116). Hershey, PA: IGI Global. doi:10.4018/978-1-5225-1947-8.ch005

Wilson, J. G. (2017). Social Psychology: The Seduction of Consumers. In C. Martins & M. Damásio (Eds.), *Seduction in Popular Culture, Psychology, and Philosophy* (pp. 206–231). Hershey, PA: IGI Global. doi:10.4018/978-1-5225-0525-9.ch010

Wu, F., Tang, X., Ren, Y., Yang, W., Takahashi, S., & Wu, J. (2017). Effects of Visual Contrast on Inverse Effectiveness in Audiovisual Integration. In J. Wu (Ed.), *Improving the Quality of Life for Dementia Patients through Progressive Detection, Treatment, and Care* (pp. 187–200). Hershey, PA: IGI Global. doi:10.4018/978-1-5225-0925-7.ch009

Wu, Z., Lin, T., Tang, N., & Wu, S. (2015). Effects of Display Characteristics on Presence and Emotional Responses of Game Players. In A. Mesquita & C. Tsai (Eds.), *Human Behavior, Psychology, and Social Interaction in the Digital Era* (pp. 130–145). Hershey, PA: IGI Global. doi:10.4018/978-1-4666-8450-8.ch006

Xie, T., Zhu, Y., Lin, T., & Chen, R. (2015). Modeling Human Behavior to Reduce Navigation Time of Menu Items: Menu Item Prediction Based on Markov Chain. In A. Mesquita & C. Tsai (Eds.), *Human Behavior, Psychology, and Social Interaction in the Digital Era* (pp. 162–187). Hershey, PA: IGI Global. doi:10.4018/978-1-4666-8450-8.ch008

Yang, C., Ha, L., Yun, G. W., & Chen, L. (2015). From Relationship to Information: A Study of Twitter and Facebook Usage in Terms of Social Network Size among College Students. In A. Mesquita & C. Tsai (Eds.), *Human Behavior, Psychology, and Social Interaction in the Digital Era* (pp. 241–258). Hershey, PA: IGI Global. doi:10.4018/978-1-4666-8450-8.ch012

Yartey, F. N., & Ha, L. (2015). Smartphones and Self-Broadcasting among College Students in an Age of Social Media. In A. Mesquita & C. Tsai (Eds.), *Human Behavior, Psychology, and Social Interaction in the Digital Era* (pp. 95–128). Hershey, PA: IGI Global. doi:10.4018/978-1-4666-8450-8.ch005

About the Contributors

Shouvik Chakraborty is a Lecturer in Computer Science & Technology and In-charge, Robotics and Innovation Laboratory at M.B.C. Institute of Engineering & Technology, West Bengal, India. He is pursuing Ph.D. in Computer Science & Engineering from the University of Kalyani, India. He completed his M.Tech in Computer Science and Engineering from the University of Kalyani, India in 2016. He completed his B.Tech in Computer Science and Engineering from Maulana Abul Kalam Azad University of Technology (Formerly known as West Bengal University of Technology), India in 2014. He received AICTE National Fellowship during M.Tech. and DST INSPIRE Fellowship during Ph.D. He secured First class First position among the university in M. Tech. He is an associate member of IRED (UACEE), USA. He is also a member of IACSIT, Singapore; IAENG, Hong Kong; ICSES; IEDRC, Hong Kong; MIR Labs, USA. His research interests include Soft and Evolutionary Computing, Digital Image Processing, Bio-medical Image Analysis, Patteren Recognition, Machine Learning and Optimization Techniques. He is the author of several book chapters and journal articles. He presented various research works in many international and national conferences.

Kalyani Mali received B. Tech and M. Tech Degree in 1987 and 1989 from university of Calcutta, India and Ph.D Degree in Computer Science and Engineering from Jadavpur University, Kolkata, India in 2005. She joined faculty of Deptt. of Computer Science and and Engineering, University of Kalyani, India in 1992. She currently holds the rank of Professor. Her current research interests include Pattern Recognition, Image Processing, Data Mining and Soft Computing. She has published 50 journal papers.

* * *

Rajalingam B. graduated B.Tech in Information Technology from Alpha College of Engineering, Affiliated by Anna University, Chennai, Tamilnadu in 2010. He got M.E. in Computer Science and Engineering from Annamalai University,

Chidambaram, Tamilnadu in 2012. He have submitted Ph.D thesis in Computer science and Engineering from Annamalai University in November 2019. He has worked as assistant professor at Aksheyaa college of Engineering, Maduranthakam, Tamilnadu from 2012 to 2016. Currently he is working as assistant professor at Priyadarshini College of Engineering and Technology, Nellore, Andhra Pradesh. He has published 20 papers in international journals and presented 20 papers in the national and international conferences. His research interest includes Medical Image Processing, Image Retrieval and Network Security.

R. Bhavani received her B.E. degree in Computer Science and Engineering from Regional Engineering College, Trichy in 1989. She received her M.E. degree in Computer Science and Engineering from Regional Engineering College, Trichy in 1992. She worked at Mookambigai College of Engineering, Keeranur from 1990 to 1994. She has been with Annamalai University, since 1994. She received her Ph.D. degree in Computer Science and Engineering at Annamalai University, in the year 2007. She presented 45 papers in International Conferences, 19 papers in National Conferences and published 55 papers in National and International Journals. She also published 1 Book and 5 Book Chapters. Her research area includes Image processing, Image Segmentation, Image Compression, Image Classification, Stenography, Pattern Classification, Medical Imaging, Content Based Image Retrieval and Software metrics.

Rohini A. Bhusnurmath, 2017 Ph.D. in Computer Science, Gulbarga University, Kalaburagi, Karnataka, India, 2002 Master of Science in Computer Science, Karnataka University, Dharwad, Karnataka, India. She was working as Lecturer at Government P.U. College for Girls, Vijayapura, Karnataka, India (2009-2018), presently working as Assistant Professor, Department of Computer Science, Karnataka State Akkamahadevi Women's University, Vijayapura, Karnataka, India. Her research areas of interest are Image Processing and Pattern Recognition. She has published 14 research papers in peer reviewed International Journals and Proceedings of International Conferences.

Prabhakar C. J. received his Ph.D. degree in Computer Science and Technology from Gulbarga University, Gulbarga, Karnataka, India in 2010. He is currently working as Associate Professor in the Department of Computer Science, Kuvempu University, Karnataka, India. His research interests are Pattern Recognition, Document Image Processing, Computer Vision and Machine Vision.

P. S. Hiremath, 1978 Ph.D. in Mathematics, Karnataka University, Dharwad, Karnataka, India, 1973 Master of Science in Mathematics, Karnataka University,

Dharwad, Karnataka, India. He had been in the Faculty of Mathematics and Computer Science of various institutions in India, namely, National Institute of Technology, Surathkal (1977-79), Coimbatore Institute of Technology, Coimbatore (1979-80), National Institute of Technology, Tiruchirapalli (1980-86), Karnataka University, Dharwad (1986-1993), Gulbarga University, Kalaburagi (1993-2014) and presently working as Professor, Department of Computer Science (MCA), KLE Technological University, BVBCET Campus, Hubli- 580031, Karnataka, India. His research areas of interest are Computational Fluid Dynamics, Optimization Techniques, Image Processing and Pattern Recognition, and Computer Networks. He has published 230 research papers in peer reviewed International Journals and Proceedings of International Conferences.

Balakrishna K. received his BE and M.Tech Degree from the VTU University, Karnataka, India in 2011 and 2013, and his Ph.D. degree at the University of Mysore, Karnataka, India in 2019. He has published about 14 research papers in reputed journals and conferences. His research interests his Image processing, Wireless Sensor Network, Communication systems. He has 5 years of Research and Teaching experience.

Priya Kandan received her B.E. degree in Computer Science and Engineering from Thiagarajar College of Engineering, Madurai in 1997. She received her M.E. degree in Computer Science and Engineering from Annamalai University, Chidambaram in the year 2005. She has been with Annamalai University, since 1999 with 20 years of experience. She received her Ph.D. degree in Computer Science and Engineering at Annamalai University, in the year 2014. She has published 60 papers in international conferences and journals. Her research interest includes Medical Image processing and Pattern Classification Methods. Life member of the Indian Society for Technical Education (ISTE) and a member of Computer Society of India (C.S.I).

Mousomi Roy is a PhD research scholar in the department of Computer Science and Engineering, University of Kalyani. She received her M.Tech. in 2016 and B.Tech. in 2014. Her research interests include data security, chaos theory, image processing, etc.

Index

Ensure Quality Research is Introduced to the Academic Community

Become an IGI Global Reviewer for Authored Book Projects

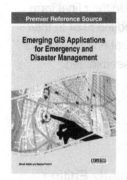
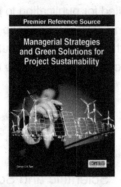

The overall success of an authored book project is dependent on quality and timely reviews.

In this competitive age of scholarly publishing, constructive and timely feedback significantly expedites the turnaround time of manuscripts from submission to acceptance, allowing the publication and discovery of forward-thinking research at a much more expeditious rate. Several IGI Global authored book projects are currently seeking highly-qualified experts in the field to fill vacancies on their respective editorial review boards:

Applications and Inquiries may be sent to:
development@igi-global.com

Applicants must have a doctorate (or an equivalent degree) as well as publishing and reviewing experience. Reviewers are asked to complete the open-ended evaluation questions with as much detail as possible in a timely, collegial, and constructive manner. All reviewers' tenures run for one-year terms on the editorial review boards and are expected to complete at least three reviews per term. Upon successful completion of this term, reviewers can be considered for an additional term.

If you have a colleague that may be interested in this opportunity, we encourage you to share this information with them.